THE INTERNATIONAL
EUCHARISTIC CONGRESSES

THE INTERNATIONAL EUCHARISTIC CONGRESSES: A SPIRITUAL ODYSSEY 1881–2016

Dear Anna

Blessings !

Fr John Allen

5/8/18

JOHN FRANCIS ALLEN

GRACEWING

First published in England in 2018
by
Gracewing
2 Southern Avenue
Leominster
Herefordshire HR6 0QF
United Kingdom
www.gracewing.co.uk

ISBN 978 085244 932 5

Typeset by Gracewing

Cover design by Bernardita Peña Hurtado

To Thomas Holland: Bishop, mentor, friend

CONTENTS

CONTENTS...ix

PREFACE...xiii

FOREWORD...xv

1 A KALEIDOSCOPE OF CONGRESSES 1881–1968...1

1881–1914...1

1922–1938...10

1952–1968...19

2 MELBOURNE 18–25 FEBRUARY 1973 37

The Congress opens...41

Words of wisdom..47

3 PHILADELPHIA 1–8 AUGUST 1976..................53

Hungers of the World: Days 1–4.....................................55

Hungers of the World: Days 5–8.....................................61

Fourteenth Street...67

4 LOURDES 16–23 JULY 1981...........................71

From all horizons the Church assembles..........................75

The Church proclaims the Word of God..........................77

The Church gives thanks to the Father............................80

The Church recalls Christ's redemptive act......................81

The Church calls upon the Holy Spirit............................86

The Church receives the Body of Christ..........................87

The Church has its part in the mission of Christ..........91

5 NAIROBI 11–18 AUGUST 1985.............97

The Congress opens...............99

The Christian Family...............104

The 'Sick and Suffering'...............108

The Pope's Message...............112

6 SEOUL 5–8 OCTOBER 1989.............119

Threats to Peace...............124

The Search for Unity...............131

The Holy Father's Prayer...............136

7 SEVILLE 7–13 JUNE 1993.............145

Presence, Sacrifice, Communion...............151

Word, Sacrament, Oneness...............158

Sacrament of Eucharist, Commandment of Love...........166

8 WROCŁAW 25 MAY-1 JUNE 1997.............171

The Eucharist makes us free...............181

Yearn, Pray for Unity...............184

Freedom in the Third Millennium...............189

9 ROME 18–25 JUNE 2000.............197

'Too good to be true'...............206

The Eucharist and human culture...............211

Eucharist and Reconciliation...............216

Bread for New Life...............222

10 GUADALAJARA 9–17 OCTOBER 2004...........229

Light and darkness...............233

Zapopan—and Eucharist and Mission...............240

Christ the King...............246

Eucharist and Ecclesial Communion.............................248
Eucharist and Evangelisation......................................255
Year of the Eucharist..258

11 QUEBEC 15–22 JUNE 2008....................263

Day of North America..267
Day of Europe...273
Day of South America...278
Day of Asia...282
Day of Africa..291
The Plains of Abraham..292

12 DUBLIN 10–17 JUNE 2012.....................301

Facing the future..304
Baptism..308
Marriage and the Family..309
Priesthood and ministries..315
Reconciliation..318
Suffering and Healing...321
Communion and Mary...324
Faith in Christ—Let it grow!.......................................331

13 CEBU 24–31 JANUARY 2016....................337

Monday: hope, persecution, St Paul............................344
Tuesday: Eucharist, faith, poverty.............................348
Thursday: cultures, migrants, youth...........................355
Friday: street children, sacredness of food, popular piety...359
Saturday: first Communions......................................363
The Statio Orbis...366

EPILOGUE..373

PREFACE

A T A theology conference at Thornycroft Hall in March 2017, during a conversation with Fr Oliver Treanor, it emerged that I had been privileged to attend all twelve International Eucharistic Congresses since 1973. Fr Treanor was enthusiastic: 'You must write a book about them. There's nothing in the English language about them all.' So I invite you to come with me on this world tour of International Eucharistic Congresses, to what I like to call a Spiritual Odyssey.

Such Congresses end nowadays with the Statio Orbis, when the Pope or his Legate presides over the final gathering. People often ask, 'But what is the *Statio Orbis*?' Indeed, what is a 'statio' or 'station'? There are bus stations, fire stations, railway stations, Stations of the Cross, the station churches in Rome, the Stations in Ireland where the priest visits homes, and so on. What they all have in common is that they are places where people stop. That isn't a surprise because the Latin word *statio* and the English word *station* come from the Latin verb *sto, stare* meaning to stand still. That is why Eucharistic Congresses

> should be considered as a kind of 'station' ['statio'], that is, a pause of commitment and prayer, to which a community invites the Universal Church, or a local Church invites other Churches of the same region or nation or even those of the entire world. The purpose is that the members of the Church join together in deepening some aspect of the Eucharistic mystery and express their worship publicly in the bond of charity and unity. (*Holy Communion and devotion to the Mystery of the Eucharist outside of Mass*, 1973, n.109).

That is what has happened at all the Congresses I've been to. The Eucharist has been considered under various aspects and people have come together to worship in unity and in all charity. I hope you will get a glimpse of this in the chapters to follow.

There are no footnotes since this book is intended for the general reader but references are given after every chapter. Perhaps the chapters will inspire budding theologians to choose Eucharistic Congresses as subjects for doctoral studies? There is certainly ample material available for that.

My warm thanks go to Cardinal Vincent Nichols for kindly writing his Foreword. The Cardinal knows well the value of these Congresses and he instigated an inter-diocesan Congress whilst Archbishop of Birmingham, as well as the National Congress to be held in Liverpool in September 2018. I thank Fr Vittore Boccardi SSS, secretary to the Pontifical Committee of International Eucharistic Congresses. He was courtesy itself and a willing helper when I consulted the Committee's archives in the Vatican. Archbishop José Serofia Palma of Cebu and Susanna Hwang Yun-gyeong of the Catholic Bishops' Conference of Korea kindly provided me with invaluable material. Fr Thomas Rosica, CEO of the Canadian Salt and Light Catholic Media Foundation, allowed me to quote some of his words. Fr Anthony Dearman patiently read the manuscripts and corrected them (though any mistakes remaining are mine only). There are two people I must thank especially. First, the late Bishop Thomas Holland who recognised the immense value of these Congresses, attended eight, and introduced me to them. And then Fr Oliver Treanor, without whom this book would never have seen the light. He has encouraged and inspired me all the time since he first suggested that it should be written. The reader must be grateful to him, as I most certainly am; grateful too to all those who had any part to play in gifting these Congresses to the Church and to the world.

FOREWORD

The International Eucharistic Congresses: A Spiritual Odyssey make up the reflections of a priest personally present at International Eucharistic Congresses from 1973 to 2016, covering a period of forty-three years. Unbroken attendance and eye-witness observations combine to produce a volume unique both for its fascinating travelogue and for the richness of its Eucharistic theology and devotion. It also explains how these Congresses have grown from humble beginnings in Lille in 1881 to the present day.

After most International Eucharistic Congresses, the host venue has published a record of its proceedings. Such a record can take various forms but normally more for the professional theologian. In any case, they are all long out of print, except one. What has been needed, and what many people have longed for, is something that everyone can access, and in plain English. Unavailable until now, here it is, and totally new!

The author's clear style will appeal to all and his distilling of the meditations of some of the finest theologians in the world will provide endless spiritual nourishment.

Here we have an opening up of Eucharistic thought over many years, closely observing the way it has developed, and bringing us nearer to Christ the Bread of Life and His Mystical Body, the Church.

For those also who may be wondering where to go on holiday this book points a way. The Congresses have been held in strategic places, in all five continents. The author shows how to combine a journey that takes in different cultures and amazing venues with an uplifting Eucharistic experience.

I thank him for this labour of love.

✠ Cardinal Vincent Nichols
Archbishop of Westminster

1 A KALEIDOSCOPE OF CONGRESSES 1881–1968

1881–1914

INTERNATIONAL EUCHARISTIC CONGRESSES had a humble beginning. That they began at all is due to the tenacity of a French woman, Mlle Marie Marthe Emelie Tamisier— 'Emelie' to her friends. Emelie had been born at Touraine in 1834. By then, France, the 'eldest daughter of the Church', had been shaken by the philosophical movements of the Enlightenment, by the Revolution, by governments hostile to the Church, and by rampant anti-clericalism. The coming of the Second Empire in 1852 seemed at first to bring a new spring into the life of the Church. Ordinations to the priesthood mounted; the old religious congregations prospered; the number of pupils in Catholic schools increased. Soon, however, the anti-clericals in government became vociferous once more. Press attacks on the Church multiplied. The writings of authors such as Strauss, Renan and Darwin shook the faith of many. In the last quarter of the nineteenth century, the French State passed a number of anti-Catholic laws, culminating in the Law of Separation of 1905.

Nevertheless, at the same time piety flourished. Bl Frederick Ozanam, St Jean-Baptiste Vianney, Ven Jean Marie de Lamennais, St Peter Julian Eymard and many others nurtured people's faith. It was the last named who influenced Emelie Tamisier. She joined Eymard's newly-founded Congregation of the Blessed Sacrament, determined that Christ in the Eucharist should be glorified. St Peter Julian Eymard saw Christ, present in the Eucharist, as the living and life-giving answer to the secularist and atheistic thought and practice of his time. Daily, and even nocturnal, adoration of the Blessed Sacrament spread rapidly. Eymard's aim was to restore Christ, dethroned by the anti-clericals and the atheistic philosophers, as the foundation and the keystone of Christian order in society. Emelie set out to realise that aim.

She would do it with the unwitting help of an Englishman, George Stephenson! His invention of the locomotive revolution-ised transport throughout the world. By the 1860s, much of the French rail network was in place, enabling people with limited resources of time and money to travel with comparative ease. Emelie organised pilgrimages to popular French shrines associ-ated with Eucharistic miracles: Avignon; Faverney; Douai. She wanted these pilgrimages to develop as congresses and conven-tions. Medical and scientific professions met in conference to exchange experiences, information, new discoveries. Why should not the Eucharist also be the subject of study and research? Emelie received support from Monsignor Louis Gaston Adrien de Ségur, whose book *France at the foot of the Blessed Sacrament* had considerable influence, and from Monsignor François-Marie-Benjamin Richard de la Vergne, Bishop of Belley and later Cardinal Archbishop of Paris. However, when Emelie tried to extend her pilgrimages to become national and even interna-tional, the French bishops were reticent; they did not want to risk confrontation with the anti-clerical authorities. The bishops of Belgium, initially favourable, also declined. The bishops of Holland when consulted were apprehensive at the prospect of 'excitable French Catholics' parading their faith in Protestant Holland. It seemed to Emelie that her dream was at an end.

A Lille industrialist, Philibert Vrau, came to the rescue. With his brother-in-law, he was highly respected for organising bene-ficial societies for working people, planning model homes for them and arranging a joint society of employers and employees. He had introduced nocturnal adoration of the Blessed Sacrament in Lille as early as 1857. Approached by Emelie, Philibert got the approval of Pope Leo XIII for a Eucharistic Congress in Lille for 28 June 1881 and, greatly daring, invited the Catholics of the world to come to it. 800 came, mostly from France and Belgium. People from 13 countries took part, including one priest from

England, Fr Basil OFM. Representatives came too from outside Europe and reported on Eucharistic developments in South America, Cuba and the Philippines. They shared in worship and workshops for three days. International Eucharistic Congresses were born.

Lille 1881 shaped the pattern of future Congresses. Throughout the three days there was daily and nocturnal adoration of the Blessed Sacrament. In the first two days discussion papers and reports tackled ways whereby Christ would be restored to His rightful place in the world: confraternities of the Blessed Sacrament; adoration; the Mass and the Sacraments; frequent communion (this at a time when frequent communion was not the practice); catechism and preparing children for first communion; preparing the sick for the Last Sacraments; publicity for Eucharistic devotions and works. These last gave the name to the first Congresses, known until the Paris Congress of 1888 as 'Congresses of Eucharistic Works'. From then on they were known as Eucharistic Congresses, apart from Jerusalem in 1893 which reverted to Eucharistic Works. Paray-le-Monial in 1897 was the first to use 'International' in its title.

Wisely, the Lille organisers formed a permanent committee to ensure the future. From now on, Congresses would be held almost every year until the outbreak of the First World War in 1914. Numbers attending grew: 5000 came to Avignon in 1882. Liège in Belgium in 1883 witnessed an outdoor procession of the Blessed Sacrament, which then became a permanent feature of these Congresses. The Congress moved to Fribourg in Switzerland in 1885, where the local government and the military publicly proclaimed Christ as the King of Society.

The Fribourg Congress reflected the Church's concern for workers. Rapid industrialisation in Europe was changing society. Catholic movements sprang up in France, Belgium, Germany, Switzerland and Italy with the aim of ameliorating the social evils suffered by the labouring or working classes. Leon Harmel, a textile manufacturer at Rheims, spoke in Fribourg on the Eucharist and Working Men. This social concern continued in other Congresses: as well as reports from the North African Missions and the Belgian Congo, Antwerp in Belgium in 1890 heard a paper on the relevance of the Blessed Sacrament to the social questions of the day. 150,000 people were present at Antwerp's closing ceremony. At Rheims in 1894 the Blessed Sacrament and the Social Question was an official Congress subject. This followed the publication in 1891 of Pope Leo XIII's famous encyclical, *Rerum Novarum.*

International Eucharistic Congresses were entering the mainstream of Catholic life.

1893 saw the Congress in Jerusalem, the first to be held outside Europe. Pope Leo XIII chose the venue himself. He wished to foster good relations with those Churches of the East not in communion with Rome. He also gained the confidence of the Catholic Eastern Rite Churches. Opposing any effort to Latinise them, he maintained that they represented a valuable ancient tradition and were a sign of the divine unity of the Catholic Church. He made this clear in his follow-up encyclical letter of 1894, *Orientalium Dignitas*: 'The Churches of the East are worthy of the glory and reverence that they hold throughout the whole of Christendom in virtue of those extremely ancient, singular memorials that they have bequeathed to us.' Only a few years previously, in 1890, the Dominican, Fr Marie-Joseph Lagrange, had founded the Ecole Biblique in Jerusalem. Leo knew its importance, and the Ecole was to play an important part in the revival of Catholic biblical scholarship throughout the twentieth century. It was in the Jerusalem Congress year of 1893 that Pope Leo issued his encyclical letter *Providentissimus Deus*, underlining the importance of the Scriptures for theological study. For the first time at such a Congress, a papal legate was present. Pope Leo gave the task to Cardinal Langenieux. By such an appointment, the Pope wanted to highlight his aspirations for unity between East and West.

Over the next decade the Congress was shared between France and Belgium: Rheims, Paray-le-Monial, Brussels, Lourdes, Angers, Namur, Angoulême. The way was being paved for the momentous decrees of Pope St Pius X. Frequent, even daily, communion and earlier communion for children were regular topics at these Congresses. At Angers in 1901, for example, there was discussion about young men and the Blessed Sacrament. Namur in 1902 set up a special committee for matters concerning young people. Fr Durand SSS year after year pleaded for early communion. The Eucharist was not only for adoration but also food 'for the life of the world'. Against this background, and to mark the twenty-fifth year since Lille, Pope St Pius X called the next Congress to Rome.

Pius X saw International Eucharistic Congresses as an ideal way to prepare for and later to implement his decrees on frequent and early communion. Speaking to those present at the Rome Congress, he stressed the importance of 'frequently approaching the Eucharistic Sacrament'. He pointed out that 'the centre of the Christian life, the soul of the Church, is to be found in the Eucharist'. Little wonder that Pope Pius XI called him the 'Pope of the Eucharist'. Various biographers of Pius X have described how he 'produced a spiritual revolution'; his eucharistic decrees were seen as 'among the most important Acts ever put forth by the Papacy'; Pope Ven Pius XII later described those decrees as 'inspired by God Himself to bring the faithful back to the ecclesiastic practice and fervour of the early Church'.

The Rome Congress of June 1905 was followed in the December by the first of a trilogy of eucharistic decrees from Pius X. *Sacra Tridentina* on 'Frequent and Daily Reception of Holy Communion' recalled the instruction from the Council of Trent: 'The Holy Council wishes indeed that at each Mass the faithful who are present should communicate, not only in spiritual desire, but sacramentally, by the actual reception of the Eucharist.' Piety however had since grown cold and the poison of Jansenism had led to a forbidding rigorism. Accordingly, 'Frequent and daily

Communion, as a practice most earnestly desired by Christ our Lord and by the Catholic Church, should be open to all the faithful ... therefore, parish priests, confessors and preachers ... should exhort the faithful frequently and with great zeal to this devout and salutary practice.' The following year, Pius X gave instructions that the sick should be given every facility to receive the Eucharist as often as possible. In 1910 came *Quam Singulari,* lowering the age for first communion to the age of 'seven, more or less'.

The Congresses held from 1906 until 1914 were especially concerned with implementing the decrees of Pius X. The Tournai Congress of 1906 was known as 'par excellence the Congress of Frequent Communion'. Topics covered included Eucharistic teaching for children; the Sunday parish Mass; the Sunday High Mass; obstacles in the way of attending Sunday Mass. The Congress in Metz in 1907 took daily communion as its central theme. Cologne in 1909 followed this theme through. Vienna in 1912 heard papers on frequent communion for school children and school leavers, and on the missal for use of children. Following on from the Jerusalem Congress, the spirituality of the Eastern Churches also featured prominently. Metz considered the eucharistic hymns of the Greek Oriental Church. Cologne studied the eucharistic teaching of St Cyril of Jerusalem and Vienna heard papers on Mass in the Early Church.

In September 1908 it was London's turn. With each passing year the Eucharistic Congress was becoming more international. That, coupled with the opening of the new Westminster Cathedral in 1903, prompted the Archbishop of Westminster, Francis Bourne, to invite the Congress committee to his diocese. The London Congress turned out to be one of the most representative and important of all the early Congresses. England was still widely thought of as a bulwark of Protestantism. Yet here was a Eucharistic Congress being held so close to the centre of Government and the Established Church! Protestant societies were horrified. They appealed to the King to forbid the proposed Blessed Sacrament Procession and called on the Government to enforce the statute outlawing such processions. In the event, and only days before the planned procession was to take place, the Prime Minister Herbert Henry Asquith, afraid of public disorder, privately asked Archbishop Bourne to call the procession off. Addressing an assembly at the Albert Hall during the Congress, Bourne disclosed what had been said. He promised that there would be a procession but without the Blessed Sacrament. Folklore has it that as the story spread throughout the country that a Blessed Sacrament had been forbidden in the capital, Catholics organised their own processions, especially in Lancashire.

It would be a mistake to overemphasise the squabble over the procession. Tolerance generally prevailed. Cardinal Vincenzo Vannutelli, the papal legate, set a pacific note in his opening address. The first legate to enter England since Cardinal Pole 350 years before him, he said:

> We meet in a most hospitable country, upon which through the ages God has heaped the most signal blessings; which deserved to be honoured by the mouth of a Roman Pontiff of great name with the title of a land of Angels rather than Angles. And if, in later days, deplorable differences arose, these have since been softened by an age which has learned to set greater store by peace. And now, for the first time in many centuries, the gates of England are open to a cardinal who is also a Papal legate. O truly wonderful ways of divine providence which are so sweetly bringing us together in this city!

With the legate were six other cardinals—Gibbons of Baltimore, Logue of Armagh, Sancha y Hervàs of Toledo, Ferrari of Milan, Mathieu of France and the Roman Curia, and Mercier of Mechelen in Belgium. Bishops, priests and people came from all quarters of the globe.

The Congress had sections in English and French. In an impressive sweep of theology and history, speakers covered many aspects of the Eucharist both in the Eastern and Western

Churches. After the closing ceremonies, Cardinal Vannutelli sent a telegram to the Cardinal Secretary of State in the Vatican:

> The Congress concluded with a great triumph today when the procession passed through the streets of London packed with crowds raising continuous cheers for the cardinal legate and the other cardinals and prelates. The Sacred Host was not carried in the procession, but I gave a final benediction with the Sacrament to the crowd from three open balconies on the façade of the cathedral. Members of the House of Lords formed an escort of honour for me. Perfect order was kept.

Following the Congress, Pope St Pius X wrote to Archbishop Bourne in glowing terms. Although the Congress was the first of its kind in England in the order of time,

> it must be accounted as without rival throughout the Universal Church for its concourse of illustrious men, the weight of its deliberations, its display of faith and devotion to the Holy Eucharist, and the splendour of its religious ceremonies.

He thanked the archbishop and all who had taken any part in the proceedings.

After Cologne in 1909, the Congress crossed the Atlantic for the first time, to Montreal. The Montreal Gazette reported 200,000 visitors for the Congress, with close on half a million attending the final Benediction on Fletcher's Field. Cardinal Vannutelli was again the papal legate at what the newspaper described as 'the greatest demonstration of any kind—historical, religious or political—which Canada has ever witnessed'.

Archbishop Bourne of Westminster however caused a storm. Speaking in the church of Notre Dame, he tactlessly argued that English should become the principal language of the Church in North America, with French being abandoned. The congregation reacted strongly. Henri Bourassa, a member of the Quebec assembly, was scheduled to speak after Bourne. He put his prepared text away and spoke extemporaneously in words still remembered today in French nationalism.

> But, it is said, you are only a handful ... We are only a handful, it is true. But in the school of Christ, I did not learn to estimate right and moral forces by number and wealth. We are only a handful, but we count for what we are, and we have the right to live.

When he finished, there was a hush in the church. Dramatically, Cardinal Vannutelli stood up and shook Bourassa's hand. People remembered how cheering then broke out, hats were waved, and many of the assembled bishops stamped their feet in applause.

Madrid and Vienna followed Montreal. From Madrid came a proposal to institute a feast of Christ, the King of Society. The twenty-fifth Congress was held in Lourdes, 22–25 July 1914. 200 bishops came from all five continents. All the themes of preceding Congresses were encompassed in a programme under the theme of the Eucharist and the Social Kingship of Jesus Christ. The papal legate, Cardinal Gennaro Granito Pignatelli di Belmonte, announced that the Congress would be 'for love and peace ... Christ wishes to reign through love, because it is love alone that will give to peoples the peace of which the nations today stand in such pressing need'.

Opening the 25th Congress at Lourdes, the President, Bishop Heylen of Namur, had announced that the Pope wanted such Congresses to be held every two years. This was intended to promote national, regional or diocesan Congresses in the intermediate years. Alas! Three days after the Lourdes Congress ended, the First World War broke out. It was to disrupt the Congresses and change the face of Europe. Nine million combatants and seven million civilians were to die in one of the deadliest conflicts in history. Paul Christophe (*When God is Silent*, 2014) wondered how French and Germans who had proclaimed their common faith together in front of the Lourdes grotto could then turn into soldiers ready to kill each other. A fair question? Should we not pity the men in the trenches and castigate rather the interests and propaganda of those in control? Pope St Pius X died less than a month after the War started. He was succeeded by Pope Benedict XV who tried in vain to bring about peace. It would be eight years before the next Congress was held, and then under the newly elected Pope Pius XI.

1922–1938

Throughout the War, Pope Benedict worked incessantly for peace. In August 1917 he approached the Allies and the Central Powers in August with a seven-point plan. He proposed a peace based on justice rather than on military conquest. While Britain and France ignored the plan, Germany steered away. The Holy See was allowed no part in the peace settlements of 1919. In the secret Treaty of London of 1915, Italy had agreed to enter the War on condition that the Vatican would be excluded from any subsequent negotiations. Even so, Benedict worked with considerable success in establishing relations with the warring powers and with the new states which had emerged. He also began preparations for the next International Eucharistic Congress to be held in Rome, but he died before it started. In May 1922, his successor, Pope Pius XI, presided at the Congress. Its theme was 'The Peaceful Reign of Our Lord Jesus Christ in the Eucharist'.

Opening the Congress, Pius XI explained its purpose: 'With this Eucharistic Congress ... will begin that full pacification which is the first and indispensable condition of all social reconstruction.' He called for a

> true regeneration ... in the return of society to Jesus Christ ... The pride and vain-glory of the human mind have driven out Jesus Christ, exiled Him, confined Him in His solitary tabernacles. Unbridled lust for worldly goods has made the minds of men mutually bitter, barbarous, hostile. Together with the banishment of the Lord, peace has left humanity.

> The sacrament of the Eucharist ... that is the remedy. Here
> it is, where the human mind bows before the majesty of
> God, offering Him the homage of faith, which believes,
> does not see, but adores and acknowledges. It is in this
> Sacrament that minds become softened and regain gentle-
> ness. It is in this Sacrament that all are seated at the same
> table and feel themselves truly brothers—great and small,
> masters and servants, rulers and ruled. Peace, the peace
> that all are seeking ... the peace the world cannot give
> because it can offer nothing more than goods unworthy of
> the human heart and insufficient for its happiness, this
> peace Jesus Christ in the Blessed Sacrament alone can give.

The Congress examined ways in which the Eucharist could
nurture this peace. It considered the individual in his intellectual
and moral life; in the family; in professional and working associ-
ations; in society; in the nation; and between nations.

After the Rome Congress, Pope Pius XI— whose papal motto
was 'The Peace of Christ in the Kingdom of Christ'—began a 'new
series of Congresses' involving the local churches in all five
continents; they took place every two years and were focused on
having a 'missionary' preparation. Following up the wishes
expressed during previous Congresses, in 1925 this Pope instituted the Feast of Christ the King for the whole Church. He made
it clear that the Kingship of Christ is about service, not domination. It is a spiritual kingdom concerned with spiritual things. It
stands for the common good and human dignity. From Christ's
Kingship, peace and harmony will follow.

The Congresses in Amsterdam (June 1924) and Chicago (June
1926) developed the themes of peace through the Eucharist. They
underlined the example of peoples who remained faithful to the
Church's teaching from earliest times. They aimed to draw others
to the Eucharist by the public profession of faith and devotion.
Cardinal George Mundelein, Archbishop of Chicago, opened the
Congress there by saying that

one of the principal purposes of the Congress is to bring the doctrine of the Church and the reason for our belief in the Real Presence to the notice of those outside the Church as well. And it is our hope that the splendour of the ritual, the eloquence of the discourses and above all the fervour of the faithful will leave a lasting impression on the millions of onlookers who, as yet, are not of this fold.

Thanks to the burgeoning film industry, the Chicago Congress— the first to be held in the United States—made an enormous impact on the 'Movie Mind'. It attracted extensive media coverage and brought in about one million pilgrims. 60,000 school children sang the *Missa de Angelis* at the opening Mass in Soldiers' Field. The largest transport enterprise in American history carried over half a million people forty miles from Chicago to the seminary at Mundelein village, with electric trains leaving every two minutes and with roads designated as one way going to and from their destination. Seven Pullman cars were repainted in cardinal red and gold for the special train that carried the papal legate, Cardinal Giovanni Bonzano, with Cardinal Patrick Joseph Hayes of New York and seven visiting foreign cardinals (and their substantial entourages) from New York to Chicago in almost exactly twenty-four hours. The first Congress since the feast was established, Chicago brought the Kingship of Christ eminently to the nation's notice.

Pius XI was impressed by the attendance of Australian pilgrims in Rome for the Holy Year of 1925 and he readily agreed to the suggestion that Sydney might host the next Congress in September 1928. The Congress opened with the consecration of the newly-completed St Mary's Cathedral. Perhaps because of that, conferences at the Sydney Congress focussed on the Eucharist and Mary. Although a number of Protestant bodies called for the Congress to be prohibited, a spirit of unity prevailed. Many Protestant leaders welcomed visitors. The Prime Minister, the Anglican Archbishop of Sydney and the leader of the Jewish community attended a garden party at Government House to celebrate the Congress and to honour Cardinal Bonaventura Cerretti, the first papal legate to set foot in Australia.

From Australia the Congress moved to Africa. Before his conversion, St Augustine had lived in Carthage for nine years, conducting a school of rhetoric there before moving on to Rome. He died as Bishop of Hippo in the year 430. The Congress in Carthage in May 1930—the first to be held in Africa—commemorated the fifteenth centenary of Augustine's death and also bore witness to the vibrant Christian presence in northern Africa prior to the Arab conquest. Christianity had come to Carthage in the second century and quickly gained converts as the Church rapidly grew. Eighty bishops from north Africa attended the Council of Carthage in 256. The see of Carthage came to be recognised as the most important in the whole of Roman Africa. When Hasan ibn Noman, governor of Egypt, captured Carthage from the Byzantines in 698 he ordered its complete destruction. A new city, the modern Tunis, grew a little to the south of ancient Carthage. Carthage was restored as an archiepiscopal see in 1884, with Cardinal Charles Lavigerie as archbishop. Six years later, on the peak of the famous Byrsa Hill, he consecrated a magnificent new cathedral dedicated to St Louis of France. There the Congress met.

Tunisian nationalism grew apace, leading to independence from France. In 1964 the Holy See was obliged to hand over to the Government all but five of the seventy or more Catholic churches in Tunisia. The Carthage of St Cyprian and the early martyrs became a titular metropolitan see. The Cathedral passed into the ownership of the Tunisian state and became a cultural centre known as the Acropolium. After 1930, there would not be another International Eucharistic Congress in Africa for 55 years—the Nairobi Congress of 1985.

In June 1932 the Congress was again in Europe. 1500 years after the arrival of St Patrick, and in celebration of the devotion of the Irish people to the Eucharist, Dublin was the chosen venue, with the theme 'The Propagation of the Sainted Eucharist by Irish Missionaries'. It was one of the largest Congresses of the century.

By all accounts, a quarter of the Irish population attended the closing Mass in the Phoenix Park, while half a million people assembled in the centre of Dublin for the final Benediction. The Mass was broadcast and relayed around the city by the most extensive PA system ever used anywhere in the world. Pope Pius XI sent his message from the Vatican, while John McCormack's rendering of *Panis Angelicus* was still spoken of generations later. The Congress was a conspicuous success for the newly-formed Irish Free State and gave its Catholic citizens new pride as they saw the world flocking to its shores.

Lectures given to packed audiences related to the Eucharist and Ireland. Meetings of overseas visitors understandably focussed on Irish connections and the work of the very many Irish missionaries. The UCD building, then in St Stephen's Green, hosted an exhibition on Irish missionary work which was attended by vast numbers and may well have led to the substantial increase in the number of men and women who came forward and dedicated themselves to missionary work over the following two decades. Following the Congress, the papal legate, Cardinal Lorenzo Lauri, wrote to the Archbishop of Dublin:

> I shall never forget the unforgettably glorious days of this Eucharistic Congress ... all have participated, all have co-operated to make this congress a triumph, government and civic leaders, as well as ecclesiastical authorities, priests, members of religious communities, men, women and children, have all united to make this Eucharistic Congress a plebiscite of love for the Blessed Eucharist, a plebiscite of devotion to the vicar of Christ.

Cardinal Lauri is also quoted as saying, *'Dopo Dublino, solamente il cielo'*—'After Dublin, there can only be heaven!' When Cardinal Lauri reported back to Pope Pius XI about the Dublin Congress, the Vatican Secretary of State, Cardinal Eugenio Pacelli, would no doubt have been present. Did he remember Lauri's words? Pacelli—later Pope Ven Pius XII—was appointed papal legate for the Congress in Argentina in October 1934. After the opening ceremony in Buenos Aires he exclaimed, 'Here we are in paradise!'

For two whole years, Argentina had prepared prayerfully and thoroughly. The Eucharistic Congress in Buenos Aires of 1934 has gone down in the story of Argentina as a defining moment in that nation. It has even been said that the history of the Argentinian Church is divided into two stages: before and after the Congress. There, for the first time, the Catholic Church was able to celebrate an event which had an extraordinary effect on public life. Until then, a liberal regime, supported by freemasonry and anti-clericalism, had sought to dominate the Church, relegating her to the sacristy and out of public life. The population of Argentina at that time was eight million. Yet more than one million people gathered for Holy Mass in Palermo Park, to hear a greeting and blessing from the Pope via Vatican Radio. At special Masses, over 100,000 children made their first Communion; 400,000 men and 700,000 women received Communion too. The Congress awakened numerous priestly and religious vocations. Fr Henrique Alla SSS was one of the Congress secretaries. He recalled how

> Men of every social class, often known for their indifference or their hostility to faith, came to God that night. Many fathers of families, who for years had resisted the supplications and tears of their loved ones, were won by grace and fell at the feet of confessors. Various journalists who had come out of professional curiosity, upon seeing those men praying and singing 'like little girls', were captured by an irresistible force and themselves joined the queues and ended up confessing and receiving communion.

Two years after the Congress a boy was born in Buenos Aires to Mario José and Regina María Bergoglio, Italian immigrants. Christened Jorge Mario, he is better known today as Pope Francis.

Pope Pius XI had instituted the feast of Christ the King in 1925 with his encyclical letter *Quas Primas* ('In the first'), with the hope that nations would see that the Church has the right to freedom, and immunity from the power of the state (31); that leaders and nations would see that they are bound to give respect to Christ (32); and that the faithful would gain strength and courage from the celebration of the feast, as we are reminded that Christ must reign in our minds, wills, hearts and bodies (33). Opposed to the Kingship of Christ were the totalitarian States emerging after the First World War: Communist Russia; Nazi Germany; Fascist Italy. In a series of encyclical letters, Pope Pius exposed their philosophies and errors. *Divini illius Magistri* ('That Divine Teacher') on education came in 1929; *Non abbiamo bisogna* ('We do not need') denouncing the worship of the fascist Italian State in 1931; *Mit brennender Sorge* ('With burning Concern') against Nazi racism and *Divini Redemptoris* ('Divine Redeemer') on Communism in 1937. He also wrote *Quadragesimo Anno* in 1931, marking the 'Forty Years' since Pope Leo XIII's encyclical *Rerum Novarum* and repeating Leo's warning against both socialism and unrestrained capitalism. The 1920s and 1930s saw many set-backs for the Church, including in Mexico, Spain and Russia. But if the Pope could have been at Buenos Aires during the Congress, he might have thought that his hope was being realised: that the Kingship of Christ was arriving.

Pope Pius XI's desire to establish world-wide the Kingship of Christ was one reason for his taking the International Eucharistic Congresses into all continents. He also had the Church's missions in mind and was known as 'the Pope of the Missions'. The explosion of missionary activity during the nineteenth century led to a huge increase in the numbers of Christians of all denominations. Pope Pius, like Pope Benedict XV before him, strongly urged the training and ordination of native clergy. In 1926 Pius consecrated six Chinese bishops in St Peter's in Rome—the first native bishops for all of East and Southeast Asia for 250 years. It was a new beginning to insert native clergy into Church leadership. The Pope named Manila in the Philippines as the Congress venue after Buenos Aires. Appointing Cardinal Dennis Joseph Dougherty, Archbishop of Philadelphia, as papal legate, Pope Pius told him that 'For the propagation of the Faith, nothing is more effective than the one sacrament and sacrifice which is rightly called "the Mystery of Faith"'.

Cardinal Dougherty knew the Philippines well. In 1903, aged just 38, he had been appointed there as Bishop of Nueva Segovia. He immediately faced fierce opposition from Gregorio Aglipay and the Philippine Independent Church. Aglipay was a Catholic priest who had been excommunicated in 1899. Allied with the most radical political parties, in 1903 he became the first 'Supreme Bishop' of the newly formed Independent Church. Bishop Dougherty won the people's trust. When an influenza epidemic swept through his diocese, he turned a number of church buildings into emergency hospitals, staffed by religious sisters, thereby saving innumerable lives. He returned the cathedral in Vigan City, occupied by the 'Aglipayans', to the diocese of Nueva Segovia and re-opened and re-consecrated many churches the schismatic group had taken. Dougherty returned to the United States in 1915 as Bishop of Buffalo and three years later became Archbishop of Philadelphia. Pope Pius XI made him Cardinal in 1921. He was enthusiastically welcomed back by the Philippine people when he came as papal legate in February 1937.

Not too many travelled to Manila from Europe or the Americas due to distance and cost. The East however was well represented, with delegations from Korea, China, Japan and Vietnam. It seems that the Philippine Government gave the papal legate no official welcome. Their snub was more than offset by the warmth of the people. The Prefect of Manila offered Cardinal Dougherty a golden key, saying 'Here is the key of the city. Know that no door is closed for the Pope's representative. If we have to use this key, it would be to close the City gates after Your Eminence has entered so that you may stay with us always.'

Luneta Park in Manila was the centre of celebrations. There an altar was erected under a canopy almost 40 metres high, supported by three white columns representing the three main island groups: Luzon, Visayas and Mindanao. Great numbers of people took part

in the five-day Congress programme which ended with a spectacular candlelight procession of the Blessed Sacrament attended by
a crowd estimated at one million. In a radio message Pope Pius XI
stressed the missionary aspect of the Eucharist:

> Among the abundant fruits of salvation which we antici-
> pate from your Congress and for which we pray, there is
> one hope of which we will make mention, the one which
> your session had particularly in view: it is our hope,
> namely, that from a more ardent love of Our Lord in the
> august Sacrament of the altar and from more frequent
> communion with him there may come a daily increase of
> devotion to missions and enterprise for the promotion of
> missionary activity. For it is from that very source that light
> is given to our minds, ardour to our souls and divine
> fruitfulness to our labours and good works.

Only fifteen months separated the last two Congresses to be held
before the outbreak of the Second World War. Budapest followed
Manila in May 1938, marking the nine hundredth anniversary of
the death of St Stephen, first king of Hungary and responsible for
the evangelisation of the Hungarian people. The Congress theme
was 'The Eucharist—Bond of Love'. Pope Pius XI gave as its
purpose 'to make reparation for the many blasphemies of those
who deny the existence of God'. In 1938 war clouds were
gathering over Europe. The Third Reich had annexed Austria just
two months before the Congress and stood poised on Hungary's
borders. Hitler forbade German Catholics to attend the Congress.
The Hungarian Nazis formed the slogan, '1938 will be our year'.
No doubt the papal legate—Cardinal Eugenio Pacelli, Vatican
Secretary of State—had this in mind in his opening speech. He
recalled how the Ottoman forces had been defeated in 1686 and
Buda won back from the Turks. He spoke of Budapest, Hungary's
capital, as 'the bastion of Christian Europe'.

Papers given at the Congress covered the Eucharist as a social
bond of charity, a family bond of charity and a national and
international bond of charity. Of Hungary's nine million inhab-

itants at this time, about six million were Catholics. They had fervently prepared for the Congress with a year's programme involving all parishes in the country. Political figures participated too, along with the Head of the Government and ministers, the Universities and the professions. While Latin was the common language of communication between priests, the general assemblies were in Hungarian, with interventions in twenty-four other languages. The highlight on Ascension Thursday was the evening Blessed Sacrament procession on the river Danube. The Blessed Sacrament, illuminated by powerful beams, was carried on the prow of a regal vessel and followed by a flotilla of boats. All along the river banks the many thousands of onlookers sang Eucharistic hymns in what was described as 'a fantastic concert of lights and songs'. A fireworks display rounded off the evening in an expression of popular joy. But before long, other fireworks would divide and decimate a Europe plunged into war.

It would be 14 years before another International Eucharistic Congress was held.

1952–1968

The 35th Congress met in Barcelona 27 May–1 June 1952. Coming shortly after the end of the Second World War, the Congress theme, not surprisingly, was 'The Eucharist and Peace'. The Congress met in a world greatly changed by the War. The dominant world powers were now the USA, the USSR and China. Germany had been split into two and Russia had taken control of East Germany, Poland, Czechoslovakia, Hungary, Bulgaria, Romania, the Ukraine, Albania, Latvia, Estonia and Lithuania. The former colonial empires of the Western Powers were dissolving. Great Britain granted independence to India and started withdrawing from Africa. Robert Schuman, Konrad Adenauer and Alcide De Gaspari, outstanding statesmen and devout Catholics, leaders in France, Germany and Italy, were determined to put an end to wars in Europe. In 1951, along with

Belgium, the Netherlands and Luxembourg, they formed the European Coal and Steel Community. Schuman said his aim was to 'make war not only unthinkable but materially impossible'. The ECSC would ultimately lead to the European Union.

When the Barcelona Congress opened, peace in Europe was fragile and there was open war in Korea. The Archbishop of Barcelona, Gregorio Modrego Casaus, had announced that 'united for the one same purpose and glorying in the name of Christ, the object of the Congress was to study the work of justice that is peace'. The theme of peace was developed each day with a different emphasis: first, peace in the family; then individual and social peace; international peace; peace in the Church. Preparatory work was rewarded when pilgrims from sixty-four nations were registered and for the first time at International Eucharistic Congresses simultaneous translation of conferences was available in Spanish, French, German, English and Italian. The Congress attracted famous speakers, among them the theologian Père Reginald Garrigou-Lagrange OP, the biblical scholar Fr Augustin Bea SJ (later Cardinal and first President of the Vatican Secretariat for Promoting Christian Unity), the writer Don Lorenzo Riber, the liturgist Dr Pius Parsch CRSA and the preacher Fr Riccardo Lombardi SJ. Pope Pius XII appointed as his legate Cardinal Federico Tedeschini, who from 1921 to 1938 had been Apostolic Nuncio to Spain.

Artistic exhibitions featured prominently in the Barcelona Congress, bringing together treasures from Toledo, Salamanca, Zaragoza, Madrid and many other cities and towns of Spain. Huge crowds enthusiastically attended the Congress ceremonies; it was estimated that the population of Barcelona, then one and a half million, doubled during the Congress. The most impressive and extraordinary event, the ordination of 810 priests, took place in the Olympic Stadium of Montjuich. Twenty-one altars were built around the edge of the sports field, at which twenty-one bishops celebrated synchronised Masses during which they each ordained about forty priests. The Archbishop of Barcelona led the liturgy from a central altar, his voice amplified throughout the stadium. The ceremony was seen by some as an experimental phase in the liturgical movement; six years later, in the decree *De Musica Sacra et Sacra Liturgia*, the Vatican Sacred Congregation for Rites forbade the practice of synchronised Masses.

Pope Pius XII relayed a message at the end of the Congress, summing up its work as

> an example to the entire world—so many nations, so many races, so many rites 'one heart and one soul'—so that seeing it the world may come to understand where lies the source of true peace, in its individual, family, social and international aspects ... Gathering together all your voices, all the wishes of your hearts, all the anxieties of your souls, we wish to concentrate them all into one great cry of peace, which may be heard the world over.

The search for peace also underlay the theme of the 36th Congress, held in Rio de Janeiro 17–24 July 1955. Its theme was 'The Eucharistic Kingdom of Christ the Redeemer'. The Congress examined the nature of this kingdom and its relationship with the individual Christian, the family, society and the Church, with particular attention to the Church of Silence—mainly Christians suffering under Communist regimes in Europe, China, Korea and Vietnam. Seats were pointedly reserved at the Congress for Cardinals Stepinac of Yugoslavia, Mindszenty of Hungary and Wyszynski of Poland, all of whom were detained by the Communist government in their countries. It was also the time of negotiations in Geneva, attempting to end the ten years of the Cold War. The main speakers at the daily conferences were all laymen. Dr Alceu Amoroso Lima expressed the overwhelming desire for peace in his paper on 'The Eucharistic Kingdom of Christ and His Church':

> During these days, the eyes of the world are turned towards two world capitals: Geneva and Rio de Janeiro, the one in the old world which is newer every day, and the other in the new world which gets stronger day by day. There, the

meeting of the 'Big Four'; here, an International Eucharistic Congress. There, men who hold in their hands the
destiny of the material world; here, men who possess in
their hearts the secret of spiritual peace by their spirit of
faith, sacrifice, justice and love. There can be no peace on
earth, on sea and in the air unless there be peace in the
hearts, minds and homes of all.

A colossal engineering feat created the Congress site. 1,900,000
metres of earth were moved, demolishing a hill close to the city
centre and forming a square with seating for 300,000 people as
well as ample standing room, looking out onto the Atlantic. As
at Budapest in 1938, the Blessed Sacrament was borne on a ship
transformed into a floating altar and escorted by hundreds of
boats. Other highlights included a blessing of the sick, following
the pattern of Lourdes, and accompanied by 20,000 nurses. It was
estimated that 1.5 million communions were given during the
Congress week. Pope Pius XII appointed as his legate Cardinal
Benedetto Aloisi Masella, who had been Nuncio to Brazil from
1927 to 1946. At the end of the Congress, the papal legate led the
consecration of Brazil to the Sacred Heart of Jesus. The secretary
general responsible for organising the Rio Congress was an
auxiliary bishop of Rio, Mgr Helder Camara, later Archbishop of
Olinda and Recife and world famous as a champion of the poor.
He has been widely reported as saying, 'When I give food to the
poor, they call me a saint. When I ask *why* they are poor, they call
me a communist!'

In 1960 the Congresses again returned to Europe—to Munich.
Munich marked a turning-point in the history of the International Eucharistic Congresses and would merit a chapter on its
own. In the previous year, Pope St John XXIII had announced
that he was calling an Ecumenical Council. Already, twenty
months after the announcement, much preparatory work for the
Council had been done. As a theology student in Rome at that
time, I remember well those heady days. Pre-Preparatory Commissions and then Preparatory Commissions flew into Rome

from around the world, meeting in fervent, sometimes hot, debate. The Munich Congress would foreshadow changes the Council would bring in the Church's liturgical and devotional life and its pastoral approach to the problems of the day. Pope John had called on the Munich Congress to pray that 'the entire social system of our day, as well as the entire way of life, be adapted to the rules of the Christian moral law'. The Congress theme was 'The Eucharist—for the Life of the World'.

It was at Munich that the term *Statio Orbis* was coined, thanks primarily to the liturgist Josef Jungmann. Jungmann recalled how it was an early custom in Rome for the Pope to celebrate Mass in a different church most days of Lent in the presence of the clergy and faithful of the city. This was known as the *Statio Urbis*, the 'Station of the City'. At International Eucharistic Congresses, the faithful gathered around the Pope or his legate from all over the world—in Latin, 'orb'. This, Fr Jungmann maintained, constituted a *Statio Orbis*, a 'Station of the World'. He had floated the idea of a *Statio Orbis* at the Carthage Congress of 1930 but it had gone practically unnoticed.

Fr Jungmann saw that the programme of a Eucharistic Congress threatened to fall into three parts: Procession, Mass, Communion. But the idea of the Statio made it possible

> to re-establish the unity of the Eucharistic Mystery and its celebration. For in this way the emphasis is placed where it had been placed from the very beginning in virtue of the institution of Our Lord: in the celebration of the Eucharist which finds its conclusion in communion and does not exclude the homage of a procession ... It is in the co-offering and co-receiving of the Body of the Lord that the congregation itself becomes discernible and visible as the Mystical Body of the Lord ... Yes, here the universal Church is seen again as the one family of God which gathers all lands and peoples and races around the one altar, at which the first priest and pastor carries out the Mystery of Faith.

Here we see a change of emphasis, away from the Eucharist in itself and onto the Eucharistic assembly. It was all in keeping with Jungmann's vision as presented at an Assisi Congress in 1956, when he spoke of the Mass as an assembly of the people, with the priest as leader, and as a celebration of the Last Supper, with stress on the community meal aspect. Later, Jungmann would say, 'It is not the Eucharist itself that is the focus of the holy event, but the People of God'. Professor Josef Ratzinger of Bonn University, attending the Munich Congress as a young priest, saw it as 'a milestone of liturgical and theological development, serving the entire Church'. In 2012, now as Pope Benedict XVI, he recalled that Jungmann had created a new model for Eucharistic Congresses, one that was revolutionary for the whole Church as well as being a preparation for the Second Vatican Council.

Pope St John XXIII adopted Jungmann's phraseology and in his letter appointing Cardinal Gustavo Testa as papal legate to the Munich Congress he wrote that it was to be

> a liturgical station of religious service, as it were, similar to the one which takes place in Rome during Lent ... Not a *Statio Urbis* but a *Statio Orbis*, a station of religious service for the whole world, where an army of worshippers will be summoned and will pray fervently to heaven for the entire suffering Church and for the sorrows of the world.

Cardinal Joseph Wendel, archbishop of Munich, gave his whole-hearted support to the new forms of liturgy which had been developing apace in the German Church. A huge free-standing altar was built on the Congress site. Mass was said *versus populum*, facing the people. The epistle and gospel were read only in German. The sign of peace was exchanged and nearly all the one million people present received Communion, distributed by hundreds of priests who made their way through the crowds. Bishop Thomas Holland (who was then secretary to Archbishop Gerald O'Hara, Apostolic Delegate to Great Britain, and who accompanied him to the Congress) remembered how

Munich too offered splendour to eye and ear—but controlled, rehearsed and harmonious. There were gorgeous uniforms, crowd formations, massed choirs and, unique to this Congress, an inspired preview of liturgical features which two or three years later found their place in the Second Vatican Council's Constitution on the Liturgy.

The unity of Christians featured strongly in the Munich Congress. Only two months before, Pope St John XXIII had established the Secretariat for Promoting Christian Unity, with the German Cardinal Augustin Bea SJ as its President. Germany was already a leader in the ecumenical field. Mutual opposition to Nazism, coupled with active persecution, had brought Catholics and Protestants together as in no other country. The *Una Sancta* Movement began in 1948, while in 1957 Archbishop Lorenz Jaeger of Paderborn founded an Institute for Ecumenism in that city. During the Congress, Catholic and Protestant theologians gave lectures at Munich's University. The pattern was set for all future International Eucharistic Congresses. In the lead up to the Second Vatican Council, the Rhine had begun to flood into the Tiber.

The structure of the Munich Congress, 31 July–7 August 1960, was simple. There was continuous adoration of the Blessed Sacrament in various churches throughout Munich. For a whole week, the Eucharist was placed within the setting of the Paschal Mystery. Four days of preparation, inspired by the rites of Holy Week, took the Congress to Thursday, the 'Day of Priesthood and brotherly love'. There were priestly ordinations in several churches, and agapes— meals in imitation of those celebrated by early Christians—were held in the city's parishes. Friday was kept as the 'Day of the Cross'. Young people went on pilgrimage to Dachau, the place of the infamous concentration camp. In the evening there was veneration of the Cross and nocturnal adoration of the Blessed Sacrament. Saturday, the solemnity of the Lord's Transfiguration, was a 'Day of Light', with many meetings and events, and in the evening the renewal of baptismal promises. The Congress climaxed with the Statio Orbis on the Sunday, followed by the Blessed Sacrament procession, Benediction and a solemn *Te Deum*, accompanied by the pealing of all the city's church bells. Munich had been a showcase of *nova et vetera*. As the Vatican Council took shape, Eucharistic Congresses would take on this new look. The wider Church in its turn would be greatly influenced by Munich.

Bombay in India hosted the next Congress, from 28 November–8 December 1964. Pope Bl Paul VI made history as the first pilgrim pope to attend a Congress outside Rome.

He was present for three days, leaving the Armenian Cardinal Gregory Agagianian as his legate for the rest of the time. The world was still gripped by the Cold War and Pope Paul VI addressed this on the flight to India. Speaking to journalists he said:

> If only countries would stop the armaments race, and put their resources and energies instead into the brotherly assistance of the under-developed nations! Let every nation, by cultivating 'thoughts of peace and not of affliction' and of war, put at least part of the sum destined for armaments into a great world fund to help with the many necessities of food, clothing, houses and health care that afflict many peoples. From the peaceful altar of the Eucharistic Congress, may our cry of distress reach all the governments of the world, and may God inspire them to undertake this peaceful battle against the sufferings of the less fortunate brothers.

Two million people lined the route to welcome the Holy Father on his way to the Congress site. The thought of peace ran through all his speeches. He praised the natural goodness of the Indian people and said:

> We come to you as a messenger of Jesus and his teaching … The people of India and of Asia can draw light and strength from the teaching and spirit of Jesus, from his love and compassion, in their efforts to help the less fortunate, to practise brotherly love, to attain peace among

themselves and with their neighbours. This is the mission
of the Church here.

When the Bombay Congress opened, three sessions of the
Vatican Council had ended. The Council Fathers had approved
momentous Constitutions—on the Liturgy, on Ecumenism, on
Oriental Churches and on the Church. There had been much
debate on Scripture and on the Church in the Modern World.
All had their impact on the Congress. Concelebration at Mass,
for example, gave bishops and priests a greater sense of their
collegiality and their unity in the priesthood. Mass was celebrated
also in the Siro-Malabar and Siro-Malankara rites. Pope Paul
recognised these traditions as 'a living witness to the Catholicity
of the Church of Christ, which is at the same time for all men,
embracing all cultures, and also expressing in a particular way
the truth and beauty which exist in each culture'. Meetings were
held with representatives of other Christian Churches and other
Faiths. The papal legate struck an inclusive note when he opened
the Congress: 'Thinkers of the noblest religions of every country
have always considered union with God as the supreme purpose
of human life ... More than any other country, India has given
the example of this long and passionate quest for God and a desire
for total communion with Him.' The image of the 'servant
Church' envisaged by the Constitution on the Church was lived
out in Bombay by visits the Congress pilgrims made to hospitals,
prisons, orphanages and the forgotten slums. Bishop Thomas
Holland, newly-appointed to Salford, enthused:

> Even two years in Bombay as port chaplain had scarcely
> prepared me for this Congress. The sub-continent flow-
> ered in homage to the Blessed Sacrament with all that is
> best and authentic in Indian art—music, dance, and the
> décor of the Cooperage (a huge open maidan in the heart
> of the city where the religious functions took place). True,
> the medium was English in the main—the commentator
> inevitably (and superbly) Fr Agnellus Andrew OFM.

The Congress theme was 'The Eucharist and the New Man', based on mankind fashioned by post-war society. Announcing the Congress, Archbishop Valerian Gracias of Bombay said:

> Today, human life is progressing in every direction to new frontiers of achievement, and a new man is emerging who is in possession of tremendous resources, but finds his life constrained, and almost destroyed, by lack of love of God and of men. The many new nations that have recently come into being are anxious to lead a new life and to make their own distinctive contribution to the new world. Among them is India, which maintains an ancient tradition that all renewal must begin with a renewal of self. By a renewal of herself in her members in the midst of the nations, the Catholic Church can make a signal contribution to the future of the world.

The Congress aimed to achieve this through its study sessions and liturgy, by fostering

> the conviction that in the Eucharist, and more particularly in the full celebration of the Mass, people of today can find the programme, the inspiration and the supernatural help they need in order to be renewed in the inner life of their minds and be clothed in the new self created in God's image, justified and sanctified through the truth.

This was not to be a purely personal renewal; it was to flourish into Christian service of the community and especially to the poor of India. The seven Sacraments were celebrated over the week of the Congress. Notable events were the First Communion Mass for 3,600 children; the ordination by Pope Paul VI of five bishops from the five continents; and the marriage of several dozen couples. 'Who can ever forget', wrote Bishop Holland, 'the shy brides in their sarees, their demure responses, the earnest young husbands and the transparent goodness of brides and grooms?'

The next Congress met in Bogotá, Colombia, 18–25 August 1968. The Church and the world had moved on since Bombay. The Second Vatican Council ended in 1965 and its reforms were being implemented. But there was growing unrest throughout the world. 1968 saw violent student protests all over Europe. Latin America was seething with unrest. Camilo Torres, a Catholic priest, socialist and member of the guerrilla National Liberation Army, was shot dead by the Colombian military in 1966. The Marxist Che Guevara was shot by a Bolivian execution squad in 1967. Argentina, in the hands of a military dictatorship, saw the emergence of the Movement of Priests for the Third World— mainly priests serving in shanty towns and poor neighbourhoods, inspired by reform ideas coming from the Vatican Council but combined with strong socialist political views. In Brazil, the 'March of the One Hundred Thousand' in Rio de Janeiro, just two months before the Bogotá Congress, came in public protest against that country's military dictatorship.

Concerned Christians in the whole of Latin America saw social justice as their main aim. Some supported violent revolution and formed groups of guerrilla fighters. The Basic Text prepared for the Bogotá Congress recognised the situation. It spoke of the problems but also the hopes and aspirations of the continent and drew attention to the importance of Pope Bl Paul VI's encyclical *Populorum Progressio*, 'On the Development of Peoples', written in 1967 and teaching that the world economy should serve all mankind, not just a few. The Text called on all to develop a social conscience, especially those persons in more responsible roles.

Pope Paul VI was clearly keen to attend the Congress, not only to celebrate with pilgrims local and from afar, but also to observe and to offer solidarity and guidance to the people. He said that he came to Bogotá, not for his own glory but to honour Christ in the Eucharist and in the poor. As he stepped from the plane at the airport of Bogotá, he knelt and kissed the ground. It was another papal 'first'. His humble gesture struck home: a local newspaper called it 'a gesture that will make history'. Two million people welcomed him along the route from the airport to the city.

The Congress theme was 'The Eucharist—the Bond of Charity'. On the eve of his departure from Rome, Pope Paul stressed that the Eucharist, as sacrifice and sacrament, was what the Congress was all about. The Congress was

> a great assembly of clergy and faithful in honour of the Eucharist, which is solemnly celebrated and adored to give public homage by faith and love to Christ, our Saviour, really present in the sacrament of the Eucharist as the victim who was sacrificed on the cross; to Christ become spiritual food for the faithful, who, in a rite in which they share the same table, recall His memory in order to live by Him in time and to merit meeting Him on the day of His final return in glory.

Was a balance subtly suggested here to the one-sided interpretations of Josef Jungmann's approach at Munich? A little later, in 1972, Pope Paul would say to the members of the permanent committee preparing for the Melbourne Congress:

> We know quite well that the Sacrifice of the Mass enjoys pride of place in the liturgy: all the documents of the Magisterium already affirm this, right up to the most recent ones. But we want also to remind all our brothers and children, that, contrary to certain recent theoretical and practical rash innovations, all kinds of eucharistic worship retain their validity unaltered, their pedagogical and formative value as a school of faith, prayer and holiness … By reviving worship of the real presence of Christ, we can revive the spirit of generosity, strength, heroicity to discover Christ in the faces and sufferings of the poor, the needy, immigrants, the ill, the dying; we serve Christ in them single-mindedly since we are sustained by the strength that comes only from the well-tried practice of familiarity with Him in prayer.

Once in Colombia, Pope Paul embraced the poor. He met with 300,000 peasants, *campesinos*, at Mosquera, just outside Bogotá. He greeted them:

> We can tell you that this encounter with you is one of the most desired and beautiful moments of this our journey:

it is one of the dearest and most significant moments of our apostolic and pontifical ministry! We came to Bogotá to honour Jesus in his Eucharistic Mystery, and we are full of joy that we have been given the opportunity to do so in your midst by celebrating the presence of the Lord among you ... The sacrament of the Eucharist offers us its hidden, living and real presence; you are also a sacrament, that is, a sacred image of the Lord among us, like a reflected representation, but not hidden, of his human and divine face. We remember what a great and wise Bishop Bossuet once said about the 'eminent dignity of the poor'. And all the tradition of the Church recognizes in the poor the sacrament of Christ, which is certainly not identical to the reality of the Eucharist, but in perfect analogical and mystical correspondence with it. Moreover, Jesus Himself has told us in a solemn page of His Gospel, where He proclaims that every man who suffers, every hungry, every sick, every wretched, every person needy of compassion and help, is He, as if He himself was that unhappy person ... (cf Mt 25: 35) ... You, dear children, are Christ for us ... We bow to you and we want to see Christ in you ... We love you! ... We love you with a preferential love; and with us you love, remember it well, always remember it, the holy Catholic Church.

Then we ask you what can we do for you after speaking so far in your favour. We do not have, you know, direct competence in temporal things, and we do not have the means or the authority to intervene practically in the matter. Yet this we say to you: We will continue to defend your cause ... with particular reference to fair pay, affordable housing, basic education, health care, and civil rights and the gradual participation in the benefits and responsibilities of the social order. We will continue to denounce the iniquitous economic inequalities between the rich and the poor; the authoritarian and administrative abuses damaging you and your community ... We are delighted to know that, as part of this great Eucharistic Congress, there is study and promotion of new and organic plans for the working classes and especially for the rural ones, for you Campesinos! And we urge all the governments of Latin America, and those of other continents, as well as all the wealthier classes, to continue generously and courageously the reforms necessary for a more just and more efficient social order ...

Promising to keep up his pressure on behalf of poorer nations, and to commit the Church to the generosity and poverty of spirit called for by the recent Council, Pope Paul also reminded his hearers that 'Man does not live by bread alone (Mt 4:4). We all need that other bread—the bread of the soul, of religion, of faith, the bread of the Word and of Divine Grace.' Their humble status was more favourable for attaining heaven.

Before ending with his blessing, Pope Paul added:

> Finally, allow me to urge you not to put your trust in violence and revolution; this is against the Christian spirit, and it can also delay, and not favour, that social advancement to which you legitimately aspire. Rather, support initiatives in favour of education ...be united and organised under the Christian sign, be able to modernise the methods of your rural work; love your fields, and value the human, economic, and civil function of the earth that you cultivate.

Bishop Holland recalled being present at that meeting with the Campesinos:

> Many are poor, many lack adequate grasp even of their one treasure, The Faith. But, so far as I could see, no privations had robbed them of the kindness of their smile ... [The Campesinos] received Pope Paul tumultuously, a vast multitude stretching faraway into the open country-side, miles from the city. There he delivered his famous address, so sensitive to their plight, so firm in rejecting violence as the remedy ... That evening I was at one of the city churches with young men. They had not yet heard what the Pope said. When I told them that the gun was

'out', that violence was not the way to peace, they went very serious.

Before leaving Bogotá, Pope Paul, speaking with the same sensitivity shown to the Campesinos, inaugurated the general assembly of the Bishops of Latin America. The papal legate, Cardinal Giacomo Lercaro, brought the Congress to a close. The Latin American bishops continued their assembly in Medellin, where they famously agreed that the Church should make a preferential option for the poor.

Four and a half years later, the Melbourne Congress was held in 1973.

References

1) Pontificio Comitato per i Congressi Eucharistici Internazionali, Vatican City, *Atti dei Congressi Eucaristici Internazionali.*

2) Pontificio Comitato per i Congressi Eucharistici Internazionali. *Report of the Nineteenth Eucharistic Congress, held at Westminster from 9 to 13 September 1908* (Sands, London & Edinburgh 1909).

3) Pontificio Comitato per i Congressi Eucharistici Internazionali. *The International Eucharistic Congresses for a New Evangelization* (Vatican City 1991).

4) Pontificio Comitato per i Congressi Eucharistici Internazionali. *Suggerimenti e Proposte per la preparazione e la celebrazione dei Congressi Eucharistici* (2010).

5) *Statio Orbis: The International Eucharistic Congress 1960 at Munich.* Vols 1–2 English translation (Munich 1961).

6) *XXVe Congres Eucharistique International tenu a Lourdes du 22 au 26 juillet 1914.* Digitized by the Internet Archive with funding from University of Ottawa (2010).

7) Afanassief, N., *Statio orbis,* (1962), No.1, pp. 65–75.

8) Arratibel, J. SSS., *Los Congresos Eucaristicos – su historia, utilidad y organizacion* (Tolosa 1940).

9) Aubert, R., *Les Congrès eucharistiques de Léon XIII à Paul VI. Concilium* (1965), No.1, pp. 117–124.

10) Bello, A. I., Congressi Eucharistici e il loro significato teologico e pastorale (Milan 2010).

11) Boylan, P., *Dublin—The Book of the Congress 1932*, 2 Vols (Dublin 1934).

12) Brouard, M., *La Dynamique des Congres Eucharistiques Internationaux depuis Lille 1881 jusqu'a Lourdes 1981* (Chicoutimi: Editions Science modern, 1981).

13) Boccardi, V. SSS., *International Eucharistic Congresses: Between history and modern times.* Paper given on 18 June 2015 at the Plenary Assembly of the Pontifical Commission in preparation for the 51st IEC.

14) Casas, J. M. C., *Experiences and Impact of the Congresos Eucaristicos Internacionales en la vida Eclesial. Pastoral Liturgica* (Mayo-Junio, 2008) No. 304.

15) Daniel-Rops, H., *Histoire de l'Eglise du Christ*, Vol 6 (France, 1960 & 1964), English translations Vols 8 & 9 (London & New York 1965 & 1966).

16) Donovan, C. F. (Ed), The Twenty-Eighth International Eucharistic Congress, Chicago, 20–24 June 1926 (Chicago 1927).

17) Feron-Vrau, P., *Les Triomphes Eucharistiques dans les 25 premiers Congrès Eucharistiques Internationaux* (Paris 1920).

18) Holland, T., *Eucharistic Congresses—A Set of Six.* Adoremus (1985) No. 1, pp. 4–13.

19) Jeune, L., *Emelie Tamisier et l'Idée Mère des Congrès Eucharistiques: 1834-1910* (Lyon 1927).

20) Jungmann, J. A., *La Pastorale, Clef de L'Histoire Liturgique* nn 47–48 (1956).

21) Jungmann, J. A., *Corpus mysticum. Gedanken zum kommenden Eucharistischen Weltkongress. Stimmen der Zeit* (1959), No. 26, pp. 401–409.

22) Jungmann, J. A., *Statio Orbis Catholici—Heute und Morgen. Statio Orbis. Eucharistischer Weltkongreß 1960 in Munchen (*1962), Vol.1, p. 81.

23) Lestra, A., *Retourner le monde—Les origines des Congrès Eucharistiques* (Lyon-Paris 1959).

24) Marini, P., *The Shape, Significance and Ecclesial Impact of Eucharistic Congresses* (2009).

25) Meehan, T. F., *Eucharistic Congresses.* The Catholic Encyclopedia, Vol.V, pp. 592–594 (New York 1913).

26) McKeon, T., *Eucharistic Congresses: An Historical Perspective.* Adoremus (1981), No.1, pp. 40–45.

27) Menozzi, D., *Eucharistic Congresses: Unsolved Identity. The News Kingdom (1997),* No. 18, pp. 523–526.

28) O'Dwyer, R., *The Eucharistic Congress, Dublin, 1932* (Dublin 2009).

29) Oury, G-M. and Andry, B., *Les Congrès Eucharistiques, Lille 1881-Lourdes 1981 (*Solesmes 1980).

30) Parker, L. A., *The International Eucharistic Congresses 1881–1981.* Adoremus (1982), No.1, pp. 3–18.

31) Pereira, T. A., *38th International Eucharistic Congress Bombay, 1964.* 2 Vols. (Bombay 1965).

32) Pratzner, F., *International Eucharistic Congresses: Experiences and Traditions* (2002).

33) Schwertner, T. M. OP., *The Eucharistic Renaissance* (Macmillan New York 1926)

34) Vecchi, E., *The Social Dimension of the Eucharist. History, roots and tradition of the National Eucharistic Congresses in Italy (*Ponteranica 2004).

35) Vecchi, E., *Eucharistic Congresses and the salvific dimension of the Eucharist at the service of humanity and of society.* Pontificio Comitato per i Congressi Eucaristici Internazionali, Plenary Assembly (2010).

36) Willke, J. C., *Eucharistic Congresses.* New Catholic Encyclopedia, Vol.5, pp. 617–618 (Washington 1967).

37) www.congressieucaristici.va

38) www.saltandlighttv.org/iec

2 MELBOURNE 18–25 FEBRUARY 1973
CONGRESS OF THE PEOPLE

L ED BY BISHOP Thomas Holland, fifty of us set off from the
diocese of Salford to go to the other side of the world. By
1973 package holidays to Spain and southern Europe had
taken off in more senses than one. Inter-continental flights though
were still something to be wondered at. Our journey took us first
to India. We stayed for a few days in Delhi, in a former palace now
transformed into a hotel, albeit showing signs of faded grandeur.

A day trip took us to Agra and the glory of the ivory-white
marble mausoleum which is the Taj Mahal. Behind the Taj, on
the banks of the Yamuna river, a religious ceremony was taking
place. St Paul's experience at Philippi and Lydia's conversion
came to mind, when Paul 'went along the river outside the gates
as ... this was a customary place for prayer' (Ac 16:13). Rivers
provided handy places for ritual ablutions. Glorious in its own
way was the nearby clinic we visited run by the Sisters of Mother
Teresa. About eighty mothers, their sarees brilliant in the sun,
patiently waited for a doctor to see their babies. The treatment
was given free of charge.

Bangkok, the capital and most populous city of Thailand, was
our next stop. The city was growing rapidly in the burgeoning
tourist trade. We visited the usual sights: the floating markets;
the Grand Palace; the Buddhist temples of Wat Arun and Wat
Pho. We also called on the Apostolic Nuncio. Portuguese and
French missionaries have taken the Catholic faith to Thailand
since the sixteenth century. Their story has see-sawed between
success and persecution. At the time of our visit Catholics made
up less than half of one percent of the total population. Nowadays
the Catholic Church in Thailand takes an active part in fighting
against human trafficking.

No visit to Thailand would be complete without a visit to 'The
Bridge on the River Kwai'. The bridge lies on the Myanmar (then

known as Burma) border. It carries the 'Railway of Death' built under Japanese orders, linking Thailand with Burma and constructed by prisoners of war and Asian slave labourers in terrible conditions. It runs for two hundred and fifty miles. Begun in the autumn of 1942 it was completed in one year at the cost of many thousands of lives. It is reckoned that one life was lost for every sleeper laid in the track. A 1957 film starring Alec Guinness, Jack Hawkins, William Holden and others brought this historic tragedy to the attention of millions of viewers worldwide.

When we visited in 1973 the bridge was fast becoming a tourist attraction. An old engine lay rusting on the track. A plate on its side proclaimed that it was made by Beyer, Peacock and Company in Gorton, Manchester—my old stamping ground as a curate at the Sacred Heart, Gorton.

Recalling Joseph Conrad's story *Youth*, in which the ship *Judea* sailed from Newcastle to Bangkok with its cargo of coal, Bishop Holland said 'We must go for a sail on the Bangkok river'. And so we did. An enterprising American had transformed a river boat into a floating restaurant. Forty people could eat on deck whilst enjoying the ever-changing scenes of the majestic river Chao Phraya. The Bishop ordered a Madras curry—the hottest of all curries—for himself. Mine was much milder. The diners were served by six beautiful Thailand ladies in traditional costume. Meal over, they all came to our table and sat on the ground round the Bishop and me. The other diners looked on in astonishment. What did these 'men of the cloth' (we were wearing our clerical dress) have over them? The reason was soon revealed. 'Tell us about God' the beautiful ladies asked. They listened with rapt attention as Bishop Holland spoke very simply about the Father who so loved the world that He gave His only Son.

From Bangkok, we came to our true destination, 'Marvellous Melbourne' as the city was once known. We found a vibrant, modern city built along the Yarra River: a city of gardens and parks, of fine architecture and culture, of business and finance. Above all we found a city with an open welcome for the Congress.

How can one do justice to a Congress which took three years to prepare and which involved many thousands of people? Perhaps by underlining the Congress theme chosen by Pope Paul VI: the 'New Commandment' of Jesus Christ, 'Love one another as I have loved you' (Jn 15:12).

But the Congress nearly did not take place. The Permanent Committee for International Eucharistic Congresses, with the knowledge and approval of Archbishop James Knox, had announced in Rome in December 1969 that Melbourne was to be the venue of the 1973 Congress. The announcement was not well received in the Melbourne archdiocese. Those were early, heady days after the Second Vatican Council (1962–1965). Opposition came from clergy who recalled Bishop Emile De Smedt's accusations of 'triumphalism, clericalism, juridicism' and who feared a Congress based on outdated theology.

It says much for Archbishop Knox's tenacity in making the Congress happen at all. His knack of identifying priests and lay people with ability paid off. He gave them responsibilities and then trusted and supported them, none more so than Mgr Kevin Toomey and Mgr Brian Walsh. They planned that Melbourne would be a 'new look' Congress—a People's Congress—in keeping with the emphases of the Second Vatican Council. The organisers paid special attention to popular participation, simplicity, the needs of the poor and underprivileged in Australia and around the world, as well as to unity among Christians.

As always with ventures of this magnitude the secret of success lies in solid preparation. The pastoral side of the Congress was in the hands of Monsignor Toomey and his committee. They worked in close consultation with the Victoria Council of Churches and worked out a three-phase operation.

The first phase began in Lent 1972 with thousands of groups of Christians all around Australia meeting four times in one another's homes to discuss the theme, 'Christians in the Community'. By the final meeting, most of those taking part claimed their faith had deepened and they wanted to know and do more.

From introspection at the start, the groups found their vision widening. They saw how Christianity affects people in two ways: as a stimulus to self-examination and as a spur to action on behalf of others. They saw that both of these were needed for a complete Christian witness.

The second phase took the form of a campaign organised by Action for World Development, a national ecumenical agency working for the Australian Council of Churches and the Australian Catholic Bishops Conference. In July 1972 about 150,000 Australians took part in four discussion meetings to study the topic of development. Another 20,000 New Zealanders took part in the programme, as well as parishes in Papua-New Guinea and the Pacific Islands. This unprecedented campaign led to many substantial personal commitments, renewal of faith and profound involvement of Christians of all denominations in shaping the social goals of the nation.

The third phase began in October 1972 with the resumption of home meetings for discussions on 'The Eucharist and Life'. This phase concentrated on the practical love and concern for others which should follow from a reception of God's Sacrament of love. Thousands of people hailed this phase as an exhilarating spiritual experience.

Some people could not join in the meetings and other activities during the year because of sickness or handicap or old age. They were invited to a special Mass in November 1972 at the Royal Melbourne Showgrounds, concelebrated by Cardinal Gilroy and all the bishops of Victoria. In this way, they were able to associate with the renewal programme and to offer up their prayers and sufferings for the success of the Congress.

Technical planning for the Congress was in the hands of Mgr Walsh and his committee. They looked after the countless details of organisation. A large network of committees and sub-committees gave long hours to preliminary arrangements. Help came from all directions, with the public authorities and the Churches giving a generous lead. The media gave the Congress more space and time as February 1973 approached.

Pope Bl Paul VI had appointed as his Legate Cardinal Lawrence Joseph Shehan, Archbishop of Baltimore, USA. On 17 February 1973, the civic and religious leaders of Australia enthusiastically greeted the Papal Legate. Cardinal Shehan proved a wise and popular choice. He spent himself unsparingly in the intense activity of the Congress week. If ever, by the way, the Cardinal had needed a lookalike he would have found one in Bishop Holland who later reminisced that wherever the Salford contingent went, 'I swam around in a warm haze of whispered "Cardinal Shehan"'s'.

The Congress opens

The Congress opened in the Gothic grandeur of St Patrick's Cathedral, Melbourne, on Sunday 18 February 1973. Built in the nineteenth century, the Cathedral is the tallest and, overall, the largest church building in Australia. In his inaugural address, Cardinal Lawrence Shehan etched the beginnings of Melbourne both as a Catholic community and as a modern and progressive city. He said: 'For all these things we may well be grateful.' He went on:

> We are, however, particularly grateful for the strength and richness of the Catholic life that has developed here and for the promise of Christian unity which we now see. With these things we shall be concerned during this week of the Congress. The centre of that life and the life of the whole Church is the Eucharist. For the Eucharist at once serves as our test of faith and supplies us the grace to deepen and vitalise that faith. It is also the bond of Christian love that binds us all to Christ and through Christ to the Father in the Holy Spirit; that joins all of us together in the spirit of forgiving love as we share in the redemptive love of Christ. It is the love of the Eucharist that has urged us even beyond those who are Christian, to those Asian peoples who are

so close to your homes and are seeking the guidance and
help of your great nation in their own efforts of human
development. It is particularly on this truth we shall dwell
during this Congress whose theme is: 'Love one another
as I have loved you'.

On the same day, many thousands of people gathered in other
parts of Australia for Mass and processions. In Melbourne, the
city's many communities of migrants gathered in their national
groups, welcoming the pilgrims sharing their language and
cultures who had come from overseas for the Congress.

The City Fathers went out of their way to give their backing
for the Congress. They provided permanent floodlighting for the
Catholic and Anglican Cathedrals. The city's trams and buses
were bedecked with flags, reminiscent of a royal review. The
Victorian Government gave a reception in the new National Art
Gallery for visiting Church dignitaries and pilgrims. The Great
Hall of the Gallery was adorned for the occasion by three
tapestries on loan from the Vatican and the Choir of the Sistine
Chapel sang. Libraries and other venues, including the Anglican
Cathedral of St. Paul, presented art exhibitions, musical recitals
and drama performances. An observer wrote:

> A stranger arriving in Melbourne in those days without
> any knowledge of what was going on would soon have been
> aware that the city was in the kind of mood of friendliness
> and joy which one normally does not expect to meet in a
> busy metropolis. The citizens were going out of their way
> to be helpful and to give a sincere welcome to their visitors.

During the week that followed, major ceremonies at central
venues attracted large numbers of people, while hundreds of
smaller events drew people of many nationalities together in a
spirit of Christian love. One of those events was a meeting at the
Loreto Training College where our English group was staying.
Before leaving home, Bishop Holland had alerted the people of
his diocese to invite any relatives or friends from the diocese now
in Melbourne to two reunions. Afterwards the Bishop recalled

'the family bond of a distant diocese that brought together close on two hundred migrants from my part of Lancashire in two happy nostalgic sessions'.

What did the week hold? Far more than can be compressed here. One thing to bear in mind is that this Congress was very much a child of its time. Coming so soon after the Second Vatican Council, when the decrees of that Council were beginning to sink into the Catholic psyche, there was much emphasis on Liturgy and on Ecumenism.

Fr Josef Jungmann made plain the liturgical slant in a preconciliar article written for the Australian Catholic Press. He had encouraged the idea of a Statio Orbis as the focal point of the Congress in Munich in 1960. He then saw the Melbourne Congress as not only a celebration 'of this city and this continent, but a Feast of the whole of Catholic Christianity...It is the common celebration of the Eucharist which must establish the central and high point of the Congress.' It may well have been his influence that persuaded the Melbourne organisers not to hold a Blessed Sacrament procession through the city streets. Fr Jungmann had argued that such a procession could be misunderstood in a cosmopolitan city where many people were not Catholics and that it would therefore be out of place. He rather disparagingly described people as spectators at a Eucharistic procession, 'a nondescript mass'. He preferred a 'celebrating congregation ... It is in the co-offering and co-receiving of the Body of the Lord that the congregation itself becomes discernible and visible as the Mystical Body of the Lord.'

Many were disappointed at the decision not to hold a Blessed Sacrament procession. The Italian and other Mediterranean peoples resident in Melbourne may well have thought the German liturgist's comments too coldly Teutonic. The decision does seem to have by-passed the guidance of Pope Bl Paul VI. In his address to the Permanent Committee for International Eucharistic Congresses in Rome on 1 March 1972 the Pope had said:

We well know that the Sacrifice of the Mass holds the first place in the liturgy: all the documents of the Magisterium say so, up to the most recent ones. But we also wish to remind our brothers and sons that ... all the forms of Eucharistic worship maintain unaltered their validity, and their pedagogical and formative value as a school of faith, prayer and holiness.

Pope Paul recalled a passage in *Mediator Dei* where Pope Pius XII had quoted St Augustine's famous dictum that 'No one eats that flesh without having first worshipped it'. Pope Paul went on to say: 'The real presence of Christ is the prolongation of the sacrificial liturgy ... this presence, and consequently Eucharistic worship outside the Mass, is of an importance that cannot be equalled.'

Nevertheless, the liturgical ceremonies at Melbourne were impressive and very varied. Melbourne was blessed in having the talented Rev Dr Percy Jones as director of music. Dr Jones was also the head of the Festival Committee for the Congress and chaired the Ecumenical Committee. He made a massive contribution to the success of the Congress.

The liturgies ranged from the solemn ordination of three bishops and five priests to renewal Masses for a number of groups: priests; the Catholic Women's League; altar servers; nurses; deaf people; religious sisters; guides and scouts. The Mass for the deaf moved many people. An observer wrote: 'Catholic and Protestant knelt quietly in prayers for the deaf and I am certain that the vision of at least one cameraman was impaired as he struggled to focus not only his own camera but his own vision through his tears.' Other celebrations also reinforced the Congress theme, 'Love one another as I have loved you.'

The Mass for Migrants was the first of several celebrations on the hallowed turf of the Melbourne Cricket Ground. The first official cricket Test Match had been played here in 1877, almost a century before, making it a revered spot for all cricket lovers. Now it would host something even more sacred!

Immigrants were numerically strong in Australia and had contributed richly to national life. At the Offertory procession in the Migrants' Mass representatives of some twenty countries in their national dress presented an explosion of colour as they brought up the gifts. Later at the same venue the Melkite and Ukrainian communities united to celebrate a Solemn Liturgy in the Byzantine Rite. Present at this celebration were Patriarch Maximos V Hakim and Cardinal Josyf Slipyj—the latter well-remembered as a long-term prisoner of the Kremlin.

Perhaps the most joyful and spectacular liturgy at the MCG was the Mass for Schools. A massive, carefully organised public transport operation conveyed 100,000 children to the Ground. The ship with the Tasmanian youngsters aboard only arrived in Melbourne half an hour before the Mass started. They were all in their places in time. The children prayed, sang and cheered at the top of their voices. Fr Harold Winstone from England, who had founded the St Thomas More Centre for Pastoral Liturgy in London and who chaired ICEL's Advisory Committee, spoke to them and said: 'To me you are not just a sea of faces but a hundred thousand heroes and heroines already set out on the great adventure of life.' He based his homily on a story about concern for others written by the Australian author, Alan Marshall. He spoke to the children of Jesus in the Eucharist, their companion through life, and the message He enables us to give: 'This is the message we give to everyone we meet in life, be they enemy or friend—"You're loved, you're needed"—for in giving this message we find God, as St Paul did, in everyone.' At the end of the ceremony the children gave the Papal Legate and Cardinal Knox a rousing and prolonged farewell.

The Sidney Myer Music Bowl, set in the lawns and gardens of Kings Domain, is a hugely popular open-air venue for gatherings of all kinds. It was the setting for one of the most memorable occasions of the Congress, the Australian Aboriginal Mass, attended by 30,000 people. The Papal Legate, Cardinal Shehan, celebrated the Mass at an altar decorated with Aboriginal symbols. He wore vestments made at the Bathurst Island Mission, off the north coast of Australia. Aboriginal singers and dancers from the north and west of Australia took part. Replacing the first Scripture reading, one hundred Aborigines in war paint and native dress interpreted the Last Supper in dance. The celebration broke new ground in the Church's liturgical renewal and led later to the formation of the Aboriginal Catholic Ministry.

A celebration for young people, 'Voices for Peace', was also held at the Music Bowl, with the Mass liturgy adapted to the minds and culture of youth. Sitting under the stars, thousands of young people sang and prayed under the leadership of The Proclaimers, an inter-Church group. The celebrant, Fr Maguire, told them they had to be builders of bridges, not of walls.

St Francis's church in Melbourne is the oldest Catholic church in Victoria, built between 1841 and 1845. It is still the most popular church in Melbourne and the busiest church in Australia. More than 10,000 worshippers attend each week and since 1929 it has been a centre of Eucharistic Life under the care of the Blessed Sacrament Fathers. It was the venue for a number of memorable Congress events. Each day large numbers of priests concelebrated Mass there. It was packed for a Pentecostal Rally. The Papal Legate attended a Eucharistic Hour for priests led by Cardinal John Wright, Prefect for the Congregation of the Clergy. Brothers from many different religious Congregations and orders filled the church on another day at a Mass celebrated by Cardinal John Cody of Chicago along with other bishops and religious superiors. Fr Anthony Lawless SSS wrote:

> Throughout the week there was never a slack moment at St Francis'. It seemed to be on everyone's list as a place to visit, not only for the liturgy, whether solemn or simple, but for music, for prayer in the hours of stillness when there was simply the monstrance enshrining the Blessed Sacrament above the altar, for Confession or just for a cup of tea.

The Melbourne Showgrounds arena was the venue for a moving Mass with thousands of sick, handicapped and elderly persons. Bedridden and wheelchair patients were brought in ambulances. Others were brought by family, friends or neighbours.

The Congress took full advantage of the new ecumenical possibilities opened up by the Second Vatican Council. That had been evident in the preparatory phases of the Congress. It reached its peak at the Melbourne Cricket Ground in the 'Meeting of the People of God', jointly arranged by the Victorian Council of Churches and the Melbourne Archdiocesan Ecumenical Commission. Cardinal Johannes Willebrands, President of the Secretariat for Promoting Christian Unity, came from the Vatican. The Reverend Dr Lukas Vischer, director of the Faith and Order Commission of the World Council of Churches, came from Geneva. They joined Catholics, Greek Orthodox, Anglicans, Presbyterians, Methodists and other Christians at the largest ecumenical service ever held in Australia. An observer described the Meeting as characterised by a spirit of joy and hope. Christians of different traditions listened to the reading of the Word of God and to homilies delivered by a leading cardinal and an outstanding Protestant ecumenist; they professed their common faith with lighted candles in their hands; and they exchanged food with each other as an expression of the fellowship of Christian love.

To avoid confusion between a Eucharistic service and an agape meal, the main participants shared yeast buns which could not be mistaken for bread, while many in the congregation shared biscuits with one another.

Words of wisdom

Aside from the liturgical celebrations, one of the highlights of the Congress for me was the public session staged at the Sidney Myer Music Bowl on 'Population and Ecology'. That night we heard three powerful speakers: Professor Sylvester Theisen, Professor of Sociology at St. John's University, Minnesota, on 'The Population Controversy'; St Mother Teresa of Calcutta on 'Care of the Destitute'; and Mr Bob Santamaria, president of the Australian National Civic Council, on 'Philosophies in Collision'. What a feast that was!

Professor Theisen argued that 'Developed nations should put more emphasis on changing their consumer patterns than on encouraging further reductions in their birth rates'. He described himself as a 'cautious optimist' on the world population situation and stressed that developed countries had damaged their environment more than could be justified by the size of their populations, necessitating a re-evaluation of the way resources are used and more planning to ensure a better quality of life for all people. He forecast that population growth would taper off as countries such as India became modernized, minimizing the danger of a population explosion. He dismissed the argument that pollution, the result of greater population, would bring disaster: 'The possibilities of controlling pollution are incredibly good. I think governments should do thousands of times more in this area.'

St Mother Teresa took the Congress motto, 'Love one another as I have loved you', as her theme. She spoke movingly about her work among the poorest of the poor. Jesus

> has identified Himself with the hungry, the sick, the naked, the homeless: hunger, not only for bread but for love, for care, to be somebody to someone; nakedness, not of clothing only, but nakedness of that compassion that very few people give to the unknown; homelessness, not only for a shelter made of stone but that homelessness that comes from having no one to call your own.
>
> Our little children come into the category of the unwanted and the unloved. Today the problem that is worrying so many people is not only that the world is getting too full of people, but what we find in the world today more and more is that they try to prove that Divine Providence cannot take care of new, unborn children. To me, if they

allow abortion in rich countries filled with materials and all that money can give, *they* are the poorest of the poor.

Bob Santamaria saw three major philosophies competing for the soul of the West: secular humanism (or libertarianism which asserts that anyone can do whatever they like), totalitarianism, and Christianity.

1. The libertarian philosophy is more commonly known as the philosophy of secular humanism, as distinct from that of Christian humanism ... Its method is to bring about a massive change in the climate of public opinion, mainly through the influence of its devotees in the education system and the media (above all in the field of television), and thus to create an atmosphere so overwhelming on issues like population control, abortion, censorship, that no political party feels it politically possible to confront it. In this context, television will be as revolutionary as the automobile has been. The invention of the automobile dissolved the compact city, created the sprawling suburbs. The invention of television dissolves established beliefs and attitudes, without discriminating between those which are right and those which are wrong.

2. The totalitarian (or for practical purposes the Communist) philosophy has a different method. For it, mastery involves the use of physical, military, political methods in order to control the State and through the coercive power of government to impose on the people conformity with historical materialism and its practical derivatives.

3. The Christian (or more generally the religious) philosophy has a familiar content. Its method is internal change in the hearts of men; and external change through the 'presence' of committed Christians in all the institutions of society. In democratic societies these include government, administration, political parties, trade unions, universities, media and the rest.

Santamaria held that

Over large areas of the conflict which rends modern Western communities, the liberal democrat is the indispensable ally of the Christian in the struggle for a human world and against 'de-humanisation'. But between the three main philosophies themselves however—the religious, the secular humanist, the totalitarian—there will never be any compromise until they cease to be what they are. They have totally different views of man. They aim to create totally different human societies. And we do no service to anyone by presenting the matter differently.

He went on 'to examine the types of world order proposed by these three forces, and to enquire into a few of the moral, legal and political principles and consequences involved in the struggle between them.' Read over forty years later, Santamaria's paper appears strangely prophetic. The Communist threat in Europe has receded but the forces of libertarianism march on.

The other highlight for me during the Congress was the opening of the new seminary of Corpus Christi College, Clayton, the regional seminary for the Catholic dioceses in Victoria and Tasmania. The seminary has since been relocated to Carlton, near St Patrick's Cathedral. Cardinal John Wright, then Prefect of the Sacred Congregation for the Clergy, gave a memorable address spiced with humour, which I have quarried many times in speaking to high school students and others. A seminary, said the Cardinal,

> is intended to increase the knowledge of those who come here, but above all to achieve their maturity. It is one of the characteristics of our generation that we are long on knowledge and short on maturity... We are a little bit retarded on the wisdom side, but we are way ahead on the knowledge side. We are jammed with knowledge and starving for wisdom... We're long on Know How and short on Know Why...

Cardinal Wright developed his theme with examples of the way Know How, without Know Why, was damaging the world. He suggested ways the seminary should impart wisdom and so bring its students to maturity. He appealed to the humanism of Greece and Rome and the Judaeo-Christian tradition. Each of these contributed two words.

> Six words summarise all there is to know about how to be a mature person ...The Greeks taught the first two: 'Know thyself' ... The Romans added two further words: 'Rule thyself' ... The eternal Son of God Himself added these two words: 'Give thyself' ... The seminary is the place where you learn to do that, and it's a tough place to do it. It's a laboratory in which to come to know yourself, to rule yourself, to give yourself, and therefore to love the rest of us.

In perfect weather, the Congress closed on Sunday evening, 25 February, with the Statio Orbis at the MCG. A congregation of 120,000 squeezed into the Ground. Cardinal Shehan, Papal Legate, was the main celebrant. He hailed the Congress as 'an extraordinary success'. He thanked the people of Melbourne for the warmth of their hospitality and their demonstration of Christian love. He saw the Congress as 'a new light of hope' for the Church in Melbourne; for the universal Church; and for the whole world. We also heard the recorded voice of Pope Paul VI. His message drove home the Congress theme:

> Love one another as I have loved you... We have said that peace is possible. Peace is possible because love is possible; and we know that love is possible because we have been given an example by the Eucharistic Lord. This then has been our wish for you, and for the world.

Hundreds of priests gave Communion among the vast crowd. Bands played, choirs sang. People were reluctant at the end to leave. With the final hymn sung, and as the Papal Legate and Cardinal Knox made a last round of the huge arena, the bands and people broke into Australia's unofficial national anthem, 'Waltzing Matilda'. It seemed a fitting end to a Congress of the People.

References

1) Allen, J. F., Personal notes and diaries.

2) Costigan, M. (Ed), *Congress of the People.* (Melbourne 1973).

3) Holland, T., *Eucharistic Congresses—a set of six.* Adoremus (1985), No.1, pp 4–13.

4) Santamaria, B. A., *Philosophies in Collision.* (National Civic Council Publication, 1973).

5) Waters, I. B., *Knox, James Robert (1914–1983)* in Australian Dictionary of Biography.

3 PHILADELPHIA 1–8 AUGUST 1976
JESUS, THE BREAD OF LIFE

O N SATURDAY 31 July 1976, some fifty pilgrims to Philadelphia, led by Bishop Thomas Holland of Salford,
checked in at the Pan Am desk in Heathrow and boarded
the flight to New York. We met and conversed with St Mother
Teresa in the airport there before a coach whisked us away to the
Hilton Hotel on South Broad Street in Philly.

Across the road from us in South Broad Street was another
hotel, the Bellevue-Stratford. The American Legion had held its
annual convention there the week before we arrived, attended by
more than two thousand Legionnaires. During the week of the
Congress we began to hear stories of the mysterious deaths of
Legionnaires who had stayed at the Bellevue-Stratford. It was
later discovered that a bacterium was found to be breeding in the
cooling tower of the hotel's air conditioning system, which then
spread it throughout the building. The bacterium was given the
name *Legionella pneumophila.* We sadly witnessed that week the
beginning of Legionnaire's Disease.

At the beginning of July, Queen Elizabeth and Prince Philip
had visited Philadelphia as part of the 200th commemoration of
the Declaration of Independence on 4 July 1776. From their visit,
and for the Congress, the city was newly bedecked with flags and
bunting. Philadelphia! Bishop Holland enthused:

> Could any city live up to such a name? The very sound of it
> is music. Its origin is the New Testament, its meaning
> 'brotherly love'. That is Our Lord's own New Commandment
> and the sign by which He wants us to be recognised as His
> disciples (Jn 13:34 and 15:12). Could any city of that name
> advance a stronger claim to host a Eucharistic Congress?

Philadelphia had not always lived up to its name. The 'Know-
Nothing' riots plagued the city in the 1800s, so much so that the

Catholic cathedral of Saints Peter and Paul was designed with no windows at street level and built with only very high clerestory windows to prevent vandalism. The largest Catholic Church in Pennsylvania, it was completed in 1864, and modelled after the Lombard Church of San Carlo al Corso in Rome. In that cathedral the Congress opened on Sunday 1 August with Mass at 12 noon.

Cardinal John Krol, Archbishop of Philadelphia, concelebrated the opening Mass with 29 other cardinals, 162 bishops and a large number of priests. Admission was restricted to invitees only. They included Princess Grace of Monaco—born Grace Kelly in a well-known Philly family—and Philadelphia Mayor Frank L Rizzo. Cardinal James Knox, the Papal Legate, gave the homily and boldly proclaimed the Congress theme, 'The Eucharist and the Hungers of the Human Family'. Knox said, 'No matter how great and varied the needs of each of the faithful, the Eucharist can meet them all.' Those needs, and their remedies, were spelt out in the week that followed.

On the evening of that opening day of the Congress, we walked in the candle-lit Blessed Sacrament procession from the cathedral down the Benjamin Franklin Parkway, ending with Benediction at the Philadelphia Museum of Art. 350,000 people took part.

The Congress week produced a wealth of great speakers. How about Cardinal Karol Wojtyla, now better known as Pope Saint John Paul II? Mother Teresa, now Saint Mother Teresa of Calcutta? Dom Helder Camara of Brazil; the social activist Dorothy Day; Archbishop Fulton Sheen; Cardinal Terence Cooke; Fr Pedro Arrupe, General of the Jesuits? The canonisation process for these last five has already started. There were others too like the farm workers' advocate Cesar Chavez. All had a lasting effect on many who heard them, such as Anne Healy Ayella who retired in 2017 after thirty-six years of service at the Community Food Program of the Archdiocese of Philadelphia: 'The Eucharistic Congress totally influenced me. It helped me to see the connection between the Eucharist and feeding the hungry. I learned so much from it.'

It was all in keeping with Pope Bl Paul VI's letter appointing Cardinal James Knox as his Legate for the Congress. Pope Paul wrote that its theme of hunger gave expression to the deepest social implications of the Eucharist, for 'those who are nourished by the divine food cannot ignore the suffering members of the same body but must feel themselves urged in every possible way to help in their needs'.

It was all in keeping too with the express aims of those who had planned the Congress. Their purpose was to bring together two fundamental teachings of the Second Vatican Council: that the 'Eucharistic Sacrifice is the source and summit of the whole Christian life' (*Dogmatic Constitution on the Church*, 11), and that all human activity finds its fulfilment in Christ's paschal sacrifice (cf *Pastoral Constitution on the Church in the Modern World*, 38). Three continuing programmes were begun: Operation Rice Bowl, a Lenten project to aid the hungry locally and internationally; Operation SIGN (Service in God's Name), in which young people offered voluntary service to the sick, elderly and disadvantaged; and Operation Faith Sharing, evangelisation through home visiting and parish open houses. As in Melbourne, the Congress owed much of its success to careful preparation. 95% of the dioceses in the United States shared in a two-year preparatory programme.

Hungers of the World: Days 1–4

Archbishop Fulton J Sheen is credited with suggesting the Congress theme. He asked, 'Have you ever thought of the starving souls all about us? There are people starving in body for food and people starving in soul for God.' In April 1975, the theme was settled: 'The Eucharist and the Hungers of the Human Family'. The various hungers of the human family were identified as follows:

- The Hunger for God (to feature on 1 August);
- The Hunger for Bread (2 August);
- The Hunger for Freedom and Justice (3 August);

☐ The Hunger for the Spirit (4 August);

☐ The Hunger for Truth and Unity (5 August);

☐ The Hunger for Understanding (6 August);

☐ The Hunger for Peace (7 August);

☐ The Hunger for Jesus, the Bread of Life (8 August).

A conference was held on each of these hungers. With the other twenty-seven affiliated Conferences and exhibits, they attracted almost 112,000 people. There were also fifty-eight major liturgies, attended by more than 950,000 people. Various churches in the city held solemn exposition of the Blessed Sacrament and offered Masses for ethnic groups and nationalities ranging from Armenians to Vietnamese. Masses were also arranged according to various themes.

Forty-seven locations in and around Philadelphia accommodated the Congress events. There was a full programme of Performing Arts; an exhibition of Liturgical Arts; and a specially commissioned bronze statue of 'Jesus Breaking Bread'—a six-foot-tall sculpture by Walter Erlebacher. During the Congress, this statue was on display in the lobby of the Philadelphia Civic Centre. After the Congress it was positioned outside the Cathedral of Saints Peter and Paul at Logan Square. The official history of the Congress placed the number of persons who participated in the Congress at 1,000,000 to 1,500,000.

Organisers ran a competition to find a Congress hymn. 'Gift of Finest Wheat' was judged the best of over two hundred entries. Written by Omer Westendorf, organist and choirmaster at St Bonaventure's church in Cincinnati, the verses use biblical images to illustrate the meaning of the Sacrament. The refrain then hauntingly repeats the dominant theme: 'You satisfy the hungry heart with gift of finest wheat; come give to us O Saving Lord, the bread of life to eat.' God's 'gift of finest wheat' is of course Christ Jesus, 'the bread of life', as found in Ps 81:16 and Jn 6:35. The hymn was sung at all the Congress-sponsored liturgies. A thousand-voice choir and orchestra provided music and accompanied the congregational singing. In Bishop Holland's words:

> This Congress came closest to the angelic choir. Voices throughout blended with a great orchestra. The mind's eye still recalls the ecstatic moments when, at the down-beat of the baton, the huge Sports Bowl swelled with glorious sound. Constantly and sweetly we were reminded of the theme: *Bread for a Hungry World.*

Thousands of families came together for Mass in the Veterans Stadium on day two. Cardinal Terence Cooke of New York gave the homily, describing the event as a celebration of strength and unity 'in the human family, in God's family, and in the individual families we call our own ... Tonight in this stadium we have living examples of husbands and wives, parents and children, whole families who have built strong, prayerful, loving relationships.' He invited them 'in a Eucharistic spirit' to help other couples and those preparing for marriage. Earlier in the day, at a Family Life Conference in the Civic Centre, Princess Grace of Monaco had said:

> To share the same basic feelings and beliefs, to have had a similar Christian background and training is of great importance in family life ... In my situation, marrying a man from a different country, different language and different cultures ... it would have been extremely difficult without the strong basic bond of our religion.

Day three, with its emphasis on Hunger for Freedom and Justice, began with a Conference in the Convention Hall and Civic Centre at which the Archbishop of Olinda and Recife in Brazil, Helder Camara, spoke. Under Camara's leadership, the Catholic Church in Brazil was an outspoken critic of the 1964–85 military dictatorship and a powerful movement for social change. He spoke of

> the great scandal of the century ... We are trying to reach other planets, leaving our own planet with over two-thirds of humanity in misery and hunger ... Like my dear brother, Martin Luther King, I have a dream. When one person

> dreams alone, it is only a dream. When we dream together,
> it is the beginning of reality.

Day three finished with a Mass in the Veterans Stadium, combined (for the first time in Eucharistic Congress history) with an American Indian ethnic liturgy. The Archbishop of Cracow in Poland, Cardinal Karol Wojtyla, gave a memorable homily. Poland was then under the control of a strict Communist regime and the future Pope took as his text:

> The Spirit of the Lord is upon me, because he has anointed
> me; he has sent me to announce good news to the poor,
> to proclaim release for prisoners, and recovery of sight for
> the blind; to let the broken victims go free, to proclaim the
> year of the Lord's favour (Lk 4:18–19).

His hearers knew well that the Cardinal was speaking with personal experience of a totalitarian State. He went on:

> We have a true vision of the man of our times and we speak
> truthfully of him, when, while remembering the physical
> hunger of millions of brothers, men of all continents, we
> intend to speak now of the hunger of the human soul,
> which is no less than the hunger for real freedom...

> ... the hunger for freedom continues to be unsatisfied ...
> In our times ... the principle of the freedom of the human
> spirit, of the freedom of conscience, of the freedom of
> religion has become much more evident. The Second
> Vatican Council has expressed it in many places and
> especially in the separate Declaration on Religious Free-
> dom. But is this principle really respected everywhere? Do
> we never meet with the case of those who are underprivi-
> leged because of their religious convictions? May we not
> even speak today of actual persecutions of those who
> confess their religion, especially Christians, persecuted as
> they were in the first centuries after Christ?

> This is what the Declaration on Religious Freedom says
> on the subject: 'Forms of government still exist under
> which, even though freedom of religious worship receives

constitutional recognition, the powers of the government are engaged in the effort to deter citizens from professing religion and to make life difficult and dangerous for religious communities' (*Dignitatis Humanae Personae*, 15).

And so today we bring to this great community of confessors of the Eucharistic Christ, gathered at the Eucharistic Congress in Philadelphia, the whole hunger for freedom which permeates contemporary man and all humanity. In the name of Jesus Christ, we have the right and the duty to demand true freedom for men and for peoples. We therefore bring this hunger for real freedom and deposit it on this altar. Not only a man, a priest, a bishop, but Christ Himself is at this altar, He who through our ministration offers His unique and eternal sacrifice.

Two years after delivering this homily Wojtyla was elected Pope. The following year, 1979, he visited Poland. His nine days visit there changed the world. Other forces too were at work. On 8 December 1991, the solemnity of the Immaculate Conception, Soviet First Secretary Mikhail Gorbachev announced the dissolution of the Soviet Union. On 25 December, Christmas Day, he resigned. By 1 January 1992, the Solemnity of Mary, Mother of God, the Communist empire was no more.

The freedom and liberty Cardinal Wojtyla so ardently wished for his own country was visible on the streets of Philadelphia. There did not seem to be any special security. Yes, armed police were there but the crowds were relaxed and very good-humoured. Famous personages mingled freely with everyone. Cab drivers, Cardinals and Catholics of every calling were on the easiest of terms. The friendliness of these Eucharistic Congresses, where people of so many nationalities are at home, becomes even more evident as the week draws on.

At these Congresses too there are plenty of opportunities to take in the local scene. Our group shared with many others a visit to historic Philly. The city had been founded on the Delaware river in the 1680s by William Penn, a Quaker. We went up Penn

Tower; walked down Penn's Landing; rang the Liberty Bell in its new pavilion on Independence Mall; visited the Betsy Ross House, where the seamstress and flag-maker Betsy Ross (1752–1836) lived when she sewed the first American Flag; and called into Christ Church, where fifteen of the signatories of the Declaration of Independence worshipped. We paid our respects to Old St Mary's church, the first Catholic cathedral of Philadelphia, built in 1763. Commodore John Barry, born in County Wexford in 1745 and known as the 'Father of the American Navy', is buried in the churchyard. Our pilgrimage took us also to Old St Joseph's, Philadelphia's oldest Catholic community, founded in 1733— though the present church dates only from 1839.

On day four Cardinal John Wright gave the homily at Mass in the Veterans Stadium 'In Petition and Thanksgiving for commitment to Religious Vocation'. The Mass was concelebrated by nearly all the bishops and priests attending the Congress. It stressed the re-dedication of priests and religious. In his very personal style Cardinal Wright spelt out the universal nature of a call from God, not limited to a vocation to priesthood or religious life, though priests and religious had a special responsibility to encourage others:

> Happily, the Spirit is not dead. Philadelphia this week is the proof of it! ... It is not any particular vocation that is in trouble or crisis; it is the sense of vocation itself; the sense of the Providence of God. We no longer look upon ourselves, as did our immigrant ancestors, as the agents of God in whatever state we are called to serve Him and all mankind. Let's look to it—beginning with the call to the priesthood—but not ending there. Here I am, O Lord! Send me!!!

It was good to meet Cardinal Wright again, three years after the Melbourne Congress, and also his secretary, Fr Don Wuerl.

Hungers of the World: Days 5–8

The Second Vatican Council, ended eleven years before this Congress began, was still very fresh in the minds and lives of many American Catholics. The Congress gave them the opportunity to experience the renewal and reform the Council had set in motion. A preparatory Committee on the Participation of Christian Churches of the Congress had been chaired by Cardinal William W Baum of Washington DC. Its vice chairmen were Bishop John Allin, Presiding Bishop of the American Episcopalian Church, and President Robert Marshall of the Lutheran Church in America.

Day five of the Congress was dedicated to the 'Hunger for Truth and Unity'. It lent itself to a memorable and moving ecumenical event. The Philadelphia Convention Hall and Civic Centre hosted an ecumenical programme when the congregation sang together, heard Scripture together, prayed together, confessed their sins together, and washed each other's feet as brothers and sisters in Christ. Unable to celebrate the Eucharist together, Christians from many traditions did what they could do until 'separate tables' are no longer required. During the hymns *Amazing Grace* and *The Church's One Foundation*, the twelve presiding leaders joined twelve circles of twelve persons each to have their feet washed. Then each of them knelt to wash the feet of the others in the circle. Following that symbolic act, Cardinal John Krol of Philadelphia urged all to share 'the peace of Christ', to 'bring us closer to the day when we share the bread of life and heal the hungers of the world'. Cardinal Jan Willebrands, president of the Vatican Secretariat for Christian Unity, gave the homily and Bishop Allin and Dr Robert Marshall jointly led a prayer before the litany of repentance.

Friday 6 August—feast of the Transfiguration—took us to the church where St John Neumann was buried. Neumann's story is more than remarkable. Born in what is now the Czech Republic, he trained for the priesthood at Charles University in Prague. His bishop announced that there would be no more ordinations at that time as Bohemia had so many priests that he could not find places for them all. So in 1836 Neumann travelled to the United States in the hope of being ordained. He arrived in New York with one suit of clothes and one dollar in his pocket. Three weeks later, Bishop John Dubois ordained him in the Old St Patrick's Cathedral in New York City. He was given a parish stretching from Lake Ontario to Pennsylvania. He joined the Redemptorist Order and was appointed Bishop of Philadelphia in 1852. His gift of languages—he could speak six languages fluently—served him well with his mixed congregations from all over Europe. Amongst his achievements is that of founding the first Catholic diocesan school system in the United States. When we visited his shrine in the church of St Peter the Apostle, he was Blessed John Neumann, having been beatified by Pope Blessed Paul VI in 1963. The same Pope Paul canonised John Neumann the year after the Congress.

On that same day, 6 August, day six of the Congress, a moment of tension was evident. It was the feast of the Transfiguration and Mass had been arranged that day for members of the military and their families. August 6 was also the anniversary of the bombing of Hiroshima. Pax Christi members and others protested that a Mass for the military should be scheduled on such an anniversary.

A conference entitled 'Woman and the Eucharist' also took place on 6 August. The main speakers were Dorothy Day and St Mother Teresa. Dorothy Day began by speaking of both physical and spiritual hunger. She spoke of her work at the House of Hospitality in New York where poor people were afforded both bodily and spiritual nourishment. She also made the point that 'Penance comes before Eucharist. Otherwise, we partake of the Sacrament unworthily'. But then she drew attention to the Mass for the military which was to be celebrated that day. Those responsible for the Congress did not seem to realise what the bombing in Hiroshima and its anniversary on 6 August meant to those dedicated to peace. The Gospel message had been turned upside down. God had given life, and given the Eucharist to sustain life, but we had used 'instruments of death of inconceivable magnitude'. She asked that 'we will regard that military Mass, and all our Masses today, as an act of penance, begging God to forgive us'.

Mother Teresa then spoke on 'Women and the Eucharist':

> God so loved the world that He gave His Son. This was the first Eucharist: the gift of his Son, when He gave Him to Our Lady, establishing in her the first altar. Mary was, from that instant on, the only one who was able to affirm with complete sincerity, This is my body. She offered her body, her strength, her whole being, to form the body of Christ. It was on her that the power of the Holy Spirit rested, and in her that the Word became flesh.

Mother Teresa developed her theme, showing how Mary shared her Son with others:

> Our Lady ... ran in haste [to help Elizabeth]. I think this is why God chose a woman to show His love and compassion toward the world. It was she, the woman, who gave evidence of her kindness by immediately sharing what she had just received. To say it in another way, she hastened to share the Eucharist.

Mary teaches us tenderness, as shown in her search when Jesus was lost; her concern for the newlyweds at Cana, exposed to the humiliation of not having wine; her anguish at the foot of her Son's cross. 'I think this is the wonderful tenderness of a woman's heart: to be aware of the suffering of others and to try to spare them that suffering, as Mary did.'

Addressing women directly, Mother Teresa continued: '...This is the source of Mary's greatness: her understanding love. You and I who are women—do we possess that great and magnificent thing, that love full of understanding? ... I believe that what we can learn from Our Lady is her tenderness.'

Drawing on her own experience, and the experience of her Sisters in Australia, Rome, Mexico and New York, Mother Teresa continued:

> God has created women for this. Perhaps he didn't create them to do great things, but certainly at least do small things with a great love. And I believe that this love is to begin in the home, coming from our hearts; in our families with our neighbours, next door, with our neighbours on the next street. And then it must be extended to all. Only thus will we be able to extend the meaning of the Eucharist. The meaning of the Eucharist is love that understands. Christ understood. He understood that we are terribly hungry for God. He understood that we have been created for loving. That is why he became the bread of life. And he said, 'If you do not eat my flesh and drink my blood, you will not be able to live. You will not be able to love. You will not be able to serve' (see Jn 6: 53). We have to eat Him. The kindness of Christ's love is His love that understands.
>
> Christ wants to offer us the means of putting our love for Him into action ... He becomes hungry, not only for bread but for love ... He becomes naked, not only for a piece of clothing but for love that understands, for human dignity. He becomes dispossessed, not only for a place of shelter but for the sincere and deep love for one another. This is what the Eucharist is all about. This is Jesus, the living bread that has come to be broken with you and with me.

Her listeners knew that, like Cardinal Wojtyla, Mother Teresa spoke from personal encounters; they took her to their heart.

A lighter note was struck on Saturday 7 August with the 'Irish Liturgy and Festival' at St Charles' Seminary in Overbrook. Cardinal William Conway of Armagh was the main celebrant and Bishop Edward Daly of Derry the homilist. Reminiscent of the Dublin Congress of 1932, when John McCormack famously sang *Panis Angelicus* before a million people in the Phoenix Park, a silver tenor rendered the same for us, with a more modest audience of 20,000. Bishops concelebrated from a raised dais.

Bishop Holland remembered, 'I was at the end of a row and in response to a persistent hiss looked down on a gentleman in a green bowler. Clearly the request was an autograph for his programme. I obliged, adding diocese and country. Was that unkind? Well, why did he pitch on the only bishop from England?'

We had been at St Charles' Seminary the evening before for a reception given by Cardinal Krol. He put on a 'frugal supper of oyster stew and a crisp Californian wine'. We met Archbishop Bernardin of Cincinnati, President of the US Catholic Bishops Conference, and were able to discuss the warm letter he had written to the English and Welsh Bishops Conference. The day was memorable not just for the fare and friendship but also for the fierce wind of hurricane force that struck the great marquee. The fury passed as quickly as it came, with no casualties. We sang a grateful *Salve Regina.*

Earlier that same day saw us at the Children's Mass in the Veterans Stadium where children dramatised the Gospel reading. Then we were off to renew old acquaintances: with Matt McCloskey III at his home at Bryn Mawr and Paul Niedringhaus and family at Wynnewood. On other days, we struck landfall with Jim and Victoria Shallow; with Bob and Bernadette Kelly (nee O'Callaghan) and infant Benjamin, exiles from Salford Diocese; and a relative of mine, Mary Hawthorne. Wonderful what these Congresses enable one to do!

I must here recall one of Philadelphia's most distinguished sons, Gerald Patrick O'Hara. Born in Scranton, Pennsylvania, in 1895, he went to school and seminary in Philly before studying in Rome where he was ordained priest in 1920. Nine years later he was consecrated as an auxiliary bishop for Philadelphia. He became Bishop of Savannah, Georgia, in 1935. In 1947 came a different and difficult appointment: whilst retaining his duties in Savannah Pope Pius XII made him regent of the Apostolic Nunciature in Bucharest, Romania. His vicar general and chancellor assumed the everyday administration of his diocese.

In Bucharest O'Hara was an outspoken critic of the Communist regime. In return, the Romanian Government accused him of espionage and expelled him from the country in 1950. He returned to Savannah but only briefly. Pope Pius appointed him Apostolic Nuncio to Ireland and then in 1954 Apostolic Delegate to Great Britain. In 1960 he visited the Houses of Parliament, the first papal representative to do so for 400 years. Archbishop O'Hara died of a heart attack in 1963. His funeral Mass was offered at Westminster Cathedral and his body then flown to Philadelphia for burial in the cathedral crypt. Thomas Holland had been his personal secretary at the Apostolic Delegation in Wimbledon from 1956 to 1960. They formed a deep friendship there. Thomas (by now Bishop) Holland accompanied the body to Philadelphia for the burial. Thirteen years later, at the Congress, he was able to re-visit the tomb and pay his respects to his former friend and 'beloved boss'.

The Congress closed on Sunday evening, 8 August, with a Parade of the Nations and States from the Spectrum indoor arena to JFK Stadium, where the Papal Legate, Cardinal James Knox, was principal celebrant and homilist. The weather was threatening, with a torrential rainstorm earlier in the day. But the rain held off, the sun came out, and we were able to savour the final ceremonies.

Before Mass began President Gerald R. Ford spoke. He described how America trusted in divine providence; cherished freedom of worship and conscience. He saluted the Catholic Church for its contribution to building a more peaceful world and giving moral direction to mankind; for upholding the values of human life. 'Our commitment to the unique role of the family relationship is also basic to our faith. There are no adequate substitutes for father, mother and children in a loving commitment to nurture and protect. No Government, no matter how well intentioned, can ever take the place of the family in the scheme of things.' He ended with a plea and a prayer that we might all 'move beyond tolerance to love'.

Cardinal Knox reminded us that 'the Statio Orbis is the focal point, the culminating event of an International Eucharistic Conference. It is at this moment the place of worship of the Universal Church, of the whole world, uniting us in bonds of faith with the Holy Father and millions of our brothers throughout the world.' He concluded with a challenge to his hearers to centre their lives on the Eucharist and to imitate the example of Christ who gave Himself for others.

At the end Pope Paul gave a televised message, reminding everyone that the Eucharist brought each of us personally to Christ in a meeting of life and love, and ending with his apostolic blessing.

Fourteenth Street

From Philadelphia our group went on to Washington, New York and finally Boston. Our drive from Philadelphia to Washington took us past the city of Baltimore, the seat of the first Catholic bishop in the States, John Carroll. Carroll was consecrated bishop in 1790 by the Benedictine Charles Walmsley, who himself had been consecrated bishop in the sodality chapel of the Venerable English College in Rome. Seeing the skyline of Baltimore as we drove by, I thought of the American pilgrims who remembered their spiritual patrimony and who came to visit and pray in the sodality chapel of the College in my student days in Rome. Their sense of history and *pietas* was impressive.

Carroll would certainly have approved of the Congress, and particularly of the liturgical offices. In his own day, he was an advocate of the use of vernacular languages in the liturgy. In 1787 he wrote:

> ...to continue the practice of the Latin liturgy in the present state of things must be owing either to chimerical fears of innovation or to indolence and inattention in the first pastors of the national Churches in not joining to solicit or indeed ordain this necessary alteration.

His hope was realised, albeit nearly two hundred years later, at the Second Vatican Council and then throughout the States.

We arrived at our Washington hotel too late for a meal. 'There's a McDonald's down the road', we were told. We weren't familiar with McDonald's—they hadn't yet spread over the UK—but Bishop Holland and I set off to see what we could find. By the time we had eaten it was almost midnight. The night was clear and warm and we saw the White House was nearby. So midnight saw us taking a look at the President's residence. In the bright lights, a cardinal bird rummaged in the ground in a fruitless search for worms. A pocket map showed that by walking down Fourteenth Street to a certain intersection we would get almost straight back to our hotel. Fourteenth Street came across as rather curious. We walked a good length and it seemed the whole of human life was there. However, most of the people lounging on the sidewalks and in the shadows were friendly enough. No doubt our collars and the bishop's chain and cross helped. 'Good night, Fathers' from all quarters accompanied our progress.

Next morning the coach arrived to take our party on a tour of Washington. The driver greeted us, and then: 'Folks, Washington is a great city but it can be dangerous. Don't go out on your own, or even in twos or threes. Go out in groups. And whatever you do, never ever go down Fourteenth Street.' Only then did we discover that Washington's Fourteenth Street was once home to the rioting that followed the assassination of Martin Luther King and then a crime hotspot with next-to-no foot traffic! How things change; forty-one years later, in 2017, it's now the city's hottest place to dine out.

We saw all the important places in Washington and then New York, though the personal reunions in New York carried more importance. My mother had told me to look up her old friend Mary Ann Cahill (nee Moroney) who had emigrated to the States from Newmarket-on-Fergus, County Clare, in the 1920s. That was the last they had seen of each other. I found her with the help of her daughter-in-law Edie Cahill (of WNBC TV fame), and her son Bill and his wife Mary and their children. Priests I had known as students in Rome some years previously also came from their various dioceses and we met in an Italian *trattoria*: Tom Candreva; Ken Boccafola; Lawrence Bock; Tom Downes. The Eucharist makes a family of people, with Congresses providing the interface.

Our group's final destination was Boston. As we arrived the bottom dropped out of the pound sterling. We only had B&B in Boston and no dollars to pay for other meals. Credit and debit cards had yet to be invented. The Franciscans at St Anthony's church came to our rescue. Fr Eric invited us to dine with them. Our hunger was satisfied. A fitting end to a Congress that perhaps lacked the spontaneity of Melbourne but had stamped on every event 'Made in the USA'.

References

1) Allen, J. F., Personal notes and diaries.

2) CatholicPhilly.com, *All Healy Ayella*.

3) De Mayo, J. B. and Casino, J. J., *The Forty-First International Eucharistic Congress, August 1–8, 1976: A History* (New Jersey 1978).

4) Guilday, P., *The Life and Times of John Carroll, Archbishop of Baltimore, 1735–1815* (New York 1922).

5) Holland, T., *Eucharistic Congresses—a set of six*. Adoremus (1985), No.1, pp 4–13.

6) Pope Paul VI, *Epistula ad Iacobum Robertum S.R.E. Cardinalem Knox 7 July 1976*.

7) Rademacher, N., *To Relate the Eucharist to Real Living: Mother Teresa and Dorothy Day at the Forty-First International Eucharistic Congress, Philadelphia, Pennsylvania*. U.S. Catholic Historian (Catholic University of America Press Fall 2009), Vol. 27, No. 4, pp. 59–72.

4 LOURDES 16–23 JULY 1981
JESUS CHRIST: BREAD BROKEN FOR A
NEW WORLD

THE 42ND EUCHARISTIC Congress held in Lourdes in July 1981 should have been a joyful celebration of the centenary of International Eucharistic Congresses. On several counts, it was a disappointment. Firstly, Pope St John Paul II had planned to come. He was brutally shot in St Peter's Square on 13 May and in July was still recovering in hospital.

Then the weather did not help. It rained … and rained … and rained … as it can in the Hautes-Pyrenees. It came down in stair rods and washed away the marquee of the Spanish speakers. One bishop withdrew his drenched youth contingent from their waterlogged mountain camp and took them home.

Nor were numbers present as at other Congresses. Lourdes itself is a small provincial town, inadequate to accommodate the huge crowds of pilgrims usually present at these events. The French authorities and tourist organisation hardly gave the Congress their full support. Because of the restricted availability of space and accommodation they discouraged people from other countries by imposing a limit on the numbers who might come. Archbishop Roger Etchegaray, President of the French Catholic Bishops Conference, expected an overall attendance limited to about 20,000. In addition, there was heightened anxiety about security.

There were theological hesitations too. 'Anti-triumphalist' organisers succeeded in eliminating from the Congress programme the traditional Blessed Sacrament Procession—in Lourdes of all places, where this daily procession is *de rigueur!* The daily transfer of the Blessed Sacrament from the altar on the Prairie to the Carmel chapel was a very low-key affair.

There were of course many high spots. The Papal Legate, Cardinal Bernardin Gantin, a close ally of the stricken Pontiff, was an inspired choice for the Lourdes Congress. The radiant joy of his features and gestures lifted very many hearts. One day, in the Missions Pavilion, he spoke of the first men to bring the Gospel to his country: Dahomey in West Africa, today known as Benin. The three priest missioners were Irish, French and Italian. Gantin said it was his father who welcomed them. Bishop Holland remembered Gantin's words: 'Years later the young Bernardin was called home from the seminary to his father's death bed. The old man recalled the day when the three holy men came with treasures from the sea.' His children were to ever hold it as the great day in their country's story and in their own personal lives. 'The Cardinal shared the experience with us, smiling and seemingly unaware of any effect on his hearers. What a page in African Mission History!'

Ordained priest in 1951, Gantin was appointed Archbishop of Cotonou in 1960 at the age of 37. Pope Blessed Paul VI called him to Rome in 1971 as secretary of the Sacred Congregation for the Evangelization of Peoples and in 1977 named him Cardinal. In 1984 Pope St John Paul II appointed him Prefect of the Congregation for Bishops, a post he retained until 1998. He was thus responsible for the appointment of bishops the world over. He was Dean of the College of Cardinals from 1993 until 2002. When Cardinal Gantin died in 2008 a period of three days of national mourning was observed in his memory. The international airport of Cotonou has since been named after him. What a page in African Mission History indeed!

A group of Anglican clergy belonging to the Church Union came to Lourdes for the Congress, bringing with them a stole which they had intended to present to Pope St John Paul. The stole was richly worked with Japanese golden silk thread and showed the papal coat of arms at the ends, the cross of St. Augustine on the chest, a dove representing the Holy Spirit at the neck. In the back where it couldn't be seen, was a sort of private message: a hidden *Ut unum sint*, a prayer for unity. They presented it to Cardinal Gantin who spoke his thanks with great charm. Pope John Paul wore that stole on his historic visit to Canterbury the following year.

During the week of the Congress a storm blew up between England and Spain. It was revealed that Prince Charles and Lady Diana Spencer would board the royal yacht at Gibraltar two days after their wedding in London. This led to diplomatic disapproval from Spain, and the Spanish Government announced that King Juan Carlos and Queen Sofia had declined their invitation to the wedding as an act of protest. Happily, such diplomatic reserves did not affect us in Lourdes. As noted above, the marquee for Spanish speaking pilgrims was washed away by the atrocious weather. That marquee was in a field next to the marquee for English speaking pilgrims. What more natural then than to offer the hospitality of ours, especially when Cardinal Munoz Vega of Quito asked for refuge? In earlier times, he had been my Rector Magnificus at the Pontifical Gregorian University in Rome. Hospitality was offered and gladly accepted.

The adverse weather conditions brought out in most the best of a spirit of *camaraderie*. That was most evident in our youth—in numbers the strongest of the British contingent. Two Benedictines from Ampleforth, Fr Jonathan Cotton and Fr Martin Haigh, succeeded admirably in building up the strength and spirit of those young people.

Another positive was the prominence given at the Congress to the Prayer of the Church. The Divine Office, as it was known, had been almost exclusively the prerogative of the clergy until the Second Vatican Council encouraged the laity, too, 'to recite the divine office, either with the priests, or among themselves, or even individually' *(Sacrosanctum concilium* 100). Each day during the Congress, a choir of Benedictine monks sang the Hours in the Rosary Chapel, joined by the laity in great numbers. Minds and voices met there in harmony.

Pope St John Paul II had given a clear-cut target to the Congress organisers. They were to go deep into the foundations of faith in the Eucharist in order to bring out the transforming effect of Christ: in individuals, in the Church and in the whole human family. Writing on 1 January 1979 to Cardinal James Knox, then the President of the Permanent Committee for International Eucharistic Congresses, the Pope quoted the Lourdes Congress theme—'Jesus Christ, bread broken for a new world'—and said:

> In order to grasp fully the specific and radical newness that Jesus Christ introduces into every member of the faithful who shares in the Eucharist, into the Church, and therefore into society, it is fitting that the Congress should especially emphasise the foundations of Eucharistic doctrine, just as this doctrine has been uninterruptedly received, meditated upon and lived, from the Apostles, the martyrs, the Fathers of the Church, from mediaeval Christendom, from the Councils, from modern piety, and from the legitimate research carried out in our own age. Like Saint Paul (cf 1 Co 11:23), the pastors and theologians of the Congress must pass on what they themselves have received from living Tradition, which is guided by the Holy Spirit. Thus there will appear, in the wholeness of its mystery, the full meaning of the 'broken Bread' … It is by beginning from this lived Tradition that the Congress will be able to deepen and to express to the people of today how and why the new world is linked with the Eucharist, and the Eucharist on its part is linked with Christ's Passion and Resurrection.

Then, as Christ gave His life for us, so too we must give up our lives for our brothers and sisters. In this way, moral and social consequences will flow from the Eucharist. 'A "new nature" (Col 3:10), a new world marked by filial relationships with God and fraternal relationships with people, let us say a new humanity: these are the fruits that we expect from the Bread of Life that the Church breaks and distributes in the name of Christ.' Unity among Christians and the service of others, especially the poor, would follow. 'The Lourdes Congress will have the task of in some way confirming all the spiritual and ethical dynamism that the

Eucharistic Christ imparts to those who feed on him with the necessary dispositions.'

Pope John Paul invoked the help of the Immaculate Virgin Mary. He concluded his letter: 'The Marian City, which is already familiar with so many admirable pilgrimages, is a matchless setting, almost unique in the world, for expressing homage to Christ in the Eucharist and for spreading his message.'

To develop its theme—'Jesus Christ, Bread Broken for a New World'—the Congress handbook used the structure of the Mass. Successive days were to focus on these topics:

☐ From all horizons the Church assembles

☐ The Church proclaims the Word of God

☐ The Church gives thanks to the Father

☐ The Church recalls Christ's redemptive act

☐ The Church calls upon the Holy Spirit

☐ The Church receives the Body of Christ

☐ The Church has its part in the mission of Christ

From all horizons the Church assembles

The Papal Legate, Cardinal Gantin, joyfully opened the Congress, recalling how 'a Christian lay person of this country, Emelie Tamisier of Tours ... initiated the celebration of the first Congress just a hundred years ago. Conscious of the fact that the Eucharist was the heart of the Church, she wanted Christians to proclaim publicly and with strength their faith in Christ present, and to come back to Him.'

Turning to the centenary Congress he said:

> Christ unites us with one another in the immense family of believers, in this living Body of which He is the Head and of which we are the members, irrespective of our country of origin, our age, culture, social status or state of health. How can we fail to be sensitive here to the presence of so many young people, so many sick people, so many

representatives of the young Churches! ... Let us this
evening confine ourselves simply to meditating on the
mystery of this assembly. It is the Church from the four
corners of the world which is here assembled. 'Assembly'
is an essential characteristic of the Church, the one which
gives her her name: Ecclesia. After Munich, Bombay,
Bogota, Melbourne and Philadelphia, it is France's turn to
welcome this assembly. It was fitting to mark the centenary
of those International Congresses started in France, at
Lille, in 1881...

More precisely it is Christ who assembles us, who calls us
together; it is He who calls the Congress into existence
('the love of Christ has called us together into one'). We
are His guests. The Church gathers around its invisible
Head, Christ crucified and glorified, source of life for all
the members of His Body, as the Bread broken. This is
already the meaning of all our Eucharistic assemblies on
Sunday, the day of the Resurrection of the Lord. But in the
course of history we need more ample manifestations of
our faith, with more universality, more depth.

Cardinal Gantin remembered how the emphases of International
Eucharistic Congresses had shifted to answer new spiritual needs
or theological developments. But the essentials remained and the
Eucharist was needed more than ever:

The more the world expands, the more nations and social
classes close themselves to one another, the more hatred
and violence spreads, the more the gap widens between
peoples of plenty and peoples of hunger, so much the more
do we need the Eucharist, the supreme testimony of God's
love and the sacrament of our unity in Christ.

The Cardinal ended his homily with a moving and heartfelt prayer
to Christ and to Mary.

The Church proclaims the Word of God

The German Professor Balthazar Fischer had been an outstanding pupil of the liturgist Josef Jungmann. In 1961, he was named consultor to the Congregation for Sacraments and Worship and helped to frame the Constitution on the Liturgy of the Second Vatican Council. He later chaired the committee entrusted with the reform of the rite of baptism for children and the restored rite of Christian initiation of adults. Dr Fischer's address on the day after the Congress opening was eagerly awaited. Nor did it disappoint. He entitled his talk, 'The Eucharist, Banquet of the Lord and Fraternal Meal'. To illustrate the title and explain it, he spoke of 're-discoveries' and 'new discoveries' in the Mass following the reforms of the Vatican Council. Perhaps anticipating objections, he said:

> Above all, I do not wish to give the impression that the Mass as our parents and grandparents knew it was celebrated on the margin of the eucharistic mystery. Oftentimes they surely lived the eucharistic celebration more intensely than we do, even if the terms in question were unknown to them. When we talk of 're-discoveries' and 'new discoveries' in relation to the Eucharist we are not referring to a new understanding of the Eucharist but rather to new insights into it.

Dr Fischer's lengthy talk was divided into several sections: the Feast of the Lord; Eucharist and Conversion; the Eucharist and the World; Thanksgiving; the Dynamic of the Eucharist; the Dynamic of Adoration; the Eschatological Dimension; Sharing the Word; the Holy Spirit; Creation; Eucharistic Adoration outside Mass; Fraternal Meal; Communion; Ministries; the Absent; Eucharist and the Sick; Music in the Eucharist; the Eucharistic Ethic.

Since the theme for this day was 'The Church proclaims the Word of God' it will suffice to quote his comments on that:

There is the re-discovery that the liturgy of the word is already the banquet of the Lord. The *Liturgy Constitution* expressly re-introduced the ancient formularies 'table of the word' and 'table of the body of Christ'. According to the assertion of the Council it is Christ himself who comes to us in the proclamation and in the interpretation of the Scriptures, and who, throughout the centuries, summons together the members of the assembly. This we always knew, but with the Counter-Reformation's concern to defend the real Presence in the Eucharist, the other more discreet, though equally real, presence in the Word remained for a period in the shade. It went so far that the catechisms used the term 'Fore-Mass' for the readings of the Mass, and attached little importance to them. Even in our own century it was usual to say in the Church that a person who arrived at Mass only at the Offertory fulfilled his Sunday obligation. How different the spirituality we find in the important theological document underlying the Congress, and how much more it affects us: 'There is question somehow of breaking and sharing the bread of life before breaking and sharing the bread [of the Eucharist] ... The liturgy of the word, therefore, is not a mere preparation for the Eucharist; it is already the pledge of participation in the action of God with a view to our salvation'.

As a 'new discovery' Fischer listed

the possibility of the faithful intervening, instead of the commissioned homilist, in order to share among them-selves the 'bread of the Word broken for a new world' by replacing preaching with their own sharing. The ruling of the German Episcopal Conference on small group Masses has expressly authorised such free sharing as a legitimate possibility alongside the homily of the minister (who must, however, as official minister take responsibility for co-ordinating the sharing). It is significant that the basic Congress document takes account of this possibility: 'When believers listen together to what the Spirit says to the Churches, whether in silence, through the homily of the priest, or through the sharing of their experiences as enlightened by faith, they discover what God is saying to them in their daily lives'.

In the light of subsequent developments, it must be said that this particular 'new discovery' was a child of its time, an idea whose time has now passed. In 1981 the topic was still being debated. Four decades later, we have the benefit of the new Code of Canon Law as well as the 2014 Homiletic Directory from the Congregation for Divine Worship and the Discipline of the Sacraments. The Code would seem to exclude group sharing during Mass while the Directory (no. 4) explains how

> the liturgy is a privileged setting because it is there that we listen to God's Word as part of the celebration that culminates in the sacrificial offering of Christ to the eternal Father... Given its liturgical nature, the homily also possesses a sacramental significance: Christ is present in the assembly gathered to listen to His word and in the preaching of His minister, through whom the same Lord who spoke long ago in the synagogue at Nazareth now instructs His people. In the words of *Verbum Domini*, 'The sacramentality of the Word can thus be understood by analogy with the real presence of Christ under the appearances of the consecrated bread and wine'.

The full liturgical significance of the homily is there revealed as integral to the link between Word and Sacrifice, to be given by an ordained minister who can speak with magisterial, teaching voice. Fr Edward McNamara, Professor of Liturgy and Dean of Theology at the Regina Apostolorum Athenaeum in Rome, has commented (ZENIT 24 August 2017) that 'the most fruitful manner of sharing the Word is not in the context of the homily of the Mass but in other situations such as a Celebration of the Word. Such celebrations also have the advantage of affording the necessary time for those who wish to share their reflections.' One might conclude therefore that the positive aspects of Dr Fischer's suggestion would be more at home outside the actual liturgy and within, for example, *Lectio Divina*.

The Church gives thanks to the Father

On the Sunday, Cardinal Gantin, as Papal Legate, presided at Mass televised throughout France and the Low Countries. His homily took up the theme, 'The Church gives thanks to the Father':

> To designate the whole of the Mass the Church has reserved the word 'Eucharist', which means 'thanksgiving'. Such is truly the meaning of the key prayer, which begins with the preface: 'Father, it is our duty and our salvation, always and everywhere to give You thanks through Your beloved Son, Jesus Christ'. Throughout the entire Mass, moreover, we praise, we adore, we give thanks. But more: our entire Christian life should be a thanksgiving.

The Cardinal sketched out several motives for giving thanks to God. Based on the Gospel reading of the day, from chapter 13 of St Matthew about the tares and the wheat, he mentioned one crucial motive for thanksgiving—'the patience, the mercy of God,' which should also be a reason for us to show patience and mercy to others. But the attitude of thanksgiving, of Eucharist, must be wider still.

> The true believer knows how to give thanks for everything. For life which comes to us from God. For the whole of creation which He has entrusted to us. For all the love with which He has permitted us to be surrounded. For the intimate covenant which He has been pleased to establish with men and which He ceaselessly renews. For sacred history, in which God intervened in order to save His people, despite its sin; is it not thus that the great act of thanksgiving of the Jews, taken up by Jesus at the Last Supper, commemorated all the great events of the Bible? For the new light brought by Jesus. For salvation, the deliverance from sin which He obtained through His

Sacrifice—His Body given, His Blood shed—and inaugurated by His Resurrection. For His Bread of life in which He gives Himself. For His grace which makes us children of God, temples of God, animated by His Spirit and destined for the glory of Christ Jesus. For the hope which He gives that we will pass through suffering and death with Him, as a road opening on to life.

The Church recalls Christ's redemptive act

We heard little if anything of the theme 'The Church recalls Christ's redemptive act' from the speakers. But Pope John Paul sent a message to the participants on the last day of the Congress in which he spoke of the Mass making the Cross present for every generation. His speech was televised and shown in the underground Basilica of St Pius X. His voice came over fairly well, though the flickering picture reminded us vividly of days when his life did likewise. He told us how he had longed to be present in person and how much he regretted his absence. Then he offered the participants what he called a private reflection on 'the breaking of the Bread' so that they in their turn could live it and pass it on to others: 'The experience you have had here during this Congress at Lourdes has invested you with a mission as witnesses, in the Church and for the world.' The Pope then gave his hearers three firm beliefs to live and to share.

He told them that the 'new world' in the Congress title

has as its foundation none other than Jesus Christ ... This new world was announced by Him during the whole of His earthly life as the Kingdom of God; it was won by His sacrifice and inaugurated by His resurrection and the gift of the Spirit ... Yes, the true breaking of Bread, that which is fundamental to us Christians, is none other than that of the Sacrifice of the Cross ... The new world depended on this sacrifice. The wall of separation was then overturned; the resurrection of the dead was confirmed; and with it, the possibility of a united humanity (cf Ep 2:15).

That was the first conviction which they had to live and to witness. Following from that came the second firm belief, that

> the Sacrifice of the Cross is so decisive for the future of mankind that Christ has accomplished it and returned to the Father only after leaving us the means of taking part as if we had been there. The offering of Christ on the Cross—which is the true broken Bread of life—is the first value to be communicated and shared. For this reason, before going to Calvary, Christ wanted, in the sacred silence of the upper room, to take time to accomplish a liturgical baptism of bread: He celebrated it with the Twelve and asked them to repeat it in His name until the day He would return to inaugurate the new times ...

The eucharistic celebration is one with the sacrifice of the Cross:

> It neither adds anything to it nor multiplies it. The Mass and the Cross are one and the same sacrifice (cf. Letter *Dominicae Cenae,* no.9). Nevertheless, the eucharistic breaking of Bread has an essential function, that of placing the original offering of the Cross at our disposal. It makes it present today for our generation. In making the Body and Blood of Christ really present under the forms of bread and wine, it makes the Sacrifice of the Cross simultaneously present and accessible to our generation. In its uniqueness, it remains the pivot of salvation history and the essential link between time and eternity. The Eucharist is thus the 'sacramental institution' in the Church which, at each step, serves as a 'connection' with the Sacrifice of the Cross, and which offers it a presence both real and active. In this way, it reveals its power of salvation and resurrection for every age... Such is the wonder of the Eucharist... 'It makes the Church' ... Our age cannot be mistaken about it; it must recognise the full place of the Eucharist in the new world's charter... There is the heart of the Church, the secret of its strength: she must guard this Mystery with a jealous concern for it and affirm it in all its integrity.

The third point Pope John Paul made concerned the practical role of priests and of all baptised people in relation to the Mass:

> The Congress has taught you to live the breaking of bread as Church, according to all its demands: welcoming, exchanging, sharing, overcoming barriers, being willing to change, the renunciation of prejudices, the concern to transform our social milieux in their structures and their spirit. You have understood that, to be true and reasonable, your meeting at the eucharistic table must have practical consequences.

The Holy Father—Mary's *Totus Tuus*—ended his message with a word about the nearness of Mary to us today, turning with her in prayer to her Son. In God's Providence, Pope St John Paul recovered. He would be at Lourdes the following year, giving thanks on France's favourite holiday, the solemnity of the Assumption of the Blessed Virgin Mary.

At the end of his message the Pope gave his blessing and then spoke a message to the sick:

> My affectionate thoughts and my prayer go out ... to you in a special way. Lourdes is the privileged place where the sick from all over the world are always accorded the first places, served by their brothers in good health, so as to offer their suffering to the compassion of our Mother, the Virgin Mary, to the mercy of Christ Jesus, and to start out again with the comfort which comes from God. You are at the heart of the Congress ... Your sufferings are not lost; they contribute invisibly to the growth of charity that animates the Church.

He told how his own sufferings had helped him to understand all the better the trials of sick people and invited them to offer their trials 'with me to the Lord, who achieves great things through the Cross'.

The Virgin Mary asked Bernadette at Lourdes: 'Go and tell the priests that a chapel should be built here and that people should come here in procession'. Every day from April to October the

Blessed Sacrament Procession finishes with the blessing of pilgrims, with the sick occupying the front rows. The sick are *the* important people in Lourdes. That was reflected in a special Mass of the Sick offered at the Congress by Cardinal Franciszek Macharski, the successor of Pope St John Paul as Archbishop of Crakow. The Cardinal referred to the absence of the Pope and the attempt on his life, and described him as 'one of the sick of the world ... weak in body, but at the same time a source of strength for others, thanks to communion in the love of Christ'. He underlined that Jesus himself was

> the sick person *par excellence*, the feeble one, the tormented one, stripped to the very depth of his soul. Jesus of Nazareth and of Bethlehem is the Jesus who emptied himself. Jesus of Gethsemane and Golgotha is the Jesus who was crushed ... Jesus is Redeemer through the foolishness of the cross, the foolishness of weakness (cf. 1 Co 1:22) ...

He had already reminded the sick people:

> The Gospel of Christ—Christ crucified and risen—is living in you and through you; it is alive in the world. You make present in the world the Cross of the suffering Christ. And through this Cross you make present the power of the wisdom of the Saviour, who by His suffering and the suffering of His Body—which we are—saves the world.

The Cardinal told the sick that they are needed; they are the power and strength of the Church, the friends of Christ. The anointing they were about to receive would give them the strength of God:

> Then, although you do not see with the eyes of your body, you will see with the eyes of faith. Then, although you do not hear, you will be open to the Word of God. Then, even though paralysed, you will be able to move freely in the wide-open spaces of a love without limit. Then, unlovely or deformed, you will be able to receive from the Holy Spirit, the Creator, beauty and wisdom of soul.

Bishop Thomas Holland of Salford led the English pilgrims at the Congress. Preaching at Mass for English speaking participants he quoted Pope St Pius X: 'Lourdes is the most splendid throne of Our Lord's Eucharistic Presence. Lourdes is the centre from which devotion to Our Blessed Lady lights up the whole world.' The Bishop took his main theme from the Acts of the Apostles, how the first believers 'persevered together in the teaching of the Apostles, in the Community, in the breaking of the bread and in the prayers (Ac 2:42).' He asked us to examine our consciences against that reading.

> Here we have four striking features of that unity of mind and heart which elsewhere we are given as the genuine image of the infant Church, clearly one reason for her amazing impact on the society in which she was born. Let us compare our performance with that authentic prototype.
>
> 'They persevered together in the teaching of the Apostles.' What about our solidarity in that same teaching? Today's authentic magisterium is precisely that: it is the 'Didache', the Teaching of the Apostles. Do we today impress the society around us with that same unanimity? How many of us are now, not only uncomfortable, but quick to express publicly our discomfort with the known teaching of the Church? ... 'They persevered together in the Community.' Are we, on the contrary, nowadays inclined to opt for cosy groups in which we can be free to do our own thing? That is community of a kind—and for certain special purposes legitimate and necessary. But not when we strain bonds that should unite us to the Household of all the faithful, under its duly constituted management. That Community alone has the breadth and warmth of our Holy Mother the Church's welcome. We risk our Catholic health of mind and heart outside that embrace.
>
> 'They persevered together in the breaking of bread.' Are we all there at Mass, not only when we have to be, but when we could be? It does matter how many of us are there at Mass and how many of us receive Holy Communion...

'They persevered together in the prayers.' Traditionally priests and religious have shouldered the official Prayer of the Church. But now no longer are they to do this apart and unaided. Vatican II put in hand the appropriate revision of the Breviary for linking the laity with this main Work of the Church's Day. Are we yet in fact drawing on this vast reservoir of the People of God? What signs are there of the Prayer of the Church really becoming the prayer of the whole Church? We really should be doing more.

The Bishop noted then with deep satisfaction the way the Prayer of the Church was offered publicly at Lourdes in the Rosary Chapel with hundreds of the laity taking part.

The Church calls upon the Holy Spirit

In the talk referred to earlier, Professor Balthazar Fischer had listed as a 'new discovery' the role of the Holy Spirit in the dynamic of the Eucharist. The eucharistic presence of Christ is an action of the Holy Spirit:

> The three new Eucharistic Prayers, in the epiclesis of the Consecration, call, in the Eastern manner, on the Holy Spirit to come upon the gifts. So, in the second Eucharistic Prayer, which is based on the old text of Saint Hippolytus ... the following has been added: 'Let Your Spirit come upon these gifts to make them holy, so that they will become for us the Body and Blood of Your Son, our Lord Jesus Christ'.

At Mass on the Tuesday, Archbishop James Hickey of Washington took up this theme, 'The Church calls upon the Holy Spirit'. Recalling the role of the Holy Spirit, he said:

> In the creation of the world ... God's wondrous power was displayed. *He spoke and they came to be; he commanded and they were created!* In our Eucharist, something even more wonderful is to take place. The gifts of bread and wine are to be completely changed into something they were not. They are to become the true flesh and blood of Christ. And this is to be brought about by the power of the

> Holy Spirit ... As the Spirit once brought it about that the Son of God became Man of the Virgin, so too the Spirit shall effect the change of bread and wine into the body and blood of Christ.

The Holy Spirit will also make us one with Christ, with the Father, and with one another.

> We pray therefore in every celebration of the Eucharist that the Holy Spirit assist us so that we may grow in our love of God and that, joined with Christ and nourished by His Body and Blood, we may reach out to one another in this congregation and beyond ... Through the power of the Holy Spirit in our Eucharist we seek to create a new world of justice and love and peace.

The Archbishop reminded us that when we call on the Holy Spirit, we do so not as individuals but as members of the Church,

> joined together in the sacraments of Christ's mercy, and governed by those pastors who stand in succession to Peter and the rest of the Apostles. We call on the Spirit also as members of the Church joined with Mary in persevering prayer and confidence in Jesus. *We receive the Holy Spirit in and through Christ's Church.* When we are joined as the People of God, the Holy Spirit sanctifies us, leads us, enriches us by His gifts.

Archbishop Hickey finished his homily by urging us to reflect 'that our openness to the Spirit, in Eucharist and in the service of our world, must always be modelled on Mary's openness to the Spirit of God.'

The Church receives the Body of Christ

This takes us to the heart of the Lourdes Congress. But what *is* the Body of Christ? We can truthfully say, in the words of the old favourite, the Penny Catechism: 'The Sacrament of the Holy Eucharist is the true Body and Blood of Jesus Christ, together with His Soul and Divinity, under the appearances of bread and wine.' That is what—better 'who'—we receive in communion at Mass. The Penny Catechism emphasises the Real Presence of Our Lord. Not yet published in 1981, the Catechism of the Catholic Church asks: 'What is this Sacrament called?' It gives various answers, including this one: '*Holy Communion*, because by this sacrament we unite ourselves to Christ who makes us sharers in His Body and Blood to form a single body (no.1331).' This answer better prepares us to consider how the Congress deepened and expressed 'to people of today how and why the new world is linked with the Eucharist' and how the Congress confirmed 'all the spiritual and ethical dynamism that the Eucharistic Christ imparts to those who feed on Him with the necessary dispositions' (Letter of Pope St John Paul to Cardinal Knox).

It was a Dublin priest, Fr Dermot Lane, who showed us how. His talk, entitled 'The Eucharist and Social Justice', put forward his basic thesis: 'There is an essential link between the liturgy and life, between the sacrifice of the Mass and social justice, between the celebration of the Eucharist by the Church and the mission of the Church in the world for the Kingdom of God.' Fr Lane called on the witness of the Old Testament prophets, on the words of Jesus himself, and on St. Paul's letters to show the link between liturgy and service. He noted how 'the Catholic Church in the latter half of this century has made a deliberate and conscious decision in favour of action for justice as an integral element of her mission in the world.'

Helpfully, Fr Lane defined the meaning of 'New World':

> The New World is the Kingdom of God announced and promised by the earthly Jesus, gained and brought into being by His saving death on the Cross, manifested in the glory of His Resurrection and inaugurated by the outpouring of the Holy Spirit. This New World which is already established in the Body of the Risen Christ will reach completion and final perfection in the fulness of time when Christ will unite all things in heaven and on earth (Ep 1:9–10). In the meantime, this New World comes into

embryonic being wherever and whenever the values of the Kingdom of God are promoted by action in the service of the cause of man. The transformation of human existence, history and the universe in the name of the Kingdom of God gives us 'some kind of foreshadowing of the new age' to come (*Gaudium et Spes*, no. 39).

Fr Lane then considered the Eucharist as Presence, Sacrifice, Meal and Memorial. In each case we must look outside ourselves:

This real Presence of Christ in the Eucharist is a presence with a purpose: that they may be one, that they may have life and have it more abundantly, that man may eat and not die (Jn 6:50). As such the real Presence of Christ in the Eucharist is pure gift offered to mankind for the saving purposes of healing, reconciling and unifying all 'in Christ'. This particular saving purpose of the Eucharist is one that brings about the creation of a New World.

The Mystery of the Eucharist is also about the sacrifice of Christ on the cross of Calvary. In the Eucharist, we renew the one and only sacrifice of Christ ... The sacrifice of the Mass leads to conversion, a change in lifestyle, a Passover to the values of the Kingdom of God: universal justice, peace and love. This personal conversion requires a commitment to changing those structures in society which deny justice, prevent peace, and suppress love. In this sense, the doctrine of the sacrifice of the Mass leads to the construction of a New World.

The mystery of the Eucharist is also a meal ... The sharing and communing that take place around the altar of the Lord symbolise the sharing and communing that should take place in the world around us. To share and commune with Christ our brother in the Eucharist without sharing and communing with our sisters and brothers in the sanctuary of the universe would be something of a contradiction ... The breaking of Bread around the altar of the Lord commits us at the same time to the breaking of earthly bread with our brothers and sisters in the highways and byways of life.

This wider sharing and communing with others, inspired and motivated by the Eucharistic banquet, leads in its own way to the creation of a New World.

The mystery of the Eucharist is also a memorial, not just of Calvary, but of the whole life, death and resurrection of Jesus ... The memory that we recall and that is represented is a memory of one who described His mission on earth in terms of bringing good news to the poor, proclaiming release to captives, giving recovery of sight to the blind, and setting free those who are oppressed (see Lk 4:18) ... The Eucharist as a memorial sends out on mission those assembled in the name of Jesus, a mission that includes the liberation of men ... In this sense, the Eucharist as a living memorial continually puts into motion the construction of that New World for which Christ gave His life in love.

And what of the 'ethical dimension' Pope St John Paul refers to? Fr Lane had this to say:

A powerful and creative link exists between the Eucharist as sacrifice, personal conversion and the Christian liberation of mankind. This means in effect that from an ethical point of view we can no longer celebrate the Eucharist with eyes closed to the needs of others. The Eucharist commits the individual and the Christian community to the transformation of the world ... The Eucharist creates a people who unite prayer with action; praise with justice; adoration with transformation; and contemplation with social involvement. The Eucharist is that unique liturgical act which brings together into a creative but disturbing unity the vertical and horizontal dimensions of Christian mission and living. It is that unity that makes up an essential part of the ethical dynamism of the Eucharist ... The celebration of the Eucharist is the assumption of new responsibilities and obligations for the coming week. These responsibilities and obligations begin at the end of Mass when we leave to go forth, to put into practice that which we have celebrated in the Church ... an organic unity exists, and should be seen to exist, between the

Eucharist and mission, between liturgy and witness, between the Sunday assembly and the Monday world.

Similar points were made, though in different ways, by other speakers, including Professor Balthazar Fischer; Dom Helder Camara, Archbishop of Olinda and Recife, Brazil; Fr Francis Frost, a priest of the diocese of Salford, at that time professor of theology at the Institut Catholique de Lille; Fr Eugene LaVerdiere, a Blessed Sacrament Father from the USA and a teacher at the Catholic Theological Union; and Fr John Aniagwu, a priest from Ibadan, Nigeria. All their talks were inspiring examples of luminous and sustained intellectual enquiry.

The Church has its part in the mission of Christ

Do parts of the above section ('The Church receives the Body of Christ') smack a little of naïve and unrealistic materialist idealism? Do they distinguish sufficiently between the Kingdom of Heaven—which is both accessible and attainable—and the earthly kingdom—whose perfection in history will always be elusive and insufficient in itself? People can be deprived economically, politically, socially. But what about the liberation of the whole human person in all his deprivation, including spiritual deprivation? A retired archbishop brings an earthy realism to a youth vigil during the Congress. He is old enough to be their grandfather. The young people listen enthralled and respond with enthusiasm. Cardinal François Marty, former Archbishop of Paris, tells them that Jesus is recruiting them into his dockyard— the mission of Christ.

'Lord, what do you want of me?' This is the one question I raise with you ... Setting sail for the year 2000 promises to be difficult. The coast will be rugged for you. The compass must be checked. It isn't the time to cut the motor; it's the time to open it up; the time to change speed. In the year 2000, you will be between 35 and 45 years old. You will be in charge of the new world. Are you going to let yourselves live, to risk a new adventure? Are you going to drift along or are you going to make history?

My faith as a pastor prompts me to challenge you in the name of Jesus Christ, living and loving in the Eucharist. He offers you the Gospel message with all its demands. Jesus seeks you and loves you. Jesus calls you to venture. Jesus recruits you to his dockyard ... To be involved with the Eucharist and the Gospel for a new world is no comfortable adventure, no holiday cruise. At the end of every Eucharist the priest says, 'Let us go in the peace of Christ'. I always wanted to add: 'Let us go in the work of Christ'.

The new world towards which Jesus directs us in the Eucharist is not going to be built on its own. It doesn't come automatically. We don't wait for it as we wait for a train at the station platform. The Eucharist incorporates us into the Body of Christ, making us share its responsibility ... The Lord supplies us with the bread, the word, the forgiveness to bring to our brothers. Pope John Paul said on his visit to Paris, 'You must not flee from the world; you must go into it with all your Christian identity' ... At the service of a new world, you must become spiritual, responsible and apostolic people.

Some reckless people have accused immigrants who come here of 'coming to eat our bread'! How dare they say that? The Eucharist calls on us to share. Christians must work for the success of their brothers at the material, human, moral and spiritual level. In the new world, everyone has a right to share in the responsibility.

Young friends, what will you do tomorrow in Christ's dockyard? Priests will be needed to authenticate and preach the Gospel message, to bring about the eucharistic sacrifice of the risen Jesus, to be ministers of God's pardon. Consecrated people will be needed like headlamps at the crossroads of life to show that the Beatitudes are possible. Lay people will be needed to carry out their responsibilities courageously, to transmit life, to build a just, unified and brotherly world. Do you have a choice? No! It is God and his Church who choose. But look first to see where the need is most urgent, where the workers are few. Christ cries out, he calls in the midst of the world...

To risk the adventure of the new world of the year 2000, there are still 1000 weeks, 1000 Sunday Masses and 7000 days of apostolic work. Mary whispers gently to you: 'Whatever he says to you, do it'. You have in front of you the witness of many bishops, priests, parents, consecrated people. They are saying to you: 'We are happy people'.

Cardinal Marty's appeal to the young people expressed in a vivid, personal way what the preparatory document for the Congress had said:

There are not two Churches, that of the Eucharist and that of mission ... There is but one Church, called to share the life and mission of her Lord, his death and resurrection, his struggle and his victory. This sharing comes to its fulness in the Eucharist. By communion with the body of Christ the Church can present to mankind the sacrament of their salvation. Being closely united in the Eucharist to the life-giving resurrection of Christ gives life-giving impetus to her mission.

No account of the Lourdes Congress would be complete without mention of the international symposium at Toulouse which immediately preceded it. Cardinal Hyacinthe Thiandoum, Archbishop of Dakar, presided over this symposium, attended by 200 people from 35 nations. There was sustained high-level teaching, reflection, practical propositions and research on the Congress theme. Commentators picked out the talk given by Mgr Anselme Sanon, Bishop of Bobo-Dioulasso in Upper Volta, as having great impact. He spoke about the anthropological dimensions of the Eucharist with special reference to African culture. The symposium contributions were published under the title *Responsabilité, Partagé, Eucharistie.*

How the world had changed since the first Eucharistic Congress in 1881! The old political and economic structures of the European Powers, together with their colonial empires, had been swept away in the wake of two world wars. Major Communist powers had arisen in Russia and China. Science and technology had shrunk the world. But this 'new world' was fragile, divided, dangerous. The centenary Congress had a message for both the Church and the new world, summed up in the closing words of Cardinal Gantin, the Papal Legate, to the Congress participants:

> The Eucharist makes the Church, and the Eucharist commits the Church to the construction of a new world, with the newness of the Gospel. This newness has its charter, the charter of the Beatitudes. Wherever the Beatitudes are lived by you, Christ will be there.

References

1) *Jesus-Christ: pain rompu pour un monde nouveau. Document de reflexion theologique et spirituelle* (Paris 1980).

2) *Congrès Eucharistique International, Manuel du Congressiste* (Millau 1981).

3) Allen, J. F., Personal notes and diaries.

4) Bouyer, L., Ratzinger, J. et autres, *L'Eucharistie, pain nouveau pour un monde rompu* (Paris 1981)

5) Defois, G., David, J. (Ed), *Eucharistie: vers un monde nouveau.* Conference episcopale française (Paris 1981).

6) Holland, T., *Homily at Mass for English-speaking participants.* Adoremus (1982) No. 1, pp. 21–24; *Eucharistic Congresses—A Set of Six.* Adoremus (1985) No.1, pp. 11–13.

7) Pope John Paul II, Letter to Cardinal James Knox (1 January 1979).

8) Ratzinger, J., *Behold The Pierced One, An Approach to a Spiritual Christology,* translated from the German original *Schauen auf den Durchbohrten* by Graham Harrison (San Francisco 1986).

9) Swayne, S. (Ed), *Eucharist for a new world: a selection of homilies, addresses and conferences from the 42nd International Eucharistic Congress, Lourdes 1981* (Irish Institute of Pastoral Liturgy 1981).

10) *La Documentation Catholique,* No.1813, 9 aout 1981.

11) *Intuitions et enjeux du 42 Congrès eucharistique international, Lourdes 16–23 juillet 1981,* (Cambrai 1982).

12) *Responsabilité, Partagé, Eucharistie. Symposium International, Toulouse 1981* (Paris 1982).

13) *Un people qui parle... Les Tables rondes au 42 Congrès Eucharistique International* (Limoges 1982).

5 NAIROBI 11–18 AUGUST 1985
THE EUCHARIST AND THE CHRISTIAN FAMILY

THE CONTRAST BETWEEN the Congress in Lourdes in 1981 and the 43rd International Eucharistic Congress held in Nairobi in August 1985 could hardly have been greater. Pope St John Paul II *did* come. The sun shone throughout, as it does on the Equator, right above our heads. The crowds were there in their hundreds of thousands. The theological input was upbeat. Bishop Holland recalled it as 'perhaps of all the Congresses, the most colourful, melodious, rhythmical, devotional, and, yes, the best prepared!'

In 1895 a priest from Manchester in England led the first band of missionaries from Mombasa, on the east coast of Africa, via Nairobi to Kampala. His name was Bishop Henry Hanlon. He was a pioneer: there were then very few Catholics in the countries we now know as Kenya and Uganda. How proud Bishop Hanlon would have been ninety years later to see Pope St John Paul II in Uhuru Park, Nairobi, speaking to a congregation of one million people of 'the young and thriving Church of Africa'!

At the Congress, Kenya's four million Catholics—about a quarter of the total population—were hosts not only to the Holy Father but to 30 cardinals, 300 bishops and many thousands of delegates from 70 countries. These Congresses combine prayer and study with the chance to travel and meet people from all over the world. Each of the Congresses written of above (Melbourne 1973, Philadelphia 1976, Lourdes 1981) had its own character but Nairobi was tops for sheer enthusiasm and vitality.

There was song (in English, Latin and Swahili); liturgical and native dance (with what graceful dignity the African approaches the Eucharist!); talk and discussion (with leading world theologians and charismatic figures such as St Mother Teresa of Calcutta). And through it all the warm-hearted, open, generous people of Africa flocked in their thousands to the great outdoor events, many of their youth walking up to one hundred miles to be there.

I had flown with Bishop Holland from Heathrow via Madrid. On board the plane were Bishop James O'Brien, auxiliary in Westminster, along with 60 members of the Legion of Mary, as well as 40 scouts and guides from Dorset coming to help the Kenyans for one month. We landed in Nairobi at 1.30 am and were met by Sisters Joan and Joanna of the Franciscan Missionaries of St Joseph. They drove Bishop Holland and me (including part way down the wrong side of a dual carriageway) to where we were staying: Ingham House on the Ngong Road. Their Congregation was begun in Rochdale in the 1880s by Alice Ingham to help with the overseas missions of the Church and Bishop Hanlon brought the first sisters to East Africa in 1903 to assist the priests of the Mill Hill Congregation. At Ingham House we met Mother Aloysius, then Mother General of the Congregation, who in 1990 would found the Rainbow Family Trust in Manchester to care for children with life-limiting conditions. Princess Diana opened the Trust's home, Francis House, the following year. Also at Ingham House for the Congress were priests from the Salford and Shrewsbury dioceses, Thomas Mulheran, Joseph Carney and Brendan McDonald.

The main venues for the Congress events were Uhuru (meaning 'Freedom') Park, the Kenyatta International Centre (known locally as the KICC), the Nyayo National Stadium and the Cathedral Basilica of the Holy Family. Uhuru is a public park, a 'vast and comely breathing space', next to the business district of Nairobi. President Jomo Kenyatta had opened it in 1969. It was an ideal venue for the large liturgical celebrations. Nairobi was justly proud of the KICC, opened in the 1970s and then the tallest building in Nairobi at 105 metres. Its largest conference room could hold over 4,000 delegates. The Nyayo Stadium, a handsome venue located near the centre of Nairobi and opened just two years before the Congress, had a capacity of 30,000. The Cathedral, just one block away from Uhuru Park, also dates from the 1960s. It impresses with its modernist architecture, high bell tower, tall abstract stained-glass windows framed in stainless steel, interior details in Carrara marble, and seating for up to 4,000 people. The City Hall also housed a number of exhibitions. Amongst the most striking were the exhibitions of African art. Famous artists from Kenya and beyond displayed works on barkcloth, paper and canvas as well as carvings in wood and stone, giving imagery to their spiritual beliefs. Posters inspired by local culture illustrated the Congress theme.

The Kenyan bishops had called on 'all Kenyans and guests from other countries to labour over the theme of the Congress'. And so they did. Every mission station in Kenya was involved. Fifty committees and hundreds of people worked for two years, guided by the Secretary General, Fr Paul Cunningham CSSP. Under the title 'A Call to Renewal' participants followed a five-part programme: The Church, the Body of Christ; Reconciliation; Matrimony; the Christian Family; and The Eucharist. The Congress Prayer became the 'second Our Father' among Kenyan Catholics:

> God our Father, You are so good in giving us the Eucharist and the Christian Family. Grant us Your Spirit to help us realise that this Sacrament of Your Son's death and resurrection is the source of love and life in the Family. Through Christ, Our Lord, Amen.

The Congress opens

The Congress opened on Sunday 10 August. We vested for Mass in the Cathedral Hall, meeting there Bishop Patrick Kelly, Bishop Holland's successor in Salford, old friends including Bishops Colin Davies of Ngong, Donal Lamont of Umtali, Zimbabwe, and Michael Harty of Killaloe, together with Cardinal Tomás Ó Fiaich of Armagh, and then moved in procession, a thousand strong (700 priests and 300 bishops) to Uhuru Park. The Irish saying, 'When God made time, He made plenty of it', was clearly part of the African culture too, for the whole event lasted nearly four hours. The Congress vestments, as well as the altar vessels, were of African design. So too was the altar area and the dais for the Papal Legate, their conical thatched shapes copying the roofing of village huts.

Pope St John Paul had appointed Cardinal Joseph Cordeiro, Archbishop of Karachi, as his Legate for the first part of the Congress. 'The uniqueness of this congress is that it is the first to be held in missionary Africa south of the Sahara,' Cardinal Cordeiro said amidst loud ululations: 'That is something that should thrill the heart of any Christian.' The Legate's opening homily, as all the others during the Congress, concentrated on an aspect of the general theme: 'The Eucharist and the Christian Family'. His was a profound but clear exposition of the relation between the Eucharist and the larger Christian family, the Church, and the individual Christian family.

He spoke of the visible and dynamic unity of the Church:

> Christ's Church on earth, the Kingdom of Heaven, can never make progress if it strays, be it ever so slightly, from the path of unity. The Catholic Church is divinely founded, but it remains very much a society on earth, liable to all the foibles and quirks of human nature. Undoubtedly it has the help of the Holy Spirit, Who can marvellously work through human channels. Yet it requires no great observation to see that a society flourishes insofar as it is a compact unity. Moreover, it needs to be a visible unity, for experience shows that otherwise it becomes subject to diverse interpretations. For us Catholics, the Holy Father is that visible unity. And it is a dynamic unity. If it were static, it would end in sterility. The needs of the Church vary; she must take account of the changing situation of the world. Now one, now another facet of the rich fabric of the Church needs to have our attention focussed on it. The Holy Eucharist is the sacramental sign of our unity in Christ. Sharing as we do in the one Bread and the one Cup,

we can ask for no greater unity, even as we strive to make that unity a sign for the world.

The Legate pointed out that the earliest celebrations of the Eucharist were in private homes.

> However, the emphasis is on the event which constitutes the community, rather than on the community which comes together to share the event. In an ordinary meal, the community creates the event. In the Eucharistic Meal, the redemptive event creates the community, which then in turn nourishes itself through the bread and wine embodying the event which brought it into being as a community...

Perhaps recalling Pope St John Paul's message to the previous Congress in Lourdes, that the Eucharist is linked with Christ's Passion and Resurrection, the Legate continued:

> The sacrifice of the Cross is so decisive for men that Christ did not carry it out and did not return to His Father until He had left us the means to take part in it exactly as if we had been present at it... The Eucharistic celebration does not affect the sacrifice of the Cross numerically; it does not add to it, nor does it multiply it. The Mass and the Cross are but one and the same sacrifice. Nevertheless, the Eucharistic breaking of bread has an essential function, that of putting at our disposal the original offering of the Cross. It makes that sacrifice actual today for our generation. By making the Body and Blood of Christ really present under the species of bread and wine, it makes, simultaneously, the sacrifice of the Cross actual and accessible to us in our day... This vast concourse of pilgrims is a most fitting environment for such a magnificent institution as is the Holy Eucharist. And yet, numbers notwithstanding, all this is still taking place in a family situation. Have we not, all of us, through faith in Christ, become as it were members of the family of God, and so entitled to participate in this mystery?

Through His Son, God has made an 'indestructible covenant' with us. Marriage and the Christian family have a special connection with this covenant:

> The Christian family, truly called the domestic Church, is therefore a covenant of relationships within the family itself, and of relationships with other families. And it is the Eucharist which makes the covenant accessible to the family, so that the relationships between the members can be totally illuminated by the source of love Himself. Who can deny today the need for this love, when we see families beset by selfishness, refusals, weaknesses and deceptions? How much the ruptures within the families need to be repaired by the love shown in faithfulness and pardon, to teach the world again the faithfulness and value of a word given and a word kept.

The Legate spoke too of the 'ministry of evangelisation' of the Christian family:

> Urged by love, the family can then become the means of breaking down barriers erected by race or tribe, caste or colour, creed or culture, and positively it can help to transform division and hatred into unity and love. We have too little understanding and appreciation of the power of the Eucharist to transform the world. The power is surely present whenever we celebrate the Eucharist, because Jesus is always present as He promised, and His desire is that the world be transformed. That transformation, however, will only happen when we bring the world to Christ... Channelling that power is our task.

Cardinal Cordeiro ended by thanking the First World for bringing faith in Christ to the Third World, suggesting that 'it would be a touching and gracious act of charity to offer this Eucharistic Sacrifice—Eucharist, after all, means thanksgiving—for God's choicest blessings on these countries, asking Him to be mindful of the heroic labours of the missionary pioneers who came from these same countries' and then commending all to the intercession of the Blessed Virgin Mary, 'the model of a perfect mother'. He declared the Congress open, expressing his thanks to the Government of Kenya and to the Archbishop of Nairobi and Congress host, Cardinal Maurice Otunga.

Cardinal Maurice Otunga was a most gracious and soft-spoken host. He has been described, by Bishop Anthony Muheria of Kitui, as

> a great and distinguished son of Africa, son of a chief, an authentic Christian, but one who was fully conscious of being first and foremost a son of God. His personal encounter with Christ replaced his human filiation with a deeper awareness of being a son of the Church, thus raising him to supernatural heights as son of the greater King and chief, Christ. This is the meaning of holiness.

Perhaps Bishop Muheria's words need the following explanation. Maurice Michael Otunga was born in 1923. He was the son of Sudi, a tribal chief, and although he was not the eldest son he was marked out by his father, because of his character and intelligence, as his successor. He was given the name Otunga, meaning 'a staff the old lean on for support'. He went to a school run by the Mill Hill Fathers and it was there that his interest in Christianity began. With the encouragement of the College rector, Fr Joannes de Reeper, a Dutch Mill Hill missionary, Otunga was baptised in 1935 and given the name of Maurice Michael. His father, together with the tribal elders, were dismayed when Maurice announced his intention of becoming a priest. They knew that Maurice Otunga would then never marry and so would not carry on his father's line. They kidnapped him from the seminary and tried to persuade him to change his mind. Maurice refused, and his religious superiors decided to send him to Rome to complete his studies. He attended the Pontifical Urban University on the Janiculum Hill where he obtained a doctorate in theology and was ordained priest during the Holy Year of 1950. A mere six years later Pope Pius XII appointed him auxiliary Bishop of Kisumu in Kenya. There was no church big enough for the crowds wishing to attend his ordination as bishop so the venue chosen was the sports field of the Kakamega seminary. Until now, his father Sudi had been estranged from Maurice. Maurice however persuaded his father to come to the ordination. He did so, recognizing that his son was now 'chief' to far more people than he would have been as head of his tribe—though Sudi remained shielded from the view of most in a specially constructed gazebo. At the end of the ordination Maurice took off his vestments and went to his father and there was a great reconciliation. Near the end of Sudi's life Maurice had the joy of receiving his father into the Church.

Maurice Otunga was Archbishop of Nairobi from 1971 to his retirement in 1997. Pope Bl Paul VI named him Cardinal in 1973. He died in 2003 and the cause of his canonisation has been introduced. He is now known as 'Servant of God'.

The Christian Family

Congress Monday served up two memorable lectures at the Kenyatta International Conference Centre: the first by Cardinal Carlo Martini of Milan on 'The Eucharist and the Christian Family', the second by the Nigerian Cardinal Francis Arinze, Prefect of the Vatican Congregation for Non-Christians, on 'One Body, Many Members'. The latter was especially easy to listen to and very balanced on the Africanisation of the Church: 'We need much prayer, patience, humility and time. Time has no respect for those who act without her.' We met at the Conference Hall other priests of Salford and Shrewsbury, John Dale and Peter Sharrocks, and then the Mother General of the Josephites, the African offspring of the Franciscan Missionaries of St Joseph. She was a Masai, named Mother Stephen.

Cardinal Martini's lecture—he called it a 'meditation'—was lengthy and closely argued. He based his text on the wedding feast at Cana (Jn 2:1–12).

> There, Jesus said that His hour had not yet come, meaning 'the supreme hour of Jesus' life and mission, the hour of

His death upon the Cross'. It is at this time that Jesus accomplishes—let us say, consummates—His love of donation to the Church; He gives His Body and His Blood, in other words, all of Himself, for her. Therefore Christ's hour is an hour of love and giving.

Martini said that at Cana Jesus 'reveals Himself as the Bridegroom of the new times'. At Cana

> nothing is taken from the newly-married couple's happiness: Jesus only gives. And how much! His presence is not to be feared. Rather it is to be desired. This is true for any marriage: the one at Cana and the ones that are celebrated in all the villages and towns, both large and small, of the world. Do not be afraid of Christ! Open your doors to Christ! This fundamental cry is meant for all human hearts. So why not make it ring out, with a deeper and more intense vibration, for the hearts of an engaged couple, when by celebrating their marriage they begin their path of love together?

> In actual fact, this is the meaning, so simple and yet so extraordinarily rich, of the marriage sacrament, on which married life is founded ... In it faith searches for, finds and enjoys a personal presence. It is the presence of Jesus Christ, the Church's Spouse, the Spouse of our souls.

The Vatican Council affirmed, in *Gaudium et Spes* 48, the fact that Jesus meets us in the Sacrament of Marriage. Martini then quoted from Pope St John Paul II's document, *Familiaris consortio* 13, which explains *how*. In the marriage sacrament 'the spouses participate in, and are called to live, the very charity of Christ who gave Himself on the Cross.' It is necessary to 'reflect on the loving donation of Christ on the Cross' in order to discover 'the relationship between the Eucharist and the couple and the Christian family'.

The Cardinal's reflection on the love of Christ covered several points: firstly, 'the logic of giving'.

> It is this love until the end, this love made up of total and
> sacrificial giving that is present and working in the Eucha-
> rist, in the Body given and the Blood spilt for us; just as it
> is present and operating in the Marriage Sacrament, as a
> divine instrument to assume, purify, save, renew the love
> of donation and the communion of the Christian nuptial
> couple.

Secondly, 'the purification and the sanctification of humanity'.
Martini quoted from Ephesians (5:25–27) to show how deeply
Jesus loved the Church: 'He gave Himself up for her, to make her
holy, purifying her in the bath of water by the power of the word,
to present to Himself a glorious Church, holy and immaculate,
without stain or wrinkle or anything of that sort.' He continued:
'It is the same aim as that intended by Jesus in the Eucharist, a
source of forgiveness of sins and of sanctification. It is the same
aim as that pursued by the marriage sacrament, with the gift of
a purified and sanctifying love.' But sin, selfishness, moral disorder bring unhappiness and separation. Conversion comes
through the Eucharist: 'Renewed participation in the Eucharist
makes husbands and wives and parents mature in the conversion
of their hearts and lives.' This participation will lead on to 'a
progressive maturing of marital and family love in all its values'.

The third point the Cardinal stressed was the ecclesial nature
of Christian marital and family love. The Marriage Sacrament
means that the family can truly be called 'the domestic Church',
sharing the 'double and unitary activity' of the Church: namely,
its 'liturgical activity that calls the Church to sing the glory of
God, and the apostolic-missionary activity that calls the Church
to reveal and communicate to men Christ's salvation.'

In conclusion, Cardinal Martini returned to Cana and spoke
of Mary's intervention:

> Mary's presence becomes a suggestive invitation to redis-
> cover the special role that women, according to God's
> eternal plan of love and the changing necessities of the
> history that it becomes, have in marriage and in the family,

and consequently in the Church and in society. Mary comes forward and intervenes, serenely, faithfully, courageously. Is this not an implicit but clear reminder to overcome those unacceptable forms of inferiority of women in respect to men with decision? So that the woman can rediscover, together with the irreplaceable values of maternity and domestic education, those many gifts that God has offered her for the good of the bigger family of God's sons and daughters and of all mankind? ... This so intense participation of Mary in the face of human suffering is still alive in the face of families' difficulties, pain, trials and sometimes dramas: just as she is the mother of the Church, so Mary is also the mother of domestic churches.

Tuesday's Mass in Uhuru Park was nearly all in Swahili, and offered 'for the poor and needy'. Cardinal Otunga was the chief celebrant, with Bishop Raphael Nzeki of Nakuru, President of the Bishops' Conference, the eloquent homilist. The celebration ended with an Agape and a distribution of food. Bishop Nzeki also announced that the Kenyan Bishops would build a home for the Aged and Destitute as a lasting memorial of the Congress.

The talks in the afternoon continued the theme of the Mass. We listened to Cardinal Bernadin Gantin, Pope St John Paul II's Legate at the Lourdes Congress and now in 1985 President of the Vatican Congregation for Bishops, and then Archbishop Gabriel Zubeir Wako of Khartoum. Cardinal Gantin examined the link between charity and justice:

> We should be aware of and make known the fact that true charity must include the struggle for justice and not be watered down into a vague form of solidarity based on condescendence. True charity sets forth the various levels of responsibility in our duty to seek truth.

Speaking of his own country of drought-stricken Sudan and the anticipated starvation of some one million people by the end of the year, Archbishop Wako called on the international community to urgently send food and personnel to stave off the famine and added: 'It is not a question of sharing or not sharing. It is a question of these people dying or not.' Someone at the Congress shrewdly observed that it was a starving Africa welcoming the world to a spiritual feast.

The 'Sick and Suffering'

Wednesday was dedicated to 'the sick and suffering'. Cardinal Laurean Rugambwa, Archbishop of Dar es Salaam in Tanzania was the principal concelebrant and the preacher at a Mass with anointing. The congregation emptied from the stands and invaded the central pitch. Almost everyone present received the Sacrament of the Sick. Nurses, doctors and hospital workers formed an eloquent offertory procession.

Talks in the afternoon from St Mother Teresa and Cardinal Joseph Bernardin of Chicago completed the day's theme of 'the sick and suffering'. Mother Teresa's address was marked by a splendid simplicity. She spoke from the heart, without notes, about the love of Jesus.

> When we look at the cross we know how He loved us. And when we look at the tabernacle we know how He loves us now. That is why He made Himself the Bread of Life: we just forget this tenderness of love. And He made Himself this Bread of Life to satisfy our hunger for His love. And as if that was not enough for Him, He made Himself the hungry one, the naked one, the humblest one so that you and I can satisfy His hunger for our human love.
>
> This is something so wonderful: the sick, the poor, the unwanted, the unloved, the lepers, the drug addicts, the alcoholics, the prostitutes: Christ in the distressing disguise. And they are—I always feel—the privileged to be in His presence twenty-four hours. He says: 'What you are doing to the least, you are doing it to me. If you receive a little child in my name, you receive me. If you give a glass of water in my name, you receive me.' Wonderful!

She described how suffering could bring a person into communion with the passion of Christ.

> I gave a talk to our lepers … and I said: 'Use the disease, the suffering, not as a punishment but as a gift of God. You are the chosen ones to be able to offer for the peace in the world, in thanksgiving for what God has done for all the others and for you.' And I went on telling those people that they are specially loved… I feel always that these people of ours are poor people who suffer so much; the sick and the dying are treasure houses for the dioceses; they are the living Christ going through the passion … What a tremendous gift of God is suffering if it helps our people to know that they are sharing the passion of Christ! It is just not a punishment—as it is explained sometimes—it is a gift of God.

Mother Teresa's message of liberating poverty has been seen as something deeply understood in Africa, at the foundation of an emerging African Christian theology. Meeting Mother Teresa was an unexpected privilege. She powerfully reminded me of the dignity of the sacred priesthood when she took hold of both my hands and kissed them.

At the same conference, Cardinal Bernardin in a wide-ranging talk explored 'some of the human hungers found in our world today' and then reflected 'upon the Eucharist as God's gracious action and upon our response to this gift.' He listed the 'many diverse threats to human life and dignity in our world, each of which gives rise to the hungers of the world's children.' The Cardinal went through countries and continents by name, 'to demonstrate the poignant reality of the individual hungers'. Then came a strong condemnation of the global expenditure on armaments:

> All the children of the world are being held hostage by the great sums of money spent each year on the worldwide arms race. They also live under the threat of nuclear warfare. They know the truth of the Kikuyu proverb: 'When elephants fight, it is the grass that suffers.' The children of the world hunger for peace! …

To satisfy these basic hungers, we will need to bring unity and harmony to our diversity—whether it is social or political, economic or religious. We will have to do so on a scale previously unimaginable. The task is enormous and dazzlingly complex. But we can accomplish whatever God's will is for us because He gives us all we need to carry out our mission. One of His greatest gifts is the Eucharist, which is the paradigm of unity and the basic source of our nourishment, guidance and strength...

In the Eucharistic assembly, God's Word both comforts and challenges us. It prompts our conversion and helps reconcile us. It develops our Christian vision and teaches us Gospel values. We learn the necessity—and therefore also the possibility—of living in right relationships: with our environment, with one another, within ourselves, and, especially, with God.

In a world that 'is rapidly becoming a global village in which all of us are increasingly interdependent', the Cardinal said that

as Catholics, nourished daily at the Eucharist, we must take our rightful place in our world as peacemakers. The Eucharist impels us to bring our moral principles and analysis with us as we participate in the development of private, corporate, and public policies which impact human lives.

Congress Thursday was the solemnity of the Assumption of Our Lady. Mass in Nyayo Stadium included the renewal of commitment for all involved in Church work, with the Brazilian Cardinal Agnelo Rossi as the main celebrant and Cardinal Bernardin the homilist. The afternoon found us at the KICC listening to the Filipino Cardinal Jaime Sin, Archbishop of Manila, and Sister Theresa Gachambi, Superior General of the Assumption Sisters. Cardinal Sin gave an extensive and illuminating address on the relation between faith and culture. He based his remarks on the Church as the Body of Christ:

It has pleased God to make men holy and save them, not merely as individuals without any mutual bonds, but by making them into a single people, the new People of God, the Church. In a similar way God has called to membership in the Church, not only individuals, but also peoples, nations and cultures.

All peoples of the earth are called to become members of the Body of Christ. Each people is expected to bring along with it its patrimony, its riches, its good customs, traditions and style; in short, its culture. Each people is expected to bring to Christ its own special contribution in His Church. Then the one Body of Christ, enriched by the patrimony of all cultures, is resplendent like a queen decorated with variety.

Sister Gachambi's topic was 'Religious Witness in the Church'. The fruitful development of religious congregations has been a feature of the Church in Africa: the Assumption Sisters were formed from the Missionary Sisters of Our Lady for Africa. Ministries of consecrated men and women have enriched the Church throughout its history. Such ministries may not be part of the Church's hierarchical structure but they work in union with it and new expressions of ministry are constantly emerging.

Friday's theme was 'Youth and Christian Love'. It was a day of prayer for young people preparing for responsibility and leadership. Fr Mutiso Mbinda, Secretary General of the Bishops' Conferences of East Africa, gave a sober but optimistic address in which he recalled that 60% of the total population of Africa was youth population, posing

a considerable problem to both the governments and the Church in this continent... The youth are very much victims of the social, cultural, historical, political and economic contexts of this continent. City life attracts the young people from rural areas for various reasons... Our education systems continue to promote the false hope that at the end of the educational tunnel there is a nice white-collar job which can only be found in the cities... The rural areas seem to be neglected year after year despite the impending food crisis... It is often said that the youth are the leaders of tomorrow's society. I refuse to accept such an attitude. Rather, the youth are the leaders of today's society in their own way, guiding it and directing to the future. The youth of today are more perceptive to the signs of the times and are well able to assume a prophetic role in society.

The Pope's Message

Friday at sunset saw the long-awaited arrival of Pope St John Paul II on his second visit to Kenya. He had left Rome eight days earlier and had already visited five countries: Togo, Ivory Coast, Cameroun, Central African Republic and Zaire. A welcome ceremony greeted him as he stepped off the plane and then walked along the red carpet to the car that would take him to the Papal Nunciature. Amongst those lining his path he spotted Bishop Holland. Stopping abruptly, he said with obvious pleasure: 'Ah! Bishop Holland! How nice to see you again' and embraced him in a bear hug. A moment to treasure!

On Saturday afternoon Pope John Paul II presided at Mass offered for married couples and young people preparing for marriage. There they were, twenty-five couples at the front of the vast Nyayo Stadium. Mass began at 3 o'clock and ended at 7 o'clock. One bride fainted. The press cameras swarmed round her but she recovered and to thunderous applause demurely regained her place. Pope St John Paul set his homily in the context of the wedding feast at Cana where Jesus was present with the newly-married couple: 'He was with them. He was for them. The Eucharist is the Sacrament in which Jesus Christ is with us today... Christ is with us to the end of time, and he is for us...'

The Pope explained

> why in every age the Church continues to teach the unchanging truth, that marriage is indissoluble. When couples freely receive this Sacrament, as they are doing this afternoon, they establish an unbreakable oneness... they are able in marriage to be a living sign of the ever-

faithful love of Christ for the Church... the truth of the
Gospel and the grace of the Sacrament of Marriage
transform and ennoble all married life if the couple follow
this truth faithfully, if they collaborate with this grace!
Above all, what is ennobled is conjugal love, that thoroughly human love which is united to the divine, and
which is for the good of both husband and wife... The fruit
of faithful love is a communion of minds and hearts.

He went on to explain something particularly relevant to the
African scene, that 'such a communion is radically contradicted
by polygamy.' Marriage should also be open to the possibility of
transmitting new life.

Together with this task of fostering a communion of persons, husbands and wives also fulfil a vital role in the service
of human life, in particular through that special honour and
duty which is theirs of bringing children into the world and
educating them. The vocation of marriage requires great
sacrifice and generosity on the part of both husband and
wife. And the fullest sign of this mutual self-giving is
expressed when the couple willingly accept children and
bring them up in the knowledge and love of God.

Pope John Paul then stressed the need to prepare young people
for marriage and urged his listeners: 'Listen to Mary, for Mary will
lead you to Christ! And it is Christ who offers you, the youth of
this land, the wonderful gift of the Eucharist. It is he, Jesus Christ,
who proclaims to you the truth of marriage and human love.'

On his visits, the Pope does not celebrate Mass more than once
in the same place. So Sunday's Mass, the Statio Orbis, was in
Uhuru Park, filled with a capacity crowd of one million. Pope
John Paul recalled the beginnings of the Eucharist: how

the disciples and witnesses of our Crucified and Risen Lord
'remained faithful to the teaching of the apostles, to the
brotherhood, to the breaking of bread and to the prayers'
(Ac 2:42) ... Thus it has also been on the African
continent since the Gospel first reached these lands

through the missionaries, and since it produced its first fruits in a community assembled to celebrate the Eucharist.

Today this community united in Christ extends over almost the entire continent. This community of seventy million people is a great sign of fruitfulness of the Eucharist; the power of Christ's Gospel has been revealed in Africa. From the rising of the sun to its setting, the name of the Lord is praised on African soil. Sons and daughters of Africa faithfully transmit the teachings of the Apostles, and the Eucharist is continuously offered for the glory of God and the well-being of every human being on this continent. The authentic living of Religious Life and the existence of millions of Christian families are proof that the grain of wheat has yielded a rich harvest to the glory of the Blood of Jesus and to the honour of all Africa.

The message of this Eucharistic Congress was an invitation to love:

The love of Christ that is received as a gift must in turn be given as a gift. Christ's love poured out upon us abundantly in the one bread and the one cup must be shared with our neighbour: with the neighbour who is poor or homeless, with the neighbour who is sick or in prison, with the neighbour who belongs to a different tribe or race or who does not believe in Christ. Christ's invitation to love, addressed to us once more in this Eucharistic Congress, is meant above all for the Christian family ... And Christ's invitation to love is especially relevant in the practice of conjugal love. The exclusive and unbreakable union of husband and wife expresses itself best in mutual self-giving. Couples who continually seek to love and support one another share in a special way in the life of the Most Holy Trinity. They reflect like a mirror the ever-faithful love of God for His people. Married love is fruitful, with a fruitfulness that is shown especially in children. And every child brings a renewed invitation to love with still greater generosity. To feed and clothe and care for each child requires much sacrifice and hard work. In addition, parents have the duty of educating their children.

Pope John Paul explained why prayer and the sacraments 'should enjoy a place of prominence in family life. Most important of all is the Eucharist, in which Christ's covenant of love with the Church is commemorated and renewed, and in which a husband and wife find strength and nourishment for their own marriage covenant.' Prayer together in the family 'opens the heart of each member to the Sacred Heart of Jesus and helps the family to be more united in itself, yet more ready to serve the Church and society.'

On his arrival in Kenya the Pope had called the Congress a sign of 'maturity and vigour in the life of the young and thriving Church in Africa ... The Church in every land rejoices with you at this new stage of dynamic life and mission.' He ended his homily at the Statio Orbis in the same vein:

> The Church sees in this Congress a particular result of all her missionary and pastoral labours since the beginning of evangelisation on the African continent, and for this result she gives thanks and praise to the Father, the Son and the Holy Spirit. At the same time, drawing from the young and lively faith of Africa, the whole Church desires to renew her missionary zeal just as the Second Vatican Council manifested it twenty years ago; for the Church is by her very nature missionary!

The Pope's homily was impressively reinforced by the renewal of marriage promises made by all the couples present.

Confirmation of 'the young and lively faith of Africa' came with the formal opening during Congress week of two Theological Institutes: the Catholic Higher Institute of Eastern Africa, and Hekima College. The Higher Institute, founded by the episcopal conferences of Ethiopia, Kenya, Malawi, the Sudan, Tanzania, Uganda, Zambia and the Seychelles, is now the Catholic University of Eastern Africa, whose mission is 'to promote excellence in research, teaching and community service by preparing morally upright leaders based on the intellectual tradition of the Catholic Church'.

Hekima College was founded as a school of theology by the Major Superiors of the Society of Jesus in Africa and Madagascar to provide a theological formation at University level for Jesuit students preparing for priesthood. Greatly expanded since its opening, it is now a Campus of the Catholic University of Eastern Africa. It was a delight at the opening to renew acquaintance with a cousin on my mother's side, Fr Cecil McGarry SJ, then the Dean of Studies, later Rector of Hekima College.

The Congress over, our party was able to enjoy Kenya's abundant fauna and flora. Such variety and beauty! Elephants, rhinoceros, lions, zebras, giraffes, monkeys, buffalos, hippopotami, wildebeests and others; cranes, flamingos, ostriches; bananas, mangoes, passion fruit, and everywhere the brilliant bougainvillea.

We crossed the dramatic Great Rift Valley and stayed in the bush in Western Kenya with priest missionaries on loan from the Salford diocese: Frs Joseph Cain, Richard O'Connor, Dermot Heakin. It was eleven years since my first visit to those same missions. Wonderful to see even in that short time the progress, not only in baptisms but in education, medical care, water schemes! The Swahili 'Harambee' (Let us all pull together) was very evident. Even out of their poverty the people gave generously. They presented us visitors at various places with two rams, three hens, over three hundred eggs, hands of bananas, paw-paws, mangoes, maize. 'But what can we give you in return?' we asked. Came the reply: 'You can give us God.'

At the Congress opening Cardinal Maurice Otunga had claimed: 'It can be said in all humility that Africa—the church of Africa—has a message for the world... We can show to the world that light can emanate here... that the church of Africa can truly enrich the world.' In Kenya, one caught a glimpse of the first Christian communities in Jerusalem and Rome and Corinth. Like them the young Church in Africa has its problems. But it is rapidly growing in confidence as well as in numbers. Who knows? Sometime in the future missionaries may reverse Bishop Henry

Hanlon's journey. In fact, they are already here. As Pope St John Paul II said as he stepped onto Kenyan soil:

> The prayers and sacrifices of the many missionaries who came here and the open hearts that received the Gospel message are now bringing forth a rich and plentiful harvest. The Church in Africa is entering a new era, an era in which she will be called increasingly to reach out generously beyond her national and continental frontiers and to place her resources and gifts at the service of the universal Church. What you have received as a gift you now wish to give as a gift.

References

1) Agunda, K. and Muchiri, M. (Ed), *The Eucharist and the Christian Family: the Theme of the 43rd International Eucharistic Congress* (Nairobi 1987).

2) Allen, J. F., Personal notes and diaries.

3) Burgman, H., *The Way the Catholic Church started in Western Kenya* (1990).

4) Gaudoin-Parker, M. L., *Towards a Programme of Pastoral Preparation for the Eucharistic Congress.* Supplement to Adoremus (1985) No.1.

5) Holland, T., The 43rd International Eucharistic Congress—My Seventh. Adoremus (1986) No.1.

6) Kenya Association for Liturgical Music (Ed), *Aleluya: liturgical hymns for the 43rd International Eucharistic Congress* (Nairobi 1985).

7) *Main liturgies: the Eucharist and the Christian family, 43rd International Eucharistic Congress, Nairobi = Liturjia kuu: Ekaristi na jamaa ya Kikristu/ Mkutano wa Kimataifa wa 43 wa Sakramenti Takatifu ya Ukaristia, English, Swahili* (Nairobi 1985).

8) Renewal Committee for 43rd International Eucharistic Congress, Pastoral renewal programmes: the Eucharist and the Christian family: 43rd International Eucharistic Congress, Nairobi, Kenya, 11–18 August 1985 (Kenya 1985).

6 SEOUL 5–8 OCTOBER 1989
CHRIST OUR PEACE

A HOP FROM MANCHESTER to Paris, then a long-range flight by Korean Airways over the polar route via Anchorage brought me swiftly to Seoul. Such rapid progress carries benefits. Does it also have disadvantages? When a scuba diver ascends too quickly he suffers decompression sickness, known as 'the bends'. Does passing so quickly from one continent to another, from Europe to South Asia in a matter of hours, cause similar 'bends' at the cultural level? No doubt it could do if minds that meet do not really meet at all. The Congress welcoming party at Seoul airport dispelled all such fears. There was much smiling and bowing, followed by the westernised hand-shaking. We were one in our humanity and, even more so, one in our faith. Ceremonies over, the small but comfortable New Naija Hotel in downtown Seoul provided a good night's sleep and shelter for the duration.

One's first impressions next morning were of an enormous city. Lying on the Han river and surrounded by mountains, Seoul embraced ten million citizens. It has been described as 'a healthy mix of Japanese industriousness, Irish religious zeal, and traditional Chinese Confucian values'. The streets heaved with life: smartly dressed, hurrying people and home-made Hyundai and Kia motors.

It has a long history, too, stretching back over 2000 years. Part of that history, though more recently, is the city's Catholic Myeongdong Cathedral, dedicated to the Immaculate Conception of the Virgin Mary. Built in the Gothic Revival style and opened in 1898, it was then the largest building in Seoul. The Cathedral became a centre for political unrest in the 1970s and 1980s when Catholic priests led protests against Korea's military rule and it was a sanctuary for protesters. When we arrived there on the opening morning of the Congress it was buzzing with activity of a different kind: delegates from every continent thronged the Cathedral Congress office; volunteer staff cheerfully and efficiently issued our passes. This was the first such Congress to be held in the Far East and in a country which had none of the five major languages of the world as its official language. This must have placed an extra burden on the organisers but they coped admirably.

Then it was off to a reception in several parish churches in Seoul. The parish for English-speaking delegates was that of So Cho Dong, dedicated to St Charles Hyun Sok Mun, martyred for his Catholic faith in Saenamto in 1846. St Charles came from a family of martyrs: in earlier persecutions, Charles's father had been martyred in 1801, his sister in 1839, and his wife and son had died in prison. Begun only in 1981 with 250 households, the parish of St Charles recorded phenomenal increase with 3,480 households by 1989. It had grown from 450 people to 9,870, helped by the 400 or so adult converts received every year. We heard tell of similar numbers of converts and similar growth in all parishes. Daily Mass attendance ranged on average from 160 to 460.

The parish priest, Fr Thomas Pak, welcomed us warmly: 'We will endeavour to show you, brothers and sisters from abroad, our church as it is, and you shall see and feel in person the true benefit and real aspects of one of the Korean Catholic churches.' We heard how the Korean people had been preparing for the Congress for the whole of the previous year. They took part in a campaign entitled 'One Heart, One Body Movement', remembering how Christ shed the last drop of his blood for us and came to heal all humanity. So they were encouraged to donate blood and donate organs of the body. They also did voluntary service. Every family was encouraged to give freely one member for one day each week to work in construction so that all people could have decent accommodation, with running water and heated floors. Heated floors? At that time the usual way to sleep in Korea was to sleep on the floor. A thick blanket was placed on the floor on which one would sleep, with a lighter blanket on top for warmth. The blankets would be folded up every morning and placed in a wardrobe until they were taken out again at night. This lifestyle has changed rapidly in Korea however: most Koreans today sleep in a bed.

A Good Shepherd Sister, a missionary from the USA, gave us an outline of the history and growth of the Catholic Church in Korea, now one of the fastest growing Churches in the world. Half the population of forty million people were Buddhists, with nearly two million Catholics, about half of whom were recent converts. The rapid growth in numbers was attributed to the example and intercession of the thousands of Korean martyrs, 103 of whom, mostly lay men and women, Pope St John Paul II had canonised during his first visit to Korea in 1984. Sister was followed by a married couple from the parish who described with enthusiasm the vitality of their community. A liturgical service and generous refreshments rounded off our visit. During the service, Fr Michael Gaudoin-Parker, the National Delegate for England and Wales, preached a homily on 'Living the Eucharist Today'. He stressed the importance of *presence*: the presence of Christ in the Eucharist, which we discover best by adoration, and then our presence with one another, the best form of evangelisation.

The Congress logo could hardly have been simpler. It was a circle, red in colour, dissected by a red cross, all done in jagged lines with brush on rice paper. But its simplicity was beguiling. Was it an encircled red cross? Or a red circle divided into four parts by the cross? Different people could see it therefore as either the four corners of the earth united by the cross, or as the whole world stamped by the sign of the cross, or as the arms of the cross embracing the world and overcoming its divisions. The colour red was striking: it spoke of fire, fervour, and the saving Blood of Christ. The white background signified the purity of the host, broken for the peace of the world. In that, the logo took account of the year, 1989, which marked the fiftieth anniversary of the outbreak of the Second World War (3 September 1939). The overriding Congress theme was 'Christ our Peace'. Speaking to national delegates to the Congress in 1988, Pope John Paul had asked for 'intense spiritual preparation through reflection and prayer for the forthcoming Congress, with a sincere opening of hearts and minds to welcome the gift of Christ's peace'. The theme, 'Christ our Peace', was especially relevant in a country still technically at war with its neighbour, North Korea.

The Holy Father's request for 'intense spiritual preparation' had been conscientiously answered by the Korean Church. Cardinal Stephen Kim had been Archbishop of Seoul since 1968. Speaking in Rome in 1988 to national delegates to the Congress he asked:

> The tragic division of Korea eloquently bespeaks the deep divisions and wounds of today's mankind caused by greed for power and possession, by ideology and discrimination. How then should the coming Congress convincingly address these great burning issues for the Church and for today's world? The main thrust of our thinking has already been set out in the Basic Text on the theme, 'Christ Our Peace'. Ultimately, I firmly believe it comes down to a simple, essential point: like our Lord Jesus Christ, we ourselves as individual believers and as Church have to become, in truth and reality, bread broken and given, 'rice' to be shared and eaten by a world hungering for true peace.

The Cardinal gave an honest appraisal of the Korean Church and suggested how the Congress could help:

> The main needs we are facing at the moment are the following: most of our Catholics are converts and many of them 'recent converts', in fact, nearly one half of our faithful are adult converts who have embraced the faith within the past seven years. Thus, they have not yet internalised our Christian memories. This leaves them vulnerable to the biased images and criteria of modern technological or old non-Christian values and images. The Eucharist will have to be the place of building and educating Christian memory for faith-life and for Christian responsibility in society. The Eucharist has to deepen the conversion of their recent initiation journey into Christ. The very experience of celebrating the Eucharist has to

provide a first taste of, as well as a guiding direction for, the work and mission of Unity and Peace.

Cardinal Kim went on to outline how these points would be tackled. He was followed by Bishop Peter Kang, auxiliary Bishop of Seoul. He too described the phenomenal growth of the Church but also the problems this had brought since 'this exterior growth was not accompanied by a corresponding interiorisation of the faith or the values of the Gospel'. Rapid industrialisation in Korea, with people working unbelievably long hours, with frequent changes of jobs and residence, presented

> formidable obstacles both to initial catechesis as well as to the on-going education of the newly converted. Given the above factors, it comes as almost a natural conclusion that many of our Catholics have only the most minimal understanding of the Eucharist and the basic spirit of the liturgical renewal of Vatican II.

He detailed how preparation for the Congress would concentrate on three major areas:

1. Education and Catechesis;
2. Renewal of the Liturgy;
3. Relationship with Life.

From the parish reception we were off to the Olympic Stadium for the reception of the Papal Legate and the opening Mass of the Congress. The design of the elegant stadium, opened in 1984, imitated the curves of a Korean vase. It had hosted the summer Olympics in 1988 and could hold 100,000 people.

When we collected our passes at the Cathedral, we were given badges on which were our names, seat numbers and the names and seat numbers of a Korean couple who would be seated near us at the opening Mass of the Congress. That evening, at the end of Mass, visiting pilgrims would be taken by Korean hosts to their homes for an evening *agape*. I regret losing the details of the family who invited Fr Joseph Carroll and me to join them. They were perfect hosts and our meal was framed within a Christian Passover setting. The youngest child, a teenage girl, asked, 'Father, why are we having a party tonight?' Seriously, her father replied, 'Because Jesus gave His life for us. The bread we eat tonight tells us that He made Himself our food.'

Threats to Peace

The friendly conversation and laughter of our meal served to hide the giant threatening shadow hanging over South Korea and the city of Seoul in particular. Only thirty-five miles to the north is the most heavily militarised border in the world. The zone dividing Korea into two is 160 miles long and 2.5 miles wide and has been there since 1953. Later in the week a few of us went on a brief tour to view part of the zone. It was a chilling experience.

The Congress theme, 'Christ our Peace', whilst having a relevance for the world, had therefore particular significance in Seoul. The basic text for the Congress had quoted Pope John Paul's address to the diplomatic corps during his first visit to South Korea in 1984: 'The anguish and pain of a divided Korea are symbolic of a divided world that lacks trust and faith to achieve reconciliation in brotherly love.' The text went on to say how 'Christ came not only to give us peace but to become, He Himself, our peace' (Ep 2:14). How?

> It was through His sacrifice on the Cross. He became our peace by the Blood of the Cross that reconciled the whole world to God and all men with one another, binding us together in the Spirit into one body. He became our peace by giving all of Himself, His life, His suffering, and His death, out of boundless love for us, thus overcoming the world, sin, and death. That is why the Risen Lord's first greeting to his disciples was, 'Peace be with you! Peace I leave you. My own peace I give you. I do not give it to you as the world gives'. He alone can give us true peace in our hearts and in our relationships with one another. Where now can we find this peace we long for? In the Eucharist.

The Eucharist renders Christ's sacrifice ever present in the world. There He continues to give His Body and Blood *'for you and for all'* as bread 'for the life of the world'. Christ's sacrifice as sacrament, the Eucharist, is the very fountain of true peace. Here He is, the Saviour; here present, Christ 'is Himself our peace'.

In their joint pastoral letter of October 1988, the Korean Bishops had said how 'this country is divided in two, each half aiming weapons at the other'. They drew an unflattering picture of their country:

> The North continues closed and oppressive, while the South, proud of its prosperity, is witnessing the rise of a radical selfishness in which people put self before the needs of others ... Nevertheless, we shall find in the life and teachings of Jesus Christ a way enabling us to set aside this anxiety and to create genuine peace. We feel that these difficulties can easily be overcome because our Korean family system teaches us to love others as ourselves, our people are uniquely rich in human kindness, and they are endowed with profound religious sentiments.

The Bishops also drew attention to what they called 'the dark side' of their Church's rapid and amazing development.

> Today we can see that the proportion of Catholics is increasing among the upper income levels while it is starkly declining among the urban poor and farmer/fishers. This means that the Good News is not being properly proclaimed to the poor, that they are not at home in the Church, that the Church is gradually ceasing to exist among them. No matter how much the Church grows outwardly, unless all practise friendliness and sharing with a deep sense of inner unity transcending all class distinctions, unless the Church becomes a truly poor Church, a serving Church, unless it is standing at their side, we shall not be able to achieve true community, we shall not attain true peace ... Today it is we who are sitting at the Lord's table. It is we who are called to participate in His Cross and

Resurrection, becoming one by receiving the Body and Blood of the Lord. Then we too have to achieve unity by sharing everything we have, laying down our lives for each other, as the faithful of the early Church did. For only by such unity can genuine peace be born.

October 4, the day before the Congress opened, had been designated a 'Peace Day', partly because of the Congress theme and partly because it was the feast day of St Francis of Assisi, long considered the patron saint of peace. Cardinal Stephen Kim gave a keynote address that day. Speaking simply, and with simple words, he drew sorrowful attention to the armaments race and the money spent on armaments, 'more than five hundred billions of dollars a year'. The world, he said, was 'in danger of exploding into nuclear conflict'. He quoted John F Kennedy's famous sentence: 'If humanity does not put a full-stop to war, war will put a full-stop to humanity.'

A peace based on a so-called balance of power provided by weapons could not be called true peace. True peace had to guarantee respect for the dignity and freedom of every person, and that could only be achieved if people were ready to share. Jesus gave us His example. 'If we really know how to live this love of Christ, if we know how to treat each person like Christ as our brother, and if we can share everything we have, we shall really be able to make peace, true peace.'

The retired Archbishop Helder Camara from Brazil followed the Cardinal. He asked 'Which are the ways leading to true peace?' Was it by preparing war? No! Was it by developing countries? That could help, but it wasn't enough on its own. The real way was to live the peace of Christ. 'He teaches us that all humanity has the same Creator and Father. We are one family, one world, in spite of the different races, languages, and countries.'

The Korean Congress was shorter than most, lasting only four days. It opened on Thursday 5 October, observed as a Day of Thanksgiving. Cardinal Kim welcomed the Papal Legate, Cardinal Roger Etchegaray, the former Archbishop of Marseilles who came from Rome where he served as president of the Pontifical Council for Justice and Peace. Cardinal Kim graciously acknowledged the debt owed to France by the Korean Church: 'From the times of the early persecutions until the present day there is no Church with which we have had such deep links in Christ as with the Church in France, that has sent us so many missionaries.'

In his homily at the opening Mass, Cardinal Etchegaray began by lamenting the divisions between the followers of Christ:

> How can we hunger for peace among peoples if we don't hunger for reconciliation between us Christians? And how can we be reconciled if we don't hunger for the Eucharist? ... The Eucharist is the surest test of our wanting peace. In the Eucharist, the Lord invites us to make with Him the great Paschal journey that leads from hate to love, from death to life. In the Eucharist, the Lord calls on us not to separate any more what He joined together on the night of Holy Thursday: the washing of feet and the sacred meal. When he said 'Do this in memory of me', Christ was thinking of those two gestures as inseparable facets of the same sacrament of brotherhood. In the Eucharist, His Word, which is always creative, makes us servants of one another, just as He was the first in washing the feet of His disciples and giving Himself as food.
>
> The Eucharist is the extraordinary place where Christians of all races, all cultures, all opinions, not only await the glorious return of Christ with new heavens and a new earth, but also proclaim before the world, as if in a festive moment when one forgets the divisions, that already peace can be enjoyed through God's forgiveness and brotherly reconciliation ... Peace is in the hands of all of us, not just in those of specialists in politics or the economy. Every day, by our way of living with others, we make a choice for or against peace ... Yes, peace is within our grasp. Yes, peace is possible. It is enough to believe it. It is enough to grasp it like a cross, with the hands of Christ!

After Mass, the Blessed Sacrament was carried through the streets of Seoul and out into the country, not in a procession but in buses and other forms of transport. Priests who had concelebrated took the consecrated Hosts back with them to their parishes, to give Communion to the waiting crowds who had not been able to attend the opening ceremony.

Friday 6 October was classed as a Day of Conversion. Archbishop Camara called us to that conversion. Listing some of the bad signs in the world going against the brotherhood desired by Christ, he mentioned the unfair distribution of food and resources and the arms race. He then remembered some of the ways Christ helps us to build up brotherhood: the Sign of the Cross, the prayer 'Our Father'. 'But a kind of help very much bigger is the Holy Mass.' He called on all present at the Congress 'to help in the suppression of misery around the world'. Distinguishing between poverty—where a human being has only the necessary, the indispensable to live with his family—and misery—where not even the indispensable is possessed—he said:

> Misery is an insult to the Creator. Misery is the reduction of human beings to the condition of animals. My good friends, my good brothers and sisters in Christ, let us put an end to the problem of utter poverty in the world! No more misery! Let all of us sign in our hearts the promise to engage ourselves in the abolition of misery in the world. Let us share what we are and have so that misery can disappear from earth.

Dr Anton Schlembach, Bishop of Speyer in West Germany, then gave a very long conference on 'Church in a Divided Land'. He described how Germany had finished up at the end of the Second World War as two hostile blocks. Then,

> The Catholic Church in the Federal Republic continues actively to support a peaceful order in Europe. It is convinced that the division of Germany and the splitting of the world must first be overcome by the unification of Europe. Although the peoples of Europe had the Christian faith as

a common foundation, they waged war against each other for centuries in excessive nationalism. This is for us a heavy burden, there must be no more war in Europe. All European nations must reconcile with each other and coalesce into a new economic, political and spiritual unity, without loss by individual peoples of their own culture and traditions. Above all, Christian politicians are seeking new forms for Europeans to live together. Their objective is more open frontiers, shorn of divisive character.

The Bishop spoke of the need to develop friendly relations with the peoples of Eastern Europe, with particular reference to Russia and the Communist bloc. He recalled the public reconciliation between Germany and Poland which began at the end of the Second Vatican Council in November 1965, 'when the Polish and German bishops shook hands and assured each other: "We grant forgiveness and we ask forgiveness." The ice was broken.' He described the help in terms of food, clothing and medicines the diocese of Speyer had sent to Poland in the last eight years and other help and contacts between the two countries. Abstaining from the use of all military force was the fundamental principle for the maintenance of peace. He also remembered how

> The seven million and more displaced persons, who came from Eastern European countries to the Federal Republic and of whom most were Catholics, stated in 1950 in a charter that they voluntarily and publicly renounced force, hatred and revenge, reprisals and retaliation for injustice. They acknowledged a united Europe and undertook a commitment to forgiveness and reconciliation, thus setting a signal for peace at a very early age.

Disarmament and development aid, the creation of the organisation Misereor and a scheme to support the Church in Latin America, all featured in the Bishop's talk, as did the need for an ecological plan. 'Care for the environment and posterity commands rational and economical energy consumption and a responsible approach to energy supply and policies.' He spoke of the social and community work carried out through the Church and its efforts to promote just social legislation. Finally,

> When the Church proclaims its message of God, Jesus Christ and His deliverance, it performs a basic service to peace. Where there is belief in Jesus Christ, where He is heard, loved, worshipped, adored, there peace is born, there peace grows, there people receive the strongest impulse to create peace and live in peace: in peace with God, with themselves, with their fellow-men, with the whole of creation: there they receive the best inspirations and impulses to develop a global culture of brotherliness and love.

St Mother Teresa of Calcutta followed the bishop with a short message continuing the theme of conversion and reconciliation. She called conversion 'love in action between God and the soul'. Looking at the Cross

> we realise how much Jesus has forgiven us, what love for each one of us has done to Him, just to make our hearts so clean as to see Him in each other and especially in the Bread of Life. When we look at Jesus in the Eucharist, the living Bread, we realise how much He loves us now, as to make Himself the living Bread to give us life.

Mother Teresa stressed the need for prayer in the family and quoted Bl Cardinal Newman's prayer, 'Radiating Christ'. She ended by telling us that since beginning an hour of daily adoration in front of the Blessed Sacrament 'we have doubled the number of vocations'.

Earlier that day, along with a group of other Congress pilgrims, I visited the Martyrs' Shrine at Chol Tu San, on a small rocky hill overlooking the Han river. The place was used for executions and thousands of Catholics were martyred here in and about the year 1866. They were beheaded and their bodies thrown into the river below. This was to be the last of the four main periods of persecution, during which it is reckoned 10,000 Catholics, most of them ordinary men and women, old and young, had died. The fact that there were only about 20,000 Catholics in Korea in 1866 helps us to understand the scale of their sacrifice. Twenty-seven of the 103 martyrs canonised in 1984 by Pope St John Paul II were executed here at Chol Tu San.

The Search for Unity

The next day of the Congress, Saturday 7 October, was classed as a Day of Unity. It was the day Pope St John Paul II arrived. His movements were slow and he showed signs of his illness, but in his speech on arrival at Seoul's military airport he immediately addressed the subject of unity and peace. He asked God to 'bless Korea and all its people with His gifts of spiritual well-being and fraternal harmony'. He greeted his Catholic brothers and sisters, saying that he had come to Korea 'to worship Christ our Peace, and to pray that our heavenly Father will bless every human heart, every family and nation, with His peace'. He then extended his 'greetings and sentiments of friendship to my fellow Christians and to the followers of other great religious traditions'. Urging all his hearers to be true to the spiritual traditions of Korea, he said 'It is as a messenger of God's peace that I have returned to Korea ... May God bless all of you and make you true instruments of His peace.'

That same day saw an ecumenical service in Seoul's Anglican Cathedral, with nearly a thousand people taking part. Cardinal Adrianus Simonis, Archbishop of Utrecht, read a sermon prepared by Cardinal Johannes Willebrands, the Dutch President of the Pontifical Council for Christian Unity, in which he said

> The very fact that we are gathered here today in an Ecumenical Prayer Service for Christian Unity is in itself a significant act of common witness for peace and unity not only in Korea but also for the entire world ... As Christians, we cannot close our hearts to the cries and yearnings of our contemporary world in search for peace and justice. Indeed, our work together in this field, as well as in others, can help

us overcome the barriers to full communion by preparing the way to a deeper mutual understanding...

All those who are baptised in the name of the Father, the Son and the Holy Spirit, are sons of God in Jesus Christ. Therefore we are engaged in the mission of proclaiming peace and bringing it about in His name and after His example. Christian engagement and Christian politics are without false illusions. We know that perfect and everlasting peace will be assured only through the universal recognition and acceptance of the Lordship of Christ over the whole creation. In the present era, the Church, being His Body, overcomes the differences of race, of rank, of sex and is called to be the sign and the source of peace among the nations, the steward of God. For this common witness and common engagement, we are called to become always more one flock, because our discords inflict damage on the most holy cause of proclaiming Christ's peace to every creature.

Rosemary Goldie, in a long out-of-print book *The International Eucharistic Congresses for a New Evangelisation*, has succinctly described how the issues of peace and unity became an integral part of such Congresses, so much so that it is now impossible to envisage their omission. Readers of earlier chapters of this book will have noticed how ecumenical and interreligious concerns grew in importance from Munich in 1960, and how they reflected the spirit and letter of the Second Vatican Council. At Bombay in 1964, Cardinal Valerian Gracias, then Archbishop of Bombay, included ecumenical and interreligious relations among the aims of the Congress there. Bogota in 1968 featured meetings with the other Christian communities present in Colombia, as well as with the Jewish community. From Melbourne in 1973 onwards, such meetings have generally been carefully built into the planning of each Congress and provide a guide for National and other Congresses.

From the airport, Pope John Paul made his way to Nonhyon-dong parish, where we delegates awaited him, to take part in an hour's Eucharistic adoration. The Pope spoke particularly to priests, taking as his theme 'pastoral charity' flowing from the Eucharist, which is 'the centre and root of the whole life of the priest' (*Presbyterorum Ordinis* 14).

> If we are to imitate Christ's gift of self, we who are priests must live and act in ways that enable us to be close to all the members of the flock, from the greatest to the least. We will want to dwell in their midst, whether they be rich or poor, learned or in need of education. We will readily share their joys and sorrows, not only in our thoughts and prayers but also in their company, so that through our presence and our ministry they can experience God's love. We will want to embrace a simple lifestyle, in imitation of Christ who became poor for our sake. If a priest is lacking poverty of spirit, it will be difficult for him to understand the problems of the weak and the forgotten. If he is not readily available to all, the poor and needy will find it almost impossible to approach him and to open themselves to him without embarrassment.

Addressing himself directly to the Korean priests present, Pope John Paul said

> Dear brothers, I know that your dedicated and zealous ministry is an important part of the Church's vigorous life in Korea. You are very involved in your parishes, in their many organised apostolates and sodalities, and in numerous catechumenate classes. Given the many demands that are made on you, it is all the more important that you be men of prayer before the Blessed Sacrament, that you 'ask God for a true spirit of adoration' (*Presbyterorum Ordinis* 19) in order to be filled with love of Christ. Only in this way can you hope to grow in the pastoral charity that makes your life and ministry fruitful.

The Pope then went for Mass with young people in the Olympic Gymnastics Hall, a huge indoor sports arena of imaginative design, built for the 1988 summer Olympics and holding 15,000 people. He was received with great enthusiasm by youth representatives of every parish in the land. Pope John Paul saluted them and also 'the young men and women of other Christian communities and of other religious traditions'. His homily was especially concerned with 'unity and peace', based on Jesus' prayer at the Last Supper and also on the example of Joseph, son of the patriarch Jacob, as described in the Book of Genesis. He invited his hearers to accept the words of Jesus at the Last Supper as spoken about them and to them.

> Christ's mission, as revealed in the Gospel and signified in the Eucharist, is always and everywhere a work of unity and peace. Your presence today in this stadium ... must become a sign of your willingness to take up this task! ... Joseph's example of forgiving his brothers can enlighten us. Here we discover an extraordinarily profound and striking dimension of human relationships: the possibility of reconciliation and pardon, the excellence of justice grounded in love and expressed in an encounter of genuine openness and brotherhood. Here we begin to see that true unity and peace are not merely questions of economic and political structures. They are, more basically, the result of human acts of sincere love and effective solidarity among individuals and peoples.

Pope John Paul explained how Christ makes true peace by the Blood of the Cross.

> It is precisely on the Cross that He shows clearly that love is stronger than hatred and violence, forgiveness is more just than retribution. This is not weakness, or mere passivism. Your martyrs, many of them of your own age, were much stronger in their suffering and death than their persecutors in their hatred and violence. Violence destroys; love transforms and builds up. This is the challenge which Christ offers to you, young people of Korea, who wish to be instruments of true progress in the history of your country. Christ calls you, not to tear down and destroy, but to transform, and build up ...

[Then, speaking to twelve young men and women who were baptised that day] As Catholic young people, you must know that the rebirth to which you aspire cannot come from hatred and violence. It must come from the transforming power of the love which Jesus pours into your hearts through the Holy Spirit who has been given to you in Baptism and which is constantly nourished in the Eucharist. The Eucharist is both grace and mission, both gift of life and call to discipleship ... The Successor of Peter begs you, in the name of Christ, 'to remain stable and steadfast in the faith, not shifting from the hope of the Gospel you have heard' (Col 1:23). My dear young people, be courageous witnesses before all the world of Jesus' reconciliation and unity, be the joyful and brave instruments of His peace!

Crossing the Cathedral square in Seoul that day, I had occasion to marvel at the growth of the Church in Korea and the fecundity of its vocations. A long crocodile of Korean young ladies in the habit of Blue Nuns was crossing in front of me. The Little Company of Mary, popularly known as the 'Blue Nuns' because of their pale blue veil, were founded in 1877 in Nottingham by Mary Potter, now the Venerable Mary Potter since her Cause for Canonisation was introduced. The Little Company of Mary combine contemplation with active service of the sick. Their work initially spread to Australia, the USA and to Rome, where in 1908 Mother Mary Potter started the first Catholic training school for nurses in Italy. It was there in 1958 that I recovered from a serious operation incurred whilst a student in Rome, and promised to join them in prayer for their vocations. As the British Isles dried up as a source of vocations, other countries like Korea took their place. Prayers can be answered in a myriad of ways. As well as in the British Isles, the Little Company of Mary can be found ministering to the sick today in South Korea, Tonga, Australia, New Zealand, Zimbabwe, South Africa, Italy and Albania.

The Holy Father's Prayer

All too quickly the Seoul Congress came to an end. On Sunday morning, 8 October, Pope John Paul celebrated Mass in the Youido Plaza in front of a crowd estimated at one million. Under a bright sun and brilliantly blue sky, the neatly ordered blocks of people filled the enormous expanse with an explosion of colours. Concelebrating with him were 23 cardinals, 218 bishops and more than 2,000 priests. Recalling the institution of the Eucharist at the Last Supper, when Christ gave us the 'Bread of Life', the Pope spoke of the Church's determination to share this Bread of Life 'with all those who thirst for the truth, for justice, for peace and for life itself'.

> The words 'Christ, our Peace' have been chosen as the theme of this Congress. We have heard what the Apostle proclaims: 'in Christ Jesus, you who once were far off have been brought near in the Blood of Christ. For He is our peace who has made us both one and has broken down the dividing wall of hostility' (Ep 2: 13–14). The Apostle is perhaps thinking of the wall in the Temple of Jerusalem which divided Jew from Gentile. But how many walls and barriers divide the great human family today? How many forms of conflict? How many signs of mistrust and hostility are visible in countries all over the world?
>
> East is divided from West; North from South. These divisions are the heritage of history and of the ideological conflicts which so often divide peoples who otherwise would wish to live in peace and brotherhood with one another. Korea too is marked by a tragic division that penetrates ever more deeply into the life and character of its people. The Korean nation is symbolic of a world divided and not yet able to become one in peace and justice. Yet there is a way forward. True peace— the shalom which the world urgently needs—springs eternally from the infinitely rich mystery of God's love, the *'mysterium pietatis'* (cf 1Tm 3:16), about which Saint

Paul writes: 'God was in Christ, reconciling the world to Himself' (2 Co 5:19).

The Holy Father then spoke of the beginnings and the development of the Church in Korea, truly remarkable in that it began through study and not directly through missionaries. Books on science and technology had been translated into classical Chinese by missionaries working in China. These books attracted the attention of young intellectuals in Korea, who began also to read translated Christian texts and who felt they had found the truth. By the late 1790s there were a few thousand Catholic believers in Korea, most of whom had never seen a Catholic priest, let alone been baptised.

> Your admirable ancestors in the Faith knew that 'in Christ' all are equal in dignity, and all are equally deserving of loving attention and solicitude. Just like the early Christians described in the Acts of the Apostles (cf *Ac* 2: 42ff), they boldly abolished the inviolable class barriers of their time in order to live as brothers and sisters. Noble masters and humble servants sat together at the same table. They shared the riches of their new-found knowledge of Christ by composing catechisms and beautiful prayer poems in the language of the common people. They held their possessions in common so as to aid those most in need. They lovingly looked after the orphans and widows of those imprisoned and martyred. They persevered day and night in common prayer, thanksgiving and fellowship. And they gladly died for each other and in each other's stead. They pardoned and prayed for those who persecuted them. Theirs was indeed a Eucharistic life, *a true breaking of the life-giving bread!*

In this great assembly of the *Statio Orbis*, we proclaim before the world that Christ, the only-begotten Son of the Father, continues to reconcile people 'to God in one body through the Cross, thereby bringing the hostility to an end' (*Ep* 2:16). *Yesu kristo-nun uri'e pyong'hwa-ishimnida.* (Jesus Christ is our peace) (cf *Ep* 2:14).

From the Eucharist springs the Church's mission and capacity to offer her specific contribution to the human family. The Eucharist effectively transmits *Christ's parting gift to the world*: 'Peace I give you, My peace I leave you' (cf *Jn* 14:27). The Eucharist is the sacrament of Christ's 'peace' because it is the memorial of the salvific redemptive sacrifice of the Cross. The Eucharist is the sacrament of victory over the divisions that flow from personal sin and collective selfishness. Therefore the Eucharistic community is called to be *a model and instrument of a reconciled humanity*. In the Christian community there can be no division, no discrimination, no separation among those who break the Bread of Life around the one Altar of Sacrifice.

As the Third Christian Millennium approaches, the urgent challenge facing Christians, in the present circumstances of history, is to carry this fulness of life, this 'peace' into the structure and fabric of everyday living, *in the family, in society, in international relations*. But we must listen carefully to Christ's words: 'I do not give (peace) as the world gives (it)' (cf *Jn* 14:27). Christ's peace is not merely the absence of war, the silencing of weapons. It is nothing less than the communication of 'God's love that has been poured into our hearts through the Holy Spirit which has been given to us' (*Rm* 5:5). Our sharing in the Body and Blood of the risen Lord cannot be separated from our own continuing efforts to share this lifegiving love through service. 'Do this in memory of me' (*Lk* 22:19): do for one another as I did for you and for all. Yes, we must not only celebrate the liturgy but actually *live the Eucharist*. The Eucharist compels us

- *to give thanks for the created world, and respect and share it in a wise and responsible way;*

- *to esteem and love the great gift of life, especially of every human life created, from its beginning,* in God's own image and redeemed by Christ;

- *to cherish and promote the inalienable and equal dignity of every human being* through justice, freedom, and concord;

- *to give of ourselves generously as the bread of life for others*, as exemplified in the '*One Heart One Body Movement*', so that all may truly be united in Christ's love.

Each International Eucharistic Congress, each *Statio Orbis* is *a solemn profession of the Church's faith* in the Good News proclaimed and realized in the Eucharist: 'Lord, through your Death and Resurrection you have set us free. You are the Saviour of the world.'

At the end of the Statio Orbis the Pope gave his Angelus message, in which he made plain his concern for North Korea and China:

At this midday hour, we turn to Mary, whom Christ gave to us as our Mother (cf *Jn* 19:27). Forever 'she stands out among the poor and humble of the Lord' (*Lumen Gentium* 55), interceding on behalf of the hungry, the weak and the defenceless. She is the hope and comfort of the children of Eve. She is 'the gracious Advocate'. In confidence we ask her to pray for us, that we may be made worthy of the promises of her divine Son.

Today in Seoul, we offer a fervent prayer that the peace of Christ will descend upon all nations and peoples. Allow me to mention in particular two peoples who are very close to my heart. Confident of Mary's tender concern for all her children, we cannot fail to recommend to her, with deep affection, hope and sorrow, the *people of North Korea and especially its Catholic community.*

We pray for those parents and children, brothers and sisters, friends and relatives who are separated, but wait with undiminished hope to be reunited as one family. May Jesus, through the intercession of his Blessed Mother, the Queen of Peace, hasten the day when all Koreans will be reconciled in mutual trust and respect, and reunited in the joy of brotherly love.

In this filial conversation with Mary our Mother, I also make mention of our *brothers and sisters in Christ living in Mainland China*. Their geographical proximity, as well as bonds of faith and culture, bring them very near to many of those assembled here. Deep within my own heart, there is always present an ardent desire to meet these brothers and sisters in order to express my cordial affection and concern for them, and to assure them of how highly they are esteemed by the other local Churches. I am deeply moved when I think of the heroic signs of fidelity to Christ and His Church which many of them have shown in these past years. Through the intercession of Mary, Help of Christians, may Christ be their consolation in every trial and in all of life's daily challenges.

May the Lord also inspire within them a firm commitment to the delicate task of fostering reconciliation within the ecclesial community, in communion of faith with the Successor of Peter, who is the visible principle and foundation of that unity. May He encourage and sustain Christian believers there, as they seek to dedicate themselves to the pursuit of the common good and the generous service of their fellow citizens, working for the progress of their noble nation.

We ask Mary to draw all mankind to the Cross of Christ, our only hope of salvation. Through her prayers, may all hearts be opened to the peace of Christ—that peace which surpasses all human understanding (cf *Ph* 4:7). And may we who have received so many of God's gifts through her intercession imitate her example and offer ourselves in union with her Son for the salvation and peace of the entire world.

Later that same day Pope John Paul met with the Korean Bishops and then with some five hundred delegates who had come to the Congress representing seventy nations. On Monday morning, 9 October, Pope John Paul left Seoul to continue his pastoral journey to the Far East in Jakarta. At the airport he thanked the Korean Prime Minister and all who had helped to organise his visit. Addressing the 'Beloved People of Korea' he also said:

> Within these next few days, all of us will be returning to our homes and our daily activities. But the great events, the moments of profound prayer, the precious spiritual consolations of the Eucharistic Congress will not be forgotten; for they have touched our hearts with *a powerful spiritual energy, an energy which comes from God himself.* The spiritual richness of these days in Seoul will have a quiet but powerful effect on the way we live our lives.
>
> Life will go on throughout Korea as well. And yet, it is my fervent hope, dear brothers and sisters, that beneath the surface of Korea's everyday life, its struggles and its achievements, a deeper, more mysterious *process of growth, nourished by a great spiritual energy,* will be taking place. It is my prayer that the seeds of spiritual renewal will be at work in the hearts of all Koreans. You, the people of Korea, are now being called to face the future with *a firm resolve to work together to heal wounds that have remained open too long, and to ensure a better, more humane and free life for your children.* As you respond to this historic challenge, may wisdom, prudence and charity infuse your thinking, your political activity and your vision of Korea's true destiny as a nation.
>
> Wisdom, prudence and charity are the fruit of a mature conscience and a life of virtue. Where these *spiritual gifts,* and the discipline of mind and heart which underlie them, are lacking, it is easy for great hopes to be frustrated and for generous spirits to become impatient at the slow pace of change. I urge all of you, especially the young, the students, parents and educators, and all those who are responsible for the political and moral life of the nation, to combine zeal for your country's renewal and progress with *the wisdom that comes from a pure heart.* With sensitivity for the complexity of human and political issues,

and respect for the dignity of every human being, may you
be *artisans of justice and peace within the ranks of your
people.* The Korea of tomorrow will be a better and more
authentically human society as a result.

Cardinal Stephen Kim, who had been the Holy Father's host in
Korea, died in 2009. He was revered as a 'father of the nation'.
Hundreds of thousands of people, Catholic and non-Catholic
alike, came to Myeongdong Cathedral to pay their respects.
During the 1989 Eucharistic Congress in Seoul he had encour-
aged Catholics to consider organ donations as a way to fulfil
Christ's love, something extraordinary in a Confucian culture. In
his will he left his eyes for transplant.

The present Archbishop of Seoul is Andrew Yeom Soo-jung,
whom Pope Francis named as a cardinal in 2014. He is also
Apostolic Administrator of Pyongyang, the North Korean capital.
The Pyongyang diocese has been vacant since the death of its last
bishop, Francis Hong Yong-ho, who was imprisoned by the North
Korean government in 1949, and who later disappeared. Cardinal
Yeom comes from a family that for five generations have lived
the Catholic faith. His great-great grandparents, Peter Yeom
Seok-tae and Kim Maria, were executed for their faith in 1850.
The Church in South Korea continues to grow. Although Sunday
Mass attendance was only 21% of all Catholics, by the end of 2014
numbers of Catholics had grown to 10.6% of the population.

The return home was more leisurely than the journey out to
Seoul, taking in days in Melbourne, North Island New Zealand,
Hawaii, with St Damien de Veuster's leper colony in Molokai,
San Francisco and New York, all the while buoyed up by memo-
ries of an enthralling Congress.

References

1) *Adoremus,* Priests' Eucharistic League (Falcon Press, Stockton, 1988 No.2; 1989 Nos.1&2; 1990 No.1).

2) *Christ Our Peace: Acts of the 44th International Eucharistic Congress,* Congress Secretariat (Ed) (Catholic Publishing House, Seoul,1990).

3) Allen, J., Personal notes and diaries.

4) Gaudoin-Parker, M., *Adore What You Receive* (Falcon Press, Stockton,1989).

5) Kelly, J., *The Splendid Cause 1933–1983, 50 years of Columban Outreach to the Korean People* (Seoul 1983).

6) Lankov, A., *Why is Catholicism important in South Korea?* (Al Jazeera 18 August 2014).

7 SEVILLE 7–13 JUNE 1993
CHRIST, LIGHT OF NATIONS—THE
EUCHARIST AND EVANGELISATION

EVERY ENGLISH SCHOOLCHILD knows—or used to know—the date 1066. Every American schoolchild knows—or should know—the date 1492, the year Christopher Columbus discovered the New World, having sailed from Palos de la Frontera in southern Spain. The evangelisation of the Americas was begun. Seville became the economic and trade centre for the New World.

500 years after the Cross was planted in lands that had never heard of Christ, the International Eucharistic Congress began in Seville with the theme 'Christ, Light of Nations—the Eucharist and Evangelisation'. Delegates assembled in Seville from all nations. They came from the Americas, North and South; from Asia and the Far East; from India; from Africa as well as from Europe. We saw a rich diversity of cultures, united within the one Eucharist.

What better place than Seville, the capital and largest city of Andalusia? The Cathedral, with the reputed tomb of Columbus and where many of the Congress events took place, is the fourth largest church in the world and the largest cathedral. The Alcázar palace complex—'a cultural sandwich, with Roman foundations, an Arab filling and a Christian topping'—holds many treasures, including the Fernandez painting La Virgen de los Mareantes, the oldest representation of the Virgin Mary as protector of sailors. Across the river, in the former Carthusian monastery, La Cartuja, Columbus resided and studied with the monks before his voyages.

To Bishop Thomas Holland, re-visiting Spain was like coming home. He had studied at the English College, Valladolid, from 1927 until 1933 and returned there as a professor for a further six years, including during the civil war. During the month of the Congress, he would celebrate his 85th birthday and the diamond jubilee of his priestly ordination. I travelled with him from Manchester to the College in Valladolid, where the rector, Mgr Paul Smith, with Fr Francis Parkinson and staff and students gave him a royal welcome. From Valladolid we went on to Seville. Fr John Gallaraga, an Opus Dei priest, met us and conducted us to the Hotel Inglaterra which would be our lodgings during the Congress.

Pope St John Paul II in 1990 had invited the Church to renew her missionary commitment (Encyclical *Redemptoris Missio*). Announcing a decade of evangelisation to prepare for the coming Millennium of the year 2000, the Pope's cry was 'Open the doors to Christ!' He identified three stages of evangelisation: first, the mission of the Church to peoples who did not know of Christ; second, the pastoral care of fervent Christian communities; third,

> particularly in countries with ancient Christian roots, and occasionally in the younger Churches as well, where entire groups of the baptized have lost a living sense of the faith, or even no longer consider themselves members of the Church, and live a life far removed from Christ and his Gospel. In this case what is needed is a 'new evangelisation' or a 're-evangelisation'.

Many parts of Europe fitted that third description. The Seville Congress would address the 'New Evangelisation' within the setting of the Eucharist. In doing so, the Congress would continue the work of the Second Vatican Council whose greatest achievement had been the Constitution on the Church, *Lumen gentium*, 'Light of the Nations'.

At a meeting to prepare for the Congress, Cardinal Paul Poupard had asked the stark question, 'How do we proclaim the Gospel of salvation and present the Church's faith in the Eucharist to people imbued with a culture based on the positive sciences and technology—a culture contrary to that of the Scriptures and two thousand years of Christian tradition?' He was echoing Pope Bl Paul VI's striking sentence in the Apostolic Exhortation *Evangelii Nuntiandi*: 'The gulf between the Gospel and culture is undoubtedly the drama of our age.' Congress speakers squared up to the issues.

Cardinal Poupard had attempted to answer his question by emphasising the presence of Christ in the Eucharist:

> Adoration of Christ present in the Eucharist is the source of life and truth for each believer and for the whole Church. The often depressing environment in which we live—with its spectacle of human dignity being subjected to degradation nearly everywhere—this pitiful situation is radically transformed in encountering the Eucharistic Christ. In the sacrament of His love, Christ regenerates in us enthusiasm and joy to impel us to go back to the world and announce the Good News: 'We have met the Lord!' Both the Church and the world stand in great need of a Eucharistic culture.

The Congress did not officially begin until the Monday evening. Before that, we went in the morning to the Municipal Sports Centre, built just five years previously and comfortably holding over 10,000 people. There, Cardinal Joachim Meisner, Archbishop of Cologne, tackled the issue head-on with a talk entitled 'Eucharist and Evangelisation'. His argument progressed from Substance, to Transubstantiation, to Communion.

What is evangelisation? Cardinal Meisner quoted the Second Vatican Council's description of evangelisation as 'the proclamation of Christ by word and the testimony of life' (*Lumen gentium* 35). Again, 'the Eucharist appears as the source and the summit of all preaching of the Gospel' (*Presbyterorum ordinis* 5). He then emphasised the essential connection between Eucharist and evangelisation.

The Eucharist 'begins with God's incarnation. The Father surrenders his Son to the people, just as the Son will surrender himself through the Eucharist into the hands of the Church and by the same gesture delivers himself to the Passion.' Whereas we place the emphasis on our *having*, the Eucharist is about *giving*: 'This is my Body, to be given for you. This is my Blood, poured out for you.' Jesus dies on the cross to show that Jesus' way of life is not to preserve but to sacrifice himself.

We see this in the life of the Blessed Trinity:

> Being love, God turns wholly 'away from Himself' and 'towards others' ... the Father never speaks of Himself but refers only to His Son ... The Son in turn always draws attention away from Himself toward His Father ... the Holy Spirit never focusses attention on Himself, always on the Father and the Son ... In the Most Holy Trinity, this turning away from oneself and being inclined toward others—this love—is total inspiration, total joy, total verticalness ... Man, marked by sin, is turned totally away from others toward himself ... He is totally earthbound in his horizontalness. But where the divine verticalness meets the human horizontalness, there is formed the Cross.

The Eucharist comes from Our Lord's sacrifice: 'The Eucharist is the fruit of the Cross. We are celebrating not only a meal but first and foremost a sacrifice. The Cross became the Tree of Life and the Eucharist the Fruit of the new Paradise.'

It is by changing the substance of our *having* into *giving* that we will achieve: 'Love in the worldly dimension always implies: forgoing self-love and giving preference to others, withdrawing oneself in order to give others more space.' The Eucharist is where this self-giving love comes from:

> Those who communicate, who become 'one flesh', become part of that inner-trinitary movement 'away from oneself toward others'. He becomes part of this mission, which in the reality of this world mission, means evangelisation ... Thus the Second Vatican Council teaches that 'charity, which is, as it were, the soul of the whole apostolate, is given to them and nourished in them by the sacraments, the Eucharist above all' (*Apostolatus laicorum* 3).

When we have celebrated the Eucharist and received Holy Communion, people should see that charity in us, helping us to follow the lifestyle of Christ:

All of us only sincerely worship the Body of Christ that was broken for many, only receive Him worthily, if we do not merely think of our own interests, but of those of others who are waiting for the preaching of the Gospel. We, central Europeans, who have adequate medical care, can only receive the Body of the Lord for our salvation if it opens us up to the needs of others, so that we allow our wealth and our skills to be effectively used to help the poor and suffering of this world ... He served us in order to make servants of us.

Such a sharing in the Eucharist, in the death of Christ, means that we share His resurrection: 'He who eats this bread comes alive. The obligation to love, which we assume when we worship and receive the body of Christ, is not a burden but a "redemption". It allows us to live a worthy human life.'

Ordinary bread is transformed in the Eucharist and we become transformed with it:

The substance undergoes transubstantiation and gives our life a dynamism that enables us to preach the Gospel to the world. The bread becomes the Body of the Lord so as to build up as the Body of Christ in the world those of us who eat it. Thus the success of the Eucharist depends on whether it makes us more alive, in other words, whether we grow in our missionary role. We have bread which enables us to give thanks and to love. It can have the effect that we can say from our own experience, like the first Christians, that 'we have passed from death to life, we know because we love the brothers' (1 Jn 3:14).

What then will communion involve? It will mean Christ sharing His life with us so that we can help others to share the faith. Calling on his experience in Cologne, where the Cardinal was asked what catechesis should be given to families coming from the formerly communist eastern part of Germany and who were seeking admission to the Catholic Church, he discounted giving any catechesis for a year. Catholic families were to share their lives with them—and thereby their faith—by spending Sundays and feast days and some of their holidays with them, to show them what faith is like when it is lived:

> Faith has never been passed on through publicity and propaganda, always through 'infection', as it were ... Anyone who comes into contact with the Eucharistic Christ, who is in communion with Him, becomes 'Christoactive', and all who come into contact with Him are themselves filled with Christoactivity. The people crowded round Christ to be able at least to touch the hem of His garment because there emanated from Him a power which healed all. The people of Jerusalem brought the sick into the streets, because even the shadow of the apostles passing by made them well again. Evangelisation means providing the world with such dispensers of life, in other words making Christ touchable for the people.

Cardinal Meisner summed up his talk:

> Thus evangelisation is not propaganda or advertising, but the consequence of creation and the Eucharist. All substance is present for transubstantiation and transubstantiation for communion. Transubstantiation takes place through the Mystery of the Cross, in that it frees us from ourselves, allowing us to serve our brothers and sisters. Anyone who, in the process of evangelisation, excludes the Cross, will never achieve his aim. We are prevented from excluding it by the Eucharist, where, through the transubstantiation of the substance, bread has become the Body of Christ sacrificed for us, to which there is no alternative and for which the people are waiting—often unknowingly.

That evening, a delightful 'Dance of the Seises' welcomed the arrival of the Pontifical Legate, Cardinal Nicolás de Jesus López Rodríguez from the Dominican Republic, as he came to open the Congress and celebrate Mass. Sacred dances have a long provenance. The second book of Samuel records how David danced in homage before the Ark of the Covenant. The Dance of the Seises in homage before the Blessed Sacrament is recorded in Seville from the early sixteenth century. At first six in number (hence the name), more recently ten boys, dressed in red and yellow doublets, with a white sash and white knee-breeches and wearing plumed hats, gravely perform a dignified dance in front of the Cathedral altar around the feast of Corpus Christi. Having first knelt before the altar and asking permission from the Cathedral Chapter to begin, they form two lines and begin their dance, accompanied by an orchestra. Country dancers of today would find their rhythmic movements familiar. The citizens of Seville hold the Seises in high esteem.

Presence, Sacrifice, Communion

Before the Legate arrived, Professor Guzman Carriquiry Lecour, Under-Secretary of the Pontifical Committee for the Laity, gave a lecture entitled 'The Eucharist, Source of the True Christian Spirit'. He brought home to us a vivid sense of continuity by reminding us of a previous Bishop of Seville—St Isidore—and his teaching on the Eucharist. Regarded as the last of the Fathers of the Church, Isidore was bishop in Seville for thirty-two years until his death in 636—and here were we, in his own city, drawing nourishment from his teaching thirteen centuries later! Dante in his *Paradiso* (X:130) placed Isidore, along with the Venerable Bede and the Scot Richard of St Victor, among the theologians and doctors of the Church: *Vedi oltre fiammeggiar l'ardente spiro d'Isidoro, di Beda e di Riccardo ... See flaming next the glowing breath of Isidore, of Bede, and of Richard ...*

> How many times [Isidore] had proclaimed and explained this sublime mystery [the Eucharist] from his *cathedra* here in Seville ... Isidore was a leading figure at a particularly crucial stage of transition between the crumbling Roman Empire and a new world which emerged from its ruins, violence and heresies. He was to spearhead the new evangelisation which would foster the endeavour to build something founded on and sustained by Christ, the 'corner stone'.

What Isidore did in his time has to be re-done in ours.

> It is not enough to rely on the residue of a heritage which
> runs the risk of becoming dried up. More than ever it is
> true what a teacher of faith highlights in our time—that
> one must not presuppose faith nor take it for granted, but
> always return to expound the faith: '*Faith must continually
> be re-lived. And since it is an act embracing all aspects of
> our existence, faith must be also re-thought and always
> witnessed afresh*' (a quotation from Hans Urs von Balthasar
> on which Cardinal Joseph Ratzinger comments in *Che cosa
> crede la Chiesa*).

Lecour then took a section of Pope St John Paul II's first Encyclical
Letter, *Redemptor hominis*, dealing with the Eucharist, where he
presented it in terms of Sacrament-Presence, Sacrament-Sacrifice
and Sacrament-Communion. Christianity, Lecour went on,

> is above all a presence—the here and now of the Lord, who
> sustains us in the here and now of the act of believing and
> in the concrete reality of the life of faith. [Christianity] is
> neither a theory, nor morality, nor ritual, but an event and,
> because of it, a real meeting with a Presence, that of God
> who has entered history and in the Eucharist is 'the
> incarnate Jesus' flesh and blood' ... If we have met Jesus
> Christ and become His disciples, we are called to desire
> always that His Presence may be the vibrant and determin-
> ing influence throughout our existence, giving it such a
> particularly evident radiant stamp that, despite our
> wretchedness, anyone meeting or living with us will ask:
> Who are these people? How are they so fully human and
> yet so different?

The Eucharist is truly a sacrifice, rooted in Christ's death. 'The
Eucharist is the memorial of this perfect and definitive Sacrifice
of the Word made flesh—that sacrifice which it calls to mind,
re-presents, makes real for people of every place and time.' Christ
is of course now risen and in glory: death has been overcome. But

without sacrifice there is no freedom, no liberation. There is nothing to fear about sacrifice—physical, moral, spiritual—because rather than being an obstacle to life, it is the condition of life. Because of sacrifice, tenderness and happiness are rendered enduring, hope is enlivened, and every act of love becomes eternal. This is what matters. God is the ultimate purpose in living! Without sacrifice, there is and can be no genuine relationship of any kind—with one's spouse, children, friends, or one's work. It is highly significant that during the Last Supper Jesus gave us the 'new commandment' as the distinctive sign of his discipleship: to love as he has loved us.

The sacrifices we make for others we unite with Christ's sacrifice in the Eucharist. Christ's presence and sacrifice leads to communion.

Credit is due to Henri de Lubac especially for drawing our attention to how the expression 'Mystical Body' originally referred to the Eucharist and that, for the Apostle Paul as well as the Fathers of the Church, the notion of the Church as the Body of Christ was inseparably bound up with that of the Eucharist. From this there follows a eucharistic understanding of the mystery of the Church or eucharistic ecclesiology, often called an ecclesiology of *communio*. This ecclesiology of communion is the heart of the Second Vatican Council's doctrine regarding the Church—a doctrine which is based both on the Church's reflection about itself and on its rediscovery of its roots. There is a complete mutual penetration of the Church and the Eucharist as the mystery of communion becomes realised, deriving and flowing from the sacrifice of the New Covenant. Thus, it becomes clear that just as the Church makes the Eucharist, the Eucharist makes the Church. By receiving Christ Himself in eucharistic communion we remain intimately bound to the unity of His Body which is the Church.

We are a 'community of sinners reconciled by the grace of God, which recognises itself in faith as the Body of Christ, bears witness and proclaims the salvation of all people.' It is, however, a temptation to distort this image of the Church, in an attempt to make ourselves more acceptable to others—or even to ourselves—

> when we remain obsessed with planning and making projects, organising structures and tasks, in such a way that inordinate confidence is placed in our human resources and everything is viewed in a perspective of efficiency ... The Church is not 'ours', it is God's! ... People do not become united as Christian community because of new undertakings, nor because of painstaking search for better means of organisation, nor because of power-sharing or distribution of responsibilities. What truly gathers and draws them into one is a living reality, a newness of shared life such as is found in the Eucharist, its 'source' and 'summit'. The Eucharist is the basis of the Church's spiritual, communal and missionary vitality. It is the central sacrament of evangelisation for which the world stands in urgent need.

Cardinal Carlo Martini of Milan opened the second day of the Congress with a long and thoughtful address on 'Eucharistic Celebration, the Summit of Evangelisation'. He stressed the *celebration* aspect of the Eucharist, taking us through the various stages of the Mass: the introductory rites; the Liturgy of the Word; the Eucharistic Liturgy; the concluding rites.

> Mass begins with an *ecclesial assembly*, whose ultimate significance is that of a divine assembly. This meaning, however, is not always clear to the minds and hearts of the laity and even, let me say quite frankly, to their pastors ... It cannot be ever impressed enough upon all the faithful how important it is for them to participate in the whole of the liturgical celebration right from the beginning. There is a vast difference, whether in the communal experience or that of each person, to begin Mass as an assembly already united and prepared, or for the most part being gathered in dribs and drabs.

In the introductory rites, we acknowledge God's mercy towards our sinful condition and praise and petition God's glory. Then we come to the table of the Word. This is itself evangelising.

> To listen to the Word which is proclaimed in the liturgical assembly offers today—for both the ecclesial community and individuals—the vivid experience of divine revelation, introducing us today to the same school of Jesus, the unique and authentic Teacher, who once taught the people of Israel, the apostolic community and the disciples ... The Second Vatican Council underlined the importance of Christ's real and living presence 'already in His Word, through which He speaks when the Church reads the Sacred Scripture'.

The Liturgy of the Word also 'teaches in a living way how to view the Old and the New Testament as belonging together as a unified whole: prophecy and gospel, psalms and spiritual canticles.' Also, 'the Liturgy of the Word *evangelises the life of the Christian community* and that of each of the faithful ...' Finally, 'the Liturgy of the Word *evangelises the Church's manner of praying* which it constantly leads back to its genuine biblical inspiration and roots. Once again the prayer of general intercession (or prayer of the faithful) has found its rightful and significant place within the course of the Liturgy of the Word.'

The Liturgy of the Word leads into the Liturgy of the Eucharist. The one, in fact, 'has to follow the other: the Word prepares for the Sacrament and the Sacrament realises the full saving power of the Word.' Cardinal Martini recalled how the threefold arrangement of the eucharistic part of the Mass—preparation of the gifts; the eucharistic prayer; communion rite—re-enact liturgically what Christ did at the Last Supper. Such is the unchangeable form of the Mass, the faithful memorial of Christ's actions.

Preparing and presenting the gifts at the altar proclaims the goodness of creation and its supernatural purpose. It helps to evangelise our contemporary Western culture so that it may 'find again a new capacity to offer praise (blessing) when viewing created things and human work; to rediscover a sense of God's providence through-out creation; to create space for gratitude and appreciation ...'

The Cardinal explained how the structure of the Mass is both the memorial celebration of God's deeds (*anamnesis*) and also the calling on the power of God to bring about salvation (*epi-clesis*). It is the responsibility of bishops and priests 'to bring about a deeper awareness of the theological and spiritual significance of the different parts and their over-all unity in the way in which we carry out the words and ritual gestures of the eucharistic or consecratory prayer entrusted to us in a special way.'

The bread and wine are consecrated and become the Body and Blood of Christ by the action of the Holy Spirit so that

> all who eat this bread and drink the chalice may 'be filled with His Holy Spirit, and become one body, one spirit in Christ' ... the real specific fruit of the Mass consists in the building of the Christian community in a communion of life—like that of a marriage—with Jesus Christ ... By being nourished with this bread every baptised person becomes drawn ever more deeply into *the meaning of the life of Him who offers Himself as food;* he learns to think, act and love according to the standards revealed by the Spirit of Christ ... Thus ... the eucharistic liturgy evangelises the Church and the world to receive in Jesus Christ God's last and definitive gift to humanity.

The Mass then ends 'by turning the congregation towards its mission of living out what it has celebrated'.

Cardinal Martini then asked the question, 'What is required to bring out the riches of the eucharistic celebration for evangelisa-tion?' His answer lay in 'liturgical education'. He quoted Pope St John Paul II who wrote: 'What is needed ... and urgently appropri-ate is to undertake again a true *education* in order to discover the riches contained in the liturgy' (*Dominicae cenae* 9). For Martini, this education would cover the *language* of celebration: 'biblical, laudatory, ritual, symbolic, gesture, iconic, etc.' Particularly impor-tant was the care to be taken in preparing children for their first

Holy Communion: 'They should learn on this occasion the ABC of Christianity and, particularly, its liturgical and sacramental language.' Within the celebration, we should bring out the best in 'words, song, gesture, silence, ministries involved, manner of presiding and conducting the liturgy, etc.' Education in the liturgy should also link 'the various forms of popular devotion and personal spirituality of the faithful ever more closely and explicitly with the celebration of the Eucharist.'

As well as the *language* of celebration, education should also cover *participation* in the Eucharist. The Cardinal rejoiced in the progress made in ministries and active participation but struck a note of caution:

> The emphasis on 'doing' or 'carrying out' the ritual cele-bration has (and does) run the risk of depriving our eucharistic liturgies—and hence the life and faith of our people—of their contemplative and prayerful spirit ... We must rediscover in a committed and creative way how to integrate into the various ministries of the word, gesture, song, etc. the ministry of silence—that silence of knowing how to remain in the presence of the Lord ...

Cardinal Martini ended by pointing out the three ways in which the Eucharist supported Christian living: it forms a community; it enables the community to listen to and proclaim the Word; it empowers the community to go out in its service of charity.

I had heard about Cardinal Martini's successful sessions with the youth of his diocese on the first Friday of each month, when he took a full cathedral for *lectio divina.* Coming out from the Conference I asked him about this and with obvious satisfaction he described how eager the young people were to pray and to understand the scriptures. Speaking later that day with a priest from the Milan archdiocese, I was told that, yes, the cathedral was full of young people for the Cardinal's talks 'but only because we parish priests work hard to get them to go!' The Cardinal lived to see *lectio divina* particularly encouraged by the 2008 Synod of Bishops on the Word of God in the Life and Mission of the Church.

Word, Sacrament, Oneness

That same day produced two other gems: the homily during Mass of Cardinal Jaime Sin, Archbishop of Manila, and an evening talk by the Superior General of the Blessed Sacrament Fathers, Fr Anthony McSweeney, on 'The Evangelising Riches of the Eucharist'. The fourteenth of sixteen children, the Cardinal was known as 'Jim'. He amused with his surname. 'Welcome to the house of Sin', he would say to his visitors. Filipino Catholics warmly referred to him as 'The greatest sin of all—Cardinal Sin'. But he was also a fluent and compelling orator. His homily had a long title: 'The Eucharist: summons and stimulus, call and challenge to evangelisation: the Eucharist as a missionary event'. At the end of the concelebrated Mass, he gave a missionary crucifix to priests and lay people going to countries of the Third World.

The Cardinal's homily was wide-ranging. He quoted from St Augustine's sermon on Psalm 95, where Augustine speaks of the human race as broken up through Adam's sin, but 'the Divine mercy gathered up the fragments from every side, forged them in the fire of love, and welded into one what had been broken.' This welding into one is achieved in the Eucharist. Quoting from the Second Vatican Council, he said how 'the Church is ultimately about bringing oneness into humanity; perhaps better, bringing humanity into oneness' (*Lumen gentium* 1). The Council insisted that Word and Sacrament must never be separated.

> Word and Sacrament are constitutive dimensions of evangelisation. The Eucharist is at the core of the proclamation of the Good News, because when the Eucharist is celebrated, that which is proclaimed, better still, He who is proclaimed and whose great deeds are announced to all, is made present: preaching yields presence. From the Lord's presence, the redemption that He accomplishes is poured out upon the world. It is the Eucharist, finally, which re-creates the broken Adam, and fashions him into one body of Christ in the Church and in the world.

St Paul took the Corinthians to task for having a contempt for community when they came together. But the Eucharist challenges us 'to ask: What are the "sins against community" which communion in the Lord's body commands us to do combat against, in ourselves and in society? Where are the gaping wounds which the Eucharist lays bare before our eyes?' Cardinal Sin listed a number of them: the division between the wealthy of this world and the poor; racism; oppression of women:

> There are innumerable stratagems of social, economic and political domination and exploitation, on every level of human relations, that we can only speak in general terms. The Eucharist proclaims the unacceptability of all of these before the cross of Jesus, before his death which we announce.

He included the abuse of young girls and boys in Asia

> catering to men from the First World ... children handed over for slave labour in lands neighbouring mine ... mineworkers in their late teens [who] cough away in airless tunnels. Enough—but you see, Christ makes all their woundedness and their victimhood His own, in the Eucharist. When we say *Amen* to the *Body of Christ* in communion, we place ourselves in solidarity with that Christ 'who bears all these in Himself'. Therefore, with Him, we must place ourselves in solidarity with all the suffering and brokenness in the world. My brothers and sisters, this is not pious rhetoric: it is the mystery of our Christ in the Eucharist! ... Thus the Eucharist tells us that to evangelise is 'to take upon ourselves the role of the servant' ... If there is so much suffering and poverty in our world, still Eucharist and Spirit renew the Church with disciples who are not afraid to follow the Lord wherever He leads them.

Cardinal Sin recalled 'yet another wound which lacerates the body of Christ, the on-going division among our Churches'. He fervently reminded us of the deep desire and prayer of Pope St

John XXIII for Christian unity which we, at this Congress on the Eucharist, should passionately share and progress.

> Those of us who have come from beyond the boundaries of Europe want to remind our brethren here that it was people from your shores who brought from the North, brought to us, the divisions of Christendom, the broken relationships which sunder Christ's body. They were not of our making; you brought them to us; they are the heritage of our past. Unless you undo them *here* among yourselves, how shall they be healed among us? Who is responsible finally, for keeping them alive? Here at this Congress, let Jesus' longing, let Pope John's anguished hope, pass through our hearts. The Eucharist challenges us to this, at this hour of grace.

The Cardinal reverted to the theme of evangelisation, 'a crucial imperative for our time'. The Asian Bishops Conference had demanded the 'Building up of the Local Church' as necessary for their part of the world.

> But in Asia, proclamation must follow the path of dialogue ... This means an immersion in the total reality of our peoples' lives, their religious traditions, their cultures, their real situations of poverty and struggle for humanity, justice and peace ... Is not this the way the Son of God came to us in the Incarnation? His immersion in our human condition was complete, sin alone excepted. And is not the Eucharist a prolongation of this same logic of Incarnation? Is not the way of the Eucharist also a Dialogue of Life, casting of His lot with ours, a total sharing of what He is for us, so that 'He may bear us in Himself', and make all of us His one body?

Finally, the Cardinal turned to inculturation as 'continuing the way the Son took, in becoming Emmanuel, God-with-us'. Powerfully using texts from the prophet Isaiah, about the nations flowing to the Lord's house and carrying their gifts, the wealth of the nations, the Cardinal asked,

And what is this wealth of the nations? May we not say, the gifts of peoples' cultures? What people create with their minds and hands, from earth and sea and sky: 'Fruits of the earth and the labour of men's hands'. Songs and stories, arts and thought and troves of wisdom: gifts of the cultures of humanity. Human cultures gather the best and deepest which the humanity of nations produce.

All these gifts of their cultures, the nations bring to worship the Lord. There, upon the holy mountain Isaiah described, all peoples shall hold festival before the Lord.

Is not all this what the Eucharist images forth for us, its very meaning and promise? The Eucharist is 'summons and stimulus' to mission, because it proclaims the death of the Lord until He comes! There on the cross, God reigns, God draws all men to Him! But is not the Eucharist also 'fulfilment of mission'? For at the Lord's table all evangelisation reaches its term, at the banquet where all are brothers and sisters, where God's love embraces all the peoples, the dream we all dream, the dream of Catholicity, the dream of *catholica unitas*!

Where else but in the Eucharistic assembly is this final messianic banquet symbolised, promised and in measure already realised? Where, but here, my brothers and sisters, around the meal of the Lord's body and blood do all the nations of the world assemble, poor and rich, high and low, of every race and colour and costume, of every age in the great history of humanity, in all the wondrous diversity of traditions and cultures, amid all the incredible richness of their gifts of mind and heart, and hands and voices, of their very souls? ... And is not this really what we experience here ... where upon each one, and upon each people, falls that amazing grace whereby each of us, and every race and nation among us, hear our own name, sounded in the symphony of the spirit which is Church, Eucharist and promise of the Kingdom to come.

Fr Anthony McSweeney's theme that evening was 'The Evangelising Riches of the Eucharist'. First, he set out his store:

> The image of the Eucharist which emerges from this story [of the supper at Emmaus, Lk 24:13–35] is that of the presence of the risen Lord to His own. He, the Christ who died, rose and is to come, the definitive word of salvation, is seated with His disciples at the table. Present sacramentally to His disciples, He is the fulfilment of all the words of the Scriptures, which are summed up in the paschal proclamation. This is the central message, the core of the Church's proclamation of faith, its *kerygma*. The whole of Jesus' life as incarnation of the Word converges on it. This *kerygma* is announced in a unique way in the Eucharist. There it finds its summit, its fullest realisation.

Then: 'The *evangelising* character of the Eucharist is not something secondary or added to it. It belongs to the very nature of the celebration of the Sacrament.' Fr McSweeney saw its evangelising riches both in the celebration and in the adoration of the Eucharist. The content of the Eucharist is the life of Jesus and its significance. As the rite unfolds, it is He who is proclaimed in the celebration of Mass, especially through the proclamation of the Word, but also through the witness of the community: '... the day to day behaviour of the community enters into the proclamatory character of its Eucharistic celebration. Christian liturgy cannot abstract from actual life ...' He stressed the need for liturgical education and renewal in the Church of today, leading into adoration:

> Prayer and devotion directed to Christ in the sacramental species will open us to the evangelising riches of the Eucharist to the degree to which they respect the movement and the finality of the celebration, namely worship of the Father through Jesus Christ in the Holy Spirit, and deeper union with Christ in his Paschal Mystery.

The riches the Eucharist yields 'introduce us into a new vision of existence in the risen Christ'. We become a 'new creation' in a renovated world. 'Jesus saw His own death as the act whereby the

Father would gather into one God's scattered children. The very being of the community, then, is inseparable from the memory of His life-giving death.'

The Eucharist also of course brings us 'into contact with Christ in the power of His resurrection and teaches us a new wisdom'. We acquire a sense of gratitude for life.

> The Eucharistic prayer is the primary prayer and formative model of the believer's fundamental attitude towards existence. This point is of crucial importance today. For we run the risk of falling into a new form of moralism when we insist, correctly, on the need for Christians to 'become eucharist', that is to say, to 'become bread broken' for their brothers and sisters. We will only perpetuate a moralistic mentality unless we make sure that becoming a gift for others is seen as a response born of a wonder-filled sense of the gratuitous character of one's own existence.

The Eucharist brings us the wisdom of the Cross when it invites us 'to nourish ourselves with the strangely bitter bread and wine of God till it transforms our outlook and re-creates our minds ... It teaches us the true wisdom, which is the knowledge of God and His ways in the world.' It transforms our desires so as 'to work for a bread which will last and will save us from death'. It leads us to contemplation.

> This contemplative dimension of the liturgy calls for moments of silence and the avoidance of excessive verbalisation, which is all too common today ... Eucharistic adoration can be seen as a prolonging of this contemplative moment or dimension of the celebration. It is a way of *dwelling* in the mystery, whereby we 'replay' it in order to taste the goodness of the Lord and to place ourselves at His disposal so that He may be formed in us.

This 'new wisdom' is to be found in the way that we cope with suffering.

> The Eucharist evangelises our experience of suffering,
> schooling us in seeing the redemptive dimension of pain
> ... The sending of the Eucharistic bread to the sick and the
> house-bound elderly, for example, is not simply a gesture
> of charity and inclusion on the part of the Eucharistic
> assembly. It is also an affirmation of their redemptive role
> in the sacrifice that they celebrate in the Eucharist.

Finally,

> the Eucharist evangelises by giving hope. Jesus lived His
> Passover in an attitude of intense waiting for the Kingdom.
> His Eucharist is marked by the same ardent expectation
> ... A eucharistic people is one which participates with
> unwavering hope in the building up of a society of justice
> and brothersisterhood, *'a civilisation of love'*, to use the
> expression of Pope Paul VI. The Christian is called to play
> his part in preparing the table for the universal banquet.

St Mother Teresa of Calcutta had planned to attend the Seville
Congress but was too ill in hospital in London. However, Sister
Juana Elizondo Leiza, Superior General of the Daughters of
Charity, argued strongly on behalf of the poor:

> Whereas humanity has never had so many resources, never
> have so many people experienced such scandalously great
> a lack of the very necessities for subsistence. While at the
> tables of the rich there is sheer extravagance, waste and
> destruction of tons of food, at the tables of the majority
> there are not enough scraps ... Merely to accept and allow
> the status quo of injustice and inequality between people
> to continue, without trying to correct it, this is truly a
> scandal that gives little credibility to the followers of Jesus
> and is tantamount to 'invalidating' the celebration of the
> Eucharist, sacrament and sign of brotherhood.

Sister Juana argued her case—that God does not allow us to forget
our brothers and sisters in their need—by appealing to the
Scriptures: the prophets of the Old Testament, especially Amos

and Isaiah, and Jesus himself and St James in the New, and then her Founder, St Vincent de Paul.

Christians had to form a community themselves in order to transform society:

> To be a Christian is to be a person of communion. This means living the reality of eucharistic brotherhood which unites a believer to the whole Christ: to live in communion with Christ and one's brethren. To receive the body of Christ, to say 'Amen' to Christ, is also to acknowledge one's brethren, to say 'Amen' to the Church, to the community.

Such a communion will reflect the very communion of God in the Blessed Trinity. In its history, the Church had formed many communities which 'have been and are a leaven not only of evangelisation but also of transformation and social development. Responding to historical needs and local circumstances, they have been and are committed to fostering culture, justice and the practice of charity.' Now, in the new evangelisation urged by Pope John Paul, the witness of the Christian community is indispensable.

> The Christian community will be more credible and contribute to the *transformation of society* if it strives to express with might and main: a style of life which offers an alternative to that in the consumer society where 'having' holds priority over 'being'; a simple and unostentatious lifestyle which recognises the proper measure of things in relation to fundamental values... Such a lifestyle has a beautiful humanising influence in an environment where everything is evaluated in terms of money, profit or usefulness.

We are not left alone in continuing the mission of Christ.

> In the Eucharist Christians encounter all the energy required to live out faithfully the significance of their baptism. Participation in and adoration of the Eucharist express the source of grace for undertaking their mission as witnesses of the Gospel ... In the celebration and adoration of the Eucharist the Church encounters the great teachings of Christ which focus and shape its own

policy for action: love, service, sacrifice, total dedication ... The Eucharist is for Christ's disciple the font from which he can draw the necessary strength to fulfil the sublime, though demanding, mission which the Master has entrusted to him.

Earlier, the Canadian Cardinal Edouard Gagnon, President of the Pontifical Council for the Family and President also of the Pontifical Committee for International Eucharistic Congresses, had celebrated a Mass for Christian Unity, attended by many thousands of people in the Cathedral. The English 'Round Table' discussion that day was 'Ecumenical Cooperation in the Mission *ad gentes*'.

Sacrament of Eucharist, Commandment of Love

Spain delights in its religious processions, and no city more than Seville. Sometimes disparaged as 'popular religion', the people of Spain would say, 'You don't understand. By these processions, we make religion itself popular!' How to describe the Seville Corpus Christi? Deeply part of the culture of the city, it has to be seen. On Thursday 10 June, after Mass in the Cathedral, came the procession: colourful, jubilant, prayerful, dignified. I stayed with Bishop Holland as, now too infirm to walk, he watched the procession from his wheelchair. About forty men known as *costaleros* and belonging to various Confraternities carried the traditional nine floats. Their movement was choreographed, with frequent stops because of the weight of the floats' solid wooden structures. Swelled by pilgrims to the Congress, the procession took about two hours to pass, wending its way slowly through the crowded streets, past houses whose windows and balconies were bedecked with aromatic flowers. Altars it seemed were erected in every street. Music played, clouds of incense rose from before the Blessed Sacrament. That evening, the Congress pilgrims enjoyed an agape in the homes of the citizens of Seville. It was a gracious ending to a day dedicated to the Eucharist.

The following day was Bishop Holland's 85ᵗʰ birthday. We attended Mass in the Cathedral, celebrated in the Hispano-Mozarabic rite dating from the seventh century. The chief celebrant was the Archbishop of Toledo and Primate of Spain, Cardinal Marcelo Gonzalez Martin. As a young man, he had been in the Valladolid seminary when Thomas Holland was on the staff of the English College there. They had been good friends and their meeting over 52 years later was warm and moving.

The arrival of Pope St John Paul II was eagerly awaited. Greeted at the airport by the King and Queen of Spain, Don Juan Carlos and Doña Sofía, and by members of national and local government, the Holy Father went directly to the Square of the Virgin of the Kings where many thousands awaited him. It was a festal scene: banners hung from buildings, bells rang, people cheered. Earlier that morning the famous 'Procession of the Virgin of the Kings' had taken place, with the beautiful statue of Our Lady dating from the thirteenth century. In his Angelus address, Pope John Paul drew attention to the two devotions 'which from time immemorial have characterised your people's Christian spirituality: devotion to the Blessed Sacrament and devotion to our Lady. Without these two devotions, the history of this Church of Seville would not make sense.'

The Holy Father then closed the solemn Eucharistic adoration in the Cathedral. He praised those responsible for organising continuous adoration in many of the city's churches, even throughout the night. He hoped that all parishes and Christian communities would establish some form of adoration of the Holy Eucharist, quoting a Spanish bishop who used to say that 'in the tabernacle of each church we possess a shining beacon, and in contact with that our lives can be illuminated and transformed.'

> Yes ... it is important for us to live and teach others how to live the total mystery of the Eucharist: the sacrament of *the Sacrifice*, of *the Banquet*, and of the abiding *Presence* of Jesus Christ the Saviour. You know well that the various forms of Eucharistic devotion are both an extension of the sacrifice

and of Communion and a preparation for them. Is it necessary to stress once again the deep theological and spiritual motivations which underlie devotion to the Blessed Sacrament outside the celebration of Mass? It is true that the reservation of the Sacrament was begun in order to take Communion to the sick and those absent from the celebration. However, as the *Catechism of the Catholic Church* says, 'As faith in the real presence of Christ in His Eucharist deepened, the Church became conscious of the meaning of silent adoration of the Lord present under the Eucharistic species' (*Catechism of the Catholic Church* no.1379) ... It is *God with us* who enables us to share His life and sends us into the world to evangelise it and make it holy! *The Eucharist and Evangelisation* is the theme of this Congress. The Eucharist really is 'the source and the summit of all evangelisation' (*Presbyterorum ordinis* 5).

Pope John Paul stressed the importance of the Lord's Day:

How important it is in today's social environment that is gradually being secularised, to promote the renewal of the Sunday celebration of the Eucharist and respect for the Lord's Day ... The Sunday rest from work, attention to the family, the cultivation of spiritual values and sharing in the life of the Christian community will contribute to making a better world, one richer in moral values, with greater solidarity and less consumerism.

I had taken Bishop Holland to the cathedral in his wheelchair for a period of adoration but without concelebrating at the Mass. We were towards the rear of the vast cathedral. As the procession of concelebrants returned from the sanctuary the Holy Father spotted Bishop Holland, left the procession and came over to greet him. They had first met and formed a friendship at the Synod of Bishops on Evangelisation in 1974. Seville, with its programme of evangelisation, would be their last meeting. It was a poignant moment.

Later that same day, in the Sports Centre, Pope John Paul ordained thirty-five priests. He told them that their ministry would be devoted to the Eucharist; to the work of forgiveness; to announcing the Word of the Lord and preaching. They would be called to intimacy with the Lord in prayer and configured to him by their celibacy. Their task would be always to evangelise, to help those who needed light and faith, the poor and those most neglected, the voiceless.

The closing Mass of the Congress—the Statio Orbis—was celebrated under a hot sun in the Seville Fairground—the Campo di Feria—and attended by the King and Queen of Spain with the royal family, civil and military authorities, many bishops and priests and 600,000 of the faithful. Pope John Paul explained the significance of the celebration: it brought together numerous pastors and faithful from the five continents into one spot, the Statio Orbis. It also included 'many brothers and sisters of other Christian Churches': already united through baptism, the Church 'prays intensely to the Lord that the long-awaited day will arrive on which, united in the faith, we can all participate together in the Eucharistic banquet'.

Remembering the role of Spanish missionaries in founding the Church in the New World, the Holy Father said it was charity that linked Eucharist with Evangelisation:

> From the Eucharistic altar, beating heart of the Church, constantly comes the evangelising flow of the word and charity. Therefore, contact with the Eucharist must lead to a greater commitment to make Christ's redemptive activity present in all human situations. Love for the Eucharist has to lead people to put into practice the demands of justice, fraternity, service, and equality among all people.

There were so many injustices in the world, continued Pope John Paul, which contradict the ideal of *koinonia*, or communion of life and love, as experienced in the Eucharist:

> The sacrament of the Eucharist cannot be separated from the commandment of love. One cannot receive the body of Christ and feel remote from those who are hungry or thirsty, who are exploited or strangers, who are imprisoned

or suffering from infirmity (cf. Mt 25:41–44). As the *Catechism of the Catholic Church* states: 'The Eucharist involves a commitment on behalf of the poor. In order truly to receive the Body and Blood of Christ given up for us, we must recognize Christ in the poor, His brothers and sisters' (CCC no.1397) ... The world has to pause to reflect that, among the many paths which lead to death, only one road leads to life. It is *the path of eternal life.* It is Christ.

With obvious delight, Pope John Paul announced that the next Eucharistic Congress would be at Wrocław in his homeland of Poland, 'in that part of Europe which after difficult trials has regained its freedom'—a reference to the fall of communism. Seville's was the first International Eucharistic Congress after the end of the Cold War.

Before continuing his pastoral visit to other parts of Spain, the Holy Father visited the Residence San Rafael, a home for the elderly in the nearby town of Dos Hermanos. The home had been opened earlier in the year as a practical application of the Eucharistic Congress. His visit was, he said, the final act of the Seville Congress, wishing 'to emphasise precisely that the Eucharistic liturgy and the liturgy of life are intimately connected'.

References

1)   Allen, J. F. Personal notes and diaries.

2)   *The Eucharist and Evangelisation, Basic Text on the Congress Theme,* Sancta Maria Abbey (Nunraw 1991).

3)   *Cristo Luz de los Pueblos (Christus Lumen Gentium),* Secretariado General XLV Congreso Eucaristico Internacional (Sevilla 1993).

4)   Pontifical Committee for International Eucharistic Congresses, *The International Eucharistic Congresses for a New Evangelisation* (Vatican 1991).

5)   *Christ, Light of Nations,* Editions Paulines (Canada 1994).

6)   *L'Osservatore Romano,* English edition, 1993, nos. 24, 25.

8 WROCŁAW 25 MAY-1 JUNE 1997
CHRIST OUR FREEDOM

F R ANTHONY CONLON, the national delegate for England and Wales, had suggested ways of preparing for the Wrocław Congress. Helped by these suggestions, the party of thirty that set out by coach from Manchester was in good spirits, ably led by Frs Tony Leonard and Francis Rice of Shrewsbury and Michael Eastwood of Nottingham. We travelled through the night to catch the early morning ferry from Calais, then on by coach to Hanover for a night's rest. A 24-hour journey along Germany's autobahns, and the new ones under construction in Poland, saw us into Wrocław (pronounced as vrots-wahf), a city which has seen bewildering changes in its thousand years of history. From a Bohemian stronghold, it became part of Poland, then after 350 years part of the Kingdom of Bohemia, then of the Kingdom of Hungary, then of the Hapsburg Austrian Empire, then part of the Kingdom of Prussia. After the unification of Germany in 1871, it was the sixth largest city in the German Empire. Until 1946 it was known as Breslau and was predominantly German and Protestant.

After World War II Poland's borders were changed. By then the Russian army already controlled all of East-Central Europe. At the Yalta Conference in February 1945, meeting with President Franklin D Roosevelt of America and Prime Minister Winston Churchill of Britain, Premier Josef Stalin of Russia insisted on retaining those lands. The new borders were then ratified in August 1945 at the Potsdam Conference and Breslau became part of Poland. Under Soviet influence German-speakers were expelled and the city filled with Poles forcibly moved from Eastern parts. Roosevelt had died in April. President Harry Truman replaced him and said later: 'I remember at Potsdam, we got to discussing a matter in eastern Poland, and it was remarked by the Prime Minister of Great Britain that the Pope would not be happy over the arrangement of that Catholic end of Poland. And the Generalissimo, the Prime Minister of Russia, leaned on the table, and he pulled his moustache like that, and looked over to Mr Churchill and said: "Mr Churchill, Mr Prime Minister, how many divisions did you say the Pope had?"' Fifty-two years later, Pope St John Paul II and the 1997 Congress in Wroclaw answered that question.

At the time, many people wondered why Wrocław had been chosen to host the Congress. If it was to be in Poland, why not Cracow or Jasna Gora? A possible answer is that Wrocław lies near the Polish borders with Germany and the Czech Republic, an area that embraces the cultures and history of many peoples. Pope John Paul had in fact drawn attention to this when he met the Congress organisers in 1995. He recalled that Wrocław was at the heart of Europe, which must find its Christian roots again for the benefit of all mankind. Its gates, he said, were also open to the East and it had an ecumenical character. He was to repeat this during his homily at the Statio Orbis. Wrocław's culture and architecture reflect its Bohemian, Austrian and Prussian past. In 2016, it was the European City of Culture. With about 700,000 inhabitants, it is the capital of Lower Silesia. It lies on the Oder River and covers twelve islands with 130 bridges. Its Cathedral, Gothic but with Baroque features and largely rebuilt over the centuries following damage from fire and war, was a worthy venue for many of the Congress events.

The 46th International Congress at Wrocław can be understood only in the light of time and world events. The time was the dawn of the third millennium. World events included the fall of Communism and the liberation of Poland.

Pope St John Paul II had set his sights on making Christ central to the third millennium. In his encyclical letter of 1994, *Tertio Millennio Adveniente*, he wrote:

> Since the publication of the very first document of my Pontificate, I have spoken explicitly of the Great Jubilee, suggesting that the time leading up to it be lived as 'a new Advent'. This theme has since reappeared many times ...

In fact, preparing for the Year 2000 has become as it were a hermeneutical key of my Pontificate.

Pope John Paul would mention the third millennium again at the Statio Orbis. In presenting the Basic Text for the 46th IEC Fr Jesus Castellano Cervera had also drawn attention

> to the celebration of the Jubilee of 2000, in the year dedicated especially to Christ the Evangeliser, who proclaims the Jubilee of freedom at Nazareth, and realises it in the Paschal mystery of which the Eucharist is the perpetual memorial in time.

He pointed out that the Basic Text 'by way of final exhortation contains certain essential points of doctrine: an invitation to set free the forces of good, in the perspective of the Jubilee of the year 2000 as a specific contribution of the IEC ...'

In May 1995 Cardinal Henryk Gulbinowicz, Archbishop of Wrocław, spoke movingly of the new freedom Poland and its neighbours now enjoyed:

> Peoples that for hundreds of years have been living in freedom, and that have never fallen into the clutches of Hitlerian or communist totalitarianism that deprives human beings of freedom and inalienable rights, now need to know the true and deep meaning of freedom. Peoples that five years ago freed themselves from the communist yoke must learn from Christ the 'sovereignty of the spirit'. A Polish poet, Adam Mickiewicz, expressed this thought in this way: 'Siberia is nothing, the lash is nothing; if the spirit of the people is corrupt, sorrow is added to sorrow'. Christian Central Europe, and perhaps also the rest of the world, must therefore be helped to regain a freedom that is just, because it is based on the wisdom of God.

The Cardinal saw the Congress as an opportunity for an exchange of ideas at international level, especially after the Second Vatican Council—an exchange that the communist power had prevented for over fifty years.

The Congress programme was very full. The Eucharistic celebration and a conference each day was usually led by a Cardinal in the Hala Ludowa, the People's Hall. Also known as the Centennial Hall, commemorating its opening in 1913 as part of the centenary celebrations of the Battle of Leipzig when Napoleon was defeated, the Hala had been renovated for the Eucharistic Congress. It held about 10,000 people. In the city, there was a rich table of theatrical, musical, poetical and artistic events and exhibitions. Thursday, Corpus Christi, saw the Blessed Sacrament procession through Wrocław's streets. On Friday, Cardinal Ruini led an ecumenical study day. Pope St John Paul II arrived on the Saturday, when there was adoration of the Blessed Sacrament and ecumenical prayer, while on Sunday he presided at the closing Statio Orbis. Throughout the week the Blessed Sacrament was exposed day and night for adoration in various churches in all parts of Poland. The whole country had been preparing well for this Congress, following a programme outlined in three pastoral letters from the Polish hierarchy. Universities organised symposia, while meetings throughout Poland reflected on the relationship between freedom and the Eucharist.

Cardinal Joachim Meisner's lecture on 'The Eucharist: Proclamation and Witness of the Presence of Freedom' was highly significant. He was born in Breslau in 1933 when it was still a largely German city. He was one of those displaced under the terms of the Potsdam Agreement. During the Congress he admitted: 'I have four parents: Silesia, Thuringia, Berlin and Cologne, but it is the first I love the most.' Now Archbishop of Cologne, he had been Bishop of Berlin before the collapse of the Berlin Wall. He began his address with reference to the French Revolution and immediately revealed his hand:

> The so-called Good News of 1789 is expressed in the slogan: Liberty, Equality, Fraternity. The meaning of this could not become fully effective because a fourth and essential dimension was forgotten, or, rather, deliberately ruled out, namely, Faith in Christ. The terms of freedom, equality and frater-

nity all stem from the New Testament. Where these terms are not deeply rooted in the reality of God, as during the French Revolution, their sense becomes distorted to mean the opposite. What is freedom without God's covenant? Its sense is quickly lost to human beings through their involvement with their own selfishness. For even if they appear to have liberated themselves from external forces imposed by some oppressor or tyrant, they are still far from being free from themselves. The history of the insanity of communism has demonstrated this in a glaring way.

Human beings, deformed by sin, are turned in on themselves. But God did not intend this. God made us in his image and likeness. Far from being 'turned in' God is 'turned out'.

In revealing Himself to humanity, God turned out to be tenderness, love, emanation, humility and compassion. The Eucharist is this substantiated love, tenderness and humility of God: it is the incarnate God Himself. The Eucharist is not a thing, but a Person.

Cardinal Meisner had addressed the Seville Congress four years previously on 'The Eucharist and Evangelisation'. Now he covered similar ground but with the emphasis on 'Freedom'. He spoke of the Trinitarian, Christological and Ecclesiological dimensions of the Eucharist.

God is Love: this is the central message of St John. But love cannot exist alone within itself since the primary focus of love is 'You' (cf 1 Jn 4:16b). Love always says: 'you'. God's saying of 'you' is not merely empty prattle. Rather, in His Son the Father faces His eternal 'You'. And since the Son is altogether and entirely Son of the Father, He cannot but re-call Himself to His Father by calling Him 'You' as well. The Father from His side reiterates this 'You' to the Son so that the paternal and filial 'You' coincide in the Person of the Holy Spirit. The Holy Trinity is the mystery of Love: 'subsistent relations', as St Thomas Aquinas says … The Father owes Himself to the Son, for without Son there is no Father. The Son owes Himself entirely to the Father, for without Father there is no Son. And the Holy Spirit owes Himself to the Father and the Son, for without Father and Son there is no Spirit of interchange and covenant.

The Holy Eucharist is rooted in this ... The eternal filial 'You' to the Father in the Holy Spirit finds its temporal extension towards people in the sacramental words of the Eucharist: this is My Body, given for you; this is My Blood, poured out for you. Thus, the Eucharist in the tabernacle is not to be regarded in a static way, as it has been formerly done in pious pictures and literature, where for example the Child Jesus or the Good Shepherd in the Host was waiting for adorers. No! Rather Christ is present in the Eucharist as the One being altogether away-from-Himself, striving towards the Father. Nearing the tabernacle, you are approaching, so to speak, the magnetic field of the Son, away-from-Himself, turned towards the Father. Consequently, the presence of the Lord in the Eucharist is a dynamic one which redeems mankind from turning around and inwards on himself; it turns him into being the living action of deliverance to the Father. Only in this way human beings become freed from themselves, free for God and for others. This is their ultimate freedom in the truest sense of the word.

Whilst appreciating the Cardinal's emphasis on what he calls the 'dynamic' presence of the Lord in the Eucharist, one might be pardoned for thinking a little extreme his strictures about a 'static' presence. Writing in the Homiletic and Pastoral Review (February 2016) about a similar comment by Karl Rahner—that 'It would be pitiful if we were to reconcile ourselves forever to the inadequate, and perhaps half-magical, misconceptions which we drag along with us from early religious instruction, and from the practices of our childhood'—Fr John McCusker OSB showed how it is necessary to emphasise 'the ontologically "static" doctrine of the Real Presence'. A reading of Pope St John Paul's encyclical *Ecclesia de Eucharistia* and Pope Benedict's *Sacramentum Cari-*

tatis should be enough to see how the 'static' and 'dynamic' are inter-related; the 'dynamic' depends on an ontological foundation. One remembers the story of the Curé d'Ars asking an old man what he did in his habitual visit to the Blessed Sacrament, and the man's reply: 'He looks at me, and I look at Him.' The 'static' presence has made the 'dynamic' possible, so that such visits, such prayers have formed saints.

Christ remains the Son, totally directed towards the Father in the Holy Spirit.

> Being this, He is entirely the expression of the Trinitarian verticality. And now, He becomes a true man in the Incarnation ... The divine Heart of Jesus is a heart turned outward and open to others. This is made visible at the cross when it was opened by the lance. The cross comes into being where the divine and the human lines meet each other. I emphasise again: true God and true man in one, totally vertical and horizontal dimensions at the same time: this is what makes up the cross. It tears the Crucified One apart. But, as its outward shape shows, only the cross makes the minus a plus. It re-qualifies death into life, loss into gain, tyranny into freedom, the negative into the positive. The merely horizontal line of the world does not offer any point from which human beings could strive beyond themselves to the heights and reach from a horizontal to the vertical plane of living. The centre-point of the cross alone is the only one in which the vertical line of God cuts across the horizontal line of the world so that a pass-over becomes possible between mankind and God. The cross, or the pain of Christ, is consequently the shape of Divine Love taking on the circumstances of the world which is bound in original sin. The eucharistic Blood flows from the pierced Heart of Jesus. The Eucharist is the fruit of the Cross of Christ, the Tree of Life.

The Cardinal showed how, in the Eucharist, God gives Himself away.

> Since, according to a saying of the Lord: 'It is more blessed
> to give than to receive' (cf Ac 20:35), it is the giving that
> makes a person blessed. God, however, does not give us
> just anything, but everything, namely, His Son Jesus Christ.
> This is why God is the All-Blessed One since He is a
> eucharistic, a blessing-giving God. He wants us to partake
> in His all-blessed state by drawing us through the Eucharist
> into His channel of giving.

Using the example of the poor widow dropping her two small
coins into the Temple treasury in Jerusalem (cf Mk 12:41–44),
the Cardinal continued:

> In this poor widow you can almost recognise God giving
> away Himself in the Eucharist. He has not just put something
> into the treasury box of this world, but the bare necessity of
> His life, His only-begotten Son. Whenever we genuflect
> before the sacred Host at the elevation this is, materially
> speaking, almost nothing. But it is before God's one and all,
> His only-begotten Son Who has been offered as a sacrifice
> for us on the cross. God cannot offer more than this! We are
> the heirs of God. What shall we inherit from Him? What
> does He have to give away? The ability to give, the possibility
> to give away, in order to admit us to His glory. 'It is more
> blessed to give than to receive'. It is here where we find real
> human liberation: to be admitted to God's life-style, to God's
> way of life, to share His own quality of being.

Cardinal Meisner then spoke of the role of the Eucharist in the
Church.

> Christ's Gospel is destined to be lived in the Church as in a
> body, but not to be enclosed in that body. Christ assumed
> a body not to redeem this body, but to redeem the world by
> this body ... The Church comprises the whole Christ, Head
> and body. It is not 'the body of Christians', but 'the body of
> Christ' through the Eucharist. A Christian who consumes
> the Host is what he eats: he becomes the Body of Christ by
> partaking of this Body; he becomes church ... By being
> incorporated into the Mystical Eucharistic Body, commu-

nicants are freed from their individual existence so that they share the ecclesial way of life of the Communion of Saints ... Apart from Jesus' institutional words proclaimed at every Mass: 'This is My Body, this is My Blood', there is still another 'consecrational' sentence which He pronounced about the weary and suffering of the world: 'Whatever you did to one of the least of my brothers, you did it to me' (Mt 25:40). By employing the indicative mood in both these statements, our Lord emphasises that He identifies Himself with the poor and needy of the world just as much as He is present in the Bread and Wine. The Eucharist frees human beings towards becoming a true and permanent civilisation of love, in which we are rehabilitated. By kneeling down before the consecrated Host, we discover how easy it is to stoop down to the weary and suffering of the world.

The Cardinal ended with a reference to Mother St Teresa of Calcutta who

> introduced an Hour of Adoration of the Holy Eucharist in her communities in order to sharpen the awareness of her sisters regarding Jesus' real presence in both the Eucharist and His suffering members. Her sisters are truly contemplatives in action. They pray their work in front of the monstrance, and afterwards they work their prayer with people. Thus, they belong to the most liberated human beings in God's world, since they have been freed through the Eucharist to serve God and other people ... The life of Christ which entered the world by His Incarnation must become a new way of existence also in our own lives. This becomes a reality when, like the eucharistic way of transubstantiation, we arrive at the point of realising that it is no longer we who live, but Christ lives in us (cf Gal 2:20). Christ is the freedom of love in person. He frees us for His incomparable freedom.

Some years before this, when Cardinal Meisner was still bishop in Berlin, I accompanied him on a day out from the Liborifest in Paderborn which we were both attending. We were part of a group visiting historical sites in that diocese but our journey included a visit to the Wall—not in the city of Berlin but in the countryside of eastern Germany. The Wall there was a truly shocking sight. Machine gun posts and high barbed wire and electric fencing prevented citizens of East Germany from leaving their State, and prevented any from the West, should they so have wished, from entering the Communist East. I mentioned to Bishop Meisner that, sadly, certain councillors in my native city of Manchester supported the PAX Association prominent in East Germany and other Communist countries. He rose in coils of wrath: 'Magnum scandalum est! Magnum scandalum!'. (We were conversing in Latin since I had no German and he no English.) PAX was a Communist front organisation, formed in Stalinist Poland in order to divide Catholics, win them over to Communism, and so break their links with the Vatican. It supported the trial and imprisonment of priests and bishops, including Cardinal Stefan Wyszynski ... I quickly tried to change the subject!

Cardinal Meisner gave his major lecture on Congress Tuesday when the day's theme was 'Witnesses of Truth and Freedom'. The Congress had opened two days before with the host, Cardinal Henryk Gulbinowicz, Archbishop of Wrocław, greeting participants from all over the world. Cardinal Jozef Glemp, Primate of Poland and President of the Polish Bishops Conference, then presided at Mass in Wrocław Cathedral where the Papal Legate, Cardinal Angelo Sodano, Secretary of State of the Holy See, explained how the Holy Eucharist makes the presence of Christ visible to us. Renewed by Christ in the Eucharist we are able to avoid evil and do good. We are no longer servants under the command of their Lord but children of a loving Father. Urged on by His love, we are able in our turn to work for freedom and social justice, in solidarity with one another. The word 'solidarity' had particular resonance in Poland. It was the name of the labour union founded in 1980 at the Lenin Shipyards in Gdansk under the leadership of Lech Walesa, and which later played a monumental part in the collapse of Communism.

The Eucharist makes us free

Congress Monday carried the theme 'Freedom of God's Children'. At a Mass introduced by Cardinal Franciszek Macharski, Pope St John Paul's successor as Archbishop of Cracow, and celebrated by Cardinal Adam Joseph Maida, Archbishop of Detroit, Bishop Karl Lehmann of Mainz, President of the German Bishops Conference, gave the homily. True freedom, he said, is born of faith and baptism which overcomes sin and transforms human life in all its aspects. Bishop Lehmann reflected the overall focus of the first few days of the Congress, on the pressure of sin restricting, even enslaving, men and women, and which faith and baptism overpower. On the same day, Cardinal Francis Arinze, then President of the Pontifical Council for Interreligious Dialogue, described how the Eucharist gives us the power to achieve true freedom and preserve it. We are only truly free when we live in the way God shows us. This is the true way which sets us free. Continuing Tuesday's theme of 'Witness of Truth and Freedom', Cardinal Bernard Law of Boston recalled in his homily the sufferings of Poland where

> the tragedy of two world wars was experienced in all its violence. Here the memory of Nazi and Communist oppression is still fresh in its horror. Here the slavery that comes with systems devoid of God has given Poland its martyrs. Here the indomitable power of God's Spirit moving in the minds and hearts of Poland's sons and daughters has brought the hope of a new spring of freedom. We come, from all over the world, to give thanks to God for the freedom that is ours in Christ Jesus.

As sacrifice, the Eucharist makes us free.

> In the Eucharist there is made present on our altars, under the appearance of bread and wine, the all-sufficient sacrifice by which Jesus Christ, both priest and victim, redeemed the world ... Jesus' sacrifice is the total gift of Himself out of love for us. Greater love than this no one

has. It is to this sacrificial love that we are called. Listen again to Jesus' words: 'If a man wishes to come after Me, he must deny his very self, take up his cross and begin to follow in My footsteps' ... It is necessary to enter into the sacrifice of Christ by offering our lives in faithful disciple-ship. It is in knowing the truth, who is God, who is revealed to us in Christ Jesus, who is present in Eucharist, that we become free. Only in leaving all to follow Him can we know freedom in the fullest sense ... Contemporary culture misunderstands freedom as an ability to choose, regardless of the object. By contrast, true freedom, as Jesus reveals to us in His redemptive death, is the freedom to love even to the point of laying down our lives for another ... The notion of sacrifice is alien to a rampant consumerism.

Also as communion, the Eucharist makes us free. 'Sin is disruptive of communion with God and communion with one another.' Giving examples of violence and discrimination from the Bible, from history and from the contemporary world, the Cardinal called them

the sin from which the Lord Jesus has delivered us. The Eucharist as communion teaches us that if we are one with our Eucharistic Lord, then we are one with one another. Again St Paul is our guide as he teaches us that 'the body is one and has many members, but all the members, many though they are, are one body; and so it is with Christ.' We receive the Body of Christ, the Risen Lord, each one of us, in the Holy Communion of this Mass. As each of us is brought into a deeper communion with the Lord Jesus, so are we brought into a deeper communion with one another. We discover one another in Him in a new way. No longer are we blinded by our differences, but we are drawn by the Lord who is present in each of us.

Speakers on Congress Wednesday, when the theme was 'Freedom from Sin', underlined the message already proposed in earlier homilies and lectures. Archbishop Zenon Grocholewski, Secretary of the Apostolic Signatura, spoke of the faith and humility with which we must approach the Eucharist, conscious that we are sharing in our Saviour's cross. Cardinal Lucas Neves of Brazil lectured on the pedagogical aspect of the Eucharist. At evening sessions in the Cathedral, several speakers who had personally experienced hardship and even imprisonment because of their faith gave moving testimony to the inner freedom they had retained. Cardinal Kazimierz Swiatek, Archbishop of Minsk in Belarus, was ordained priest in 1939. Persecuted by the Nazis, he was imprisoned by them in 1941 and then by the Soviets when they took over Belarus. He was sentenced to forced labour in Siberia and spent from 1944 to 1954 in a gulag there. Only after the fall of the Iron Curtain was he appointed Archbishop of Minsk, a see that had been vacant since 1925. Cardinal Miloslav Vlk, Archbishop of Prague, described how the authorities in Communist Czechoslovakia had cancelled his authorisation to work as a priest. For eleven years, from 1978 until 1989, he lived in Prague, most of the time as a window cleaner, but secretly carrying out his priestly ministry with small groups of the faithful.

Congress Thursday dawned, the solemnity of Corpus Christi. The day's theme was 'Eucharist, The Source of Freedom'. Cardinal Edouard Gagnon, President of the Pontifical Committee for International Eucharistic Congresses, was the main celebrant at the morning Mass in Hala Ludowa. The Blessed Sacrament Procession then formed, led by representatives of the different continents: Africa, Australia, America, Europe and Asia. The weather in Wrocław that week had been problematic, with a cold wind and an abundance of rain. But the sun shone on the procession as it made its colourful, musical and prayerful way through Wrocław's streets to the Cathedral, with tens of thousands of people taking part. That afternoon, Polish families welcomed delegates and pilgrims into their homes.

Congress Friday's theme was 'Christ Frees and Unites'. There were ecumenical meetings in different languages in various Wrocław churches; the celebration of a Greek-Catholic Mass; an Armenian Pontifical Mass; and a Christian Unity Conference with Cardinal Ruini, President of the Italian Bishops Conference, as the main speaker.

Yearn, Pray for Unity

Saturday was the feast of the Visitation of Our Lady; the Congress theme was 'Mary—the Model of Freedom'. Cardinal Bernard Law, Archbishop of Boston, gave the homily this day at Mass for English-speaking pilgrims. He addressed a topic common to most Eucharistic Congresses, the scandal of Christian disunity. Setting the scene historically—'This city embraces a span of time of over a thousand years'—and geographically—'Pope John Paul II, steeped in the authentic Marian piety of the Church which he learned from his earliest years in Poland'– the Cardinal showed how Mary leads us to Jesus.

> In visitation, Mary set out, proceeding in haste into the hill country to be with her cousin Elizabeth. Mary is the icon, the image of the Church. In her we see what we should be. In charity, in love, she set out in haste—without concern for her own convenience and comfort. She went into the hill country, which means it was not an easy journey. She went to be with her cousin who was in need. The Church today is called to be on a journey of love to our brothers and sisters who are not in full communion of faith with us. The way often appears steep and difficult. Convenience and comfort can easily hold us back. Like Mary, however, we must proceed in haste.

> Mary never comes alone. How beautiful and rich are the words of Elizabeth! 'Blessed are you among women and blessed is the fruit of your womb. But who am I that the Mother of my Lord should come to me? The moment your greeting sounded in my ears, the baby stirred in my womb for joy.' We must go in visitation with Mary to our Orthodox brothers and sisters, with gratitude for their fidelity to the truth that Mary is Theotokos, bearer, Mother of God. We must go in visitation to our Protestant

brothers and sisters, and ask them to read in prayer with us this passage of the Scriptures they so reverently honour. May we understand together that it is the same Spirit of God that filled Elizabeth which will enable us to say that Mary is Blessed among women, that she is the greatest among all human beings because of her unique relationship to the Incarnate Word of God, that she is Mother of God and our mother. It is the Spirit who will shed light on the truth about the ministry of Peter in the Church, the truth about the Eucharist.

The Visitation has a particular message for our times when a culture of death threatens us all. Elizabeth said: 'The moment your greeting sounded in my ears, the baby stirred in my womb for joy.' How powerfully God speaks to us in this word, urging us to ponder the dialogue of love between Jesus and John the Baptist while both were still in the wombs of their mothers. Small wonder that our Holy Father has called us to be unconditionally pro-life. This feast urges us, as Catholics, to be in haste and heedless of the obstacles in serving the cause of human life. The Church must be with unborn children and their mothers and fathers; the Church must be with the terminally ill, with the disabled, with the refugee, the stranger, the poor, with whoever is in need; and the Church must come with Mary to bring the Lord who alone can bring joy to the human spirit. The Church is called to the visitation of all who suffer from whatever cause in this world. How much more effectively could we be the instruments of God's healing, strengthening presence if we were the Church united! How much more clearly and convincingly could we proclaim to the world the greatness of the Lord if the divisions between East and West, Protestant and Catholic were overcome! The difficulties of the task must not cause us to hesitate in the ecumenical journey to which the Holy Father calls us. In this Eucharist, may we pray for the movement of the Holy Spirit within all Christians so that together we might proclaim, with Mary, the greatness of the Lord, so that together, in full integrity of faith, we might proclaim that Jesus Christ is Lord, yesterday, today and forever.

The 'movement of the Holy Spirit' in inspiring, moving and enabling all Christians to share the same eucharistic cup was given major importance at the Wrocław Congress. Pope St John Paul II and Cardinal Edward Cassidy, the Australian President of the Pontifical Council for Promoting Christian Unity, both spoke about it.

'May the Holy Spirit enable the Word of God, which we have heard with obedience of faith, to bear fruit.' So Pope John Paul began his address in the People's Hall during an ecumenical service: 'The principal theme of this Liturgy of the Word is contained in what Jesus included in his priestly prayer the day before his Passion and Death on the cross. It is the prayer for the unity of his disciples.' He continued:

> When they listen to the voice of the Holy Spirit, the Churches and Ecclesiastical Communities feel called irrevocably to the search for an ever more profound unity, not only interior but also visible. A unity that becomes a sign for the world to see, so that the world may believe. There is no turning back on the ecumenical path! ... My thoughts willingly return to our last meeting in the church of the Most Holy Trinity in Warsaw in 1991. At that time I said that we need tolerance, but that among Christians tolerance alone is certainly not enough. What kind of brothers and sisters are people who only tolerate one another? We also need to accept one another. Today I recall these words and resolutely confirm them. But we cannot be content even with mutual acceptance. For the Lord of history is bringing us to the third millennium of Christianity. A great hour is striking. Our reply should be equal to the great moment of this special *kairos* of God. Here, in this place, I wish to say: Tolerance is not enough! Mutual acceptance is not enough! Jesus Christ, He who is and who is to come, expects from us a visible sign of unity, a joint witness ...

The West so much needs our deep and living faith at the historic stage of building a new system with many different points of reference. The East, spiritually devastated by years of a programme of doing without God, needs a strong sign of trust in Christ. Europe needs all solidly united round the cross and the Gospel. We must read the signs of the times carefully. Jesus Christ expects from all of us the witness of faith. The future of evangelisation is linked to the witness of unity given by the Church ...

The difficult path of reconciliation leads to joint witness, without which unity is impossible. Our Churches and Ecclesial Communities need reconciliation. Can we be fully reconciled with Christ without being fully reconciled among ourselves? Can we bear joint and effective witness to Christ if we are not reconciled with one another? Can we be reconciled with one another without forgiving one another? Forgiveness is the condition for reconciliation. But this cannot take place without interior transformation and conversion, which is the work of grace. 'The commitment to ecumenism must be based upon the conversion of hearts and upon prayer' (*Ut unum sint* 2) ... With sincere prayer let us support our ecumenical commitment. In this our second millennium, in which the unity of Christ's disciples has suffered tragic divisions in the East and in the West, prayer for the rediscovery of full unity is a special obligation of ours. We must yearn for the restoration of the unity willed by Christ, and we must pray for this unity: for it is a gift of the Most Holy Trinity. The stronger the link which unites us to the Father and the Son and the Holy Spirit, the easier it will be for us to deepen our mutual brotherhood ...

In recent years the distance which separates the Churches and Ecclesial Communities from one another has diminished significantly. Even so it is still too great! Too great! Christ did not will it so! We must do everything possible to restore the fulness of communion. We cannot stop along this path. Let us turn once again to Jesus' priestly

prayer, in which He says: 'That they may all be one; even
as you, Father, are in me, and I in you ... so that the world
may believe that you have sent me' (Jn 17:21). May these
words of Christ be for us all an exhortation to make an
effort on behalf of the great work of unity, on the threshold
of the Year 2000 which is drawing to a close.

Immediately before the Holy Father, Cardinal Edward Cassidy in
a lengthy talk rejoiced in ecumenical progress already achieved.
He described Jesus as the 'new Moses'; freeing us 'from our sins,
from our fears, from our false securities, from worshipping false
idols, He draws us ever closer to Himself. And the closer we come
to Him, the closer we come to one another.' He emphasised that
salvation comes through Christ:

> 'For of all the names in the world given to men, this is the
> only one by which we can be saved' (Ac 4:10). So important
> is this teaching of our Christian faith that it became even
> a matter of division among Christians. Any indication that
> salvation might be obtained in any other way than by faith
> in Jesus Christ and through His sacrifice became anath-
> ema. Today at last through the theological dialogue,
> especially between Catholics and Lutherans, Christians
> are becoming once again united in a common belief in the
> understanding of Christ and the Church.

There had been great progress also in our relations with more
ancient Churches.

> This truth about Jesus, that in His person there is realised
> a mysterious union of two natures, the divine and the
> human; that He who walked on this earth was fully God
> and fully man, true God and true man, is such an extraor-
> dinary revelation that right from the earliest centuries the
> Church had to insist that one could only be Christian if
> one were ready to make such a confession. The Councils
> of Ephesus in 431 and Chalcedon in 451 were called upon
> to declare the Church's faith in this truth. Separations
> resulted and from that time on some of the great, ancient

Churches lived in isolation from the rest of the Christian world because of their reluctance to accept the dogmatic definitions of these two Ecumenical Councils. With what immense joy Popes Paul VI and John Paul II signed with the Heads of those Churches—Coptic, Syrian, Ethiopian, Armenian and Assyrian—Christological declarations that, after a period of 1500 years, brought to a close the misunderstanding of the fifth century.

Freedom in the Third Millennium

Earlier in the day, Pope John Paul had been welcomed at Wrocław airport. He went straight to the Cathedral to take part in Eucharistic adoration. In his address, he explained how

> Eucharistic Congresses are celebrated precisely for this reason, to remind the world of this truth: 'Do not labour for the food which perishes, but for the food which endures to eternal life' ... We are here in order to profess, together with the whole Church, our faith in Christ the Eucharist, in Christ the living bread and the bread of life ... Along with physical hunger man has within him another hunger, a more basic hunger, which cannot be satisfied by ordinary food. It is a hunger for life, a hunger for eternity. The sign of the manna was the proclamation of the coming of Christ who was to satisfy man's hunger for eternity by Himself becoming the 'living bread' which 'gives life to the world'. And see: those who heard Jesus ask Him to fulfil what had been proclaimed by the sign of the manna, perhaps without being conscious of how far their request would go: 'Lord, give us this bread always' (Jn 6:34). How eloquent is this request! How generous and how amazing its fulfilment! ... Now, on the threshold of the Third Millennium, we wish to give a particular expression to our gratitude.

> This Eucharistic Congress in Wroclaw has an international dimension. Taking part in it are not only the faithful of Poland, but faithful from throughout the world. Together we all want to express our deep faith in the Eucharist and

our fervent gratitude for the Eucharistic food which for almost two thousand years has nourished whole generations of believers in Christ. How inexhaustible and available to all is the treasury of God's love! How enormous is our debt to Christ the Eucharist!

The following day, Sunday 1 June, the Congress reached its high point: the Statio Orbis, with the Church in every continent of the globe spiritually gathered around the Congress open-air altar in the centre of Wrocław, in front of the Hotel Wrocław. The weather had turned bad again, with a cold wind and steady rain. In his homily, Pope John Paul again situated the Congress within the preparations for the Third Millennium and the fall of Communism.

This Congress is part and parcel of the context of the Great Jubilee of the Year 2000. In the programme of spiritual preparation for the Jubilee, this year is dedicated to special contemplation of the Person of Jesus Christ: 'Jesus Christ, the one Saviour of the world, yesterday, today and forever' (cf Heb 13:8). So could this year have lacked this Eucharistic profession of faith by the whole Church? In the series of Eucharistic Congresses which crosses every continent, it is now the turn of Wrocław—Poland and east central Europe. The changes that have taken place here have begun a new era in the history of the modern world. The Church in this way wishes to give thanks to Christ for the gift of freedom regained by all those nations that have suffered so much in the years of totalitarian oppression. The Congress is taking place in Wrocław, a city rich in history, tradition and Christian life. The Archdiocese of Wrocław is getting ready to celebrate its millennium. Wroclaw is a city situated practically at the meeting point of three lands which through their history are very closely united to one another. It is, as it were, a city of encounter, a city that unites. Here there meet in a certain way the spiritual traditions of East and West. All of this gives a particular eloquence to this Eucharistic Congress, and especially to this Statio Orbis. My eyes and heart embrace the whole of our great Eucharistic community, the character of which is authentically international, worldwide. Through her representatives, the universal Church is present today at Wrocław.

The Holy Father then meditated on the Last Supper and chapter six of St John's Gospel, before facing one of the pressing problems of the day.

During this Statio Orbis we need to recall the whole 'geography of hunger', which includes many areas of the world. At this moment many millions of our brothers and sisters are suffering from hunger, and many are dying of it—especially children! In an age of unprecedented development, of advanced systems and technology, the tragedy of hunger is a great challenge and a great indictment! The earth is capable of feeding everyone. Why then today, at the end of the twentieth century, are thousands of people dying of hunger? There is needed here a serious and worldwide examination of conscience—an examination of conscience regarding social justice, elementary solidarity among human beings.

We do well to recall here the fundamental truth that the earth belongs to God, and all the riches it contains have been placed by God in man's hands, to use them in the right way, so that they can serve the good of all. This is the purpose of created goods. The very law of nature bears testimony to this. During this Eucharistic Congress there cannot fail to be a joint invocation for bread in the name of all who are suffering from hunger. We address it first of all to God, who is Father of all: 'Give us this day our daily bread'! But we make it also to the politicians and economists, upon whom rests responsibility for a just distribution of goods, on both the worldwide and the national levels: we must finally put an end to the scourge of hunger! May solidarity prevail over the unrestrained desire for profit and ways of applying trade laws which do not take into account inalienable human rights. Upon each one of us there rests a small part of responsibility for this injustice. Each of us in some way has firsthand experience of the hunger and poverty of others. Let us learn to share our bread with those who have none, or who have less than we do! Let us learn how to open our hearts to the needs of our brothers and sisters who are suffering because of poverty and neglect! ... This is also the lesson taught to us by the Eucharist, the bread of life.

Finally, Pope John Paul addressed the overall theme of the Congress.

Freedom has a flavour all its own, especially here in this part of Europe, which for many long years was sorely tried by being deprived of freedom under Nazi and Communist totalitarianism. The very word 'freedom' now makes the heart beat faster. And this is certainly the case because during the past decades a high price had to be paid for freedom. Deep are the wounds that remain in the human spirit from that period. Much time must yet pass before they will be completely healed. The Congress exhorts us to look at human freedom from a Eucharistic perspective. In the Congress hymn we sing: 'You have left us the gift of the Eucharist to re-order inner freedom'. This is a most essential affirmation. We speak here of the 'order of freedom'. Yes, true freedom demands order. But what kind of order are we talking about here? We are talking first of all about the moral order, order in the sphere of values, the order of truth and goodness. When there is a void in the area of values—when chaos and confusion reign in the moral sphere—freedom dies, man is reduced from freedom to slavery, becoming a slave to instincts, passions and pseudo-values.

It is true that building the order of freedom demands hard work. True freedom always costs dear! We each have to keep making this effort. And here arises the following question: can man build the order of freedom by himself, without Christ, or even against Christ? This is an exceedingly important question, but how relevant it is in a social context permeated by ideas of democracy inspired by liberal ideology! In fact, attempts are being made to convince man and whole societies that God is an obstacle on the path to full freedom, that the Church is the enemy of freedom, that she does not understand freedom, that she is afraid of it. This is an unprecedented falsification of the truth!

The Church never ceases to be in the world the proclaimer of the gospel of freedom! This is her mission. 'For freedom Christ has set us free' (Ga 5:1). For this reason, a Christian is not afraid of freedom, nor does he flee from it! He takes it up in a creative and responsible way as the task of his life. Freedom, in fact, is not just a gift of God; it is also given to us as a task! It is our vocation: 'For you were called to freedom, brethren' (Gal 5:13), the Apostle reminds us ... Modelled on the Eucharist, in what does this order of freedom consist? In the Eucharist Christ is present as the one who gives Himself to man, as the one who serves: 'having loved His own ... He loved them to the end' (Jn 13:1). True freedom is measured by readiness to serve and by the gift of self. Only when it is understood in this way is freedom truly creative, only then does it build up our humanity and create interhuman bonds. It builds and does not divide! How much the world, Europe and Poland need this freedom that unites!

Pope John Paul's peroration was heartfelt and stirring.

The Eucharistic Christ will ever remain an unattainable model of the 'pro-existence' attitude, that is to say the attitude of the person who lives for others. He lived completely for His Heavenly Father, and in the Father He lived for every individual person. The Second Vatican Council explains that man finds himself, and therefore also the full meaning of his freedom, precisely 'through a sincere gift of self' (cf *Gaudium et Spes* 24). Today, during this Statio Orbis, the Church invites us to enter this Eucharistic school of freedom, so that gazing at the Eucharist with the eyes of faith we will become builders of a new, evangelical order of freedom—deep within our-

selves and within the societies in which we live and work
... What great value man has in the eyes of God, if God
feeds him with His Body! What vast spaces the human
heart conceals within itself if they can be filled only by God!

From Wrocław Pope John Paul continued his Polish visit, to
Gniezno to take part in the commemorations for the millennial
commemoration of the martyrdom of St Adalbert in 997, then on
to Potsdam, Jasna Gora, Zakopane and Cracow. Our party left too,
visiting Auschwitz, Jasna Gora, Nowa Huta, Wadowice (where
Karol Wojtyla was born and grew up), Kalvaria Zebrzydowska and
Cracow. Kalvaria had a special place in Karol Wojtyla's early life.
His mother died when he was only eight years old. It is recorded
that his father took him on pilgrimage to Kalvaria and there, in
front of the icon of Our Lady, told him that she would be his
mother now. Later, as Pope, John Paul II made several visits to
Kalvaria, repeating there the words of his motto: *'Totus tuus ego
sum, et omnia mea tua sunt. Accipio te in mea omnia. Praebe mihi
cor tuum, Maria.'* ('I belong entirely to you, and all that I have is
yours. I take you for my all. O Mary, give me your heart').

The Wrocław Congress brought home to us pilgrims the deep
devotion of the Polish people to the Blessed Sacrament; their
kindness and hospitality, as personally experienced from the Blaiha
family; their noble culture; and the fun and joy of their youth.

References

1) Pontifical Committee for International Eucharistic Congresses, *The Eucharist and Freedom, Basic Text for the 46th International Eucharistic Congress, Wrocław, Poland 1997,* published in weekly English edition of L'Osservatore Romano 3 November 1996.

2) Allen, J. F., Personal notes and diaries.

3) Cervera, J. C., in La Nuova Alleanza, pp. 27ff, January 1996.

4) Gulbinowicz, Cardinal H., Pontifical Committee for IEC, *Address to National Delegates,* May 1995.

5) Janiak, E., Deren, A., Francuz, M., *For freedom, Christ has set us free. Texts of the 46th International Eucharistic Congress* (Wrocław 2000).

6) *In Christ's Freedom,* Adoremus 1996, No.2, pp. 4–15.

7) Pratzner, F., in Cenacolo, March 1997, pp. 12–15.

8) *Talks at the Eucharistic Congress,* Adoremus 1997, No.2, pp 4–20 and 1998, No.1, pp. 4–22.

9 ROME 18–25 JUNE 2000
JESUS CHRIST THE ONLY SAVIOUR OF THE WORLD, BREAD FOR NEW LIFE

'AND SO WE came to Rome' (Ac 28:14). Paul had appealed to Caesar. His epic, storm-filled journey from Palestine to Italy, under guard from a Roman soldier, is recounted in the Acts of the Apostles. It took several months and included a shipwreck off Malta. Speaking at his trial before King Agrippa, Paul had recounted his vision on the road to Damascus, and how the Lord Jesus had told him to

> get up and stand on your feet, for I have appeared to you for this reason: to appoint you as My servant and as witness of this vision in which you have seen Me, and of others in which I shall appear to you. I shall rescue you from the people and from the nations to whom I send you to open their eyes, so that they may turn from darkness to light, from the dominion of Satan to God, and receive, through faith in Me, forgiveness of their sins and a share in the inheritance of the sanctified.

Paul then proclaimed the mission of Christ:

> I was blessed with God's help, and so I have stood firm to this day, testifying to great and small alike, saying nothing more than what the prophets and Moses himself said would happen: that the Christ was to suffer and that, as the first to rise from the dead, He was to proclaim a light for our people and for the gentiles.

Nearly 2000 years later, we too came to Rome, to celebrate the International Eucharistic Congress—the third to be held in Rome and the first ever in a Jubilee Year—and to proclaim that same saving mission of Jesus Christ, as set out in the Congress theme: 'Jesus Christ, the only Saviour of the world, Bread for New Life'.

On Trinity Sunday, 18 June, a riot of colour cascaded through the streets of Rome, as people from all over the world converged on St Peter's Square, with Africans, Bangladeshis and Koreans especially in brilliant array. As Rome's bells pealed out over the city, 30,000 members of confraternities and sodalities came from different parts of Italy, laden beneath their processional 'cars' all adorned with flowers. Five hundred arrived with their 'Pasos' (floats) from Spanish Granada, while seventy national delegations were led by their respective bishops. Looking out over the assembly, with the sun declining in an azure sky behind the great basilica, Pope St John Paul II opened the forty-seventh International Eucharistic Congress, inviting those present to bend their knees 'in thoughtful adoration' before the mystery of Christ present in the Eucharist. Quoting St Paul, the Pope reminded us that 'There is one body and one Spirit, just as you were called to the one hope that belongs to your call' (Ep 4:4):

> At the Last Supper, Jesus, who was born of the Virgin Mary 2,000 years ago, wanted to leave us His Body and Blood, sacrificed for all humanity. The Church, His Mystical Body, gathers round the Eucharist, the sacrament of His love for us. See: Christ and the Church, one Body, one great mystery! The mystery of faith! ... In the heart of the Great Jubilee and at the beginning of this week dedicated to the Eucharistic Congress, we return to that historic event which marked the fulfilment of our salvation ... In the days ahead, it will be in the Upper Room especially that we will pause to reflect on what Christ Jesus did and suffered for us. At the Last Supper, while celebrating the Passover with His disciples, Christ offered Himself for us. Yes, gathered for the International Eucharistic Congress, the Church returns in these days to the Upper Room and remains there in thoughtful adoration ...

> The Apostle Paul speaks of the Church, the community of believers gathered together in the unity of one body, enlivened by the same Spirit and sustained by sharing the same hope. Paul is thinking of the reality of Christ's

Mystical Body, which finds in His Eucharistic Body its own vital centre from which the energy of grace flows to all its members. The Apostle says: 'The Bread which we break, is it not a participation in the Body of Christ? Because there is one Bread, we who are many are one Body, for we all partake of the one Bread' (1 Co 10: 16–17). Thus all of the baptised become members of that Body and therefore individually members of one another.

As so often, Pope John Paul ended with a plea for the unity of Christians.

The Eucharistic Congress also invites us to renew our faith in the real presence of Christ in the sacrament of the altar: *Ave, verum Corpus!* At the same time, we receive the urgent appeal for the reconciliation and unity of all believers: 'one Body ... one faith, one baptism'! Divisions and disagreements still rend the Body of Christ and prevent Christians of different confessions from sharing the one Eucharistic Bread. Therefore, let us pray together for the healing power of divine mercy, which is superabundant in this Jubilee Year.

The following morning, continuous Eucharistic adoration began in certain churches in all five parts of the Diocese of Rome. Cardinal Camillo Ruini, Vicar General of the Diocese, presided at the first Mass of the Congress in Rome's Cathedral of St John Lateran. He reminded us that, though often known by that name, the Cathedral's full dedication is to 'the Most Holy Saviour and St John the Baptist and St John the Evangelist'. As such, the title was very relevant to the Congress theme of 'Jesus Christ, the only Saviour of the world, Bread for New Life'. 'The connection between the Eucharist and life is essential,' said Cardinal Ruini, 'as is the connection between the Last Supper and the Cross and the Resurrection. The Eucharist invites us to be holy.' In the days that followed, many of the main sessions of the Congress were held here in Rome's cathedral church.

When Mass was over we listened to representatives of all five continents reporting on the state of Eucharistic devotion in their territories: 'a breath of universality, of catholicity, in the deep unity expressed and realised in the Eucharistic mystery', Cardinal Ruini called it.

Bishop Peter Sarpong, Bishop of Kumasi in Ghana, opened the proceedings unpromisingly with the sentence: 'Africa has many problems.' He recalled how the world 'is aware how time and time again Africa has to face terrible ethnic conflicts that result in untold hardships and misery for thousands of people.' He quoted Pope St John Paul II who had also spoken of 'famine, epidemics and destruction, not to mention massacres, scandals and trage- dies of refugees' that marred the face of Africa. The Pope had encouraged the Church in Africa to aim at building up the Church as Family of God. This was an expression of the nature of the Church 'particularly appropriate for Africa. For this image emphasises care for others, solidarity, warmth in human relation- ships, acceptance, dialogue and trust.' Bishop Sarpong then contrasted 'ethnocentrism' with 'ethnicity':

> Ethnocentrism is a deadly phenomenon. It denies the very assistance of other people. It is inward looking and turns to create divisions and hostilities. It exaggerates and, in the process, negates the values of ethnicity. Ethnicity is a gift from God. It legitimately acknowledges one's roots. It gives dignity and honour to one. It provides a point of reference, of refuge and of acceptance for the human being. But it accepts the humanity of others and respects it.

The Bishop showed how the Eucharist, considered under various aspects, overcame divisions: as covenant; as communal meal; as reconciliation; and through the Kingship of Christ:

> In Africa, many societies have what are called *blood-pacts*. A person enters into a blood-covenant with another person and becomes more closely associated with him than with his own natural relatives, father, mother, brother or sister. This person will do everything for his blood-partner,

including laying down his life. The description of the Eucharist as a covenant of the New Testament therefore means something weighty and comprehensible to the African. 'This is the Cup of the new and everlasting Covenant. It will be shed for you and for all so that sin may be forgiven.' We Africans understand the offering of blood and of serious covenants ...

Africans also have a wonderful appreciation for and give great premium to communal eating, coming together to share a meal. To refuse to eat with somebody is tantamount to declaring yourself his enemy. Therefore, for the African the common celebration of the Eucharist is the powerful sign, the ritual anticipation and the sacramental preparation for the eating and drinking at Jesus' table in the Kingdom ... By giving His own Body and Blood for our food, the African appreciates how Jesus demonstrates a love that can never be equalled. Through that food, the African knows that Jesus unites us, for 'to eat from the same bowl is to be in a cordial relationship that is strong, genuine and life-saving' ...

The African appreciates reconciliation. The African knows the value of helping one another to bear our problems. Hence for the African the Eucharistic assembly is a pledge of the coming Kingdom, because it is here and now a sign of the present growth of the Kingdom. This Kingdom of God comes into being wherever and whenever men accept one another as Christ accepted us; wherever men bear one another's burdens as Christ bore ours. The Kingdom thrives on forgiveness and mutual understanding. Most African societies have institutionalised ritual means of effecting forgiveness and reconciliation, and for us true forgiveness means forgetting what has happened. The Asante would say 'after vomiting there is no nausea'. African Catholics see the Eucharist playing the role even more perfectly ...

The Eucharist also plays yet another significant role in the life of the African Catholic. Africans have special respect for authority, the sacred and the aged. They pay special reverence to their leaders. For them the Eucharist provides a concrete social symbol of a God to be adored and praised. Among my people, the Eucharist, on the feast of Christ the King, is presented as a King and treated as if we were seeing the King in flesh and blood. The Eucharist then becomes the medium of encountering our King in a special way ...

The Eucharist, like the food we cherish so much, is for the African the strength of our life and of our character, and the meal of salvation. We believe that it is only through the Eucharist, this powerful source and symbol of unity, that Africa can continue confidently to construct the Kingdom of peace, of justice, of unity, of grace, of humility, of mercy which Pope Paul VI has called the 'Civilisation of Love'.

Archbishop Agnelo Geraldo Majella of San Salvador da Bahia in Brazil followed, speaking for South America, and recalling how many of the faithful living in the rural villages in his vast country would walk for miles to take part in the Sunday Eucharist. The Mass was for them the inspiration for their lives. In the cities also, where people could be anonymous and marginalised, the Eucharist strengthened them to trust God, 'Who walks with His people, and never abandons them'.

'Several thousand miles—and a variety of cultures—separate the Churches of Asia from the See of Peter, but we take great comfort from its interest in our endeavours to "draw all to the Bread of Life".' So began Archbishop Diosdado Talamayan of Tuguegarao in the Philippines. Asia too had its problems:

Corruption is endemic in many societies of Asia, up to the highest levels of officialdom, and it can hardly be denied that there is a direct relation between corruption and the abject poverty of most Asian countries. While talent and native ability are by no means wanting or in short supply, opportunities are severely limited ... Asia has traditionally been the home to many of the world's great religions. In different forms these religions continue to survive. In countries where Christianity, particularly the Catholic

Church, has taken root, we see bountiful harvest of the
Spirit, if not in the number of converts, then certainly in
the fervour and ardour of the members of the Church ...
Because of the economic and political profile of Asia, many
of the Asian Churches have explicated the Church's
'option for the poor' and have been directly involved in the
struggle for justice and for the respect and recognition of
human rights and fundamental liberties.

The Archbishop gave a brief account of the Eucharist as celebrated and lived in Korea, Japan, China, the Philippines, Malaysia,
Indonesia, Sri Lanka, Bengal, Pakistan and India. He concluded:

The peoples of Asia rejoice in the great gift that is the
Eucharist. In their struggle for dignity and the vindication
of their rights, they draw strength and inspiration from it.
In their aspiration for a just society, they take their bearings
from it. They are inspired by the knowledge that divergent
though cultures may be, their brothers and sisters stand
around the same Table, sharing the same Bread and partak-
ing of the same Cup. Though true to their traditions and
proud of their rich cultural heritage, they pray for the unity
of the one Body of Christ that manifests itself in the unity
of one Family gathered around the Table of the Lord.

Archbishop Sigitas Tamkevicius of Kaunas in Lithuania spoke
for Europe—more precisely, for those countries recently liberated
from Communist government and oppression. He recalled how,
along with millions of Catholics in the Soviet Union and Eastern
Europe, they had suffered persecution because of their faith. It
had been a 'practical genocide of the nation and of the Church',
with massive deportations, arrests and massacres. Churches had
been closed, hundreds of priests who would not collaborate with
the Communist power had been imprisoned. The Government
did all it could to separate the local Church from Rome and to
destroy its influence on believers.

Priests were persecuted for preparing children for their
first Communion. The powerful Communist rulers, with

their missiles and atomic bombs, were scared of the religious practice of children and their closeness to the Eucharist. Given that parents were unable to prepare their children for the sacrament of penance and their first Communion, that was done by a large number of priests who risked losing their liberty. Fr Joseph Zdebskis was up before the judge for a second time for preparing children for their first Communion. When the judge asked him why he did not keep the law forbidding the teaching of the faith to children, he answered with the words of the apostle Peter: 'We must listen to God and not to men.'

Fr Zdebskis was offered his freedom if he would simply say that he had made a mistake. He declined, so that people would realise the importance of preparing children in the spiritual life and see that the meeting with Christ in the Eucharist was the most important moment in the life of children. He, and other priests like him, were then able to minister to prisoners of conscience exiled in Siberia, as well as to Lithuanian soldiers serving in the Soviet army.

In the 1970s Sister Edwige Stanelyte formed a 'Union of Friends of the Eucharist'. The Soviet authorities looked on this Union as a powerful enemy and imprisoned her, but this could not stop the Eucharistic movement which renewed the spiritual life of very many people. Fr Zdebskis continued:

In 1983 I was arrested for publishing 'Chronicles of the Catholic Church in Lithuania'. The first part of my imprisonment, before being judged, was passed in the KBG prison. Detained there with me were thousands of believers and hundreds of priests and some bishops: Metchislovas Reinys, Vincent Bonsevicius and Theophile Matulionis whose causes of beatification have been opened. My brightest memory of that difficult time is of the sacrifice of the Mass offered in the prison cell. When I celebrated Mass there for the first time, it seemed to me that I had not experienced such a joy since the day of my first Mass. I don't know how the Lord felt upon my 'altar' set in the cupboard of the prison and with a plastic cup instead of a chalice, but I felt wonderfully well. The Eucharist came with me in my deportation and never allowed me to be tempted to be released ... To those who ask me today how to learn to respect the Eucharist, I reply with a smile that the Soviet prison is very useful for that ... For many Catholic Lithuanians, the years of persecution were not years of abandonment by God but a gift of our Father in heaven. We recovered our freedom ten years ago and it has given believers the possibility of publicly practising their faith and taking part in Sunday Mass. Nevertheless, this has not strengthened our faith. I often sadly notice a lack of respect for the Eucharist in the life of energetic priests who toil at the works of God but forget the God living in the Eucharist. I confess that I often look back wistfully to those difficult days when persecution purified the faith of people. All the same, I note a renewal of respect and attention of the people for the Eucharist ... Preparing for this Eucharistic Congress has rekindled the religious life of many believers.

'The history of the Catholic Church in Australia is centred on the celebration of the Eucharist. This reflects efforts of the priests, bishops and parish communities to provide, often at great personal sacrifice, the presence of the Eucharist in every parish, even in the most distant parts.' So Bishop Barry Collins of Willcannia Forbes in New South Wales began his report on Australia. Given the geographic size and isolation of the country, it was decided that the emphasis during the Year of the Jubilee would be mainly at the diocesan and parish level. Nevertheless, a number of national celebrations were held, including 'Journey to the Heart', a day of prayer and reconciliation with a pilgrimage from the capital Canberra to Uluru, known also as Ayers Rock, in the centre of the continent, a place held in veneration by the Aboriginal people as an especially sacred site.

In recent years, with the reduction in the number of clergy, there has been a reduction in the number of places able to celebrate weekly and daily Masses ... In many a diocese and parish, this year has been celebrated by the development of Eucharistic ceremonies such as Holy Hours, times of adoration and the celebration of Benediction. These are nationwide and therefore too difficult either to number or document. Diocesan newspapers and parish bulletins are being used by bishops and parish priests to emphasise the importance and the reality of the Eucharist and to encourage a devotion to the Mass and the Eucharist outside of the Mass.

Bishop Collins ended by saying that 'in the other nations of the Pacific or Oceania similar celebrations are taking place which will enhance the importance of and devotion to the Eucharist in our Church'.

That rapid overview from the five continents did provide that 'breath of universality, of catholicity' Cardinal Ruini had described in his introduction. In a small way, I shared in that overview. With Fr Kevin Cull, a priest friend from the Hamilton diocese in Ontario, I stayed in the Canadian College in Via Crescenzio for the duration of the Congress. There, we gained an insight into the Canadian Church, thanks particularly to Mgr Emilius Goulet, the then rector, and Mgr Marc Ouellet, then in residence.

'Too good to be true'

Monday 20 June saw the first public catechesis of the Congress on the theme 'The Eucharist, presence of Christ among us', given by Cardinal Francis George, Archbishop of Chicago. Some years previously, he said, a man had told him that the Christian gospel was 'too good to be true'.

I have thought of this man and prayed for him in the years since that conversation. I do not know if he ever came to believe in the God revealed through Jesus Christ, but what he said was correct. It's too good to be true, except for those whose hearts and souls and minds have been somehow touched and moved by a God Who loves us more than we could ever love ourselves, Who is closer to us than we are to ourselves.

'The Word became flesh and dwelt among us.' The Prologue of the Gospel according to St John proclaims that the Eternal Logos, the only begotten Son of God, chose to enter into the very heart of God's temporal creation so that everything can be a sign and invitation to enter into the communal love of God's Trinitarian life. Jesus Christ, our Saviour, does not stand apart from creation. He enters into its very life so that all God has accomplished can be seen to exist for the sake of our salvation. Too good to be true? Yes, except for those who, with the eyes of faith, see the world as Christ sees it.

The Scriptures also tell us that the one born of the Virgin Mary, suffered, died, and is now risen ... He is perfectly free. The Risen Lord is, therefore, free to keep his promise to His disciples: 'I will be with you always, until the end of the world.' The Risen Lord will never abandon His people. Those who find their personal identity in relation to Him will never be alone or abandoned. How could they be? The Risen Lord is wherever He wills to be. Having assumed human nature as the new Adam, He now fills the cosmos as Risen Lord. Too good to be true? Yes, unless one's aspirations have been transformed by the hope of glory in which the Risen Lord lives and which He offers to us.

Jesus, the Risen Lord, does not act alone. He has established the Church as a community of believers, to be 'the means for God's saving love to transform all creation'. He continues to work through the sacraments.

Each of the sacraments is an action of the Risen Christ, gathering with His Body, the Church. In a unique fashion, the Eucharist is both the action and the abiding presence of the Lord. In the Eucharist, Christ gives Himself as food for our journey, as our daily bread, as a banquet, which brings us together as pilgrims. Christ never comes to us alone. Christ comes to us with the Father and the Holy

Spirit. Mary, the mother of Christ and our mother, accompanies her Son. All the angels and the saints, who have gone before us in faith, together with the souls in purgatory, join in the great communion. Moreover, all those who are the visible Body of Christ throughout the world today are united in the divine gift of love. We therefore never go to Jesus alone. In the Eucharist, we are most clearly members of a Body, living stones of a temple, a gathered people of God. Too good to be true? Yes, except for those whose hearts have been turned inside out by the unity given to those who know they are loved by God and who have come to sense their unity with the many, who are brothers and sisters of the Risen Lord.

The Cardinal then considered the Eucharist in the life and thought of the Church. Christ is truly present in the Eucharist. As described in chapter six of St John's Gospel, Jesus made no attempt to soften His language in the face of His disciples' confusion.

The Eucharistic realism was clearly understood and accepted by the apostolic Church. By sharing in the real, sacrificed, and risen flesh of Christ and in His blood shed on the cross, the Church becomes a living body. Not a body in an organisational or sociological sense: the Church becomes a real body, brought into existence by the Eucharist (1 Co 10:16 ff). In St Cyril of Alexandria's words, precisely through the Eucharist, through 'eating the flesh of Christ', we are made into a 'living flesh'. Cyril's realism even compares the union between Christ and the recipient of the Eucharist to a fusion of two globs of sealing wax. Christ desires to be as close to us as nourishment is to our bones ...

This inseparable link between Eucharistic realism and ecclesial union gives rise to the great Patristic vision of the Eucharist as the bond of charity, unity and peace, those signs of an authentic civilisation of love. St Augustine in particular placed strong emphasis on this 'social' function of the Eucharist, 'social' in the sense that the bond of love, unity and peace among the baptised is a participation in the *communio* of the Trinitarian life of God ... The Eucharist discloses the divine *communio* of Trinitarian love and invites our participation. In this sense, it is a perpetual proclamation of God's transcendence and power, manifest most fully in the life, death and resurrection of Jesus Christ the Lord (Ph 2: 6–11). This is true both when the Eucharistic liturgy is being celebrated and breaks the limits of time and history, and also when the Eucharist is in the tabernacle, where the drama of salvation is not immediately being re-enacted, but where Christ is still present for our contemplation and prayer. St Thomas expresses this contemplative dimension of the Eucharist in a phrase redolent of Aristotle: 'It is the law of friendship that friends should live together' (*Summa theologiae* III q75 a1). That is why devotion to the Eucharist, apart from the Eucharistic liturgy itself, is an indispensable element of Catholic spirituality. It is also why all devotional life should, in some way, be linked to the Eucharist.

Cardinal George ended by describing the action of the Holy Spirit in the Eucharistic liturgy, giving the liturgy its 'profound, evangelical depth'. 'We live more and more in a globalised society. In economics and politics, in culture and communication, the human race is more connected than ever before. But a connection is not necessarily a personal relationship.' This is where the Eucharist can be 'the sacrament of the unity of the human race'.

Jean Vanier, founder of the International Federation 'L'Arche', followed the Cardinal with a most moving personal testimony, not easy to transcribe here. L'Arche, now present in 37 countries, is for people with disabilities and those who care for them. Vanier regards people with disabilities not so much as burdens but as our teachers, because in them we see Christ Himself. We think that Jesus loves us because we are good. There are handicaps that we can see but also handicaps inside us: difficulties in forgiving, in sharing. We are doubly poor.

I see the tears in Jesus' eyes. It's here that He reveals His secret: 'The one who eats my flesh and drinks my blood

has eternal life.' What vulnerability! According to St
Thomas [Aquinas], friendship is to stay with one another.
Friendship is vulnerability. In Jesus, God makes Himself
vulnerable, hidden, eatable: mystery of the Incarnation,
mystery of the Eucharist ... The Eucharist is the mystery
of the hidden God who wants to live with the suffering
people of the world ... We must make spaces where Jesus
lives to comfort, to dry tears, in prisons, in psychiatric
centres. It is very important that there are these places
where Jesus can live, He Who has said: 'Come to Me, and
I will give you rest.'

In the decade before the year 2000, the city of Rome and the
Vatican had been preparing for the Jubilee Year. Billions of lire
were spent on public works: the cleaning of hundreds of buildings, restoration of monuments and archaeological sites and
churches, the updating of museums. The result was a Rome
gleaming in white marble and more welcoming to the visitor,
since new railway and metro lines had been built, buses were
more disability and environmentally friendly and better parking
for motor vehicles was available near the Vatican. The façade of
St Peter's, under scaffolding for many months, shone resplend-
ently in the Roman sun now that centuries of grime had been
removed. Here, on the Wednesday morning of 21 June, Pope St
John Paul II gave his first catechesis since opening the Congress.
Speaking firmly at the weekly audience just one month after his
eightieth birthday, but showing signs of his illness, he described
the Eucharist as the source of the Church's missionary work.

That evening we went out to St Paul's outside the Walls, where
Cardinal Jozef Tomko, Prefect of the Congregation for the
Evangelisation of Peoples, recalled his visit earlier in the year to
northern Kenya. There he had met a missionary from Sudan who
had come from a camp catering for refugees from Ethiopia and
Somalia, a vast area suffering from drought and famine. The
missionary told him that when he had distributed all the food he
had been given the people asked him: 'Father, speak to us of God'!

The Cardinal identified a double hunger among people: 'hunger of the body, hunger of the spirit'. It was a world problem that in a century of progress millions of people were suffering from over-eating and obesity while other millions were dying from lack of a piece of bread or grain of rice. The Eucharist, 'Bread broken and divided for the life of the human race', satisfied our hunger for God and also brought with it 'the sharing of bread and material goods, because such is the spirit and the law of the love of Christ, the Bread of life'. Along with Christ, missionaries took his love of brotherhood, solidarity, charity—to satisfy both spiritual and corporal hunger.

Jesus had described the Eucharistic Bread as His flesh, given for the life of the world. Yet in today's world only 30% of people are Christians, 18% Catholics.

> Given this situation, the Holy Father's observation seems most realistic: 'The mission of Christ the Redeemer, which is entrusted to the Church, is still very far from completion.... this mission is still only beginning ... we must commit ourselves wholeheartedly to its service ... When we consider this immense portion of humanity which is loved by the Father and for whom He sent His Son, the urgency of the Church's mission is obvious' (*Redemptoris Missio* 1,3) ... The best result [of this Jubilee Year] must be a renewal of our missionary pledge. The final command [at Mass] of *Ite, Missa est!* (Go, the Mass is ended) must mean and really become *Ite, Missio est!* (Go, this is your Mission).

Cardinal Tomko's address had a special resonance, delivered as it was beside the tomb of St Paul, Apostle of the Gentiles.

The Eucharist and human culture

Thursday 22 June was the solemnity of Corpus Christi. That morning, in the Basilica of St John Lateran, Cardinal Jean Marie Lustiger, Archbishop of Paris and Member of the Pontifical Council of Culture, gave the second public catechesis, with the theme, 'The Eucharist, source of culture'. But what is culture?

The twentieth century favoured a narrow approach to culture, identifying culture with what human beings have created and which may be preserved in museums. Cardinal Lustiger demurred:

> This account of the notion of culture does not exhaust its richness. John Paul II, who set up the Pontifical Council of Culture on 20 May 1982, stated in Paris: 'In the cultural field, man is always the first fact: man is the prime and fundamental fact of culture' (Discourse at UNESCO, 2 June 1980). [The Pope's next sentence, not quoted by Cardinal Lustiger but filling out his meaning, was: 'And he is so, always, in his totality: in his spiritual and material subjectivity as a complete whole.'] Man, the Son of Man, is the source of culture in His Eucharist, in His Passover.

The Cardinal then approached his theme by reflecting on the liturgy of Holy Thursday. A convert to Catholicism, he made no reference here to his Jewishness. However, his insight into that Passover meal in the Upper Room at Jerusalem was compelling.

> In considering the Eucharist as the source of culture, we get a more vivid vision still of the events of our spiritual history. This enables us to recognise that the notion of sacrifice has deep roots in human cultures; in our century this notion has tended to be misunderstood ... The love that Jesus gives in the sacrifice of offering His life frees us from our sins. In becoming our nourishment, this love calls us to be eager to carry out the same loving offering, here and now, two thousand years away, in the circumstances in which the Lord has placed us. In offering our lives with His, we unite with the Risen Christ, who continues to give His life in the Eucharist for the life of the world ... The cultural revolution required by the Eucharist consists in this: to transcribe into our human condition the supremacy and beauty of this charity of God.
>
> The Catholic liturgy of Holy Thursday adds only one rite to the normal Eucharistic celebration. It is the washing of feet ... Down the course of the centuries and across different cultures, the ritual of the washing of feet remains

a prophetic and, as it were, a sacramental sign of what Jesus accomplished once and for all during His mortal life, so that we may love one another with the love with which He has loved us. 'I have given you an example, so that you may copy what I have done to you' (Jn 13: 15). Obedience to this command of humility has not been without having its impact on the history of Christian practice: the service of the poor and of the common good, the wonderful discovery of serving the least—these are qualities making up a Christian culture. They are not restricted to only one epoch; they belong to all times in which a heart full of love encounters human misery ... The liturgy of Holy Thursday reminds us of this. The celebration of the Eucharist in all its breadth throughout the centuries faithfully carries out in its essential rites the words and gestures of Jesus. It is clear that these gestures pertain to *one* single story, that of Israel's two millennia, that of Jesus.

Cardinal Lustiger commented how 'today technical progress is bringing to birth a new culture: a culture of the image instantly transmitted. The world is rapidly moving towards uniformity.' But whatever the age may call 'culture' and store up in its museums 'can all fall down into the dust of death, unless transfigured by the Paschal light of sacrifice'. He finished by listing some of the characteristics of a culture nourished by the Eucharistic mystery:

> [Among other things, such a culture] will ceaselessly tend towards overturning the order of values set up by human society: those distinctions between the powerful and weak, clever and ignorant, masters and slaves ... will value the gift of life ... will teach people to give thanks and enjoy the gifts that they do not cease receiving by turning towards God, our Creator and our Father ... will lead people to appreciate the Messianic mystery of salvation ... will initiate them into that divine compassion which is the source of communion among people that brings about respect and peace ... point out the beauty of the world,

since in all things there is the resplendent reflection of the glory of the invisible God Whose Image is revealed to us. But nothing of the world can suffice to express the unspeakable beauty of which the Eucharist is both the revelation and at the same time the veil.

The Cardinal's catechesis was followed by a testimony given by the Secretary of the Pontifical Council of Justice and Peace, Bishop Francis Xavier Nguyen Van Thuan, in which he described the thirteen years he was held captive by the Communist government in Vietnam, nine of those years spent in solitary confinement. He told a story of Eucharistic devotion and missionary zeal. He described how he was guarded by two policemen who never spoke to him. He was denied any visits from family; no radio or newspaper, telephone or TV. He had moments of despair: why had the Lord allowed this to happen to him, a young bishop, condemned without trial or sentence?

He was allowed to write a few lines to ask for clothes or toothpaste. He wrote asking for 'a little wine and medicine for his stomach'. His friends understood and sent the items in, labelled 'Medicine for the stomach'. His captors allowed him to have them, and so

> With my greatest joy, those Masses are the most beautiful of my life. I offered the sacrifice every morning in the palm of my hand, with three drops of wine and one of water. By doing that, every day I could tell the Lord of my new and eternal union as a priest.

Bishop Van Thuan described how he managed to give Communion to other Catholic prisoners; how he would smuggle a consecrated Host to other groups of prisoners who would then make a holy hour of adoration to sustain them in their trials; how he and the other prisoners would sing in low voices the hymns *Lauda Sion* and *Ave verum Corpus* and how much these hymns helped them, giving them courage and even enabling the laymen to instruct and baptise others in the prison. 'With the Eucharist, prison is changed. It becomes a school of faith and catechesis.' The Bishop held up for us the small wooden cross he had made from some wood in the prison and which he now wore as his pectoral cross, along with the 'chain' to carry it which he had managed to make out of a piece of electric wire. It was a truly charged moment! Bishop Van Thuan was made a cardinal in 2001 but died of cancer a year later in Rome. The cause of his beatification was opened five years after his death.

That Thursday evening, many thousands had gathered in front of the Basilica of St John Lateran for the Holy Father's Mass, concelebrated with thirty-eight Cardinals, over two hundred Bishops and more than a thousand priests from Rome and every corner of the world. In a short homily, the Pope spoke of the institution of the Eucharist, the sacrifice of Melchizedek and the multiplication of loaves.

> This is an amazing miracle which marks in a way the beginning of a long historical process: the uninterrupted multiplication in the Church of the Bread of new life for the people of every race and culture. This sacramental ministry is entrusted to the Apostles and to their successors. And they, faithful to the divine Master's command, never cease to break and distribute the Eucharistic Bread from generation to generation.

> The People of God receive it with devout participation. With this Bread of life, a remedy of immortality, countless saints and martyrs were nourished and from it drew the strength to resist even harsh and prolonged sufferings. They believed in the words that Jesus once spoke in Capernaum: 'I myself am the living bread come down from heaven. If anyone eats this bread, he will live forever' (Jn 6: 51) ... We would like to stay with Christ and for this reason we say to Him with Peter: 'Lord, to whom shall we go? You have the words of eternal life' (Jn 6: 68). With the same conviction as Peter, let us kneel today before the sacrament of the altar and renew our profession of faith in the real presence of Christ.

This is the meaning of today's celebration, which is given special emphasis by the International Eucharistic Congress in the year of the Great Jubilee. This is also the sense of the solemn procession which, as it does every year, will shortly make its way from this square to the Basilica of St Mary Major. With humble pride we will escort the Eucharistic Sacrament through the streets of the city, close by the buildings where people live, rejoice and suffer; between the shops and offices where they work each day. We will bring it into contact with our lives beset by a thousand dangers, weighed down by worries and sorrows, subject to the slow but inexorable wear and tear of time. As we escort Him, we will offer Him the tribute of our hymns and prayers.

Thousands of coloured flower petals, forming the logos of the Jubilee Year and of the Congress, had been arranged in the square in front of the Lateran. From there, as daylight faded, Pope St John Paul accompanied the Blessed Sacrament in procession to the Basilica of St Mary Major, along the Via Merulana thickly lined by Romans and visitors alike. Children walking in front of the Blessed Sacrament strewed flowers in its path. The Pope gave the final Benediction on the steps of the Basilica, with the beautiful thirteenth-century mosaics of the façade in the background. I went from there with retired Archbishop Couve de Murville of Birmingham to Da Mario's trattoria next to the Chiesa Nuova for a pizza. It was a pleasant end to a long but inspiring Corpus Christi day.

Eucharist and Reconciliation

On Friday 23 June we considered how, with the sacrifice of Christ, we are brought back to the love of the Father. At the Lateran, Cardinal Christoph Schonborn, Archbishop of Vienna, gave the third public catechesis on 'The Eucharist, conversion and reconciliation'. He set out his stall with great clarity in his opening words:

The Lord has given us in His Paschal Mystery two gifts of incomparable value: the *Eucharist* on the night before His Passion, and the *remission of sins* on the evening of the day of His Resurrection. Both gifts were put in the hands of the apostles in order that they might be enabled to carry on His mission: 'As the Father has sent me, even so I send you' (Jn 20:21). Both these gifts are from the beginning connected to the ministerial priesthood. Both spring from the most intimate centre of God's heart, from the heart of the Blessed Trinity, because both provide in holy signs, in sacramental signs, what God wishes to give to the world through His Son's mission, namely, the reconciliation of human beings with God in order that they may share His life—so that they may have eternal life (cf Jn 3:15–16).

Jesus came so that we may live, so that we may have life abundantly (cf Jn 10:10). God wants us to be happy. 'God, infinitely perfect and blessed in Himself,' created us so that we may share in His happiness (Catechism of the Catholic Church 1). In Him, happiness has its true meaning. He is our beatitude and without Him there is no joy. Separated and apart from Him, our life dries up like branches cut off from the vine (cf Jn 15:1–6).

Left to ourselves, we cannot attain such fulness of life with God. Sin blocks us off from God. It separates us even from one another.

For this reason, on Easter Sunday evening the risen Lord gave His disciples the most precious Paschal gift: the gift of forgiving sin in His name through the power of the Holy Spirit and the authority of God. He even endowed them with the authority to withhold absolution from sins where the right dispositions are lacking: 'If you retain the sins of any, they are retained' (Jn 20:23). Both the Eucharist and the Remission of sins are fruits of Jesus Christ's Passover, of His suffering, of His death and resurrection. But what is their relation to one another? ... In both sacraments God's love comes to meet us; God longs to give Himself to us, He wants to help and heal us ... But do we need to be reconciled? Are we irreconcilable? If we see how the practice of going to Confession has decreased (at least in some countries of Europe), we should ask ourselves if this has not something to do with the loss of a 'sense of sin'.

It can obviously be objected that the Sacrament of Reconciliation is strictly speaking necessary only for the situation of mortal sin, that is, for sins that indicate a real break in our relationship with God and the Church, and that can be overcome only through sacramental reconciliation with God (cf CCC 1856). 'Venial sins' do not necessarily require the Sacrament of Reconciliation in order to obtain forgiveness (cf CCC 1458, 1863) ... Why does the Church recommend that we regularly confess even our 'daily faults', our 'venial sins'? In the Catechism of the Catholic Church we can find the reason for this: 'Indeed regular confession of our venial sins helps us form our conscience, fight against evil tendencies, let ourselves be healed by Christ and progress in the life of the Spirit. By receiving more frequently through this sacrament the gift of the Father's mercy, we are spurred to be merciful as He is merciful' (cf Lk 6:36, CCC 1458).

The Cardinal based the connection between the two sacraments of the Eucharist and Reconciliation on the fact that God is holy and we are sinners. St Peter's reaction in coming face to face with the holiness and greatness of God was to say 'Depart from me, for I am a sinful man, Lord' (Lk 5:8).

This is constantly the experience of various people of the Bible. They see their own sinfulness in becoming aware of God's holiness. Before the Lord enters 'our house' in Communion, we also say in the words of the Roman centurion: 'Lord, I am not worthy that You should enter under my roof, but only say the word and my soul shall be healed' (cf Lk 7:6). The more we become aware of the One who comes to meet us in the Eucharist, the clearer becomes our sense of unworthiness ... The more profoundly we understand in faith how incredibly great is the compassion, mercy and love of Him who wants to give

Himself to us in the Eucharist, the greater must be our trust in Him ...

We recognise what sin is by looking on God's love. Only then are we struck by that 'sorrow of the soul' (CCC 1451) for not having responded to God's love, for having loved so little.

What irony it is that as sacramental confession declines in the West, public confessions proliferate!

Today a kind of public confession becomes ever more fashionable on television. In what are called 'talk shows', the most intimate concerns, conflicts, wounds become aired in public. It is not at all clear if this exhibitionism results in some form of healing. In the secrecy of the Sacrament of Reconciliation on the other hand, confession of our sins can be a decisive step towards healing. For this sacrament is not meant only to lay bare mistakes and sins, but to heal and transform our lives. As in all the sacraments, and above all in the Eucharist, so also in the Sacrament of Reconciliation, what is at stake is the bringing about of a true change and renewal of the person.

In the simplest words of *absolution*, something takes place that can be compared with the mystery of consecration in the Mass: during Mass through the simple words 'This is My Body, this is My Blood' such very ordinary and fragile elements as bread and wine become transformed into the substance of the real, risen and glorified Body of Christ. In the mystery of absolution, through the simple words 'I absolve you from your sins ...' the frail, broken, wounded and guilty person of a sinner becomes re-constituted; his flesh, soul and spirit become re-integrated into the whole glorified Body of Christ, into the Church. What Christ does for the *whole* Church, he does for every individual member of the Church ... Through the word of the forgiveness of sins that the priest pronounces with Jesus's authority—because only God can forgive sins—the sinner is *transformed*, renewed, becoming truly a *living* member of the Church and of the Body of Christ. Now we can approach again the Lord's table, to share in the festive banquet of those reconciled with Christ ...

We have perhaps regrettably lost sight of the fact that Communion, so to speak, requires preparation. Should this preparation always be by means of the Sacrament of Reconciliation? Certainly not, because strictly speaking this is necessary only if mortal sin separates us from God and the Church. But at the same time, experience shows that if we overly neglect Confession we run the risk of becoming accustomed to our 'little' mistakes and sins and, not being sensitive to these any more, our hearts become hardened and love grows cold. Jesus has shown the extent to which love grows cold in the parable of the Good Samaritan, where He describes the attitude of the priest and the Levite who pass by on the other side, casting a blind eye at the man struck down by brigands (cf Lk 10: 30–32). Jesus also gives the example of the wicked rich man who was insensitive to the plight of the poor Lazarus, who languished at his door covered with sores (cf Lk 16: 19–31) ... By means of both His Paschal gifts, the Remission of sins and the Eucharist, [the Lord] wants to make us 'missionaries of His love'.

Paola Bignardi, President of Italian Catholic Action, followed the Cardinal with a testimony on 'The Eucharist and Reconciliation: transformation of our life in love'. We are used to thinking of the change of bread and wine into the Body and Blood of Christ. But our lives too are changed when we come into contact with the Eucharist. We become aware of the love Christ freely gives us. If we entrust ourselves to this love, then

from having someone near us who loves us, believes in us, wants to be part of our lives, we know by experience the strength we receive to confront very difficult situations. Then we know that we find an unsuspected energy inside us, an extraordinary strength to stand up to the hardest things in life, to look evil in the face, to acknowledge our shortcomings, to recognise our sin ... At every Eucharist we experience a living encounter with a Person who wants to be with us every step of the way, so that we can fully be ourselves in freedom, in joy, in love.

Receiving and celebrating the Eucharist makes us want to share it. We do that by seeing Jesus present in other people and showing them His love. Paola Bignardi described several areas where the love of Christ, working through His followers, transformed relations between people: in family life; between men and women; in seeing the human family as one; by recognising Jesus in the poor; by seeing all that is good in the world.

There followed a video link with Mother Antonella Perugini, Abbess of the Poor Clare Capuchins of Sant'Urbano, speaking of the connection between the Eucharist and the contemplative life.

It may seem strange, but we who live a cloistered life feel ourselves to be very close to what is happening in the world, nourished as we are by the Eucharist, bringing us close to the mystery of the Incarnation, the mystery of Easter and the Resurrection. So the human story and the end times meet together in our Eucharistic life.

That evening penitential services took place in seven Roman basilicas, catering for seven different language groups. Fittingly, the English-speaking pilgrims found themselves in St Paul's Outside the Walls. Before the Reformation St Paul's was under the special patronage of the kings of England, who were honorary members of the Chapter here. The Abbot of the monastery at St Paul's was a member of the Order of the Garter, whose insignia is found in the arms of the basilica. Bishop Matthew Ustrzycki, auxiliary bishop of Hamilton in Ontario, led the service. He was leaving Rome the next day and he invited the Australian Mgr Brian Walsh, Fr Graham Keep of the Diocese of London, Ontario, and myself to join him for a farewell supper at the *Domus Sanctae Marthae* where he was staying. It was an unmissable opportunity to visit the building in the Vatican opened just four years previously under Pope St John Paul. Having suffered two very uncomfortable conclaves when cardinals slept in draughty corridors near the Sistine Chapel, the Pope commissioned this Domus to house the cardinals attending future conclaves. At other times it is used by those visiting the Vatican in connection with meetings and events organised by the Holy See. The Domus has been described by a former US Ambassador to the Holy See, Mary Ann Glendon, as 'comfortable but by no means deluxe'. Pope Francis has his residence there now.

Bread for New Life

Cardinal Norbert Carrera, Archbishop of Mexico City, gave the final public catechesis of the Congress on Saturday morning at the Lateran. He spoke about the 'Eucharist and the Lord's Day' and was followed by an impressive testimony given by Giuseppe and Silvia Dolfini, a married couple who looked after the Casa Betania (Bethany House) in Rome, a family home for mothers and children in difficulty and for children on their own or with disabilities. This Saturday also saw the perpetual eucharistic adoration begun in certain Roman churches the previous Monday come to an end. Most impressive had been the numbers taking part and their prayerfulness. Pope St John Paul referred to this in his Angelus message on Sunday 25 June:

> In basilicas and parishes, in monasteries and many other places of worship, there have been numerous liturgical celebrations, but also moments of adoration, and a great number of people have paused to pray before the presence of Christ in the Sacrament of the Altar. We can say that the entire Church, in a sense, has gathered here in Rome to remain in the Upper Room, listening and contemplating the Eucharist.

> Christ is the Bread of salvation for man, a wayfarer and pilgrim on earth. This is why on the feast of Corpus Christi the Eucharist is carried in procession through the streets, among the homes and buildings of daily life. In the

Eucharistic mystery the Risen One, in fact, has wished to continue dwelling in our midst, so that every human being can know His true name, His true face, and experience His boundless mercy.

We firmly believe that Christ is the only Saviour of the world. He is the Mediator of the new and eternal Covenant (cf Heb 9: 15), which fulfilled the Covenant God made on Sinai with the chosen people. It is a Covenant open to all peoples, in view of the great eschatological banquet foretold by the prophets of Israel. In the light of this truth, the Church does not scorn what human beings do in their various religious expressions to approach God and to be purified by Him; instead she encourages fruitful interreligious dialogue. At the same time, however, she cannot fail to state clearly that Christ is the only Redeemer, the Son of God, who became incarnate for us, died and rose again.

The Pope announced that the next International Eucharistic Congress would be in Guadalajara, Mexico, in 2004. Finally, he turned in prayer to Our Lady:

May Mary, who lived in intimate and constant communion with Jesus, the Word made flesh, help every Christian to recognize in the Eucharist the living presence of her divine Son, to receive Him with faith and to call upon Him with love. Invigorated by the Eucharistic Bread, no Christian will hesitate to serve his brothers and sisters, in order to build a new, more just and fraternal humanity.

That evening, in St Peter's Square, the Holy Father presided at the Statio Orbis, the liturgy to close the Rome Congress. Ten thousand children who had recently received their first Holy Communion were present, along with many thousands of the faithful from Rome and around the world. Bishops, cardinals and about a thousand priests concelebrated Mass with Pope John Paul. The area in front of the altar was decorated with an *infiorata*—a floral picture symbolising the Eucharist, made up of thousands of flower petals by artists from Genzano, a town near Rome famous for its annual Flower Festival on the feast of Corpus Christi, when the entire main street is carpeted with flower petals in preparation for the procession of the Blessed Sacrament. The tradition dates back to 1778 and is passed on from parents to children.

This Congress in Rome would be the last at which Pope St John Paul was present in person. His homily bears quoting at length. He based it on the covenants made between God and His people. The covenant made by God with Moses at Mount Sinai was sealed with the blood of animals offered in sacrifice. At the Last Supper Christ told His apostles: 'This is my Blood of the covenant, poured out for many' (Mk 14:24).

> The Apostles, then, understood the reference to the old covenant. But what did they understand of the new? Certainly very little. The Holy Spirit will have to descend to open their minds: then they will understand the full sense of Jesus' words. They will understand and rejoice...
>
> There is an illuminating passage in the Gospel of Luke. Speaking of the two disciples on the way to Emmaus, the Evangelist notes their disappointment: 'We had hoped that He was the one to redeem Israel' (Lk 24:21). The other disciples must have also shared this sentiment before meeting the risen Christ. Only after the resurrection did they begin to understand that human redemption had been achieved in Christ's Passover. The Holy Spirit will later guide them into the full truth by revealing to them that the Crucified One had given His Body and poured out His Blood as a sacrifice of expiation for the sins of human beings, for the sins of the whole world (cf 1 Jn 2:2).
>
> The author of the Letter to the Hebrews again offers us a clear synthesis of the mystery: 'Christ ... entered once for all into the Holy Place, taking not the blood of goats and calves but His own Blood, thus securing an eternal redemption' (Heb 9: 11–12).

The Holy Father then brought out the link between the Mass and this new Covenant:

Today we affirm this truth at the Statio Orbis of this International Eucharistic Congress, as, in obedience to Christ's command, we do again 'in his memory' what He did in the Upper Room on the eve of His Passion. 'Take; this is my body... This is my blood of the covenant, which is poured out for many' (Mk 12: 22–24). From this square we want to repeat to the men and women of the third millennium the extraordinary message: the Son of God became man for us and offered Himself in sacrifice for our salvation. He gives us His Body and Blood as the food of a new life, of a divine life that is no longer subject to death.

With deep feeling we once again receive from Christ's hands this gift, so that through us it may reach every family and every city, places of suffering and the workshops of hope in our time. The Eucharist is the infinite gift of love: under the signs of bread and wine we acknowledge and adore the one perfect sacrifice of Christ offered for our salvation and that of all humanity. The Eucharist is really 'the mystery that sums up all the marvels wrought by God for our salvation' (cf St Thomas Aquinas, *De sacr. Euch.*, ch. I).

In the Upper Room the Church's Eucharistic faith was born and is continually reborn. As the Eucharistic Congress now draws to a close, we want to return spiritually to these origins, to the moment of the Upper Room and of Golgotha, to give thanks for the gift of the Eucharist, the priceless gift that Christ left us, the gift by which the Church lives.

Finally, the Pope greeted and thanked everyone and looked to the future:

Our liturgical assembly will soon disperse, enriched by the presence of faithful from every part of the world and made even more attractive by this extraordinary floral display. I greet you all with affection and cordially thank everyone!

Let us leave this gathering reinvigorated in our apostolic and missionary commitment. May participation in the Eucharist make you, the sick, more patient in your trials; you, married couples, more faithful in your love;

you, consecrated persons, more persevering in your holy intentions; you, First Communion children, and especially you, dear young people, who are preparing to take personal responsibility for the future, stronger and more generous. From this Statio Orbis my thoughts are already looking ahead to the solemn Eucharistic celebration that will close the World Youth Day. I say to you, young people of Rome, Italy and the world: carefully prepare yourselves for this international youth gathering, in which you will be called to take up the challenges of the new millennium.

And You, Christ our Lord, who 'in this great sacrament feed Your people and strengthen them in holiness, so that the family of mankind may come to walk in the light of one faith, in one communion of love' (Preface of the Holy Eucharist II), always make Your Church more steadfast and united, as she celebrates the mystery of Your saving presence.

Pour out Your Spirit upon all who approach Your sacred Table and make them bolder in bearing witness to the commandment of Your love, so that the world may believe in You, who one day said: 'I myself am the living bread come down from heaven. If anyone eats this bread, he shall live' (Jn 6: 51). You, Lord Jesus Christ, Son of the Virgin Mary, are man's only Saviour, 'yesterday, today and for ever'!

As at other Congresses, adoration of the Lord in the Eucharist extended into a permanent provision for the poor. This took the form of a clinic at Rome's Termini railway station, serving the needy, including non-EU citizens and the homeless, with food and medical care.

The Congress programme contained some vibrant and inspiring contributions. To be part of all that; to be immersed in the climate of the Jubilee Year; to witness the universality of the Church in communion with the successor of St Peter; to share in the liturgies; to absorb the beauty of the buildings, the art, the culture of the Eternal City; to renew old friendships—all these things and more helped the Rome Congress, celebrating the birth of Christ 2000 years ago, to show that He is still truly alive and well.

References

1) Vicariato di Roma, *Gesu Cristo Unico Salvatore del Mondo, Atti dei Congressi Eucaristici Internazionali. Roma 18–25 giugno 2000* (Roma 2000).

2) Allen, J. F., *In His death we shall find life*, Catholic Times 9 July 2000, plus personal notes and diaries.

3) Vecchi, E., *Eucharistic Congresses and the salvific dimension of the Eucharist at the service of humanity and of society* (Rome November 2010).

10 GUADALAJARA 9–17 OCTOBER 2004 THE EUCHARIST, LIGHT AND LIFE OF THE NEW MILLENNIUM

EXUBERANCE! If one word captures the Mexican Congress, full of energy, excitement, and happiness, that is it. Exuberance! One heard everywhere the rhyming cry: Se ve, se siente, Jesús está presente! We see, we feel, Jesus is here! But how to do justice to this vibrant, pulsating Congress, set in a country of beautiful people from so many diverse backgrounds and with such a convoluted history? We started in Mexico City itself.

'We' were a disparate group organised by Fr Ralph Kleiter, of Ministry to Tourism fame, and led by Bishop Albert LeGatt of Saskatoon. Canon Kevin O'Connor and I had flown from Manchester to join the group in Toronto. There we met twenty-one others, mainly lay people, from various parts of Canada. Bishop LeGatt represented the English Sector of the Canadian Bishops Conference, while the Abbé Jean Picher and his party represented the French Sector. We were to meet up with them and with other Canadian groups at the start of the Congress.

After an overnight stay in St Augustine's Seminary in Toronto, the Canon and I flew with the English Sector to Mexico City. It was the Monday before the Congress began. The National Anthropological Museum, surely one of the top museums in the world, was our first stop. Artefacts there cover the ancient Olmec and Mayan civilisations. There we saw the Aztec Sun Stone and the model of the former Aztec capital Tenochtitlán, the site of modern-day Mexico City. The upper floor of the Museum covers Mexican culture since colonisation by Spain. A tour of the city followed. And what a city! A metropolitan area of over twenty million people, built on the site of the old Aztec capital at an altitude of 7,350 ft (2,240 m). It seemed to go on and on and on.

The high spots were undoubtedly the Cathedral, set in its majestic square, the Constitution Palace and the Government Market. The Cathedral is the largest in the Americas and was the first to be built. Aptly described as 'a symphony in stone', its building has encompassed three centuries, and in various styles: Renaissance, native Baroque, Neo-classical. Its interior is breathtaking; its twenty-five bells fill the city with their sound. It replaces a temple to the Aztec god of war, destroyed by the Spanish. The huge square fronting the Cathedral has been the city centre for 700 years.

An even more important spot we found in Tepeyac, now a suburb of Mexico City. Here is the shrine of Our Lady of Guadalupe. The story of Our Lady's appearing to a poor Indian peasant is well-known. His name was Cuauhtlatoatzin. He received the name Juan Diego when he was baptised in his 50's. Asked by Our Lady to tell the Bishop that she wanted a church to be built at the place of the apparition, Juan Diego duly obeyed. Not surprisingly, Bishop Zumarraga treated his story with caution and dismissed him. Juan Diego came back. This time the Bishop told him to ask the Vision for a sign. At the next apparition Juan Diego was told to go to the top of the hill of Tepeyac and gather the flowers growing there into his tilma or cloak. He was then to take them to the Bishop. It was the middle of winter when no flowers were expected but Juan Diego discovered a profusion of flowers blooming in the frozen soil. Gathering them into his tilma, he came again into the Bishop's presence. Opening his tilma, the flowers fell away to reveal an image of the Lady he had seen at Tepeyac.

It was the image of a mestiza girl or young woman with high cheek bones and straight black hair, unbraided and parted in the middle. Her dress was pink and blue-green, studded with stars. She stood on a crescent moon, with rays of the sun behind her. The native Indians saw many important symbols in the image and heard the motherly message Our Lady gave to Juan Diego. The miracle of the tilma and Our Lady's message led to the conversion within a very few years of nine million Indians. St Juan Diego was canonised by Pope St John Paul II in 2002. He is the patron saint of Indigenous people.

Bishop Zumarraga saw to the building of a temporary shrine at Tepeyac. Eventually a great basilica was built there, housing the tilma over the high altar. When this basilica was sinking into disrepair a modern church was built next to it and opened in 1976 to hold 10,000 people. Our group celebrated Mass there before venerating the tilma, now framed in black and gold, and so positioned that it can be seen from any point within the circular floorplan. A slow-moving pathway took us closely past it, along with a large group of pilgrims, part of the estimated twenty million who visit the shrine every year.

That same day our group visited Tenochtitlán, the ancient capital of the Aztec empire. When the Spaniards under Hernán Cortés arrived in 1519 they marvelled at the sight of this great city. One wrote:

> It was like the enchantments in the book of Amadis, because of high towers, rues [pyramids] and other buildings, all of masonry, which rose from the water. Some of the soldiers asked if what they saw was not a dream.

The city must have been one of the largest in the world at that time. It contained the palace of Montezuma II, with its 300 rooms, and hundreds of temples. Its people worshipped many gods who had to be satiated with blood and human sacrifice. Ross Hassig, an American historical anthropologist, claims that 'between 10,000 and 80,400 persons' were sacrificed over the course of four days for the dedication of the Great Pyramid in Tenochtitlán in 1487. Cortés and his troops destroyed the city in 1521 and began the foundations there of the modern Mexico City. It quickly became the headquarters of Spanish power in the New World. Its jurisdiction took in California and Texas to the north, Panama to the south and the Philippines to the west. The Hospital of Jesus of Nazareth, the oldest hospital in the western hemisphere, was built there, and the school which became the National Autonomous University. Excavations in recent years of the ruins of Tenochtitlán enabled us to get a glimpse of what that city was like before.

We left Mexico City by coach on our way to Guadalajara, the host city of the 48th International Eucharistic Congress. The northerly route we followed covered about 350 miles, with our first stop at Tepotzotlán. The area enjoyed some autonomy under Spanish rule and was part of a 'Republic of the Indians'. The Jesuits founded a famous college there which today houses the National Museum of the Viceroyalty, with a magnificent golden Baroque church and a most impressive collection of art and artefacts. From there we drove to San Miguel de Allende, some 170 miles from Mexico City and now a World Heritage Site, birthplace too of the Mexican General Ignacio Allende, one of the leaders of the Mexican War of Independence.

That War began in nearby Dolores Hidalgo. We visited the church where Don Miguel Hidalgo y Costilla began the uprising against colonial rule with his famous 'Grito de Dolores', a 'Cry from Dolores', on 16 September 1810. New Spain, as Mexico was then called, was feeling the effects of revolution in Europe. Napoleon had invaded Spain, deposed the Spanish King Charles IV, and proclaimed his own brother Joseph as king. The mother country's economic policy was causing great unrest in New Spain, particularly among the native Indians and the Creoles. Political and philosophical ideas of the previous century, along with the example of the United States' overthrow of colonial rule, undoubtedly played a large part in preparing the ground for revolution. The War dragged on for eleven years before Independence was finally achieved. Don Hidalgo's legacy lives on in the town in the form of the ceramics industry he started. Half the population derive their income from it today.

Winding mountain roads took us through striking scenery to Guanajuato, often called the 'most beautiful city in Mexico', capital of the State of the same name, boasting some splendid architecture, its colourful houses cascading down the hillsides, and world famous for its silver mines. One mine, La Valenciana, was still active, though at a much reduced rate from the time when it produced 30% of the world's silver. Through old shafts, we descended into one of the oldest mines, that of San Ramon, sensible of the awful demands such mining made on those who worked there.

The final leg of our journey, from Guanajuato to Guadalajara, a distance of about 160 miles, took us past Leon and on to a visit to San Juan de Los Lagos, set in rolling hills about 5,700 ft above sea level. Over seven million pilgrims each year visit the Cathedral to venerate the small image of Our Lady kept here. Our Lady's help is invoked in cases of mortal danger or serious illness and many miracles have been ascribed to her intercession.

Light and darkness

We came to Guadalajara, capital of the Mexican state of Jalisco, on Saturday 9 October and joined the queue at the Congress office to confirm our registrations. Canon O'Connor and I discovered that we had wrongly been registered as bishops! Despite our protestations the official in charge insisted that we keep our allotted mitres and chasubles.

The Congress opened on the Sunday evening, 10 October. Before that, we were able to take in some of the sights of the city, Mexico's second-largest with over five million people in its metropolitan area, 'homeland of the "mariachi" and the tequila, and also of a people's Church, with a strong and joyful faith'. One of the most popular and successful football teams plays here, Club Deportivo Guadalajara, known as 'Chivas', fielding exclusively only Mexican players. It was at their ground, the Jalisco Sports Stadium, that Slovakian Cardinal Josef Tomko, Papal Legate, celebrated the opening Mass and introduced the Congress theme, 'The Eucharist, light and life of the new millennium', by setting out some of the lights and darkness of our age:

We come from a world full of light but also of dark shadows. On the one hand, we can see the search for something that will unite humanity as we saw happen at the last Olympics: the longing for peace, the rediscovery of the beauty of creation, the defence of human rights, sensitivity for social justice, etc.

In the Church herself, we note the reawakening of young people to whom the Holy Father has entrusted the wonderful task of being 'morning watchmen' and who are enlarging and developing the young Churches; after a century of great Popes, John Paul II is ever more widely recognized as the highest moral authority, not only by Catholics but by all humanity, whom he continues to teach by his example as well as his words; everyone can perceive the Church's constant commitment to peace, human dignity, justice and the poorest and weakest, to the culture of life against the culture of death, to the inestimable value of every human person and also to ecumenism and inter-religious dialogue, to mention but a few of the lights.

Not everything however was light:

But we come from a world that is also troubled by dark shadows: wars known and wars forgotten, declared or smouldering, various kinds of violence and conflict, the ideological attack on marriage and the family and even human life from its conception to natural death, now also threatened by euthanasia with the legalized killing of the elderly, the sick and even new-born infants, the clouding of the moral conscience, the loss of the capacity to love faithfully and constantly, terror that becomes horror, a loss of the sense of sin that is a sign of the loss of the sense of God, the 'silent apostasy' from Christ of certain Christian regions, a secularisation that excludes God from social life and even from individual consciences, an agnosticism that leaves no room for religion and becomes worse than atheism, while manifestations of sectarian and fanatic religiosity, which are often fundamentalistic, proliferate.

We come from this world to seek light to live by, certainty for our doubts, courage to bear witness to our faith among our brothers and sisters in difficulty, nourishment for our lives and those of our neighbour. 'We want to see your face, Lord'. We too, with Peter, desire to demonstrate and profess our faith in Jesus Christ: 'Lord, to whom shall we go? You have the words of eternal life' (Jn 6: 68). Jesus himself said: 'I am the light of the world; he who follows Me will not walk in darkness, but will have the light of life' (Jn 8: 12). And again: 'I am the bread of life' (Jn 6: 48). Light and life, these are what our world needs.

The following morning continued the Congress theme. Representatives of the five continents reported on the 'lights and shadows' characterising their own *ambiente*. First came Bishop Jean Baptiste Kpiele Some of Diébougou in Burkina Faso, speaking for Africa, referring with gratitude to the Congresses as 'part of the Tradition and spiritual treasures of the Catholic Church'. He identified 'doctrinal and anthropological convergences' between the Eucharist and African culture: in the family; in respect for life; in respect for the human body; in the importance of the spoken word; and in the reality of the invisible world. He developed those five points, honestly noting the need he felt in Africa for deeper catechetical, doctrinal, liturgical, pastoral and spiritual formation. The Eucharist was a true spiritual reality in the lives of the Catholics there, even if they still had some way to go.

Archbishop Carmelo Morelos of Zamboanga in the Philippines then spoke for Asia. Pointing out that Asia represented 57.5% of the world's inhabitants, but Catholics in Asia were only 2.89%, the Archbishop said that the Church there had to proclaim Jesus Christ through dialogue with other world religions and through the witness of Christians themselves:

> For the majority of the people of Asia, the face of Christ can be contemplated only in the life testimony of the Christian community. The Christ that we present to you is the Christ they see. Our Christian faith must be solidly

founded on the fact that we are called to be witnesses, as well as martyrs.

Living in a globalised society, where an 'economic system free of political control cannot avoid promoting wild inequalities that tear apart the social fabric', and in a secularised society, where 'people have forgotten the time when they could be happy without money and without current technology', underlined the centrality of the Eucharist:

> In the Holy Eucharist, the Sacrament of sacraments, it is not only grace that we receive, but the very source of grace ... In this sacrament, barriers do not exist. In Christ, 'there is no longer Greek or Jew; neither slave nor free; neither man nor woman, since you are all one in Christ Jesus' (Ga 3: 28) ... When we come together to celebrate the Eucharist, we recognise that creation is full of meaning and purpose.

The Church in Asia is poor in terms of numbers; it has many failures; and it is seen as a foreign religion, even though it began in Asia. But Archbishop Morelos saw the poverty of the Church as its strength. 'Stripped of the inessentials, we are able to find the true treasure, Christ Himself, in the Eucharist. No other provision is necessary for our journey as pilgrims, because with Him we have everything.'

Oceania consists of many countries bound together by the Pacific Ocean. It includes large countries like Australia and New Guinea and many small countries and islands scattered over a vast area of water, with hundreds of languages and cultures, both traditional and modern. Archbishop Barry Hickey of Perth, Western Australia, welcomed delegates from Oceania and spoke on their behalf. He listed some of the shadows:

> Some countries like Australia and New Zealand are strongly influenced by a form of modern secularity that seeks to undermine what has been built up over many years, particularly attendance at Sunday Mass, Eucharistic devotion and vocations to the priesthood and religious life.

Recent surveys have confirmed our experience that the strong faith of our forefathers is not as strong in more recent generations. This has given rise to considerable concern and demands a vigorous response in terms of the new evangelisation.

Nevertheless, there were many lights:

Despite the decline in numbers, those who are faithful are being drawn closer and closer to God through the Blessed Eucharist and coming to understand how the Eucharist can affect their daily lives. The numbers of those attending daily Mass is steadily growing in many parts of Oceania ... Whereas Sunday Mass is a joyful community celebration with good music that lifts the heart and willing participation by the people in the liturgical action, daily Mass has a different character, a silence and a spirit of interiority that is treasured ... It is a source of great joy that so many people receive Holy Communion each time they attend Mass, and that they prepare themselves to do so as worthily as they can. After some years of uncertainty, the people are returning with great enthusiasm to the practice of Eucharistic Adoration.

Archbishop Hickey showed how the Eucharist should lead us to serve others: 'the poor, the homeless, the addicts, the persecuted and the rejected people of the world'.

Coming back round the world, Cardinal Carlos Vallejo, Archbishop of Seville, painted a stark picture of Europe. He quoted from Pope St John Paul II's letter, *Ecclesia de Eucharistia* 10, and applied it to Europe:

In some places the practice of Eucharistic adoration has been almost completely abandoned. In various parts of the Church abuses have occurred, leading to confusion with regard to sound faith and Catholic doctrine concerning this wonderful sacrament. At times one encounters an extremely reductive understanding of the Eucharistic mystery. Stripped of its sacrificial meaning, it is celebrated as if it were simply a fraternal banquet. Furthermore, the necessity of the ministerial priesthood, grounded in apostolic succession, is at times obscured and the sacramental nature of the Eucharist is reduced to its mere effectiveness as a form of proclamation. This has led here and there to ecumenical initiatives which, albeit well-intentioned, indulge in Eucharistic practices contrary to the discipline by which the Church expresses her faith. How can we not express profound grief at all this? The Eucharist is too great a gift to tolerate ambiguity and depreciation.

Almost the whole of the Cardinal's presentation was taken up by quotations from recent documents. Having set the scene, he used those documents to suggest how the situation in Europe might be remedied:

The Church in Europe has a universal vocation and strong commitment to fidelity to its roots and its Christian history. The Church and Christianity cannot be relegated to a marginal space in Europe. She has something to say to society and its culture. It is not about directing, much less imposing, but about offering the values and criteria that flow from the light of the Gospel. ... The Church in Europe, on her pilgrimage through history, goes to the Eucharist, 'the source and summit of the whole Christian life', and there she finds the source of hope. Only by looking to Christ can Europe find the only hope that can give full meaning to life.

Speaking for North America, the Archbishop of Boston, Cardinal Bernard Law, covered much the same ground as did Cardinal Morales. Fewer Catholics went to Mass on Sundays; Sunday had been devalued; people seemed to consider it their right to receive Holy Communion at all times by just being present at Mass, even without recourse to the Sacrament of Penance when that was needed; many are insufficiently instructed in the faith.

On the positive side, the practice of frequent Communion remained, as proposed by Pope St Pius X. May we not see here the influence of earlier Eucharistic Congresses? Also, all present at Mass are now able to 'participate fully, consciously and actively in the liturgical action'. Adoration of the Eucharist outside of Mass was also on the increase. We had the example too of the Holy Father: 'The papacy of Pope John Paul II will be remembered for his constant devotion to three Christian mysteries: the universal mission of the Church; the Sacrament of the Eucharist; and the Virgin Mother of God.'

The Archbishop of Yucatán in Mexico, Emilio Berlie, summarised the position of the Church in Latin America. Founding his talk on the doctrine and pastoral guidelines related to the Eucharist coming from meetings of CELAM, the Council of the Latin American Episcopate, and also on the teachings of Pope St John Paul II, the Archbishop neatly described the Eucharist as, 'since apostolic times, the presence of the risen Christ in His Church'. He gave a long list of 'lights and shadows', corresponding closely with some of those given above. One novelty worth noting was his statement that in Mexico 'there are already more than four million faithful associated with nightly adoration'. He expected that number to increase as a result of the Congress and ended his talk with reference to Our Lady:

> The Holy Father has a beautiful paragraph where he connects the 'fiat' of Mary with the 'amen' that each believer says when he receives the Body of the Lord. Mary was asked to believe that the one she would conceive 'of the Holy Spirit' was 'the Son of God'. In continuity with the faith of Mary, in the Eucharistic mystery we are asked to believe that the one she conceived of the Holy Spirit was the Son of God and the Son of Mary. We are asked to believe that Jesus is present in his total humanity and divinity under the signs of bread and wine. When we say yes to the Host, we are saying, 'I believe in Jesus Christ who at this moment is coming to my heart'. Body of Christ, Amen. Body of Christ, Yes. Body of Christ, 'Fiat'. How important a small word can be when it expresses the greatness of faith and love!

Zapopan—and Eucharist and Mission

The next day brought a fresh exuberance to the Congress. At dawn on Tuesday 12 October, crowds assembled, with bands and singing, for the 'Romería Festival' in honour of the Virgin of Zapopan. Her statue, representing the Blessed Virgin Mary under the title of her Immaculate Conception, is tiny: just over thirteen inches, thirty-four centimetres, tall. But her importance is immense! Made of pieces of cornstalk, cemented together by glue, and with hands made of wood, the image was fashioned in the sixteenth century and brought to Zapopan by Franciscan missionaries, Antonio de Segovia and Miguel de Bolonia. Fra Antonio, wearing the image around his neck, went among the warring Indians, urging them to make peace with the Spaniards. They did so, perhaps persuaded more by the rays they saw streaming from the image of Our Lady than by his preaching. From this comes one of the titles of the image, La Pacificadora, 'She who makes peace'. In times of epidemics and storms, the image has been carried in processions and the prayers of Our Lady successfully invoked.

Our Lady of Zapopan is hailed as the Patroness of Guadalajara and every year her image is brought in June from Zapopan to Guadalajara, a distance of just a few kilometres, to be taken round all the parishes before returning in October in a grand procession to Zapopan Cathedral. It was this procession in which we took part, along with a crowd reliably estimated at two and a half million. The Indians in traditional dress, the mariachi bands, the beautiful singing of a boys' choir, all added to the brilliance of the occasion. On arrival at Zapopan, the Archbishop of Guadalajara, Cardinal Juan Sandoval Iñiguez, blessed us all with the image of Our Lady and then celebrated Mass in the open square in front of the cathedral. Dancing and other festivities followed, rounded off with evening fireworks. Our long day was completed by a visit to the parish of San Jerónimo for discussion and catechesis for English-speaking pilgrims. In the afternoon, visiting cardinals, bishops and priests had gone to hospitals and prisons in the state of Jalisco to comfort patients and inmates with Jesus' message of salvation.

Wednesday 13 October began with the Nigerian Cardinal Francis Arinze celebrating Mass in Expo Guadalajara, a spacious conference centre only a few years old and a key venue for the Congress. In his homily, the Cardinal pointed out that the Eucharist makes us one with Christ Who then sends us out on a mission.

> The Holy Eucharist, more than the other Sacraments, favours our union with Christ. For good reason, one of the names by which it is known is 'Holy Communion'. In the mystery of the Holy Eucharist, Jesus not only unites us with Himself but also unites us with our neighbour. At the same time, He sends us on a mission ... The mission of the Church is to approach every human being, so that all may know the one true God and Jesus Christ Whom He has sent (cf Jn 17:3).

> The Church works so that all may find salvation in Jesus Christ, the only Saviour of all mankind. The Gospel of Jesus Christ makes it possible for all peoples to worship, praise and glorify God, to ask for forgiveness for their sins and to plead for their spiritual and temporal needs.

> This mission of the Church has a horizontal dimension. The Church, as a witness of Christ, also works to heal divisions between peoples because of or for reasons of race, social classes, economic or political factors and for other reasons. Refugees and exiles, socially marginalised and homeless people, need to be rehabilitated, to see themselves accepted as full members of the human family. This is also true for the sick, the elderly, the dying. Reconciliation and reciprocal forgiveness can then bring the harmony, justice and peace which the human heart calls for ... Taking part in the Eucharistic celebration, especially through a well-prepared reception of the Body and Blood of Christ, gives life and spiritual energy to our active mission as lay faithful, as consecrated or as clergy.

In words strongly reminiscent of some used by St Thérèse of Lisieux, the Cardinal ended:

> It is the Eucharist, therefore, which makes it possible for the Church to bear witness to Christ; for the martyrs to give their lives for Jesus and for the missionaries to go to distant lands to proclaim Christ. It is the Eucharist that strengthens the virgins to bear witness to a love consecrated and sacrificed by Jesus; the priests to spend their own strength to make Christ known; the spouses to live their conjugal life in an exemplary manner; the faithful lay people to bring the spirit of Christ to the various secular environments of daily life, vivifying them from within, as belonging to this world; young people to be sentinels of the dawn, to lead people to Christ, the Light, the Way, the Truth and the Life.

Another African Cardinal, Archbishop Peter Turkson of West Coast, Ghana, gave a lengthy and far-reaching public catechesis that morning, taking the same theme as Cardinal Arinze: 'The Eucharist, Mystery of Communion and Mission'. He began by quoting St Thomas Aquinas: 'The only-begotten Son of God, wishing to enable us to share in His divinity, took our nature so that by becoming man He might make us gods' (Opusc 57: 1–4). But how? Jesus called His apostles, empowered them in His name, revealed to them the mysteries of the Kingdom of God.

> But it is only when they eat the flesh of Jesus and drink His Blood that they are said to live by Him, they abiding in Him and He in them (cf Jn 6: 56–57). Jesus best and supremely shares His life with humanity when He becomes its food; and this is in reference to the Eucharist. The Eucharist, in which Jesus gives us Himself, immolated but as food (as bread and wine), becomes the end of a process which would begin with His Incarnation. One might say that the Incarnation of Jesus Christ was in view of the Eucharist. He took our nature, becoming 'like unto us' so that He might give Himself to us, 'making us like unto Himself'. The life that Jesus shares with His followers is

the life which He shares with His Father, by which He and the Father are One ...

The Eucharist, then, in response to and in fulfilment of the Incarnation (God's design in sending His Son) refers to the communion of life between the Father and the Son, and seeks to fashion the same between the followers of Jesus and God (the Father and the Son), and between the followers themselves ...

Thus the Eucharist, as the scope of the Incarnation and in the life of the Church, is intimately related with the communion of life within the Trinity, as both deriving from it and as being the locus [place] of its revelation. It is equally intimately related with the life of communion within the Church, i.e. among the followers of Jesus, as its origin, its sustenance and its perfection; and to the extent that this 'fellowship of life with the Incarnate Son of God' is the vocation of all humanity, the Eucharist also founds and underlies the mission of the followers of the Incarnate Son of God, the Church.

Cardinal Turkson then examined, 'for the pastoral and practical living of our Eucharistic faith, how the Eucharist mysteriously represents and enacts our life of communion as a Church, and founds her mission'. He saw our life of communion as a life of sonship with the Father; as rediscovered brotherhood and sisterhood among believers; as giving us harmony within ourselves and with the world of nature.

... 'sonship' expresses the relation of Jesus to the Father and the Spirit, and the form under which He shares a common life with the Father and the Spirit. The Jesus of the Passion, the Jesus of the Eucharist, is the Son of God Who was living out His son-ship: His relation within the Trinity and the way He shared life with the Father and the Spirit. Jesus, Who suffered and was crucified, was Jesus Who was being true to His nature, to His being a Son in the Trinity; and the way of the Son was His total submission to the will of the Father (cf Mt 26: 39; Lk 22: 42) ...

It was in so submitting to the will of the Father that Jesus entered His Passion to atone for the sins of humanity and to reconcile humanity with God. In other words, it was in Jesus' acceptance and the living out of His sonship to the Father (recognition and upholding the fatherhood of God) that He reconciled humanity to God, breaking down the barriers between God and man and restoring the communion of life between God and humanity. Jesus' sonship as one of total submission to the will of the Father becomes the principle of our reconciliation and communion with God ...

[The Eucharist] is the memorial of a sacrifice, whose celebration invites us to a rediscovery of the life of divine (adopted) sonship as a life of total submission to God, and to a rediscovery of the fatherhood of God, which lays total claim to our lives. This is how the Eucharist reconciles us to God and introduces us into communion with God. Its celebration becomes our invitation, first, into communion with Jesus, becoming what we receive, namely, the attitude of sonship (cf Ph 2: 5–11), and through Jesus, into communion with the Father, whose fatherhood we now accept in and with Jesus.

By sharing His sonship with us, 'our common son-ship leads to the discovery of our common brotherhood and unity in Christ (cf 1 Co 10:16–17). Restored to sonship of God in Jesus, we discover ourselves as brothers and sisters, who must now live in fraternal communion.' Using examples from the New Testament, Cardinal Turkson showed how this 'fraternal communion' was lived by believers in apostolic times with Jesus and among themselves; in unity of faith; in charity; in mutual respect; in moral living.

Jesus was also 'a well-focussed person, in full harmony with Himself' ... In the Eucharist, Jesus 'shares this disposition with us!'

Otherwise, human existence is plagued by internal dishar-mony. It suffers many distractions from sources external to it (such as the lures and attractions of the world) but especially from sources within it and which are at war with our members. We are exposed to an inner conflict which Paul describes very well (Rm 7: 15ff). This indeed is a wretched state from which only the Eucharist of Jesus Christ brings release, for the law of the Spirit of the life of Christ Jesus, which sets us free from the law of sin and death (Rm 8:2, cf also 7: 6, 25), comes from the Incarnation and the atoning death of Jesus Christ (cf Rm 8: 3–4).

Cardinal Turkson also offered a perspective on 'Eucharist and Ecological Communion':

> In his letter to the Colossians, Paul affirms that Jesus Christ is supreme over all creation, and that it is in Him that 'all things hold together' (Col 1:17). Indeed, according to Paul, Jesus is not only the Word through Whom everything was created. It is also through Him that 'God was pleased to reconcile to Himself all things, whether on earth or in heaven, by making peace through the Blood of His Cross' (Col 1:20). Thus, the death of Jesus, which the Eucharist celebrates and of which it is the memorial, does not reconcile only mankind to God: it reconciles his world too to God. Jesus is our peace; He is also the peace of the world. Accordingly, one cannot find Christ and live His life without also fashioning harmony with, and living in communion with, the world. Our celebration of the Eucharist involves us, again in Christ, to fashion harmony with, and to live in respect and communion with, our environment and the world.

Finally, the Cardinal explained how the Eucharist founds the mission of the Church:

> The 'Ite, Missa est' which concludes our Eucharistic celebrations addresses a missionary charge to us. Having touched God, we are charged to share Him with our world. Having celebrated our sonship of God in Jesus of the Eucharist, we are sent out to seek other sons and daughters of God who will become our brothers and sisters in Christ.

Having been introduced into communion with God in the Eucharistic Christ, we are reminded of His prayer and wish to make fellowship with Him and His father complete by bringing others to share in it (cf Jn 17:20–21; 1 Jn 1:3–4). Finally, having become 'sons of God' in Jesus, we receive the missionary charge He once gave to His followers: 'As the Father has sent Me, so do I send you' (Jn 20:21). The Eucharist would seem then to be the source and summit of the Church's missionary task (evangelisation), since its goal is the communion of all mankind with Christ, and in Him, with the Father and the Holy Spirit ...

The Eucharist ... is a celebration of communion of life on all levels of human existence: with God; with other human beings; with oneself; and with one's world. Since the Eucharist is Christ Himself, its celebration also becomes the celebration of the recapitulation of all things in Christ, when Christ will be all in all ... to the glory of the Father.

Christ the King

'When Christ will be all in all.' Time and again during the Guadalajara Congress, we heard the cry '¡Viva Cristo Rey!', 'Long live Christ the King!' Individuals, groups, would happily sing it out as they walked along the roads. The cry was clearly ingrained in their memories. Such had been the cry of the Cristeros and of ordinary Catholics during La Cristiada—the time of organised rebellion against the persecution of the Church by the Mexican government, especially from 1926 to 1929. Before writing *The Power and the Glory*, his most acclaimed novel, Graham Greene had travelled to Mexico. He called the attack on the Church there 'the fiercest persecution of religion anywhere since the reign of Elizabeth'. The American historian Donald Mabry described that period as 'a virulent anticlericalism that has seldom been surpassed in any other country'. The State of Jalisco, with its capital Guadalajara, mounted the strongest opposition. As a Mexican bishop said at the opening of the Congress: 'Guadalajara will never deny its Catholic origins ... For all this, it has been chosen as the venue, for the first time in our country, of an International Eucharistic Congress.'

As noted in Chapter Two of this book, Pope Pius XI had established the feast of Christ the King in 1925. Mexico's Catholics made that title their motto as they faced an increasingly hostile government led by atheists, liberals and Freemasons who in 1917 had approved an extremely anti-Catholic Constitution. Church schools were outlawed. All educational services were to be secular, without any religious teaching. The Mexican State seized much Church property. No public religious services were permitted. The State would regulate the number of priests in each region; forbade the wearing of clerical dress; and excluded offenders from trial by jury. Matters came to a head in 1926 when a new Mexican President, Plutarco Calles, came to power. Calles applied the laws strictly throughout the country, expelling all foreign priests, closing monasteries, convents and religious schools, and reducing the number of priests allowed to stay in the country. Only one priest, for example, was given permission to stay in the whole State of Chihuahua.

In response, the Catholic bishops suspended all public worship and encouraged an economic boycott against the government. Peaceful measures failing, many Catholics—the Cristeros—took up arms and fought government forces. A compromise settlement was reached in 1929. Many anti-Catholic provisions continued in force for years after that, though most were removed as recently as 1998. People remembered those who suffered under Calles and others like him. The Jesuit Fr (now Blessed) Miguel Pro became a legend. Arrested, and facing a firing squad without any trial, Fr Pro stretched his arms out in the form of a cross and said, 'May God have mercy on you. May God bless you. Lord, You know that I am innocent. With all my heart I forgive my enemies. Long live Christ the King!'

An important exhibition of sacred art was held at the Cabanas Cultural Institute during the Congress. It displayed 570 pieces of art kept inside churches and convents for more than 400 years, and helped explain the strong Catholic tradition of western Mexico and its bravery under persecution.

Eucharist and Ecclesial Communion

After morning prayer on Thursday 14 October, Cardinal Ricardo Vidal, Archbishop of Cebu in the Philippines, gave a catechesis entitled 'The Eucharist: Mystery of Communion and Centre of the Life of the Church'. He recalled something Pope St John Paul II in *Ecclesia de Eucharistia* (8) wrote about the Mass:

> ... even when it is celebrated on the humble altar of a country church, the Eucharist is always in some way celebrated on the altar of the world. It unites heaven and earth. It embraces and permeates all creation. The Son of God became man in order to restore all creation, in one supreme act of praise, to the One who made it from nothing. He, the Eternal High Priest who by the Blood of his Cross entered the eternal sanctuary, thus gives back to the Creator and Father all creation redeemed. He does so through the priestly ministry of the Church, to the glory of the Most Holy Trinity. Truly this is the *mysterium fidei* [mystery of faith] which is accomplished in the Eucharist: the world which came forth from the hands of God the Creator now returns to him redeemed by Christ.

Taking that as his starting point, Cardinal Vidal said:

> In this catechesis, I have been commissioned to elaborate the centrality of the Eucharist in the Life of the Church. I will develop this theme according to the following scheme: first, the Eucharist unites us with the Paschal Mystery of Christ; second, the Eucharist builds Ecclesial Communion; third, the Eucharist unites us with one another as brothers and sisters.

The Cardinal again referred us to Pope John Paul's same encyclical (11–12).

When the Church celebrates the Eucharist, the memorial of her Lord's death and resurrection, this central event of salvation becomes really present and 'the work of our redemption is carried out'. This sacrifice is so decisive for the salvation of the human race that Jesus Christ offered it and returned to the Father only *after He had left us a means of sharing in it* as if we had been present there. Each member of the faithful can thus take part in it and inexhaustibly gain its fruits. This is the faith from which generations of Christians down the ages have lived ... What more could Jesus have done for us? Truly, in the Eucharist, He shows us a love which goes 'to the end' (cf Jn 13:1), a love which knows no measure.

This aspect of the universal charity of the Eucharistic Sacrifice is based on the words of the Saviour Himself. In instituting it, He did not merely say: 'This is My Body', 'This is My Blood', but went on to add: 'which is given for you', 'which is poured out for you' (Lk 22:19–20). Jesus did not simply state that what He was giving them to eat and drink was His Body and His Blood; He also expressed *its sacrificial meaning* and made sacramentally present His sacrifice which would soon be offered on the Cross for the salvation of all. 'The Mass is at the same time, and inseparably, the sacrificial memorial in which the sacrifice of the Cross is perpetuated and the sacred banquet of communion with the Lord's Body and Blood' (CCC 1382) ... 'The sacrifice of Christ and the sacrifice of the Eucharist are *one single sacrifice*' (CCC 1367).

The Cardinal explained:

I believe that this is the key to understanding the kind of communion that the Eucharist brings about in our souls. The Eucharist transports us in time and space and takes us to the true source of our salvation, to the very act of the revelation by Jesus of the love of the Father. Although he experienced the abasement of the Cross in the deepest way, it was in this supreme act of obedience to the will of the Father that he was most united to God, and with Him to our sinful humanity. The Lord is present to us in the form of bread and wine, but we are also present to the Lord at the supreme moment of this saving act ...

Therefore ... we are already united when we celebrate Mass together or separately, because the celebration of the Eucharist in itself unites us in communion with the Trinity and among ourselves, regardless of personal feelings or our state of mind. Because Christ offers Himself and is offered, the celebration of the Eucharist, in any place and circumstance, is always the same Mass, because there is only one Paschal Mystery made accessible through the Eucharistic Mystery. Therefore, all the Masses offered yesterday and today, and those that will be offered tomorrow throughout the world, are one and the same sacrifice. As expressed in the third Eucharistic Prayer, 'You never cease to gather a people to Yourself, so that from the rising of the sun to its setting a pure sacrifice may be offered to Your name'.

And this according to the wishes of Jesus: in the upper room, during that decisive night in Jerusalem; in the Roman catacombs; in prison cells of China and Vietnam; in the European cathedrals; in the Filipino towns; in the slums of South America; and in the African villages, we are all gathered around the universal altar.

Cardinal Vidal's second point, that 'The Eucharist builds up Ecclesial Communion', was illustrated by personal stories and based strongly on the 'new commandment' Christ gave his apostles at the Last Supper, 'the commandment to love one another as He loved us'.

This commandment has roots in the Eucharist, not only because it was commended to the apostles during the Last Supper (Jn 13:34), but because the Eucharist is its expression and its fulfilment. It is in the Eucharist that Jesus shows us how much He loved us, giving us His Body and Blood as food and drink. The Eucharist is the sign of

Christian love. Just as Jesus loved us by giving His life for us, so we must give our lives for our friends: 'in the sacrament of the Eucharistic bread, the unity of the faithful, who form one body in Christ (cf 1 Co 10:17), is both expressed and brought about ... the actions and words of Jesus at the Last Supper laid the foundations of the new messianic community, the People of the New Covenant' (*Ecclesia de Eucharistia*, 21).

To further his point, the Cardinal might well have continued the quotation from Pope John Paul's encyclical:

The Apostles, by accepting in the Upper Room Jesus' invitation: 'Take, eat', 'Drink of it, all of you' (Mt 26:26–27), entered for the first time into sacramental communion with Him. From that time forward, until the end of the age, the Church is built up through sacramental communion with the Son of God who was sacrificed for our sake.

The Cardinal continued with an article from the Catechism of the Catholic Church (1396):

The unity of the Mystical Body: the Eucharist makes the Church. Those who receive the Eucharist are united more closely to Christ. Through it Christ unites them to all the faithful in one body—the Church. Communion renews, strengthens, and deepens this incorporation into the Church, already achieved by Baptism.

He explained why we do not share the Eucharist with 'the ecclesial communities that are not in total communion with us', while at the same time pointing out that 'The Eucharist itself, as the sacrament of unity, urges us to discover the positive values in churches and ecclesial communities that are not in total communion with the Church, but share the same faith in the Eucharist.' He then moved on to consider how 'the Eucharist unites us with one another as brothers and sisters'.

While the Lord is present in a special way in the Eucharistic species, He is no less present in our brothers and sisters. Therefore, to recognize the Lord in the bread and wine and ignore Him when He becomes present in the poor, the sick and the prisoner is to separate the Eucharist from the context of communion and the Christian life. To paraphrase the first letter of John, whoever does not love his brother or sister whom he can recognize in the flesh cannot love Jesus Who must be recognized in bread and wine (1 Jn 4:20).

In the same way, the Eucharist cannot be separated from the presence of the Lord in daily life. The Eucharist is the summit and centre of the Christian life. But without a base there cannot be a summit: without a setting, there can be no centre. Separated from daily life, devotion to the Eucharist could become pietism. Because how can we appreciate the real presence of the Lord in the Eucharistic species if we do not see His presence in the poor, if we ignore it in the community, if we refuse to meet in its name, and if we do not recognize it in the minister who presides over the Mass? ...

The Eucharist can only be at the centre of the life of the Church if our community radiates service to the needy. The Lord does not like the treasures we can put at His feet if in the process of acquiring those riches we have deprived thousands of people of their just wages ...

The Real Presence is the centre of the Eucharistic Mystery, and yet the Gospel of John does not narrate the institution of the Eucharist and in exchange includes the washing of the feet of the disciples. 'Do you understand what I have done with you? You call Me Master and Lord, and so I am. If I, being Lord and Master, have washed your feet, you must wash one another's feet. I have given you an example that you also should do as I have done to you' (Jn 13:12–15). Service cannot be separated from presence and communion ...

We who have been told to 'Do this in memory of Me' should never separate the celebration of the Eucharist from the command to love and serve. Only through presence, communion and service can the Eucharist be the Mystery of Communion and Life of the Church.

We heard two testimonies, the first from the delegation from Mali, the second from a Korean couple, Thomas Han and Catherine Ryu. Both spoke of the growth of the Church in largely non-Christian societies. That same day during evening Mass, the Japanese Cardinal Stephen Fumio Hamao, President of the Pontifical Council for the Pastoral Care of Migrants and Itinerant People, kept up the theme of service, dwelling on the new commandment given by Jesus, 'to love one another as I have loved you'.

> To be recognized as disciples of Jesus in the midst of contemporary society: this is something very important for all Christians. And the words of Jesus indicate the only authentic sign that allows us to be recognized as His disciples, as Christians ... Among the poor, weak, small ... there are today in the world masses of refugees, emigrants, victims of human trafficking, especially women and children. In a spirit of Christian solidarity, we must nurture in ourselves the spirituality of communion which St Paul describes in the first letter to the Corinthians. Most of us who are here today come from Asia and Oceania. Almost two thirds of the world's population live in these regions. Among them we Christians form a little flock, but we have the strength of the Holy Spirit Who, through the sacrament of the Eucharist, makes us move forward with courage in faith, gives us hope and exhorts us to the charity of Jesus Christ to build and spread, in these immense continents too, the Kingdom of God.

The Mass was celebrated in the large open space in front of Los Arcos, two majestic arches once marking the entrance to Guadalajara city. A Blessed Sacrament procession followed through the streets of the city to its historic centre, where Benediction was given in Liberation Square. And what a procession! Two million people took part, exuberant, singing, praying. Processions like this had been banned under Mexican law. This was the first in the city for over one hundred years and the people were determined to enjoy it. The Blessed Sacrament, in a monstrance two metres high, was carried on a mobile platform and surrounded by a golden circle. Streets along the three-mile route were decorated with lights and banners, with white and yellow balloons, and thronged with happy adorers. Throughout the procession, the city's church bells rang out. It was a glorious night.

Friday 15 October saw two Cardinals in action. The German Joachim Meisner, Archbishop of Cologne, gave the homily at morning Mass, followed by a catechesis from Carlos Vallejo, Archbishop of Seville. Both stressed the connection between the Eucharist and sharing: Meisner by expanding on the words used at the consecration of the Mass, where Jesus *took* the bread, and *broke* it, and *gave* it; Vallejo by showing how in Christ everything is new:

> Everything becomes new in Christ: a new humanity freed from sin; a new people, the Church enlivened and helped by the Holy Spirit; a new law, that of the new commandment; a new sacrifice, that which announces the death and resurrection of the Lord; a new man, the one redeemed by the Blood of Christ; a new food, the Eucharist; a new evangelisation, that invites us with greater enthusiasm and hope to offer the good news of Christ for all peoples; a new civilisation, that of love.

Cardinal Vallejo's talk brought to life the *freshness* of Easter, of Christ rising on that 'truly blessed night, worthy alone to know the time and hour when Christ rose from the underworld. This is the night of which it is written: The night shall be as bright as day, dazzling is the night for me, and full of gladness.'

That evening, several parishes in the city hosted the various language groups attending the Congress. We were made very welcome in the parish of San Jerônimo for a service of reconciliation and a Holy Hour. Throughout the Congress we were also able to visit the Templo Expiatorio, a huge neo-Gothic church dedicated to perpetual exposition and adoration of the Blessed Sacrament. Day and night, men and women members of the Nocturnal Adoration Society spend time there in prayer before the Blessed Sacrament.

The Society was founded in Rome in 1810, in the church of Santa Maria in Via Lata, and has since spread to thirty-six countries forming an international Federation. Mexico is the largest member of the Federation with four million members, fifty thousand of them in Guadalajara.

Eucharist and Evangelisation

On Saturday 16 October the Expo Centre hosted its final Congress sessions. Cardinal Marc Ouellet celebrated Mass and preached on the Eucharist as the source of evangelisation: when we are at Mass, our prayer ensures that we take part in the ascending movement of God's love, while we share His descending love by our charity and Christian witness.

Cardinal Francis George, Archbishop of Chicago, then gave the final catechesis. He too spoke of the Eucharist as the source of evangelisation, and gave three reasons for that. Firstly, the Eucharist creates unity; secondly, it brings us into contact with Christ's sacrifice of Himself; thirdly, because the Holy Spirit Who transforms bread and wine into the Body and Blood of Christ transforms the world. Enlarging on his third point, the Cardinal explained how in the central part of the Eucharist we invoke the Holy Spirit to change the elements of bread and wine into the Body and Blood of Christ. The Holy Spirit provides a channel of grace changing the lives of those who receive Communion. Without the action of the Holy Spirit, the Eucharist would simply be a remembrance of past events and nothing more. The Cardinal remembered how in earlier times the Blessed Sacrament was reserved in churches in a receptacle made in the form of a dove, representing the Holy Spirit.

How well, Cardinal George asked, do we understand the final word of the Mass, 'Go!'? Jesus told His disciples to wait for the coming of the Holy Spirit and *then* make disciples. The Holy Spirit always goes before, giving missionaries courage and enabling people to hear the Word of God. After receiving such a wonderful gift of the Eucharist, it must be our desire to share it. The first millennium, he said, was concerned with the evangelisation of Europe; the second millennium with that of America and Africa. He prayed that the third millennium would lead to the evangelisation of Asia.

On the Saturday evening, the young people present at the Congress gathered in their thousands in the huge square in front of the basilica of Zapopan. Cardinal Giovanni Battista Re, head of the Congregation for Bishops and the Pontifical Commission for Latin America, spoke to them about the two disciples who discovered the risen Christ while on their way to Emmaus. And when they recognised Him they immediately rushed back to Jerusalem to tell the others that Christ was risen and alive.

> It's nice to see those two young people who before were tired and just walking and then, after having recognized Christ in the breaking of the Bread, they started running, even though the road from Emmaus back to Jerusalem was uphill. From meeting with the Risen Lord, recognized in the breaking of the Bread, comes the commitment to evangelisation.
>
> Every young person must draw from the Eucharist the desire to be an active and dynamic person in his own community, who bears witness to Christ through his word and his style of life. So the Eucharist becomes a source of Christian commitment and of missionary spirit and makes every young person not only a friend of Christ Jesus, but also a friend who wants to make other friends in his circle of study, play and work ...
>
> In the recent Apostolic Letter for the Year of the Eucharist, the Holy Father invites every Christian to bear 'more forceful witness to God's presence in the

world'. The Pope invites Christians not to 'be afraid to speak about God and to bear proud witness to our faith' (26).

The Eucharist was born of Christ's love for us. The existence of the Eucharist explains why Christ loved us and gave Himself for us. The evangelist John introduces the account of the institution of the Eucharist saying: 'Having loved His own, He loved them to the end' (Jn 13:1).

Over the centuries a huge river of charity has flowed from the Eucharist. The Eucharist has always been a great school of charity, solidarity, love and justice to renew the world around us in Christ. Also for today's society, marked by so much selfishness and so much hatred and violence, and even by terrorism, the Eucharist is a call to love, to knowing how to forgive, to knowing how to love; it is an invitation to solidarity and commitment for the poor, for the suffering, for the little ones, for the marginalized; it is light to recognise the face of Christ in the face of the brothers.

Cardinal Re then urged his young hearers to be true to Sunday Mass:

> Dear young people, put Christ present in the Eucharist at the centre of your life. He is the way, the truth and the life. He wants to be light and life for you for the new millennium. Put the Mass at the centre of your Christian life, especially Sunday Mass. Yes, the Mass is the privileged moment of meeting with the Lord, who makes Himself present to us in the Eucharistic mystery, like the traveller on the road to Emmaus.

> Sunday Mass is very important for a Christian: without it, faith weakens and Christian witness vanishes. If we miss Sunday Mass, we cannot call ourselves Christians, because gradually we will be without Christ. It is in fact in the Mass that we meet Christ alive and present in the mystery of His Body and of His Blood given to us. We will miss the Word of God, which nourishes our daily life with truth and meaning. Our relationship with the Christian community is missing, so that without Mass we are more and more

alone and isolated in a secularised world, which tends to ignore God. The light and strength of our faith is missing, the support of our hope, the warmth of our charity.

Sunday must really be the day of the Lord. When Sunday loses its basic meaning of 'Lord's Day' and simply becomes 'weekend', a simple day of escape and fun, one remains closed in an earthly horizon, so narrow that it no longer allows us to see the heavens (see *Dies Domini* 4).

The forty-eight Martyrs of Abitene, a small town near Carthage, when they were interrogated in the year 303 and then condemned by the judge for attending Mass on Sunday, replied: 'We cannot live without celebrating Sunday'. We too cannot be Christians without meeting on Sunday to celebrate the Eucharist. The reality of Sunday must be rediscovered, welcomed in all its richness, as the day of the Lord, as a day of joy for Christians. Fidelity to the Sunday Eucharist gives life a Christian dynamism, which leads us to look to heaven, without forgetting the earth, and to look at the earth, in the perspective of heaven.

Dear young people, your faith must become a presence and a witness in today's society. Help to build a new society, inspired by human and Christian values. Help to build a society founded on unity, justice, solidarity, forgiveness and love. Do not waste the gift of life, but face your existence together with Christ, recognized in the breaking of Bread. Your life will be such a wonderful adventure.

The twenty-five thousand young people present then took part in a Mass offered by the Papal Legate, Cardinal Josef Tomko, before remaining in adoration of the Blessed Sacrament until six o'clock the next morning.

Year of the Eucharist

That morning of Sunday 17 October began without much sun. In the freshness of the day crowds gathered in the Jalisco Stadium for the final Mass, the Statio Orbis, celebrated again by Cardinal Tomko:

We come from the world, from the whole world; we represent the people of God who live on all continents. We are the Church gathered to adore its Lord Who is present with us in the Eucharist. Today is the day of the Statio Orbis. It is the solemn moment, in which the Vicar of Christ, our beloved Pope John Paul II, will join us with his image and message, whom I have the joy of representing here ...

We start from this Eucharistic Congress to bring Christ to the world, to our world at the beginning of the third millennium. We must be aware that the evangelisation of the world is still in the beginning and that two thirds of humanity do not yet know Jesus Christ, the Christ Who died for all and Whom we in the Congress have celebrated as 'light and life of the new millennium'.

It is He Who sends us on mission. It is the Eucharist, in which He gives life for our world, which inspires us, nourishes us and impels us to carry this immense gift of God to all humanity.

Therefore, this our stop before the Eucharist, this Statio Orbis makes us reflect on whether in truth 'we announce Your death, Lord, we proclaim Your resurrection, until You come again' ...

The Eucharist is a sign that 'God so loved the world that He gave His only Son, so that everyone who believes in Him might not perish' (Jn 3:16). In the Eucharist Jesus 'loved his people to the end'. Every one, each of us can say: 'He loved me and gave Himself for me' (Ga 2:20). It is necessary to announce this great love: 'We proclaim Your death, we profess Your resurrection, until You come again'.

On the cross, Jesus died for all, gave His life for all humanity. In the Eucharist He offers today His salvation for the life of the world, for the salvation of those who believe and those who do not yet believe. The Eucharist makes this gift of salvation sacramentally present in the course of history. We must take this 'good news' to all the nations ...

Because the Eucharist, as the Second Vatican Council
teaches, is 'the source and summit of the whole Christian
life' (*Lumen gentium* 11), but also 'the source and summit
of all evangelization' (*Presbyterorum ordinis* 5) ... The
Eucharistic Congress ends as a celebration, but it continues as the *Eucharistic Year*, which starts with our
Congress. We are called to be pioneers of this Year, as
sentinels of the new dawn, of the new missionary and
eucharistic growth.

The hot sun was now shining, making those on the field try to
find something with which to shade themselves, until at the end
of Mass we were linked by huge television screens to St Peter's
Basilica in Rome. There, Pope St John Paul II was presiding at a
Mass for the opening of the Year of the Eucharist. Guadalajara's
Congress was the first one he had missed since his enforced
absence from Lourdes in 1981. Looking older and stooped, but
still rock-like, he now spoke to us:

I greet all of you who are gathered at Guadalajara to take
part in the conclusion of the International Eucharistic
Congress ... The television link-up between St Peter's
Basilica, the heart of Christianity, and Guadalajara, the
venue of the Congress, is like *a bridge that spans the
continents* and makes our prayer meeting an ideal *Statio
Orbis* in which the believers of the whole world converge.
The meeting point is Jesus Himself, truly present in the
Most Holy Eucharist with the mystery of His Death and
Resurrection in which heaven and earth are united and
peoples and different cultures meet. Christ is 'our peace,
who has made us both one people' (Ep 2:14) ...

The Eucharist is light! In the Word of God constantly
proclaimed, in the bread and wine that have become the
Body and Blood of Christ, *it is precisely He, the risen Lord,*
who opens minds and hearts and makes us recognize Him,
as He made the two disciples at Emmaus recognize Him,
in the 'breaking of the bread' (cf Lk 24:35). In this convivial
gesture we relive the sacrifice of the Cross, we experience

God's infinite love, we feel called to spread Christ's light among the men and women of our time ...

Dear brothers and sisters, the needs of our many brothers and sisters call us into question. We cannot close our hearts to their pleas for help. Nor can we forget that 'one does not live by bread alone' (cf Mt 4:4). We are in need of the 'living bread which came down from heaven' (Jn 6:51). Jesus is this bread. Nourishing ourselves on Him means welcoming God's life itself (cf Jn 10:10) and opening ourselves to the logic of love and sharing.

I desired this Year to be *dedicated especially to the Eucharist.* In fact, every day, particularly Sunday, the day of Christ's Resurrection, the Church lives this mystery. But, in this *Year of the Eucharist,* the Christian community is invited to become more aware of it through a more deeply felt celebration, prolonged and fervent adoration and a greater commitment to brotherhood and the service of the least. The Eucharist is the source and manifestation of *communion.* It is the principle and plan of *mission* (cf *Mane Nobiscum Domine* 3 and 4). Therefore, in the footsteps of Mary, 'woman of the Eucharist' (*Ecclesia de Eucharistia* 6), the Christian community lives this mystery! Strengthened by the 'bread of eternal life', it becomes a presence of light and life, a leaven of evangelisation and solidarity ... Stay with us, Lord! Stay with us! Amen.

At the end of his Address, the Holy Father announced that the next International Eucharistic Congress would be celebrated in Quebec City in 2008. 'May this prospect inspire in the faithful an even more generous commitment to live with intensity the current Year of the Eucharist.'

The Statio Orbis erupted in an exuberant outburst: mariachi in their wide-brimmed sombreros led the music; white and yellow balloons in their thousands were released into the sky; doves were released as a sign of peace. Those of us who came from a Europe which had grown tired and cold in faith were left marvelling at the warmth and hospitality and vibrant faith of the Mexican people.

It is a faith matured by the blood of many martyrs: their cry 'Long live Christ the King' was heard time and again throughout the Congress week. A lasting memorial to the Congress is the Cardinal José Garibi Rivera Foundation, designed to help the poorest people.

Rather reluctantly, our group left Guadalajara to return to Mexico City by a south-easterly route, staying in Morelia—a UNESCO World Heritage Site—and travelling on via Toluca. Another visit to Guadalupe for Mass was possible before flying on to Toronto and welcome lodgings at the Oratorian church, through the kindness of the Provost, Fr Jonathan Robinson, a fellow-student from Roman days. We sat up late, remembering those days but even more pondering the blessings of the Mexican Congress and a country 'complete with rich customs and beauty'.

References

1) Pontifical Committee for International Eucharistic Congresses, Basic Text for the 48th International Eucharistic Congress, Guadalajara, 2004.

2) Allen, J. F., Personal notes and diaries.

3) Johnston, F., *The Wonder of Guadalupe* (San Rafael, 1981).

4) Meyer, J., *The Cristero Rebellion: The Mexican People Between Church and State 1926–1929* (Cambridge University Press 1976).

5) *Programa General* and *Celebraciones Liturgicas*, XLVIII Congreso Eucaristico Internacional (Guadalajara 2004).

6) Memoria, *La Eucaristía, Luz y Vida del Nuevo Milenio* (Guadalajara 2005).

7) http://www.vatican.va/roman_curia/pont_committees/eucharist-congr/archive/index_en.htm

11 QUEBEC 15–22 JUNE 2008
THE EUCHARIST, GIFT OF GOD FOR THE LIFE OF THE WORLD

After Guadalajara, the Quebec Congress might seem minuscule. Though well-organised and with very good content, numbers could simply not compare. The Archbishop of Quebec, Cardinal Marc Ouellet, had anticipated as much. Speaking at the end of the Mexican Congress he said,

> There is much difference between the living of the faith of Mexicans and those of Quebec. Here one still perceives a Christian people, Catholic, which has a quite widespread and celebrated popular piety, virtues which we have lost in part, because over the last thirty years there has been a rapid process of secularisation, of estrangement from the Church, by the faithful … It will be a great challenge for us to evangelise our people again, with new means, new impetus, new ardour.

Over the next four years the Church in Canada set out to meet that challenge. First, Cardinal Ouellet had to win over his fellow bishops, still paying off their debts from the Toronto World Youth Day. Then, together with the other bishops, he arranged a widespread catechesis on the Congress theme, helped by numerous lay catechists.

There was a strong commitment to involve young people. It was in fact a youth who suggested there should be a symbol of the Congress, something like the World Youth Day cross. A group of young people and religious came up with the idea of an Ark of the New Covenant, recalling the most sacred object in ancient Israel: the wooden chest, covered in gold, and containing the tablets of the Ten Commandments, a pot of manna and Aaron's rod, all overshadowed by God's presence. The Congress Ark, made also of wood and richly adorned with icons, represented Our Lady Mary, who bore Christ, the New Covenant. The Ark began its journey to Quebec in 2005, visiting firstly every diocese in Canada and the Northwest Territories. In March 2008 it began its final journey, a one thousand kilometre walking pilgrimage from Midland, Ontario, to Quebec. The journey took sixty-four days and, in the words of one of the porters, back-tracked 'the journey taken by the Canadian Martyrs who left Quebec to carry the Eucharist to the rest of Canada'. Cardinal Ouellet and the Papal Legate, Cardinal Jozef Tomko, welcomed the Ark at the opening of the Quebec Congress.

About 11,000 pilgrims had registered for the Congress, mainly from Canada and the USA. Mexicans came in numbers, as well as representatives from Africa, Asia, Australia, India and Korea. Most European countries were represented too, but very few from England or, surprisingly, Italy. Canon Kevin O'Connor, Fr Kevin Griffin and I (all from Salford diocese) were invited by an old friend, Fr Kevin Cull, to join the group from his diocese of Hamilton, Ontario. We flew from Manchester to Toronto and were then generously guested at Cathedral House in Hamilton for a few days before joining the diocesan pilgrims for the twelve-hour coach ride to the Hotel Clarendon in Quebec. Before that, Niagara Falls, very near Hamilton, made for a spectacular day out.

Quebec is a wonderful old city and the Congress coincided with the 400th anniversary of its founding. It was also the first Catholic diocese north of Mexico when Bishop François de Laval (beatified by Pope St John Paul II in 1980) was appointed in 1658. Founded by French settlers Quebec was an important part of New France. The Church founded hospitals and schools and from the city missionaries spread to other parts of the country. The nineteenth century saw phenomenal growth in the Catholic Church, making its demise in the last fifty years all the more striking.

With all its historic buildings, Quebec also boasts some impressive recent ones. Such is the Pepsi Coliseum, built as a stadium for ice hockey and seating over 15,000 people. Here the

Congress opened in the afternoon of Sunday 15 June. I can't better Fr Thomas Rosica's description of the opening:

> For one week in June 2008, I rediscovered what extraordinary Eucharistic miracles are all about, only this time it wasn't in theology books or Basilicas of old Europe. Along with 15,000 other people from throughout Canada and 75 other countries of the world, I saw the Eucharist come alive in a very powerful way in a hockey arena in Quebec City's Pepsi Coliseum—transformed into a National Catholic Cathedral during the 49th International Eucharistic Congress ... In a richly choreographed ceremony that featured contemporary music, dance, giant marionette figures of Saints and Blesseds of Quebec moving slowly through the huge assembly, plumed Knights of Columbus escorting the now famed Ark of the New Covenant borne by the young portageurs, we knew that we were in for something special over the next week. But the powerful images of those Saints and Blesseds, towering over the assembly and moving gracefully yet purposefully through the Coliseum, spoke volumes. The Saints came marching into our lives that night. Something was changing in Canada...

The theme of the 49th International Eucharistic Congress was 'The Eucharist, gift of God for the life of the world'. The Congress organisers were surely inspired in their choice of this theme by Quebec City itself. The French explorer credited with founding the city, Samuel de Champlain, came on a vessel named Don de Dieu (Gift of God), the name now on the coat of arms and motto of Quebec City: 'Don de Dieu, feray valoir' (I shall put God's gift to good use).

The Slovakian Cardinal Josef Tomko, Papal Legate at Guadalajara in 2004, was again appointed Legate for Quebec in 2008, this time by Pope Benedict XVI. His homily immediately took up the Congress theme at the opening Mass on Sunday:

> The Eucharist is a gift of God. Not as an object, as the other gifts of God, but a very special one, because it is the gift of

God Himself. The Eucharist is Christ Himself, a Person with His divine and human nature, given to us. It is the Body and Blood of the Risen Christ present with us under the sacramental signs of bread and wine.

Before leaving this world, Jesus wanted to leave to His Church and to the whole of humanity the gift of His Presence. He has chosen the form of bread and wine. Since the beginning of His public life, in Capernaum, He has promised the bread of life: 'The bread I will give is My flesh for the life of the world' (Jn 6:51). On the eve of His passion, in the Upper Room He took the bread and solemnly declared: 'This is My Body given up for you'. And He said over the wine: 'Drink from it, all of you, this is My Blood of the covenant, which will be shed on behalf of many for the forgiveness of sins'. He has accomplished only a few hours in advance of, and in a bloodless, sacramental manner, the sacrifice offered in a bloody way on the Cross at Calvary. Jesus therefore instituted the Eucharist as His redemptive sacrifice. The Eucharist is a sacramental form of the sacrifice of Jesus on the Cross. The Upper Room and Calvary are just one sacrifice 'for the life of the world'.

This sacrifice happened only once, but Jesus wanted to apply and to perpetuate it through the centuries. Therefore He gave a commandment to His apostles: 'Do this in memory of Me'. It is a memorial and a command: not only to remember Him with speeches and words, but to do what He has done. From that time, the priests of His Church accomplish this sublime command doing the same action and pronouncing the same words. Through two thousand years the same words of Jesus consecrating the bread and wine resound in every church. As Saint Paul testifies about the church of Corinth: 'For as often as you eat this bread and drink this cup, you proclaim the death of the Lord until He comes' (1 Co 11:26). In every celebration of the Mass, Jesus Christ Himself is present with us in the form of sacrifice, as the Lamb of God who takes away the sins of our world, of our community: our sins. When the priest proclaims after the consecration: 'This is the mystery of faith', the people profess their faith in Christ's sacrifice that is renewed at the altar: 'We proclaim Your death, O Lord!'

It is not a show, not a pure commemoration or remembrance, it is the sacramental representation of this salvific event, a continuing memorial bringing its fruits to the faithful. The Sunday Mass is such a memorial. If we understand in depth the meaning of our weekly Eucharist, we will revise our frequency at it. It will become clear for us why the martyrs of Abitene in Northern Africa declared to the pagan judge: 'We cannot live without the Sunday Eucharist' (*'Sine Dominico non possumus vivere'*) and why they offered their lives for this conviction.

Cardinal Tomko ended by saying that our main response to God's gift is to make use of it: by our attendance at Holy Mass, by our Communion and our adoration. The chalice he used at this opening Mass was the one given by the King of France, Louis XVI, to the first Bishop of Quebec City, François de Laval. Our prayer and praise was led by an impressive 700-voice choir.

Each day of the Congress, when Mass was over, a time of adoration of the Blessed Sacrament followed. Then the Blessed Sacrament was placed in a monstrance on the Ark of the New Covenant and taken in procession to various churches where adoration continued during the week.

The Congress timetable followed a similar pattern each day, opening with Morning Prayer of the Church, then catechesis and testimonials and Mass. The afternoons and evenings included adoration, exhibitions, workshops and round tables, plus heritage and cultural activities. Each day had its specific theme and was dedicated to a different continent.

Day of North America

The theme for Monday 16 June was 'The Eucharist, Gift of God *par excellence*' and was dedicated to North America. Archbishop Donald Wuerl of Washington DC was at pains to show how, when 'the Church celebrates the Eucharist, she commemorates Christ's Passover and it is made present: the sacrifice Christ offered once for all on the Cross remains ever present'. He illustrated how all four Gospels and the letters of St Paul put Christ's atoning death at the centre. '... in the four Gospels, nothing has more significance than does the account of Jesus' offering of Himself as the sacrificial lamb given in ransom for His people'. The Last Supper took place in the context of the Passover meal, commemorating Israel's liberation from slavery in Egypt. Now Christ gives us a new memorial. However:

> Unlike any other form of remembrance or commemoration, the Mass, the Eucharistic Liturgy, thanks to God's gracious gift, the outpouring of the Holy Spirit, has the power to make present the very reality it symbolises. In the Eucharist, Jesus has instituted the sacrament in which His Passion, Death and Resurrection would be made present again in our lives in a way that enables us to share in the benefits of the Cross. We speak of our dying to sin and rising to new life because we participate in the mystery of Christ's Death and Resurrection. The Church uses the word 're-present' to speak of what is happening in the Mass. The term 'holy sacrifice' of the Mass is also exact because sacramentally, but really and truly, the Death and Resurrection of Christ are once again made present.

> Moreover, when we are at Mass 'we are not bystanders, but rather participants', coming in faith, hope and charity.

> As guests who have been invited not only to witness the memorial of our redemption but actually participate in it, what do we bring? Certainly, we do not come empty-handed to the table of the Lord. The first gift we bring as we approach this extraordinary memorial is our own lively faith. Like Peter, we can reply when Jesus asks us, 'Who do you say that I am?' that 'You are the Christ, the Son of the Living God'. We can reply as Martha did when Jesus proclaimed that He was the resurrection and the life and asked her, 'Do you believe this?' With her, we proclaim,

'Yes, Lord, I have come to believe'. When we come forward to receive the Eucharist and the host is presented with the declaration, 'The Body of Christ', we can reply with lively, animated faith, with confidence in the Lord's word, with trust in Christ's revelation, 'Amen. I believe!'

We also bring the gift of hope. Because we believe, because we see with the eyes of faith, because we place our trust in the words that Jesus has spoken to us, we can with confidence live out our faith. As Pope Benedict XVI reminds us in *Spe Salvi*, his encyclical on Christian hope, 'The one who has hope lives differently; the one who has hope has been granted the gift of new life'.

We can also approach the altar with hearts filled with love. At that Last Supper Jesus taught us that since we were sharers of His Body and Blood we were members of the same family and brothers and sisters to each other ... Our faith calls us to be willing to recognize Christ not only in the Eucharist but in one another and to do so in a way that manifests Christ's love now and until He comes in glory. It is for this reason that our Holy Father, Pope Benedict XVI, in his encyclical, *God is Love*, reminds us that 'the Church's deepest nature is expressed in her three-fold responsibility: of preaching the word of God, celebrating the sacraments, and exercising the ministry of charity' ...

As he concludes his apostolic exhortation on the Eucharist, our Holy Father calls us to reflect on how 'the Eucharist makes us discover that Christ, risen from the dead, is our contemporary in the mystery of the Church, His Body'. Here, three of the great mysteries of our faith are woven together. It is in the Eucharist that we not only encounter Christ, but are invited into His Death and Resurrection, not as something beyond or outside us, but rather as members of His Body in which Christ truly is present today: He is our contemporary. The Church is the enduring presence of Christ in the world today. Through the celebration of the Eucharist in the Church this central event of salvation becomes truly present and the work of

our redemption is carried out. The Lord of history and
Saviour of the world is at work among us now precisely in
His Church and in the Eucharist.

Jean Vanier, founder of L'Arche communities and son of a former
governor general of Canada, came next with a moving testimony,
showing how 'people with a handicap guide us toward God'. He
described first the work of L'Arche:

> Jesus came to break the walls around our hearts and to
> make of us, His disciples, builders of peace. The great thirst
> of Jesus is unity: 'May they be one as the Father and I are
> one'. Our communities of L'Arche, which gather people
> who are weakened by a mental handicap and people who
> have chosen to live with them, want to be the sign that love
> is possible; they want to be communities of peace and
> unity. During my forty-four years in L'Arche, I am privi-
> leged to have lived this mission of Jesus: proclaim the Good
> News to the poor and the despised and to free them from
> the oppression of rejection and hatred by helping them
> discover that they are loved as they are, that they are
> precious, that they have their place in society and in the
> Church.

Speaking he said as a voice for the voiceless, Monsieur Vanier
gave two examples of how handicapped people can help us to see
God. The first was a man called Eric, the second an unnamed
young boy:

> We met Eric at the psychiatric hospital forty kilometres
> from our community. He was deaf, silent, unable to walk,
> he was suffering from a severe mental handicap. I had
> never met a youngster with such deep anguish. He had
> been abandoned by his parents who were distraught facing
> a child whose body and intelligence were so deeply injured.
> But like all of us, Eric had a heart, a heart wounded by the
> rejection. Because he didn't feel loved, he didn't feel
> lovable. We understand the suffering of the parents but
> we must also understand the suffering of those who feel
> they are a disappointment and a burden on their parents

and on society, who don't feel accepted or loved as they are.

Eric not only needed capable and generous professionals to help him. He was thirsting for an authentic relationship, a communion of hearts that would reveal his worth, his importance, his kindness and his deep beauty. Friendship and communion of hearts are not the same as generosity. In generosity, I keep the initiative; I decide what I give. Friendship implies a certain equality; we become brothers and sisters, present to each other and vulnerable.

That life of relationships transforms the Erics, who discover they are loved, respected and appreciated as they are. They can therefore advance in life and develop physically and spiritually. Those who live with them and become their friends are also transformed ...

A few years ago, a young boy with a handicap was making his First Communion in a church in Paris. After the Eucharist, there was a family gathering. The uncle, who was also the child's godfather, told the mother: 'What a beautiful liturgy, how sad that he didn't understand a thing'.

The child heard these words and his eyes filled with tears. He said to his mother: 'Don't worry Mum, Jesus loves me just as I am'. That child had a wisdom that his uncle didn't yet attain: that the Eucharist is a gift from God *par excellence*. That child is a witness that the handicapped person—sometimes very seriously handicapped—finds life, strength and consolation in and through communion with Jesus in the Eucharist.

Isn't this a call that the whole Church must hear? In L'Arche and Faith and Light we have experienced that if we pay attention to the deepest needs of the handicapped person, we can discern their desire at the moment of the Eucharist. Isn't there a cry for communion with Jesus in the Eucharist hidden in their cry for a communion of hearts?

Jean Vanier ended his talk hoping that the International Eucharistic Congress would serve to rediscover 'the profound gift of Jesus' friendship in His Real Presence in the Eucharist, and that we all try to live a real presence close to frail and rejected people':

> Paul writes (1 Co 12) that the weakest people in the Church, those who are least presentable and that we hide, are essential to the Church and should be honoured. Becoming a friend to the poor is therefore not an option, or even preferential; it is the true meaning of the Church. The poor with their cry for relationships disturb and upset us. If we listen to them, they awaken our hearts and minds so that together we form the Church, the Body of Christ, source of compassion, of kindness and of forgiveness for all human beings.

In his homily at Mass on the same morning, Cardinal Marc Ouellet struck a contemporary note:

> We celebrate this great International Eucharistic Congress at a time when all of humanity faces the possibility of a food crisis which is sudden and disastrous. Certain basic foods, like rice and corn, have seen their prices doubled or tripled in a few weeks, and this to the great anguish of the poor who do not have the capacity to buy these foods at exorbitant costs. This situation is intolerable. A quick and concerted action by governmental instances and by the United Nations is necessary and urgent in order to help those who are hungry, and to re-establish the balance in food production and in trade relationships. Let us pray so that the understanding of justice overcomes the greed for profit among those who hold economic power.

> We ourselves who now celebrate the Bread of Heaven, the gift of God for the life of the world, cannot take this Bread of Life without concerning ourselves also about the fate of those who are hungry. Let us now seek to know and understand the causes of this food crisis and let us call for some kind of political action, all the while committing ourselves for a greater and more just distribution of basic

foodstuffs, without forgetting water, so that the poorest are not excluded from the common table.

A 'round table' in the afternoon brought together six cardinals who reported on how the Eucharist was celebrated and lived in their part of the world.

Day of Europe

Tuesday 17 June was Europe's Day, with the theme 'The Eucharist, Memorial of the Paschal Mystery'. Cardinal Philippe Barbarin, Archbishop of Lyons and Primate of France, had a reputation for plain speaking. 'Turn off the TV and turn on the Gospel' was the challenge he threw down on arriving in his diocese in 2002. Nor did his catechesis on this day, entitled 'Memory and Sacrifice', disappoint. First, he described how the Eucharist brings together 'at the same time, the joy of the Paschal meal, the drama of Golgotha and the mystery of the morning of Resurrection'.

> We are truly at Jesus' side, like those who surrounded Him on the evening of Holy Thursday. It is a marvellous moment of friendship and sweetness ... But the Eucharist also makes us contemporaries of Good Friday. It is the hour of the supreme sacrifice, when the Lord shed His blood on the Cross, for the remission of our sins ... Finally, the celebration of the Eucharist is above all the mystery of Easter morning when, in spite of so much hatred and injustice, God's love triumphs. The Body of Jesus, living and resurrected, is held before us, still bearing the marks of His wounds. The doors of the Kingdom open, and the Holy Spirit is given to us as a strength and a source of forgiveness.

Cardinal Barbarin explained how we have inherited the concept of 'memorial' from the Jewish people. Unlike a memorial which simply evokes a memory of the past, a memorial for the Jews and for us 'is an act of faith in the active presence, the action of God who saves us today as in the past'. It is at its height with the words Jesus used at the Last Supper, 'Do this in memory of Me'.

The event of the Paschal Mystery occurred in Jerusalem, at a given moment in the history of the Jewish people and the Roman Empire, but it also transcends history. It crosses continents and centuries, and it comes, as an eternal act, to 'touch' each place where the Eucharist is celebrated, as a 'memorial' of the Lord's Passover.

Thus, even if the Paschal Mystery of Jesus took place two thousand years ago, Christians believe that with each Mass, they are like the Apostles brought together around the Lord for the Last Supper. They are like Mary, at the foot of the Cross, with the faithful women and the disciple whom Jesus loves; they are like the witnesses of Jesus' Resurrection appearances. They believe, but some also have doubts, and Jesus takes the time to strengthen their faith by showing them the truth of His Resurrection, in the same way that He did with His disciples, by showing them His wounds or by offering them something to eat.

It is right to teach children to say in their hearts, at the moment of the Elevation, the exact words of St Thomas, finally expressing his act of faith before the Lord, eight days after Easter: 'My Lord and my God' (Jn 20:28). It seems that in Ireland they say these words aloud. Perhaps by paying attention to the structure of chapter 20 of St John's Gospel in two parts, feminine and masculine, we could teach girls to say in their hearts the 'Rabboni' ('Master') (v 16) of Mary of Magdala, and teach the boys the words of St Thomas.

After developing the point that the true celebrant of the Sacraments 'is Jesus Himself', the Cardinal asked 'But what is a sacrifice?'

Often, when teaching children to do small sacrifices, we tended to focus only on suffering and deprivation. But sacrifice does not exclude joy. It evokes an interior attitude of offering that is lived as much in times of light as in times of darkness. In the Bible and in the liturgy, we meet expressions like 'the sacrifice of the broken and contrite heart' and 'the sacrifice of praise', which shows that praise and sacrifice do not necessarily belong to two different worlds. In fact, the main characteristic of sacrifice is love. It is about an offering given to someone out of love ... Jesus offered Himself because He wanted to do so ...

What the Lord lived among us is nothing other than the expression in a human heart of the offering that He, the eternal Son, is living at the heart of the Blessed Trinity. He gives back to His Father all that He receives from Him. The Eucharistic sacrifice has its source in the Trinity. It is this same movement that we live in our turn as we offer to God in thanksgiving all the gifts that we have received.

Three key words summarise the Eucharistic mystery and indeed all our Christian faith: 'Presence, Sacrifice, Communion'.

On Holy Thursday, we see that the Church is a family in which we receive and learn communion. On Good Friday, we turn our eyes toward Jesus crucified; His sacrifice is the salvation of the world. And on Easter Sunday we see the presence of the risen Jesus. Death did not get the better of him; it did not keep him captive ...

Since Christ, risen from the dead, remains *present* among us, we go forth with assurance. We unite ourselves with his *sacrifice*, so that the world may be saved. And *communion* is the result of that sacrifice which will never let us rest. All children of God must be able to find interior unity, to be at peace with themselves and with their families. This is the object of communion and of our unending mission as 'workers of peace' in this world.

Cardinal Barbarin then drew some practical conclusions for the life of a disciple of Christ, in the light of Christ's words, 'This is My Body given up for you ... This is the Cup of My Blood of the new and everlasting Covenant'.

Entering into the movement of the Mass is living together with the inner attitude of the sacrifice of Jesus. These words sum up the life of Jesus. They correspond to the most important thing that each member of the assembly does. Let us begin with the priest. When he pronounces the words of the Institution, he speaks in the name of Christ. But he could well say the same of his own life too. That priest here in front of you has given his entire life to you to serve you. The commitment to celibacy required in the Latin Church gives more power and truth to the words: 'This is My body given up for you'. Like You, Lord, this priest has given his life for us. He is a living word for his brothers and sisters.

It is good to look at the whole assembly and see that these words express the thoughts of each one of those present. For some, all is joy; for others, these words suggest a struggle or suffering. But for all, the Eucharist corresponds to the great adventure of love in our lives.

Let us look at that expectant mother who repeats with her child the words of the Lord, 'This is My body given up for you'. And let us think of the child in the womb, beginning his life, who from inside his mother takes all that he needs to form his body and to progress toward the day of his birth.

Let us then turn our eyes towards the married couples who attend Mass side by side, as they hear this sentence which brings their marriage to mind, that sacrament by which God gave them to each other. In Christ's offering they understand increasingly, as the years go by, to what extent 'to love is to give everything'. The Eucharist helps them to base their lives on this foundation.

I want now to talk about the young people who have not yet chosen their course in life. They know, thanks to these words of Christ, that the gift of their body is a gift of their life to their spouse, if they are intended for marriage, or to the Lord if they are called to the priesthood or consecrated life. We know that for them it is a struggle. We acknowledge the strength they need in the present-day world, to be faithful to the call of Christ, to chastity, and we assure them of our prayer that they may prepare with love, from their youth, the offering of their lives. The youth of the new generation await a clear testimony from the Christians of their age.

We must not forget those for whom these words of offering and love mean suffering and pain: the people who would like to marry and who have not yet had that grace; those who doubt their body and do not know to whom it could be given because they are disabled by handicap or for another reason; widowers and widows, as well as all those who were forsaken, also suffer much. Through the years, they lived the Mass with a spouse who is not there anymore! And they no longer know to whom their body is now given. For all of us, in joy or in sorrow, the memorial of the Passion of the Lord is a sacrifice of love and an offering of our lives.

The Cardinal ended his talk by speaking of the Cistercian monks of Tibhirine Monastery in Algeria. They knew all along they were in mortal danger. Having formed bonds with the Algerians 'that nothing will be able to destroy, not even death', they chose to remain. They were assassinated in 1996.

Their presence was an offering, simple, discrete and understood by all. And their sacrifice touched the whole world. To present Christianity without the Cross, without speaking of the Eucharistic sacrifice and saying where it can lead us, would be a lie …

The Lord said in His discourse at the Last Supper, 'As the Father loves me, so I also love you' (Jn 15:9). We can put that sentence in parallel with the one Jesus said to the Apostles in the appearance on the evening of Easter: 'As the Father has sent me, so I also send you' (Jn 20:21). The verbs 'to love' and 'to send' are interchangeable in these two sentences and in all Christian thought. The truth is that when God loves us, He brings us into the great adventure of the salvation of the world. Our mission is to love. That is what we learn from the life of Christ, and most particularly from the sacrifice of His Eucharist.

The rest of the morning was filled with a witness given by Fr Nicolas Buttet and Mass celebrated by Cardinal Stanislaw Dziwisz, Archbishop of Krakow and former secretary to Pope St John Paul II. Fr Buttet, a Swiss priest and founder of the Eucharistein Fraternity—a community inspired by St Francis of Assisi—sprinkled his talk with humour.

> Now is the time for us to discover the face of Christ in each one of us. They tell a story of an artist who came to Pope Leo XIII and said, 'Holy Father, would you allow me to paint your portrait?' And the Holy Father said: 'Of course!' So a little later, the artist came with the painting, but clearly he had little talent. And the Holy Father, seeing the result, said very charitably: 'Thank you very much. Would you just add a biblical quotation to the painting?' The artist, very happy, said: 'Of course, anything you wish!' 'Just one little reference', the Pope said, 'John 6:20'. When you look at this verse, you find it is the moment when Jesus spoke to the Apostles who were terrified and assured them: 'Don't be afraid, it's Me!' Sometimes, we don't reflect the beautiful face of Jesus, and yet this [in the Eucharist] is where we need to discover Jesus.

Day of South America

Wednesday 18 June was the day of South America, with the theme 'The Eucharist Builds up the Church, the Sacrament of Salvation'. That morning was memorable for the catechesis given by Cardinal Jorge Bergoglio, Archbishop of Buenos Aires and Primate of Argentina, now Pope Francis, and also for the Divine Liturgy, the Eucharist celebrated according to the Byzantine Rite. Cardinal Bergoglio's talk was entitled 'The Eucharist and the Church, Mystery of the Covenant', and in his characteristic style he structured his theme in three steps:

> The first step will be a brief meditation on the Covenant. I think of this as a key to better understanding our theme today.

The second section will be a contemplative synthesis in the course of which we will have the opportunity to experience and admire a few representations of Our Lady, as woman of the Eucharist.

In the third section I will aim to draw a few pastoral conclusions to help us in our personal lives in the Church.

The Cardinal's text was complicated but his 'brief meditation on the Covenant' eventually sank home. The clue to understanding him is found in one sentence: 'The Lord's entire Passion is anticipated and summed up in the Last Supper and in every celebration of the Eucharist.' It is therefore precisely through the Eucharist that we share the redemption Christ has won for us. Without the Eucharist, the death of Christ on the Cross would certainly have been an act of God but an isolated event. With the Eucharist, however, we can be one with Christ at all times. We can have the 'time and space of holiness where this new Covenant [proclaimed at the Last Supper] will be lived out forever'. The Cardinal based his thoughts on Pope St John Paul II's insights in his encyclical *Ecclesia de Eucharistia* 3:

> The Church was born of the paschal mystery. For this very reason the Eucharist, which is in an outstanding way the sacrament of the paschal mystery, stands at the centre of the Church's life ... At every celebration of the Eucharist, we are spiritually brought back to the paschal Triduum: to the events of the evening of Holy Thursday, to the Last Supper and to what followed it. The institution of the Eucharist sacramentally anticipated the events which were about to take place ...

Cardinal Bergoglio then reasoned:

> If the Church is born and journeys for the life of the world, the most important moment for its task is therefore the institution of the Eucharist. Its foundation sums up the entirety of the Easter Triduum. All is contained and summed up in the Eucharist. Jesus Christ has entrusted the Church with the permanent actualisation of the Easter

mystery. With this gift, He instituted a mysterious oneness in time between the Easter Triduum and the Church's life through the centuries. Each time we celebrate the sacred mystery, the wellsprings of the Church are anticipated and summed up in the Eucharist. It is through this gift that the Lord brings about that mysterious oneness in time between Himself and the centuries that pass. The encyclical invites us to marvel at the possibility of redemption; the entire life of the world is summed up in this event.

By instituting the Eucharist as the new and eternal Covenant *before* His Passion, Christ intended to prepare the disciples for His Passion.

The Lord's act of total self-giving on the Cross was received in the hearts of those who had already welcomed it in the gift of the Eucharist. This concentrates the Passion by giving it a form and scale appropriate to our ability to receive it. That is why the entire Passion can be seen as salvific, because it is part of communion and the saving love manifested by the Lord. It is a breakthrough joining the small and large, the everyday and the exceptional. The Lord's love is made available for our faith while ensuring that this extraordinary salvific act neither escapes from us nor is diluted into banality.

The Cardinal had called this first section of his talk 'The Ecclesial and Nuptial Dimension of the Eucharist'. He explained why:

There is a profound similarity here to the sacramental formula of marriage in which spouses give themselves to each other and promise to be faithful in all that awaits them in their lives. Just as in the anticipated institution of the Eucharist, bride and groom anticipate their love and the difficulties they may encounter along the way.

Section two of Cardinal Bergoglio's talk, 'Mary, Woman of the Eucharist', also drew heavily on Pope St John Paul's encyclical. He quoted the Pope's words, 'If we wish to rediscover in all its richness the profound relationship between the Church and the

Eucharist, we cannot neglect Mary, Mother and model of the Church', the Cardinal spoke of the presence, the trust and the hope of Mary in relation to the Eucharist. Hers was a 'presence shared', 'total trust' and 'Covenant as hope'.

> These three images of Mary show us what it means to live in anticipation and what a promise can be. Pope John Paul II wrote: *'In her daily preparation for Calvary, Mary experienced a kind of "anticipated Eucharist"—one might say a "spiritual communion"—of desire and of oblation, which would culminate in her union with her Son in His passion.'* In our will to oblation we transform ourselves into the likeness of Mary by becoming open vessels, so that the Word can become incarnate in our lives.

Cardinal Bergoglio's third section was taken up with pastoral conclusions for individuals and for the Church as a whole. Contemplating the Eucharist with Mary, we seek the 'grace to lovingly believe in order to remake our life in the image of the One we receive'. The Divine Word chose to live in Mary and in the Church. So, 'when Christians look at the Church, they want it to be simple and pure like Mary. They see the Church as the Body of Christ, the receptacle that perfectly preserves what is put in it.'

That morning, the Divine Liturgy according to the Byzantine Rite was celebrated in the Pepsi Coliseum, with Ukrainian, Melchite and Byzantine Slovak Catholics taking part, as well as the representative of the Catholic Patriarchs and Bishops of Lebanon. During the splendid and colourful celebration, lasting three hours, prayers were chanted in Greek, Arabic, Ukrainian, Spanish, French, English, Slovak, Hungarian and Romanian: just some of the languages in which that ancient Divine Liturgy is now celebrated throughout the world.

Archbishop Lawrence Huculak, Ukrainian Catholic Archeparch of Winnipeg and Metropolitan for Ukrainian Catholics in Canada, presided and gave the homily. Remembering that in past times relations between the various Rites had led to opposition and division, now however from our diversity we come together in a sacred unity through the invitation of Jesus Christ who calls us to receive the one Eucharistic Bread. We, members of the various Eastern Catholic Churches, are happy to be part of this International Eucharistic Congress, and we are especially happy to lead you in this celebration of the Divine Liturgy. It is our prayer that this celebration will be another example of the power of the Holy Eucharist and how it can change our lives.

The Holy Eucharist calls us to continued conversion, sanctification and unity in the most holy Trinity. It is our sincere prayer that by our participation today we will be brought to the spiritual unity of which we hear in the concluding doxology of the anaphora, or Eucharistic canon: 'And grant that with one voice and one heart we may glorify and sing the praises of Your most honoured and magnificent name, Father, Son and Holy Spirit, now and for ever and ever.'

From the splendour of the Divine Liturgy, our group that afternoon sampled the architectural splendour of the church of St-Jean Baptiste, built in the 1880s in the Second Empire style and featuring seven different Italian marbles. An exhibition mounted for the Congress included paintings showing the origins of Christianity and also highlighted the magnificent stained-glass windows in this most ornate church.

Day of Asia

Bishop Luis Tagle, Bishop of Imus in the Philippines, gave the catechesis on Asian Day, Thursday 19 June, on the theme 'The Eucharist, the Life of Christ in our lives: Spiritual Worship and Authentic Adoration'. How can one do justice to his presentation? It sparkled with wit and good humour but just as keenly denounced wrong-doings. We were to hear him again, as Archbishop of Manila in 2012 at Dublin and as Cardinal in 2016 at Cebu.

Bishop Tagle set the scene with a thoughtful survey of the sacrifice of Jesus. His obedience to the Father 'makes the gift of self an act of worship. Secondly, His worship includes His solidarity with feeble sinners'.

> In summary, we can say that the worship of Jesus is the sacrifice of His own life offered to fulfil the Father's will to save sinners, whose weaknesses he shares in order to lift them to the mercy of God as a compassionate High Priest and Brother. Obedience to God and compassionate action on behalf of sinners form one unitary act of worship. They cannot be separated from each other. Jesus' intercessory life for weak humanity before God is his priestly worship that fulfils God's will. Ultimately, we see in Jesus' worship the embodiment of loving God with one's whole being and loving one's neighbours as oneself. Every time we come to the Eucharist, Jesus renews his unique sacrifice and invites us to share in his worship of self-oblation.

> We can do that because we have been baptised. 'Like Jesus, we are to offer a living sacrifice not made up of calves, goats and grain but of lives dedicated to God.' Our living sacrifice will make ethical demands on us. As St Paul put it, we are not to be conformed to this world's standards but our minds are to be transformed. The sacrifice we offer will be the same as that offered by Jesus Himself.

> Jesus suffered on account of His self-offering for those loved by God. But He never wavered in His sacrifice. In the process He exposed the false gods that people worshipped, erroneous notions of holiness and the blindness of righteous people to the visitations of God. Jesus' sacrifice uncovered the link between the worship of false gods and insensitivity to the needy. An idolater easily loses compassion for the weak. Though He was judged, Jesus was the one actually judging the untrue worship that kept people blind and deaf to the true God and the poor. The Church that lives the life of Christ and offers His living sacrifice cannot run away from its mission to unearth the

false gods worshipped by the world. How many people have exchanged the true God for idols like profit, prestige, pleasure and control? Those who worship false gods also dedicate their lives to them. In reality these false gods are self-interests.

To keep these false gods, their worshippers sacrifice other people's lives and the earth. It is sad that those who worship idols sacrifice other people while preserving themselves and their interests. How many factory workers are being denied the right wages for the god of profit? How many women are being sacrificed to the god of domination? How many children are being sacrificed to the god of lust? How many trees, rivers, hills are being sacrificed to the god of 'progress'? How many poor people are being sacrificed to the god of greed? How many defenceless people are being sacrificed to the god of national security?

Church people too must be faithful in their obedience to God and in compassion for the poor.

Like those who opposed Jesus in the name of authentic religion, we could be blind to God and neighbours because of self-righteousness, spiritual pride and rigidity of mind. Ecclesiastical customs and persons, when naively and narrowly deified and glorified, might become hindrances to true worship and compassion. I am disturbed when some people who do not even know me personally conclude that my being a bishop automatically makes me closer to God than they could ever be. My words are God's words, my desires are God's, my anger is God's, and my actions are God's. If I am not cautious, I might just believe it and start demanding the offerings of the best food and wine, money, car, house, adulation and submission. After all, I am 'God!' I might take so much delight in my stature and its benefits that I might end up being callous to the needs of the poor and the earth.

Turning to 'authentic adoration', Bishop Tagle saw worship and adoration as one.

The sacrifice or spiritual worship of Jesus on the Cross is His supreme act of adoration. In the Eucharist, the Church joins Jesus in adoring the God of life. But the practice of Eucharistic adoration enlivens some features of worship. We believe that the presence of Christ in the Eucharist continues beyond the liturgy. At any time we can adore the Blessed Sacrament and join the Lord's self-offering to God for the life of the world.

Adoration connotes being present, resting, and beholding. In adoration, we are present to Jesus whose sacrifice is ever present to us. Abiding in Him, we are assimilated more deeply into His self-giving. Beholding Jesus, we receive and are transformed by the mystery we adore. Eucharistic adoration is similar to standing at the foot of the Cross of Jesus, being a witness to His sacrifice of life and being renewed by it. Aside from the Blessed Mother and the Beloved Disciple who kept vigil with the dying Jesus, the Roman centurion who had been watching over Jesus when He died could also be a model of adoration. Probably the centurion guarded Jesus from his arrest to his death. Seeing Jesus betrayed, arrested, accused, humiliated, stripped, and brutally nailed to the cross, he surprisingly concluded, 'This man is innocent' (Lk 23:47), and 'Truly, this is the Son of God' (Mt 27:54; Mk 15:39). Already hardened by many crucifixions he had supervised, he must have seen something new in Jesus.

In great detail, the Bishop talked us through the Roman centurion's vigil, from the betrayal of Jesus by Judas, the desertion of His friends, the lies of the Sanhedrin, the callous surrender of Pilate to the mob, the spitting, the stripping, the carrying of the cross, right up to crucifixion and death.

We learn from the centurion's 'adoration' that Jesus' sacrifice of life cannot be appreciated for what it truly is unless the horror of the Cross is confronted. Mark's gospel says the centurion stood facing Jesus. Like any leader of guards, he kept careful watch over this criminal Jesus. He did nothing but look at Jesus. Physical nearness was not enough however. He had to be intent, vigilant and observant so that he could account for every detail. We learn from the centurion to face Jesus, to keep watch over Him, to behold Him, to contemplate Him ...

The centurion saw incredible cruelty from friends, leaders, and even from a distant God. Betrayal, inhumanity, and viciousness continue up to our time in the many crucifixions of the poor and of creation. We cannot help but wonder why friends, leaders, and God are unresponsive. But I also believe that in Jesus the centurion saw incredible love, love for the God who had failed to remove this cup of suffering from Him, and love for neighbours. For His enemies, He begged the Father's forgiveness (Lk 23:34). To a bandit He promised paradise (Lk 23:43). For His mother He secured a new family (Jn 19:26–27). And to the God who had abandoned Him, He abandoned Himself, 'Father, into your hands I commend my spirit' (Lk 23:46).

The centurion saw love blooming in the aridity of inhumanity. Amidst the noise of ridicule and lies, this man Jesus uttered words of fidelity and truth. Everywhere people were shouting 'no' to Jesus, but the centurion heard from Jesus only 'yes' to the Father, 'yes' to neighbours, 'yes' to mission. In this horrible cross of hatred and violence, the centurion found love, unwavering love, a love that refused to die, a love that was strong as steel against evil, yet tender before the beloved. Jesus remained faithful to His mission. Thus His death was transformed into life ...

In Eucharistic adoration, let us join the centurion in watching over Jesus and see what he has seen. Let us cringe in horror at the sight of destructive evil. Let us marvel at the reality of spotless love, of pure sacrifice and worship. I wish that Eucharistic adoration would lead us to know Jesus more as the compassionate companion of many crucified peoples of today ... Let us adore Jesus who offered His life as a gift to the Father for us sinners. Let us adore

Him for ourselves, for the poor, for the earth, for the Church and for the life of the world.

Bishop Tagle was followed by Elizabeth Nguyen Thi Thu Hong, youngest sister of the late Cardinal Van Thuan who (as recorded in chapter nine) had spoken at the Jubilee Congress in Rome in 2000. Elizabeth witnessed to her brother's life, which 'was firmly rooted in an extraordinary union with the Living God through the Eucharist, his only strength. It was also to him the most beautiful prayer, and the best way to give thanks and sing the Glory to God ... This unshakable faith in the Eucharist was always the guiding force in his life, the strength and food for his long journey in captivity.' Elizabeth recalled her brother describing how he had prayed whilst in his nine years of solitary confinement: 'He always carried in his shirt pocket the little container holding the Blessed Sacrament. He would repeat "Jesus, You in me and I in You" adoring the Father.' She remembered the Cardinal's visit to Sydney during his final illness, to be with his mother on her 100th birthday:

> Each day with our mother and the rest of the family he celebrated the Eucharist in the living room facing the beautiful harbour. Everyone present during those mornings remained deeply touched by the reverence, the serenity, and the perfect harmony of that moment of adoration after Communion. All the worries, all the sufferings and joy, all the uncertainties were lifted up to God as a total Yes to His Divine will.

In the late morning a group of professional actors took part in a Service of Reconciliation, presenting the parable of the Prodigal Son, while hundreds of priests heard individual confessions well into the afternoon. It was said that the 'Eucharistic City' became a 'City of Forgiveness'. After Mass in the late afternoon, a procession of the Blessed Sacrament formed at the Pepsi Coliseum and followed a five-kilometre route through the city streets. Some 15,000 people walked, whilst others looked on and often knelt in the street as the Blessed Sacrament passed. The procession ended with Benediction at the Agora, an outdoor amphitheatre in the Old Port. The Quebecois newspaper *Le Soleil* reported: 'Such an assembly has not been seen since those organised by Fr Lelievre in 1950'.

Cardinal Telesphore Placidus Toppo, Archbishop of Ranchi in India, gave the catechesis on Oceania Day, Friday 20 June. As the first Adivasi (tribal) Indian to be created a Cardinal, the Congress programme said, 'Cardinal Toppo has dedicated his life to relieving the misery of his people through his vast social work ... for example, through detox programmes, education for the poor, and the rehabilitation of lepers'. After hearing him, I wrote on the copy of his address 'Vatican 2 in action!' He developed his topic, 'Eucharist and Mission', at some length but with clarity and a sure touch. Very simply, he set out his stall:

> The Church is the community that, following in the footsteps of those first disciples and apostles, continues down the centuries to fulfil this mission in the world. When we celebrate the Eucharist, we proclaim the great redemptive act of Christ and we commit ourselves to continue His work in the world by living a life of love and sharing.

The Cardinal used his own people as an example of missionary zeal and success. Until the mid-1800s the tribal peoples of Central and North East India had not heard of Jesus. They were poor and illiterate, oppressed and exploited. Missionaries among them had laboured in vain until the arrival of a Jesuit, Fr Constant Lievens, now known as 'the apostle of Chotanagpur, the land of the Tribals. When this Jesuit came, there were just fifty-six Catholics in the territory. He lived only seven years but by the time he died, due to overwork, exhaustion and tuberculosis, there were 80,000 baptised Catholics and more than 20,000 catechumens in the area!' The Cardinal wondered aloud how this could have come about:

> What was the difference between these Jesuit Missionaries and the first missionaries who came thirty years before

them? The answer is: The Eucharist. The way the Catholics understood, celebrated and lived the Eucharist made all the difference. Many of the first Christians embraced the Catholic faith because of this ... This young Church in the tribal lands has grown so much that today it constitutes 10% of the whole Catholic population of India which is 18 million. Though materially poor, it is nevertheless self-sufficient in many aspects and has its own nuns, priests and bishops. One of the characteristics of this Church has been that these tribal Catholics became bearers of the Faith wherever they went. For this reason, this extraordinary growth of the Church in the tribal lands has become known as the 'Miracle of Chotanagpur'.

Two of the Jesuits working among the Tribals in Ranchi were Albanians. On a visit home they gave talks to school children, promoting missionary vocations and raising funds for their work. One of those who heard them was a teenage girl called Agnes. She listened attentively and made up her mind to go to India to work among the Ranchi tribes. She came to India as a Loreto nun. We know her now as St Mother Teresa of Calcutta.

Cardinal Toppo based much of his talk on the Second Vatican Council's Pastoral Constitution on the Church in the Modern World, *Gaudium et Spes.* He highlighted three areas in which the Church carries out her mission: the socio-economic disparity; religious pluralism; and diversity of cultural identities. The Council gave a lead in all these too. Considering the Church's liturgy, the Council also gave a new lead:

The Second Vatican Council's constitution on the liturgy ushered in a change in the life of the worship of the Church. It transformed the Eucharistic celebration by insisting on three main aspects of that celebration: Eucharist as an act of the community ... the faithful participate actively in the celebration of the Eucharist ... the effect of participating in the Eucharistic celebration is the building up of a community of love and sharing ... The Good News

that the world needs today is a society based on brotherhood and sisterhood and lived in sharing. Then the true
God, the Father of Our Lord Jesus Christ, who has made
us also His children in Jesus Christ, will appear in our
midst. Our Eucharistic celebration should enable us to
work towards that ideal.

Obviously influenced by the Council's teaching, the Cardinal then
described how the Eucharist builds up the Christian community
and inspires the Church's mission.

From the very beginning of the Church we see that the
Eucharist builds communities of mission, whether this
mission is exercised in the form of proclaiming the Gospel
or as a martyrdom of faith witnessing, as we have seen, for
example, in China and many other countries in the past
century. The connection between the Eucharist and the
communities of mission rests on a basic characteristic of
Christian mission itself. The Christian missionary is first
and foremost a witness of Christ and not a mere pupil who
has learnt the truths about Christ. A witness is one who
has experienced what he communicates. The Eucharist is
the source of this witnessing power. There the Christian
meets the living Christ and becomes capable of proclaiming what he has seen, heard and touched ... The end of the
Mass is not the conclusion of an act of worship. It is the
beginning of the mission of the Church ... At the end of
every Mass, when the celebrant takes leave of the assembly
with the words *Ite, Missa est,* all should feel they are sent
as 'missionaries of the Eucharist' to carry to every environment the great gift received ...

We go out into the world after the Eucharist challenged
by the word of God, prophetically charged by the Spirit of
the risen Lord and committed to work for the transformation of the world. This is the meaning of the phrase: We
proclaim Your death, O Lord, until You come. That is, we
are going out to continue the work of Christ to bring about
the Kingdom of God, where Divine love will be translated

into human love, where Divine life will be manifested in communion, where creation will be transformed into a new earth and new heaven in which all the peoples of the world will live as brothers and sisters. The Eucharist empowers us to do this. This is the ultimate goal of all our Eucharistic celebrations.

A kaleidoscope of sparkling events filled the rest of the day's celebrations: a charismatic witness by José Flores, founder and director of the San Andres School of Evangelisation, followed Cardinal Toppo's talk, before the Bishop of Hong Kong, Cardinal Joseph Zen Ze-Kiun, celebrated Mass. That evening, the Pepsi Coliseum witnessed a most joyful occasion—the ordination of twelve priests. Eight of these came from the Marie-Jeunesse Family, a new Catholic community of consecrated men and women and priests which began in Quebec in 1982.

Quebec has many venerated institutions and shrines. The most famous is that of Sainte-Anne-de-Beaupré, thirty kilometres from Quebec City and attractively situated on the St Lawrence River. The shrine is credited with many cures of sick and disabled people and draws half a million people each year. Crutches and walking aids left behind by people who have visited and prayed there cover the wall at the entrance to the imposing basilica. We three pilgrims from England felt privileged to be part of the Hamilton diocesan pilgrimage to the shrine.

Day of Africa

Saturday 21 June was Africa Day, with the theme 'Witnesses of the Eucharist in the midst of the World'. Cardinal Christian Tumi, Archbishop of Douala in Cameroon, applied the Lord's description of His followers, 'salt of the earth and light of the world', to the contemporary scene. The Church had to be involved in the struggle for justice and peace. A practical example was given in the testimony of Marguerite Barankitse, founder of Maison Shalom in Burundi, dedicated to helping child victims of war. Marguerite's message was 'Love always triumphs. Evil will never have the last word', while in his homily at Mass that morning the Nigerian Cardinal Francis Arinze spoke strongly of the Church's mission to both the bodily and the spiritually hungry people of our time. He emphasised the relationship between the celebration of the Eucharist and social commitment, quoting from the 2005 Synod of Bishops, that 'all who partake of the Eucharist must commit themselves to peace-making in our world scarred by violence and war, and today in particular by terrorism, economic corruption and sexual exploitation'. He then quoted from Pope Benedict in *Sacramentum Caritatis* 89: 'the Eucharist becomes in life what it signifies in its celebration. As I have had occasion to say, it is not the proper task of the Church to engage in the political work of bringing about the most just society possible; nonetheless she cannot and must not remain on the side-lines in the struggle for justice.'

Saturday ended with a lively prayer vigil led by the papal legate, Cardinal Tomko, in which a thousand young adults took part. Cardinal Ouellet was there too and told them he felt as if 'raised from the dead'!

The Plains of Abraham

The Quebec Congress was marked by rain. Every day! Some saw it as 'a cleansing of Quebec'. But however heavy the rain had been during the week, it was as nothing compared with the deluge on the final day, Sunday 22 June, the day of the Statio Orbis.

The outdoor Mass for this was prepared on the Plains of Abraham, an historic site extending to the west of the city along the St Lawrence River. The battle that took place there in 1759 signified the end of New France and the creation of Canada. How vividly Fr (later Bishop) Geoffrey Burke had re-constructed that battle for us in his history lessons at St Bede's College in Manchester! Now on the actual site, we could almost see and hear the hour-long battle between the opposing armies led by General Wolfe and General Montcalm, both of whom were mortally wounded that day. After losing the battle, France ceded most of her possessions in eastern North America to Great Britain. That year was afterwards known in Britain as the 'Annus Mirabilis'.

A different, peaceful army now ascended the Plains of Abraham, heavily outnumbering the British and French combatants of 1759. At first the sun shone and they came in good humour. At 8.30 am the Jerusalem Community led the Office of the Resurrection, followed by music and song. The sky began to cloud over and as the procession of celebrants entered the rain started to fall. Cardinal Tomko presided at the Mass, with some thirty cardinals occupying the sanctuary and with bishops and nearly two thousand priest concelebrants in front of the altar area. Pope Benedict XVI gave the homily, transmitting from the Vatican and visible to all the assembly on large screens. In his usual courteous style, the Holy Father greeted those present before pulling together the different strands of the Congress. He called the Eucharist 'our most beautiful treasure':

> It is the Sacrament par excellence; it ushers us into eternal life in advance; it contains the entire mystery of our salvation; it is the source and summit of the action and life of the Church as the Second Vatican Council recalled. It is therefore particularly important that pastors and faithful be constantly committed to deepening their knowledge of this great Sacrament. In this way each one will be able to affirm his faith and carry out his mission in the Church and in the world ever better, remembering that the Eucharist bears fruit in one's personal life, in the life of the Church and the world.

Pope Benedict immediately reminded us of the social implications of the Eucharist:

> The Spirit of truth bears witness in your hearts; may you too witness to Christ among men and women ... Thus, participation in the Eucharist does not distance our contemporaries. On the contrary, since it is the expression par excellence of God's love, it calls us to join forces with all our

brothers and sisters to confront today's challenges and make the earth a place that is pleasant to live in. This requires that we constantly fight to ensure that everyone is respected, from conception until natural death, that our rich societies welcome the poorest and restore dignity to all, that everyone has food and can enable his family to survive and that peace and justice shine out on all the continents. These are some of the challenges that must mobilise all our contemporaries, and from the Eucharistic mystery Christians must draw the strength to confront them.

The Pope then appealed to all believers to deepen their knowledge and reverence of the Eucharist, to revitalise their Eucharistic instruction and to enter ever more closely into communion with Christ and with His Church:

> I would like everyone to make a commitment to study this great mystery, especially by revisiting and exploring, individually and in groups, the Council's text on the Liturgy, *Sacrosanctum Concilium*, so as to bear witness courageously to the mystery. In this way, each person will arrive at a better grasp of the meaning of every aspect of the Eucharist, understanding its depth and living it with greater intensity. Every sentence, every gesture has its own meaning and conceals a mystery.

> I sincerely hope that this Congress will serve as an appeal to all the faithful to make a similar commitment to a renewal of Eucharistic catechesis, so that they themselves will gain a genuine Eucharistic awareness and will in turn teach children and young people to recognize the central mystery of faith and build their lives around it. I urge priests especially to give due honour to the Eucharistic rite, and I ask all the faithful to respect the role of each individual, both priest and lay, in the Eucharistic action. The liturgy does not belong to us: it is the Church's treasure.

> Reception of the Eucharist, adoration of the Blessed Sacrament—by this we mean deepening our Communion, preparing for it and prolonging it—is also about allowing

ourselves to enter into communion with Christ, and through Him with the whole of the Trinity, so as to become what we receive and to live in communion with the Church. It is by receiving the Body of Christ that we receive the strength 'of unity with God and with one another' (St Cyril of Alexandria, *In Ioannis Evangelium*, 11: 11; cf St Augustine, *Sermo* 577).

We must never forget that the Church is built around Christ and that, as St Augustine, St Thomas Aquinas and St Albert the Great have all said, following St Paul (cf 1 Co 10:17), the Eucharist is the Sacrament of the Church's unity, because we all form one single body of which the Lord is the head. We must go back again and again to the Last Supper on Holy Thursday, where we were given a pledge of the mystery of our redemption on the Cross. The Last Supper is the *locus* of the nascent Church, the womb containing the Church of every age. In the Eucharist, Christ's sacrifice is constantly renewed, Pentecost is constantly renewed. May all of you become ever more deeply aware of the importance of the Sunday Eucharist because Sunday, the first day of the week, is the day when we honour Christ, the day when we receive the strength to live each day the gift of God.

'Receive the Eucharist with a pure heart' may well have been the heading for Pope Benedict's homily, as he continued and opened up the possibility of a Communion of desire:

I would also like to invite pastors and the faithful to take a renewed interest in their preparation for receiving the Eucharist. Despite our weakness and sin, Christ wants to make His dwelling place in us. This is why we must do everything in our power to receive Him with a pure heart, continuously rediscovering through the Sacrament of forgiveness that purity which sin has stained, 'that (our) minds be attuned to (our) voices' (cf *Sacrosanctum Concilium* 11), according to the Council's invitation. Sin in fact, especially serious sin, impedes the action of Eucharistic grace within us. Moreover, those who cannot receive Communion because of their situation will find a saving power and effectiveness in a Communion of desire and from participation at the Eucharist.

Naming many of the saints of Canada, Pope Benedict urged his hearers to learn from them

and, like them, be fearless; God accompanies and protects you; every day make an offering for the glory of God the Father and play your part in the construction of the world, proudly remembering your religious heritage and its social and cultural outreach and taking care to spread around you the moral and spiritual values that come to us from the Lord.

Pope Benedict reminded us of our part in our covenant with God, asking us to pray for priestly vocations.

The Eucharist is not a meal with friends. It is the mystery of a covenant. 'The prayers and rites of the Eucharistic sacrifice revive the whole history of salvation continuously before the eyes of our soul, in the course of the liturgical cycle and make us enter its significance ever more deeply' (St. Teresa Benedicta of the Cross (Edith Stein), *Wege zu inneren Stille, Aschaffenburg* 1987, p 67). We are called to enter into this mystery of a covenant by conforming our lives ever more closely each day to the gift received in the Eucharist. It has a sacred character, as the Second Vatican Council recalls: 'every liturgical celebration, because it is an action of Christ the Priest and of His Body, which is the Church, is a sacred action surpassing all others. No other action of the Church can equal its efficacy by the same title and to the same degree' (*Sacrosanctum Concilium* 7). In a certain way, it is a 'heavenly liturgy', an anticipation of the banquet in the eternal Kingdom, announcing the death and Resurrection of Christ 'until he comes' (1 Co 11:26).

In order that the People of God may never lack ministers to give them the Body of Christ, we must ask the Lord to make the gift of new priests to His Church. I also ask you to pass on the call to the priesthood to young men, so that they will joyfully and fearlessly respond to the Lord. They will not be disappointed. May the family be the origin and cradle of vocations.

Before giving us his blessing, Pope Benedict announced that the next International Eucharistic Congress would be held in Dublin in 2012. By this time the rain had become incessant and troublesome. At the moment of Consecration, the heavens really opened with deafening thunder and lightning, and the sheeting rain drenched us all. The Plains of Abraham turned into a quagmire. Cardinals on the altar and participants in the fields vainly tried to shield themselves. Giving Holy Communion to the people was a nightmare. Mass quickly came to an end, with the Papal Legate describing the rain as 'rain of grace' and Cardinal Ouellet bravely speaking of it as a 'flood of Divine Goodness'! A celebration and picnic time had been planned to end the day. The organisers had even stated in the official booklet that 'the celebration will take place regardless of weather conditions. Please dress accordingly'. Saturated Congressists had other ideas. The Plains emptied as they ploughed their way to their coaches. The celebration was cancelled.

It would be wrong however to finish this chapter on a damp note. There were so many positives about the Quebec Congress. Fr Thomas Rosica again:

> The real problem in Quebec has been the spiritual void created by a religious and cultural rupture, a significant loss of memory, bringing in its wake a family crisis and an educational crisis, leaving citizens disoriented, unmotivated and destabilised. One day during the Congress in Quebec, the daily rainfall compelled me take a taxi to the Pepsi Coliseum. The young driver, an Algerian Muslim man, asked me where I came from, and then spoke to me about the Congress, having encountered so many of the delegates on the streets of Quebec. 'What are they giving your people to eat these days?' he asked me. I looked

puzzled and asked him to explain. He said: 'I have never seen so many happy people in Quebec since I emigrated here ten years ago. There has to be something in the food and drink. It must be awesome!' I told him that it was certainly awesome!

The Congress has been a privileged opportunity for Canada to re-actualise the historic and cultural patrimony of holiness and social engagement of the Church, which draws its roots from the Eucharistic mystery. In his 2003 encyclical letter *Ecclesia de Eucharistia* Pope John Paul II wrote: 'The Eucharist builds the Church and the Church makes the Eucharist'. The International Eucharistic Congress in Quebec did just that.

We dried out on the twelve-hour coach ride back to Hamilton. The Congress had lasted for eight days and was notable for its liturgies and inspiring conferences. It had been a great pleasure to meet up again with old friends like Monsignor Brian Walsh from Melbourne and Fr Graham Keep from London (Ontario). Canon O'Connor, Fr Griffin and I then took The Canadian across Canada, through the Rockies, to Vancouver. The three-day memorable train ride gave us ample proof of the vastness of the country. Denis and Darlene Horgan and their lovely daughter Marie took us under their wing and showed us some beautiful places including Whistler and Vancouver Island. We stayed in Delta BC with the Augustinian Fathers who could not have been more hospitable.

References

1) Pontifical Committee for International Eucharistic Congresses, *The Eucharist, Gift of God for the Life of the World,* Basic Theological Document for the 49th International Eucharistic Congress, Quebec, 2008.

2) Congress publications:
   - Guide for Congress Pilgrims CEI 2008
   - Magnificat 15–21 June
   - Laudamus
   - Statio Orbis

3) Allen, J. F., Personal notes and diaries and Congress releases.

4) Pontifical Committee for International Eucharistic Congresses, 49th International Eucharistic Congress, Quebec, 2008, Reflection and Recommendations.

5) *The Eucharist, Gift of God for the Life of the World,* Acts of the 49th International Eucharistic Congress, Quebec 2008 (Ottawa 2008)

6) *The Eucharist, Gift of God for the Life of the World,* Acts of the International Theology Symposium, Quebec, 11–13 June 2008 (Ottawa 2009)

7) http://www.vatican.va/roman_curia/pont_committees/eucharist-congr/archive/index_en.htm

8) http:// www.saltandlighttv.org.

12 DUBLIN 10–17 JUNE 2012
THE EUCHARIST: COMMUNION WITH CHRIST AND WITH ONE ANOTHER

MEDIA REPORTING IN Ireland was generally guarded before the Congress, giving it a somewhat 'medium hello'. *Pace* Joyce, there was no suggestion that the Dublin Congress of 2012 might be written in the hearts of the people. In the event, for the welcome, the organisation, the quality of its liturgies and conferences, the Dublin Congress of 2012 was right up there with the best of them. Bishop Terence Brain of Salford had encouraged his diocesans to attend the Congress and a good number did. I stayed with Canon Kevin O'Connor at his cousin's house near All Hallows but spent much time with the Davins, Sean and Margaret, at their home in Ballsbridge, conveniently near the RDS, the Royal Dublin Society.

Inevitably, people made comparisons with the Dublin Congress of 1932. That Congress was surely the most remarkable public event of the whole twentieth century in Ireland. The sheer scale of the planning, the organisation, the festive enthusiasm—all left a lasting impression on everyone then alive. It was reckoned that a million people, over a quarter of Ireland's population, were present at the closing Mass of the Congress in the Phoenix Park. Count John McCormack's singing of *Panis angelicus* has gone down in folklore. The papal legate, Cardinal Lorenzo Lauri, was reported as saying: *'Dopo Dublino, solamente il cielo!'* 'After Dublin, there can only be heaven!'

The 2012 Congress came at a sensitive time for the Irish Church. The Congress President, Archbishop Diarmuid Martin of Dublin, wrote in May 2010:

> I am very conscious that these are difficult, painful times for our Church and for our society. Our first reaction might be one of anger, quickly followed by disillusionment

and the temptation to walk away from it all. Similar feelings led some of the disciples of Jesus, after the events of Good Friday, to put as much distance as possible between themselves and Jerusalem. It was while they were making their way, in great sadness, to Emmaus, that they encountered Jesus on the road. He listened to them, opened the Scriptures to them, and came in and broke bread with them. My prayer for all of us, especially for all who have suffered through the failures of the Church or of our social structures, is that we may encounter Jesus on the road of our lives during this next two years, and that, like the disciples, we will experience His presence with us as a source of healing and encouragement.

Later, in November 2010, Archbishop Martin addressed the Pontifical Committee for International Congresses in Rome: 'The 1932 Congress ... was an event which responded to the need for affirmation of the Catholic community in Ireland finding its way in the newly independent State. Today Irish society has changed and Irish piety has changed.' He pointed out that the 1932 Congress was 'a strong moment of reconciliation' for many who had been alienated from one another in the 'brutal and divisive civil war' of the early 1920s.

> The Eucharistic Congress which is planned for Dublin in 2012 takes place at another crucial moment in the history of Ireland and of the Irish Church. The Irish Church is in many ways a wounded Church and a Church which seeks new direction. Like many European countries, Ireland has undergone rapid social change in these years. Ireland today has become a highly secularised society ...

Acknowledging the scandal of abuse of children by members of the Church in Ireland he said:

> For many in Ireland, then, the Church is an institution which has failed to live up to its mission ... It is in this context that the Church in Ireland proposed the theme of the 2012 Eucharistic Congress as: *The Eucharist: Com-*

munion with Christ and with one another. The aim is to recall the attention of individuals and society to the fact that the fulness of our belonging to Jesus is attained through participation in the Eucharist, which builds at one and the same time communion with Christ and communion with one another.

Archbishop Martin said that, following on the teachings of the Second Vatican Council, the Congress intended to show how communion with Christ gathers people together and helps them to 'bring the good news of Jesus to others ... There can be no division between participation in the Eucharist and caring for the excluded.'

For the next two years, Fr Kevin Doran, as General Secretary for the Congress, and Anne Griffin as Programme Manager worked with the main planning committee through six groups, responsible for pastoral and liturgical planning; communications and media; volunteer management; services and logistics; finance and administration; and special events. Delegates from every diocese in Ireland formed a National Eucharistic Committee to ensure that people of every parish in the land could be involved. A Theological Committee prepared the basic document for the Congress and a National Finance Committee provided external financial control. All Congress resources were made available in electronic format.

Four stages of preparation from 2010 to 2012 explored the Congress theme. The stages considered how 1) Christ gathers us as a Eucharistic Community; 2) Christ gathers us to listen, to hear, to be nourished and to be formed into community by God's Word; 3) Christ gathers us to be nourished by the Bread of Life; 4) Christ gathers and strengthens us for Mission by the Word and the Bread of Life. Readers of earlier chapters of this book will recognise familiar themes here. Also in 2010, Pope Benedict XVI spoke of the 'happy circumstances' adding significance to the Dublin Congress.

The 2012 Dublin Congress will have a jubilee character. In fact, it will be the 50th Congress, and it will be held likewise 50 years from the opening of Vatican II, to which the theme makes explicit reference, recalling chapter seven of the dogmatic constitution *Lumen Gentium*.

The Dublin RDS—the Royal Dublin Society—was the main Congress venue. The RDS describes itself as 'an iconic, accessible and flexible venue located on a beautiful 42-acre site, close to Dublin City Centre. It is regarded as Ireland's premier venue for exhibitions, conferences, meetings and entertainment events.' With its plentiful number of halls, meeting rooms, eating places and open spaces, the RDS should have proved an ideal site. For the most part, it did. Unfortunately, the rooms were not big enough for all the people who wanted to attend many of the seminars and workshops. Even queuing for some time did not guarantee admission, leaving some people frustrated.

Facing the future

The Congress opened on the afternoon of Sunday 10 June. After a rain-filled week, the sun shone as 12,000 people filled the arena for the opening Mass, presided over by the Papal Legate, Cardinal Marc Ouellet of Canada, Prefect of the Congregation for Bishops. The Congress Bell rang out and representatives of 123 countries processed into the arena, along with parishes and groups from the four ecclesiastical provinces of Ireland, all waving their flags and banners. Voices told of the Irish Christian heritage, of saints and heroes from long ago, illustrated with drama and music and poetry. In his homily, Cardinal Ouellet said:

> How fitting it is that, in God's providence, this gathering takes place here in Ireland. This is a country known for its natural beauty, its hospitality and its rich culture, but most especially for its long tradition of fidelity to the Catholic faith. Ireland's strong history of faithfulness has enriched not only these shores, but has, through her missionary sons and daughters, helped to bring the Gospel to many other, far-distant shores.

Now the Church in Ireland is suffering and faces many new and serious challenges to the faith. Well aware of these challenges, we turn together to Our Lord, who renews, heals and strengthens the faith of His people. I know from my own experience of the last International Eucharistic Congress in Quebec City that an event such as this brings many blessings to the local Church and to all the participants, including those who sustain it through prayer, volunteer work and solidarity. And so we pray with confidence in the Eucharistic Lord that this, the fiftieth occurrence of this great universal Church event, may bring a very special blessing to Ireland at this turbulent time and to all of you. We come here as God's family, called by Him to listen to His holy Word, to remember who we are in light of salvation history and to respond to God through the greatest and most sublime prayer ever known to the world: the Holy Eucharist. May the Holy Spirit help us to be fully conscious of just how blessed and privileged we are.

Reflecting on God's covenant with Moses, sealed by blood, Cardinal Ouellet said: 'The blood of Christ has this power of redemption and purification because it is a blood shed out of perfect love for God and for humanity, a divine blood that brings the covenant to perfection, not only for Israel but for all people.' God calls us together every Sunday:

Our gathering is an act of faith in the Holy Eucharist, the treasure of the Church, which is essential to her life and to our communion as brothers and sisters in Christ. The Church draws her life from the Eucharist, she receives her own identity from the gift of Christ's own Body. In communion with His Body, the Church becomes what she receives: she becomes one body with Him in the Spirit of the new and eternal covenant. What a great and marvellous mystery! A mystery of love! The risen Lord has disappeared from our sight, but His love is closer than ever. His risen Body has acquired new freedom and new properties which make possible the marvel of the Holy Eucharist. By the power of His divine word and Spirit He changes this bread and wine into His own real Body and Blood. As Pope St Leo the Great teaches us: 'Our Redeemer's visible presence has passed into the sacraments' (*Sermo 2 de Ascensione* 1–4: PL 54, 397–399). When we receive Communion, the Spirit of the Lord present in Christ's Body passes into our hearts and into our bodies, making us one new ecclesial body, the mystical body of the Lord. This ecclesial body is our deepest identity.

The Cardinal then reminded us of the notion of a 'spiritual communion':

> At these gatherings we come as we are, poor sinners, and we may not always have the proper disposition to receive Communion. But, as the preparatory document for this Eucharistic Congress reminds us, everyone is able to live what is called 'a spiritual communion' in the sense of an act of worship, uniting themselves with the self-giving movement that is being celebrated at Mass (cf. *The Eucharist: Communion with Christ and with one another* 12). Even when we do not receive sacramental Communion, we can share in the grace that flows from the Body and Blood of Christ to His ecclesial body. This active and conscious participation means belonging to the one body and receiving from it love, peace, hope and courage to go forward, accepting our own share of suffering. Pope Benedict tells us, 'Even in cases where it is not possible to receive sacramental communion, participation at Mass remains necessary, important, meaningful and fruitful' (*Sacramentum Caritatis* 55).

We might note that this interesting suggestion was in fact raised before the Dublin Congress by two recent Popes: St John Paul II in *Ecclesia de Eucharistia* n.34 and Benedict XVI in *Sacramentum Caritatis* n.55. Pope Benedict wrote that where it is not possible to receive sacramental communion 'it is beneficial to cultivate a desire for full union with Christ through the practice of spiritual communion, praised by Pope John Paul II and recommended by saints who were masters of the spiritual life'. Pope John Paul expanded his teaching in paragraph 35 of the same document, *Ecclesia de Eucharistia*:

> The celebration of the Eucharist, however, cannot be the starting-point for communion; it presupposes that communion already exists, a communion which it seeks to consolidate and bring to perfection. The sacrament is an expression of this bond of communion both in its invisible dimension, which, in Christ and through the working of the Holy Spirit, unites us to the Father and among ourselves, and in its visible dimension, which entails communion in the teaching of the Apostles, in the sacraments and in the Church's hierarchical order. The profound relationship between the invisible and the visible elements of ecclesial communion is constitutive of the Church as the sacrament of salvation. Only in this context can there be a legitimate celebration of the Eucharist and true participation in it. Consequently it is an intrinsic requirement of the Eucharist that it should be celebrated in communion, and specifically maintaining the various bonds of that communion intact.

Three days earlier, Cardinal Ouellet had opened a Theological Symposium at Maynooth, where 370 theologians from 31 different countries deliberated on aspects of the theme, 'The Ecclesiology of Communion 50 years after the opening of Vatican II'. He surveyed past, present and possible future features of such an ecclesiology, underlining the important ecumenical understandings it provided. He evoked three themes he considered to merit particular attention: 'the relation between the universal Church and the particular Churches; the theology of Christian initiation; and the integration of modern forms of Eucharistic piety.' He proposed an ecclesiology of communion in a nuptial perspective; an examination of the relationship between Mary, the Eucharist, and the Church; and of the place of charisms. The symposium also heard from Cardinal Kurt Koch, President of the Council for Promoting Christian Unity, and Metropolitan Emmanuel Adamakis of France, President of the

Conference of European Churches, on the ecumenical dimension of a Eucharistic ecclesiology.

Baptism

Each day of the Congress focussed on a sacramental theme. Monday was the turn of baptism, seen as a common vocation of Christians. It was therefore also an ecumenical day, with the Anglican Archbishop of Dublin, Michael Jackson, presiding over a liturgy of Word and Water and the Prior of Taizé, Br Alois Löser, speaking on 'Communion and Baptism: A Passion for the Unity of Christ's Body'. Earlier in the day, Archbishop Diarmuid Martin of Dublin and President of the Congress delivered a widely-reported address on 'The Church in the Modern World':

> The particular challenge in Ireland is to learn to know who Jesus is. Many nominal Catholics, including some who, notwithstanding regular attendance in church, have never reflected personally on the faith they have assimilated through societal and familial influence ... The Church has to find new ways of being present in a new Irish society. To do that the Church must re-discover its own sense of communion and sense of common purpose, overcoming its internal divisions in a spirit of love of the Church and in a dialogue of charity ... My hope is that this Congress may be a signpost as to how our Communion with Christ in the Eucharist can generate a new understanding of our communion with each other in a modern world which is today very different to that of the 1960s and in a future which will be even more different and challenging.

Groups from England met on the Monday morning in the Newman University Church on St Stephen's Green. We concelebrated Mass, led by Bishops Mark Davies of Shrewsbury, David McGough, auxiliary in Birmingham, and John Arnold, auxiliary in Westminster. What a stunning church this is, in neo-Byzantine style! Unpretentious on the outside, the interior is breathtaking. Founded by Blessed John Henry Newman in 1856 for the Catholic

University of Dublin, it was paid for from money left over from donations he received to pay for his conviction in the Achilles trial.

That same Monday evening, Bishop Mark Davies of Shrewsbury gave a catechesis for young people in the Chiara Luce Youth Space. Chiara 'Luce' Badano, born in 1971 at Sassello in Italy, was only 18 when she died of a rare kind of bone cancer. She was active in the Focolare youth movement and dedicated her life to Christ. Her strong faith has inspired many young people, captivated by her joyful, down-to-earth holiness. A Cardinal who visited her in hospital asked her, 'The light in your eyes is splendid. Where does it come from?' Chiara simply replied, 'I try to love Jesus as much as I can.' Pope Benedict XVI beatified her in 2010, two years before the Dublin Congress. Over the week, forty-one speakers would deliver addresses in the Youth Space for young people between 18 and 25 years old.

Marriage and the Family

Congress Tuesday was dedicated to marriage and the family. The retired Archbishop of Perth, Barry James Hickey, gave a catechesis on 'Eucharist and the Christian Family'. He was happy to speak because

> preparing this talk has immersed me once again in the beauty of our Catholic faith. I reflected again on the awesome communion with God that we experience through the Risen Lord and the Holy Spirit, when we are taken up into the life of the Blessed Trinity. It has caused me to reflect again on the beauty of Christian Marriage, and on how absolutely necessary it is for us to proclaim to the world the gift that Christian Marriage is. I saw an opportunity to say in this very public forum that Christian marriage is now under fierce and hostile attack, and that we cannot let that deter us from affirming the great vision of Jesus and St Paul to a world desperately in need of it.

Archbishop Hickey quoted from chapter five of St Paul's letter to the Ephesians, where Paul speaks of 'a deep secret' now revealed that the loving union of husband and wife is so unique that it is to be an image of the union between Christ and His church, based on love. This was and is a very disturbing statement. Marriage in St Paul's time was not always based on love. In both Jewish practice and the ways of the Roman Empire, marriage was based more on perpetuating family ties or inheritance or property or status rather than on love. St Paul had absorbed Jesus' own teaching on the permanence of marriage as the original intention of the Creator, by reflecting theologically on the importance of love and self-giving in Christian Marriage.

From Scripture, the archbishop turned to the teachings of Popes St John Paul II and Benedict XVI.

Pope John Paul II wrote in *Familiaris Consortio* in 1981 'that God in himself lives a mystery of personal loving communion'. He goes on to say that if we are created in the image of God, we also have the capacity and the obligation of love and communion. To love, therefore, becomes the vocation of every human person, and in marriage especially, involving as it does, the human body as well as the human spirit. Thus he sanctifies the intimate love and embrace of husband and wife in marriage as they give themselves totally to each other. This is the image of God's love for us, as St Paul taught. The Holy Father points to the role of the Eucharist in the life of the family. Not only does the Eucharist nourish marriage and family life and deepen its union with Christ, it also includes the aspect of sacrifice, which is central to our understanding of the Eucharist. The Eucharist is a re-presentation of Christ's sacrifice of love for the Church, and was sealed with his blood on the cross. The Eucharist is the source of strength for couples who know without exception that committed love requires a spirit of self-sacrifice, freely and joyfully given. The knowledge that Jesus' love for us involved the ultimate price empowers and motivates couples to fully commit themselves to their vocation as spouses and parents, no matter what the cost.

We turn to the exhortation of Pope Benedict XVI called *Sacramentum Caritatis* or the Sacrament of Love, meaning of course, the Blessed Eucharist. It could also mean the Sacrament of Matrimony, which is also a Sacrament of Love. The Holy Father argues thus: If the Eucharist is the abiding sign of the covenantal love between God and the Church, that love is indissoluble—it will never be broken. It cannot be broken because God is always faithful to his promises. Christian marriage must therefore be indissoluble if the love of God for his church is to be compared to it. 'What God has joined together let no one put asunder' (Mk 10:9).

The Eucharist, symbol of God's unfailing love, is also the symbol of the unfailing love of Christian marriage. It also provides the strength and the grace to nourish the marriage. The Holy Father goes on to say that the force of this teaching reveals its 'radical newness'. It reveals how different Christian marriage really is compared to the diversity of human relationships we see around us. It is new in its permanence and in the quality of the union between husband and wife. We are speaking of God's original plan which was modified by Moses, as Jesus said, because of their hardness of heart. Jesus restored the marriage bond as it was meant to be. The hardness of the human heart has not changed much. Marriage continues to fail because of it. Sin enters and causes huge damage. Nevertheless, we must call people to a higher vision despite human weakness, and point to the Blessed Eucharist as the source of strength and grace, and the very presence of the healing Lord within the life of the family. The pastoral problems facing the Church and its pastors when marriages break up are very real, says the Holy Father. At the same time the pastors must offer guidance that respects the truth, and urge people in painful situations to continue to attend Mass and to pray for an answer that respects the truth, knowing that they have in our Eucharistic Lord a compassionate Saviour.

The respect of truth must extend also to the matter of children. Truth is not respected when couples defy Church teaching on contraception. It sets up an inner conflict which undermines faith, and causes mistrust of Christ's mandate to teach on matters of human sexuality. It undermines one's own prayer-life and eventually our trust in God. The wisdom of the world has chosen to ignore, even ridicule Catholic teaching on the matter of openness to children, and has taken a different and tragic path. Artificially separating sex from its possible consequences has led to the separation of sex from marriage itself and has led to the proliferation of casual unions, to the exploitation of young women, to false hopes that sexual activity will lead to love, and to the abandonment of marriage by millions of people around the world. Faced with this, the Church can either compromise and face irrelevance, or continue to teach Christ's truth about marriage, life and love, and pray that the world will listen.

In the face of so many problems of our day,

the gift we give to a world of broken relationships and unloved children is the beauty of Christian marriage and the desire to reach out to the victims of broken marriages. Jesus has entrusted to us this pearl of great price. Care for it, as it is a rare treasure.

Cardinal Andre Vingt-Trois, Archbishop of Paris, presided at Mass and treated us to a softly-spoken meditation on the Gospel message of being 'salt of the earth and light of the world'.

Christians are called to enhance the taste and the richness of the realities of this world. On the other hand, if the Christians immersed in the life of this world lose their specificity, then they become useless. If we forget the One who sends us into this world and what our vocation involves, if we allow ourselves to be absorbed into this world without displaying anything distinctive, if we simply live like everybody else, then our very existence is vain and that of the world has no flavour ... Yet, how could we bear witness to the novelty and hope of Christ if we neglected to go back to the source of our communion? The Paschal Mystery of the death and resurrection of Christ, as it is celebrated in the Eucharist, and particularly in the Sunday Mass, is not a detail in Christian life. Without this celebration, Christian life unavoidably becomes flavourless ... We know that the testimony of Catholic families is especially decisive to add the salt of the Gospel at the core of today's world. To be the salt of the earth cannot mean accepting that all behaviours are equally good, or that the various combinations existing nowadays all make up genuine families. Rather, it seems to me that the wealth and grace of the sacrament of marriage provide Christians with the words and the means to bear witness to the greatness of the family as the stable union of a man and a woman in order to bring up their children before those who believe as well as before those who don't ...

The image of the light in the Gospel offers another insight on the presence of Christians in this world ... The light radiates from 'good deeds' of Christ's disciples. If we do not do the good that the Scriptures call us to do, Christ's light will remain invisible, however loudly we speak on the public square, on the radio or on television. Our mission is not to vie with other messages competing for the public's attention. It is to bear witness to God's love in the world. We know that 'the excellency of speech or of wisdom' (1 Co 2:1) or the strength of our beliefs is not enough to make our 'good deeds' shine. If they do shine, it is because the power of God's Spirit manifests itself through them. Then, if God's love is at work in our lives, however modestly and discreetly, the life of the Spirit will reveal itself and we will be listened to! In the field of family life, we must not rule out anything of all that can be done publicly to defend the value of the family. But the first mission of Christian families is to live concretely by these values, by 'reconciliation, mutual acceptance and joy in giving one's life for one's loved ones'. The strength of our testimonies lies in the examples we give. The Church will be heard and respected inasmuch as she helps Christians remain irreversibly faithful, confident enough to welcome new lives, tirelessly kind to the oldest and to the most vulnerable, and respectfully open to the ones who are alone.

Earlier in the day, Cardinal Marc Ouellet travelled to Lough Derg at the request of Pope Benedict XVI for a day pilgrimage and to meet with victims of clergy sexual abuse. He was joined by Archbishop Charles Brown, Apostolic Nuncio to Ireland. Speaking there the Cardinal said:

> Lough Derg in Ireland is the symbol of conversion, penance and spiritual renewal. Many people come here to pray, to fast and to apologize for their sins ... I come here with the specific intention of seeking forgiveness, from God and from the victims, for the grave sin of sexual abuse of children by clerics. We have learned over the last decades how much harm and despair such abuse has caused to thousands of victims. We learned too that the response of some Church authorities to these crimes was often inadequate and inefficient in stopping the crimes, in spite of clear indications in the code of Canon Law. In the name of the Church, I apologize once again to the victims, some of whom I have met here in Lough Derg. I repeat here what the Holy Father told to the victims in his Letter to the Catholics of Ireland: 'It is understandable that you find it hard to forgive or to be reconciled with the Church. In her name I openly express the shame and remorse that we feel. At the same time, I ask you not to lose hope. It is in the communion of the Church that we encounter the person of Jesus Christ, who was himself a victim of injustice and sin' ... As members of the Church, we must have the courage to ask humbly for God's pardon, as well as for the forgiveness of those who have been wounded: we must remain close to them on their road of suffering, seeking in every possible way to heal and bind up the

wounds following the example of the Good Samaritan. From the context of this International Eucharistic Congress, I reaffirm the commitment of the Catholic Church to create a safe environment for children and we pray that a new culture of respect, integrity, and Christ-like love would prevail in our midst and permeate the whole society.

Priesthood and ministries

Congress Wednesday's theme was 'Priesthood and Ministries serving Communion'. Fr John Cusick of Chicago—'Catholics: Why we do what we do'—and Dr Tim O'Driscoll of Virginia—'Priests after His Own Heart'—gave excellent seminars in the morning, with Archbishop Michael Miller of Vancouver leading the afternoon catechesis on 'Priesthood in service of Communion'. Archbishop Miller summed up his talk as follows: ... the ministerial priesthood is born *from* the Eucharist, is directed *to* the Eucharist and bears fruit *because of* the Eucharist.' He made

> three major points about the priesthood: first, ministerial priests are at the service of the priesthood of all the faithful; second, priests are men of communion called to foster unity and healing in the ecclesial community; and third, priests, as servants of the Eucharist, provide the laity with the strength to carry out their mission in the Church and in the world.

Cardinal Rodriguez Maradiaga, Archbishop of Tegucigalpa in Honduras, celebrated evening Mass for the feast of St Anthony and spoke of the saint's Eucharistic devotion and teaching:

> There is a profound relationship between celebrating the Eucharist and proclaiming Christ. To enter into communion with Him means, at the same time, to be transformed into missionaries of the event that the celebration makes real. It involves making it contemporary in every age, until the Lord comes. For that reason, the saints, each one in a unique way in his or her own particular context, reveals

or manifests Christ. St Anthony of Padua lived an intimate and passionate personal relationship with the Eucharist, which marked his life, filling it with confident hope. The life of Anthony of Padua, so rich in supernatural gifts and in extraordinary happenings, was founded on a radical Eucharistic piety. The expression 'You yourselves, give them something to eat' (Lk 9:13) had a great significance in his own life, since in the many situations in which a multiplication of bread did happen, there was to be seen a consistent extension of his intense union with Christ and of his uninterrupted prayer.

Two personal testimonies given on this day should be recorded. Mrs Noreen Carroll, a retired primary school teacher, gave an affirmative talk on 'Priesthood: Gift and Mystery', speaking of

> my own experiences of the work, example, giftedness and compassion of the many faithful and committed priests whom I have had the privilege of meeting and knowing and who through their ministry have shown me the presence of God. These priests have, in their own unique ways, helped me on my faith journey. They have strengthened my belief in God and have given me hope in times of darkness. Many of them would not even be aware of the effects of their words, their actions, their example or witness on this struggling Christian, so if any of them are present here today, my testimony should reassure them that God is truly with them and that their life of service is a precious gift to all of us. The way in which each priest makes Christ present to all of us who seek God is the great mystery of priesthood.

Sister Conchita McDonnell, a religious sister for over 50 years, spoke on 'Consecrated Life—a Life of Communion'. Speaking affectionately and gratefully of her childhood in a loving family, she continued:

> In my own experience of living religious life I have come to the conviction that I needed a community to keep me living in the truth of who I am and who God is. One's

prayer can be delusional and requires testing in the ups and downs of life and most especially among those with whom we live in community. The closeness brings out the raw reality and directs us back to the Eucharist for the forgiveness, strength and inspiration needed to fulfil the mission to love. The emphasis on the common life and the common good challenges our innate self-centredness and urges us to live and to witness to communion ... The community we lived together as religious sisters was nurtured and sustained by the celebration of Eucharist which had to be lived each day. St Paul links community and Eucharist and suggests, as a recent writer Daniel O'Connell put it, that a unified community is the necessary basis for a proper celebration of the Eucharist. He goes so far as to say that a divided community is an affront to any celebration of the Eucharist. This was vividly illustrated for me by an African priest who told me of having removed the Blessed Sacrament and stopped celebrating Eucharist temporarily for a religious community which refused to attend to extreme dissension and disunity among them. Like St Paul he saw the divided community as the antithesis of all that Eucharist signifies.

That evening saw a public procession of the Blessed Sacrament, following a route of 2.5 kilometres in streets near the RDS. Fr Kevin Doran explained: 'The purpose of the procession is to allow the faithful to walk with the Blessed Sacrament as an expression of our desire to walk with Christ as his witnesses on the journey of life. The procession is a way of extending the worship of Christ in the Eucharist outside of the Mass, in keeping with the desire of Pope Benedict XVI.' The Procession left the RDS Main Arena at 7.30pm, taking about two hours to complete and engaging about 15,000 people. A most efficient PA system relayed prayers and music from the Main Arena around the procession route, whilst pilgrims remaining in the Main Arena could view the procession on the large screens beside the main Altar.

Reconciliation

Thursday's Congress was devoted to 'Communion and Reconciliation'. The energetic Ghanaian Cardinal Peter Turkson, President of the Pontifical Council for Justice and Peace, gave the homily during a two-hour Liturgy of Reconciliation. His words hinged on the story of Sister Genevieve, a survivor of the Tutsi genocide in Rwanda in 1994. Many of her family were killed while seeking refuge in their parish church. But three years later, a Catholic group of women brought her to two prisons. The 'Ladies of Divine Mercy' were preparing the prisoners for the Great Jubilee of 2000 and their message to prisoners and survivors was:

> If you have killed, commit yourself to ask forgiveness from the survivor; in this way, you can help the victim free himself from the burden of vengeance, hatred and rancour. If you are a victim, commit yourself to offer forgiveness to those who harmed your family; in this way, you can free the perpetrator from the weight of his crime and the evil that is in him. This message had an immediate effect upon one of the prisoners ... and then upon me. A prisoner stood up in tears, came to me, fell to his knees before me and loudly begged 'Mercy! Mercy!' I was horrified, petrified, to recognize a family friend who had grown up with us and shared everything with us. He admitted to having killed my father. He told me details of the deaths of my family members. A feeling of pity and compassion invaded me. I lifted him to his feet, embraced him in tears and said to him, 'You are my brother and always will be.' Then I felt a huge weight lift off of me and, in its place, *flowing inner peace*. I thanked the man I was embracing. To my great surprise, he cried out, 'Justice can do its work and condemn me to death, for now I am free!'

Cardinal Turkson asked us, 'Could this be my story, your story, too? St Paul, if he had heard Sister Genevieve's testimony, would exhort us with all his heart, "Rejoice. Be perfect. Admonish or encourage one another. Have the same mind and attitude. Live in peace, and the God of love and peace will be with you" (2 Co 13:11).' The Cardinal then explored those five exhortations, bringing out their meaning for people today, finally urging his hearers to 'Hear deeply those profoundly astonishing words of the priest: "I absolve you from your sins in the name of the Father, and of the Son, and of the Holy Spirit". This absolution restores us to communion with God and with one another. It is the grace of restored membership in the household of God.'

The Canadian Fr Thomas Rosica was at his finest in speaking this day, 'Towards a Renewed Vision of Priestly Ministry and Identity'. He had been asked to speak about the joy of priesthood. Nor did he disappoint. A forthright communicator, acknowledging that 'the priesthood has suffered much over the past few years, and this biblical image of service and divine authority have been blemished, tarnished and in some cases obliterated', he shared with us 'six perspectives or pillars of a renewed priestly vocation and mission. I wish to consider the priest as the man of the Eucharist, a bearer of joy, a beacon of hope, a model of compassion, and an agent and translator of the New Evangelization, and of holiness'.

Fr Rosica told us 'not to be discouraged by the sins and failings of some of her members. The harm done by some priests and religious to the young and vulnerable fills us all with a deep sense of sadness and shame. But think of the vast majority of dedicated and generous priests and religious whose only wish is to serve and do good!' His closing words give some impression of the quality of his talk:

> Priesthood is not, first and foremost, something we do, but someone we are. It is not an earned trophy. It is about an intimate relationship to the vine who is Christ. The Character of Christ the High Priest is branded on our hearts. We must never imagine that it is ourselves alone, in new-found power and privilege, who accomplish saving actions. It is Jesus, the Christ, who baptizes and preaches and spreads the feast of His Body and Blood and provides for the helpless and heals the hurt and grants us peace. He

does it through weak, human beings like you and me. Who of us can ever be worthy of such a great calling? To victims, we must be an advocate; for the aimless, we must be shepherds; for the disheartened, heralds of good news; for sinners, disturbers of conscience; and for the guilty, forgivers. Let us take heart and be encouraged by the witness of the apostles and martyrs of the Early Church and the contemporary Church and never be afraid of giving our lives whole-heartedly to the Lord of the harvest, to Him who came to serve and not be served, to the one who laid down His life for us, His friends. May we do the same for others.

Cardinal Sean Brady, Archbishop of Armagh and Primate of All Ireland, continued the theme of 'Eucharist and Reconciliation' when he celebrated Mass that evening 'in the language and music of the Irish tradition'. He began his homily by speaking of the spirit of the Congress.

What a great joy it is to come together to listen to God's Word and to experience the beautiful, peaceful presence of the Lord in this Eucharist *and* in our communion with one another. As I have been walking around the Congress Campus, as I meet you on the streets nearby, I am moved by the great spirit of joy and peace and helpfulness to one another that are so present among us. We should not be surprised. These *are* the fruits of the Blessed Eucharist.

He spoke of the Sacrament of Penance, and then:

There is a much larger stone that sits in a place of honour here before this altar. It will serve as a reminder of those children and young people who were hurt by a Church that first betrayed their trust and then failed to respond adequately to their pain. The words of the Gospel echo in my mind: 'It is not the will of your Father that any of these little ones should be lost'. May God forgive us for the times when we as individuals and as a Church failed to seek out and care for those little ones who were frightened, alone and in pain because someone was abusing them. That we did not always respond to your cries with the concern of the Good Shepherd is a matter of deep shame. We lament the burdens of the painful memories you carry. We pray for healing and peace for those whose suffering continues. I want to take this opportunity of the fiftieth International Eucharistic Congress to apologise for the times when some of us were blind to your fear, deaf to your cries and silent in response to your pain. My prayer is that one day this stone might become a symbol of conversion, healing and hope.

The stone Cardinal Brady referred to, standing before the altar and known as 'The Healing Stone', is a large piece of Wicklow granite, shaped and inscribed with the words of a prayer composed by a survivor of clerical abuse. Various groups agreed that the stone would be an appropriate symbol for the Congress. It has since found a permanent home on the island of Lough Derg in County Donegal, a place of prayer and penance known as 'St Patrick's Purgatory', and a centre of pilgrimage for over 1,000 years. Cardinal Brady ended his homily:

Every Eucharist rolls away that heaviest of all stones, the stone in our heart that keeps us back from friendship with Christ and with one another. Every Eucharist proclaims 'Christ is risen—Our God is alive!' He lives in you and me. Through his Holy Eucharist he continues to reconcile us to one another. In the memorial of his passion and death, made present in every Eucharist, he continues to reconcile the whole world to himself. Let us therefore be reconciled with God. Let us bring that reconciliation to others. For in this is our peace; in this lies the greatest hope for our world.

Suffering and Healing

Friday was the solemnity of the Most Sacred Heart of Jesus. In the Congress it was a day dedicated to 'Communion in suffering and healing'. The Latin Patriarch of Jerusalem, Archbishop Fouad Twal, presided at evening Mass and gave a moving homily, telling us that he came as the shepherd of Christ's little flock (Lk 12:32) who suffer in the land of the promise, the land of the new and modern promises and international resolutions, that were never fulfilled. It is the land that first witnessed the fulfilment of God's plan, to redeem His creation in the Incarnation, suffering, death, Resurrection and Ascension of the Son of Mary, our Virgin Mother. I am Patriarch of the city of Jerusalem, where the Sacrament of the Eucharist took place, and where our Lord took bread ... broke it and gave it to [His disciples], saying 'This is my Body which is given up for you. Do this in memory of Me' (Lk 22:19). The Eucharist originated in the Upper Room, in my Diocese of the Holy Land, where the miracle started, where your Mother Church is, and where your roots are. We renew in this Eucharistic Congress the event that happened in Jerusalem. I feel at home with you, as we continue to celebrate the same event here in your midst. We are profoundly linked to this event.

Patriarch Twal recalled that,

Much has changed in this world after two thousand years. Yet the story is the same as it ever was. The Christians in Jerusalem at the beginning of the Church were very few and found courage only in the presence of Christ. Today, we too need to realize that Christ is with us, and find courage in His Presence. Though we are very few and diminishing in number, may we Christians in Jerusalem, as well as all Christians, remain faithful where the Lord has placed us! ... I often have the opportunity to pray on Golgotha, the very place where our Lord was crucified, which is now under the roof of the same Church that covers the place where Jesus was buried and rose from the dead. As I stand and meditate on that spot, I hear the cry of Jesus 'My God, my God, why have you forsaken me?' (Mt 27:46) And today, we can hear the same cry through the sufferings of people: the victims of war, poverty and injustice, and the many refugees in the Middle East. This is the cry of a suffering human being, a cry that did not yield to defeat, but went on to victory, because 'we are more than conquerors through him who has loved us' (Rm 8:37). Resisting the tendency to see ourselves as victims leading to self-pity is strong, and requires patience and determination. While we may feel alone, Christ is our hope, joy and freedom.

The Patriarch showed how the Eucharist transforms suffering into hope. He told how there were many projects and pro- grammes helping Christians in the Holy Land.

> However, before all projects, the real help for us and for all Christians comes from prayer, in recognizing and receiving our Lord in the Eucharist. He is indispensable and the Eucharist is that most substantial and mysterious means chosen by Him for us to enter into His companionship, where we can live in His communion with the Father by the power of the Holy Spirit … Joy makes us delightful, our toils make us strong, meanwhile, sufferings help us to be more human, and failures and disappointments are lessons in humility. With the Lord, we move on and we keep going.

Earlier that day Archbishop Patrick Kelly of Liverpool gave a seminar entitled 'Eucharist as Viaticum'. He was justly proud of his diocese's stand in the exhibition hall which attracted many visitors interested particularly in Liverpool's baptismal pro- gramme. He spoke of the beginning of St John's Gospel, and how the Word of God always leads us on to the Father.

> Pope Benedict teaches us that Jesus present among us in the Mass is not just standing there, with us standing near him. Jesus is always leading us onward to the Father. Whenever we receive him, whenever we come to him, he leads us, sometimes supports us when we are weak, always toward God our Father. That shows us why the most important, most joyful, most complete receiving of Our Lord is not our first but our last. Every other time we receive him is leading us to the last, to the journey home to heaven. And that communion has a special name:

Viaticum. It means, with you on the way, with you for the final journey.

Communion and Mary

Forget that this Saturday was 'Bloomsday'. In a land steeped in devotion to Our Lady, it was fitting rather that the day was dedicated to 'Communion in the Word through Mary'. The Guinean Cardinal Robert Sarah, President of the Pontifical Council for *Cor Unum*, was the main celebrant at Mass. His moving homily began, 'It was through the body of a young Jewish girl, living in a tiny village called Nazareth, that Jesus, the divine Word, was made flesh ... Her Immaculate Heart—the Feast we keep this day—prompted a total giving of herself to God and included the gift of both her body and her heart'. The Cardinal spoke of Mary's faith which sustained her through her whole life. She uttered not one *'Fiat'* but two: one to the angel at the Annunciation, the second on Calvary:

> Mary, like us, did not have infused knowledge about God's plans. But, in the face of life's events, rather than rebel or stumble in the dark, it was faith that enabled her to come into the light. She needed that faith to remain at the foot of the Cross. As the soldier thrust his lance through Jesus' side, the sword of suffering pierced her heart, too. Here, Mary made her second fiat. She consented to God's 'unsearchable judgments' and 'inscrutable ways'. Mary stood before the atrocious sufferings of her Son. She watched His unthinkable defeat and the apparent victory of Satan. She might have been tempted to flee from the Cross or invite Jesus as the Son of God to climb down. Instead, it was precisely at this moment of greatest trial that Mary's fiat attained its supreme confirmation ... What a precious lesson the Blessed Mother offers to us! Our lives, too, are marked frequently by the obscurity of faith. On a personal level, some of us are afflicted by bodily sufferings or difficult relationships; on a national and global level, we face unprecedented moral challenges, which threaten our

> Christian foundations and the very fabric of society; trying economic times place our livelihoods at risk and we find it ever more difficult to make ends meet; even in the Church, sins and scandals mar the call to holiness. Only faith in a God who ultimately triumphs can give birth to a hope that sustains us through all darkness, allowing love of God and even whatever presents itself to us as an enemy to enter as light into the world (*Deus Caritas est* 39).

People often speak in Ireland of a 'nice, soft day', meaning the rain is coming down. It came down with a vengeance during the Mass and we were very wet. Cardinal Sarah provoked laughter and applause when he said at the end, 'Having just received a shower of divine grace let us now receive God's blessing ...'

That day Archbishop Luis Tagle of Manila gave the main catechesis. He began,

> The fiftieth International Eucharistic Congress has been providing us with a wealth of reflection on 'The Eucharist: Communion with Christ and with one another'. Having explored communion in baptism, in marriage and family, in the priestly ministry, in reconciliation and in suffering and healing, we now turn to communion in the Word through Mary. Allow me to develop this fascinating theme in two parts. In the first section I will dwell on communion in the Word of God, and in the second I will meditate on Mary's experience of communion in the Word as a model for the Church.

Archbishop Tagle started simply enough: our ordinary way of connecting with another human being, of communing with that person, is through conversation or dialogue. This is how the Church communicates too:

> This simple process called communion in the word is at the heart of the mystery and mission of the Church. St John vividly portrays it in his first letter (1:1–4): 'What was from the beginning, what we have heard, what we have seen with our eyes, what we looked upon and touched with our hands

concerns the Word of life—for the life was made visible; we have seen it and testify to it and proclaim to you the eternal life that was with the Father and was made visible to us—what we have seen and heard we proclaim now to you, so that you too may have communion with us; for our communion is with the Father and with His Son, Jesus Christ. We are writing this so that our joy may be complete.'

What St John is describing is similar to the ordinary experiences of communion between two or more human beings we mentioned earlier. But St John's account involves a special person, called an apostle, who proclaims a special word to a listener. Their converse blossoms into communion with each other, which in reality is their communion with the Father and with Jesus Christ, the Word made visible in the flesh. What a great mystery unfolding in a quite ordinary human experience! Let us delve deeper into this beautiful text.

What word does the apostle share with his listener? It is the Word of life, present with the Father and made visible. The word that the apostle proclaims is Jesus Christ, the Word made flesh. Simply put, the apostle's word is Jesus Christ … Whether it is Peter, Paul, Stephen, Philip or Mary of Magdala, the joyful story told is that of Jesus Christ and the destiny of the world in Him who is Divine Saviour and Messiah … Those who have listened to Jesus can tell this story to others in a credible way. Then their listeners accept Jesus into their dreams, joys, pains, hopes, frustrations, questions and wisdoms. They bring all these that comprise their worlds as they listen towards communion …

All well and good, said the Archbishop. But the apostles and others were eye-witnesses. What about us, so much later?

How can we who are separated from Jesus by centuries talk meaningfully about Him? Let us not forget that Jesus is alive. He is truly raised from the dead! He is with us now. He rules the world. He continues to visit the homes of many Marthas and Marys of our time to enjoy a restful meal. He continues to weep at our tombs the way He did at the tomb of Lazarus His friend. He continues to quietly call on the Zacchaeuses of our age to pay back what they have stolen. He continues to have compassion for widows who carry their children to the grave. He continues to see the hungry crowds and asks us to feed them with our five loaves and two fish. He continues to welcome the weary and heavy burdened to find rest in Him. He continues to cry out to God with the suffering victims, 'My God, my God, why have You forsaken Me?' My brothers and sisters, please do not say we have not seen, heard, looked upon and touched Jesus. Yes, we have. If only we could listen to Him more attentively, we will have stories of Jesus to tell.

Our communion with Christ leads us to the Father:

We believe that this communion with Christ is the action of the Holy Spirit Who teaches and reminds us of all that Jesus taught (Jn 14:26). The same Holy Spirit enables us to confess, 'Jesus is Lord' (1 Co 12:3). The Spirit 'assimilates' us with Jesus Christ so that as children in the Son we can also cry out, 'Abba, Father' (Rm 8:14–15). Now it is clear that communion with Jesus in the Holy Spirit brings about communion with the Father. Jesus reveals the Father to us so that whoever sees Him sees the Father also (Jn 8:9). As the Way (Jn 14:6), Jesus gives us access to the Father (Ep 2:18) and to the Father's house where He prepares a place for us (Jn 14:2–3).

What a marvellous communion in the Word that gives us weak and sinful human beings a participation in the eternal communion of the Father, Son and Holy Spirit! This is the mystery of the Church celebrated in the Eucharist where the Word proclaimed and received is the same Word become flesh eaten as the Bread of life. Communion in the Word, experienced at every Eucharist, is one contribution of the Church to the building up of a world of unity and peace.

The Archbishop then focussed on how Mary came to communion with her Son. She learned about Him through what others said about Him: the angel Gabriel; her kinswoman Elizabeth; the shepherds at Bethlehem; the old man Simeon. 'The Blessed Virgin Mary experienced communion in the Word in an utterly unique way. As a listener to and the bearer of the Word made flesh, she is the model and teacher for the Church.'

At Gabriel's annunciation, Mary uttered her Fiat. Similarly, 'By being in communion with the Word, the Church like Mary will actively promote God's saving plan in the world—not advancing its own projects but the will of God.' When she visited Elizabeth, Mary sang her *Magnificat*. 'By being in communion with the Word, the Church like Mary will be the companion of the poor so that they could recover their voice and sing for joy.' At Bethlehem, Mary listened to what the shepherds had to say and kept it all in her heart. Likewise, 'By being in communion with the Word, the Church like Mary will gladly listen to the lowly and the poor with reverential silence, listening to God speaking through them.' Meeting Simeon in the Temple, Mary heard of the joys and sorrows her Son would bring. 'By being in communion with the Word, the Church like Mary will proclaim Jesus in season or out of season, whether accepted or rejected, joyful with Him, sorrowful with Him' (2 Tm 4:2).

After this, the messenger who will speak to Mary about Jesus is Jesus Himself. Along with many other pilgrims, the Holy Family had gone to Jerusalem for the annual Passover Feast. Festivities over, Mary and Joseph left with the caravan. The twelve-year-old Jesus stayed behind without them knowing. They found Him in the Temple after three days of searching. To Mary's question, Jesus said: 'Why were you looking for Me? Did you not know that I must be in My Father's house?' ... Mary listens and accepts Jesus' enigmatic word to her, even if she does not understand ... By being in communion with the Word, the Church like Mary will look for Jesus among the lost, wounded, tired and abandoned and lead them with rejoicing to the Father's house.

Near the start of His public ministry, Jesus and His disciples attended a wedding in Cana. Jesus' mother was there. When the wine ran out, she gently told Him, expecting perhaps some intervention. He seemingly rebuffed her.

> Mary listens, accepts and utters her own words to the servers, 'Do whatever he tells you'. They obey her and Jesus ... Mary, who is obedient to her Son's word, now asks the servers to give Jesus full obedience as well. In the communion of obedience to the word, miracles happen. We run out of wine too: the wine of wisdom, understanding, insight, energy and meaning. God seems to be unreachable at times. When those moments come, know that Mary is close by. She sees our empty jars. She approaches Jesus. If we listen to Jesus and do what he tells us, those jars will overflow with unbelievably good wine. By being in communion with the Word, the Church like Mary will be attentive to the emptiness experienced by our age and lead people not to us but to Jesus for He alone can make miracles happen through His word.

> According to the gospels, the last time Jesus talks to Mary is before he breathes his last on the cross (Jn 19:23–28) ... 'Woman, behold your Son'. Then He says to the disciple, 'Behold, your mother'. Jesus reveals and creates His mother as the mother of the new family of disciples, of those who hear the word of God and act on it (Lk 8:21). Jesus' death, freely embraced in communion with God and with sinners, does not destroy community but gives birth to a new family. By the word of Jesus, Mary becomes the mother of both His disciples and the people called to believe in Him. She responds to Jesus by doing what He says—she goes to the home of the beloved disciple.

> Even now Jesus beholds mothers and fathers who lose their children to hunger, diseases, wars, illegal drugs, sex tourism, immorality, false philosophies and empty utopias. Jesus tells us to take care of the sorrowful mothers and fathers for they are our parents too. He tells us to look after the lost children of the world, for they are our daughters and sons too. No wound is so great that it could not be healed by love. By being in communion with the Word,

> the Church like Mary will be the seed of the new family of justice, healing and peace ...
>
> After Jesus' ascension into heaven, the extended family of disciples with Mary went to the upper room to await the promised Holy Spirit who would remind us about Jesus (Ac 1:13–14). I would like to think that with the help of the same Spirit that overshadowed her at the annunciation, Mary could now understand better the things about Jesus that she had kept in her heart. Now she could proclaim her stories to her new sons and daughters: what she has heard, seen with her eyes, looked upon and touched with her hands concerning her Son, the Word of life. She must have ended every story by saying, 'Do whatever he tells you'. Like Mary, go and tell the good news of Jesus to the ends of the earth. And do whatever He tells you. Amen.

I hope these extracts give the flavour of Archbishop Tagle's fascinating and deeply moving talk. We were to hear more from this young vibrant archbishop at the Cebu Congress in 2016. And maybe we will hear even more in the years after that?

John Monaghan of the St Vincent de Paul Society gave a thoughtful and passionate seminar based on Christian solidarity.

> The first [commandment] is to love God with all our heart and the second is to love our neighbour as ourselves. So these two great intertwined and inseparable commandments indicate that we cannot say we love God if we do not simultaneously love our neighbour in a very tangible way, in other words through showing solidarity. Consequently, in loving God we are all expected to look beyond our own personal needs, spiritual and worldly, and actively reach out to our neighbour, whoever and wherever they might be ... While the principles of the Social Teachings of the Church are all very noble they do need a 'human face' to bring them alive. They have to be conveyed in words and images that move the heart of each one of us to live out the Eucharist in Christian Solidarity.

In 2011 the SVP in Ireland had spent more than 75 million euros in answer to calls for assistance. Mr Monaghan drew the conclusion that 'the three principles of the SVP Mission: offering love and friendship; helping people achieve independence; and working for social justice are more than ever necessary in the Ireland of 2012.'

All too quickly, the Dublin Congress was drawing to a close. Abandoning the RDS we made our way on Sunday for the Statio Orbis in Ireland's national stadium, Croke Park. After Barcelona's Camp Nou and London's Wembley, Croke Park is the largest stadium in the world, holding 82,300 people. The stands were filled and the centre field of the stadium also held thousands of people and concelebrants. Before Mass various groups and singers performed, including the Three Tenors, The Priests and opera soprano Celine Byrne. We also saw a documentary of the 1932 Dublin Congress, complete with the voice of John McCormack. Thankfully the rain had passed and a warm June summer sun shone today.

Faith in Christ—Let it grow!

The papal Legate, Cardinal Marc Ouellet, presided and preached at the Mass. He kept his homily short, referring to the message we would hear from Pope Benedict at the end of Mass. The Cardinal's message was one of greeting to those present and of thanks to those who had prepared the Congress. It was also a call to faith in Christ: '... the Church is called, and we are called, to bear witness to the Lord by pleasing Him, that is, preaching the Gospel, living in fraternity and praising God for the gift of salvation.' He deftly observed that, after a week of Eucharistic reflection, celebration and adoration,

> we are certainly more aware of God's call to communion with Him and with one another. Let us bear witness to this grace by calling others to faith in this communion. The Irish bell, which resounds from Lough Derg, from Knock and

Dublin, must resound in the whole world. Let's ring the bell further through our personal testimony of renewed faith in the Holy Eucharist. Faith is the most precious gift we have received with Baptism. Let's not keep it private and fearful! Let it grow as a splendid tree through sharing everywhere! Even if we are sometimes tested in our faith, do not be afraid, and remember who we are: the body of Christ intent on loving God over and above all things, intent on living in the Spirit of the new and eternal covenant.

The Irish bell Cardinal Ouellet mentioned was the Congress Bell specially made for Dublin 2012. It is said that St Patrick left a bell in each church he consecrated as a way to call people to the Eucharist. And as the Olympic torch summons people to the Games, so the Congress Bell went around Ireland and Europe, calling people to be ready for the Congress. Pope Benedict XVI welcomed it to Rome on St Patrick's Day, 2012, and rang it. Its first port of call in England was at my parish of Our Lady of Grace, Prestwich, where there was a special service of welcome.

To thunderous applause, Pope Benedict appeared on the big screen as he gave his video message at the Statio Orbis. Succinctly, he spoke of the Congress theme. Then he reminded us:

> The Congress also occurs at a time when the Church throughout the world is preparing to celebrate the Year of Faith to mark the fiftieth anniversary of the start of the Second Vatican Council, an event which launched the most extensive renewal of the Roman Rite ever known. Based upon a deepening appreciation of the sources of the liturgy, the Council promoted the full and active participation of the faithful in the Eucharistic sacrifice. At our distance today from the Council Fathers' expressed desires regarding liturgical renewal, and in the light of the universal Church's experience in the intervening period, it is clear that a great deal has been achieved; but it is equally clear that there have been many misunderstandings and irregularities. The renewal of external forms, desired by the Council Fathers, was intended to make it easier to enter into the inner depth

of the mystery. Its true purpose was to lead people to a personal encounter with the Lord, present in the Eucharist, and thus with the living God, so that through this contact with Christ's love, the love of his brothers and sisters for one another might also grow. Yet not infrequently, the revision of liturgical forms has remained at an external level, and 'active participation' has been confused with external activity. Hence much still remains to be done on the path of real liturgical renewal. In a changed world, increasingly fixated on material things, we must learn to recognize anew the mysterious presence of the Risen Lord, which alone can give breadth and depth to our life.

With typical courtesy, Pope Benedict XVI lauded the past achievements of the Irish Church:

Moreover, the Eucharist is the memorial of Christ's sacrifice on the Cross, His Body and Blood given in the new and eternal covenant for the forgiveness of sins and the transformation of the world. Ireland has been shaped by the Mass at the deepest level for centuries, and by its power and grace generations of monks, martyrs and missionaries have heroically lived the faith at home and spread the Good News of God's love and forgiveness well beyond your shores. You are the heirs to a Church that has been a mighty force for good in the world, and which has given a profound and enduring love of Christ and His blessed Mother to many, many others. Your forebears in the Church in Ireland knew how to strive for holiness and constancy in their personal lives, how to preach the joy that comes from the Gospel, how to promote the importance of belonging to the universal Church in communion with the See of Peter, and how to pass on a love of the faith and Christian virtue to other generations.

Our Catholic faith, imbued with a radical sense of God's presence, caught up in the beauty of his creation all around us, and purified through personal penance and awareness of God's forgiveness, is a legacy that is surely perfected and nourished when regularly placed on the Lord's altar at the sacrifice of the Mass. The Eucharist is the worship of the whole Church, but it also requires the full engagement of each individual Christian in the Church's mission; it contains a call to be the holy people of God, but also one to individual holiness; it is to be celebrated with great joy and simplicity, but also as worthily and reverently as possible; it invites us to repent of our sins, but also to forgive our brothers and sisters; it binds us together in the Spirit, but it also commands us in the same Spirit to bring the good news of salvation to others.

Pope Benedict's pain at recent events showed in his next words:

Thankfulness and joy at such a great history of faith and love have recently been shaken in an appalling way by the revelation of sins committed by priests and consecrated persons against people entrusted to their care. Instead of showing them the path towards Christ, towards God, instead of bearing witness to His goodness, they abused people and undermined the credibility of the Church's message. How are we to explain the fact that people who regularly received the Lord's body and confessed their sins in the sacrament of Penance have offended in this way? It remains a mystery. Yet evidently, their Christianity was no longer nourished by joyful encounter with Jesus Christ: it had become merely a matter of habit. The work of the Council was really meant to overcome this form of Christianity and to rediscover the faith as a deep personal friendship with the goodness of Jesus Christ. The Eucharistic Congress has a similar aim. Here we wish to encounter the Risen Lord. We ask Him to touch us deeply. May He who breathed on the Apostles at Easter, communicating His Spirit to them, likewise bestow upon us His breath, the power of the Holy Spirit, and so help us to become true witnesses to His love, witnesses to the truth. His truth is love. Christ's love is truth.

To the delight of the Filipino pilgrims, who cheered and waved flags, Pope Benedict then announced that the next Congress in 2016 would be held in the city of Cebu.

Also looking to the future, the Archbishop of Dublin, Diarmuid Martin, concluded:

> The fiftieth International Eucharistic Congress was not just a seven-day event. Over the past year a great deal of catechesis has been carried out across Ireland in preparation for this week. Tomorrow we must start our catechesis anew to prolong the fruits of this Eucharistic Congress through a dynamic of New Evangelisation. The extraordinary interest that was shown in these days for the workshops and catecheses of the Congress tells us just how much thirst there is in our Catholic community to deepen the understanding of our faith. We must go away from here with a renewed passion for the Eucharist... We go away deepened in our faith ... We go away from here committed to build a Church of communion and service after the model of Jesus Christ. It is Jesus Himself who will renew His Church. It is Jesus present in the Eucharist who will be food for the journey of purification and renewal to which we commit ourselves as we leave this Fiftieth International Eucharistic Congress strengthened in our desire to deepen our Communion with Christ and communion with one another.

In a short chapter it is impossible to do justice to the 223 speakers, including 38 in the main arena, who took part in the Congress and to the 160 workshops featuring talks, reflections, concerts and plays. But no chapter on the Dublin Congress would be complete without the warmest encomium for the 2,000 volunteers. With unfailing courtesy and cheerfulness they guided, cajoled, shared the *craic*—and helped us all to pray. Triona King who attended the whole Congress spoke for many when she said, 'It was like being on Mount Tabor and you don't want to come down. We wish it would never end.' A word of appreciation too for Monsignor Brian Walsh from Australia. He masterminded the 1973 Congress in Melbourne and became a firm friend. He was an adviser to all subsequent Congresses. Dublin was to be his final one. May he rest in peace.

References

1) Allen, J. F., Personal notes and diaries and Congress releases.

2) Pontifical Committee for International Eucharistic Congresses, Basic Text for the 50th International Eucharistic Congress, Dublin, Ireland, 2012.

3) Programme and Pilgrim Guide, Dublin 10–17 June 2012 (Veritas, Dublin 2012).

4) *50th International Eucharistic Congress: Vols. 1–3 Proceedings of Plenary Sessions; Selection from Concurrent Sessions; Proceedings of the International Symposium of Theology* (Veritas 2013).

5) Weekly English edition of *L'Osservatore Romano* 13 June 2012, pp. 6–7; 20 June 2012, pp. 6–9.

13 CEBU 24–31 JANUARY 2016
CHRIST IN YOU, OUR HOPE OF GLORY

NOT SINCE GUADALAJARA in 2004 had we seen anything like this! Quebec in 2008 and Dublin in 2012 could both be rightly pleased with a Congress well-prepared and successfully brought to pass. But Cebu in the Philippines had the numbers, the vitality, the exuberance, yes, and the faith that rocketed it to the heights. The official logo of the Congress, designed by a nineteen year-old fine arts student, Jayson Jaluag, from Mandaue City, Cebu, spoke volumes:

> The Sun symbolises our hope of glory; it is a symbol of a new beginning. It also symbolises the Philippines because the sun is the principal symbol in the Philippine flag. The seven rays of the sun symbolise the seven gifts of the Holy Spirit. The cup and bread call to mind the sacred species of the Holy Eucharist. The monogram 'IHS' (*Iesus Hominum Salvator*) symbolises the Holy Name of Jesus. This also symbolises Cebu since the former name of Cebu was Villa del Santísimo Nombre de Jesús. The boat, a common mode of transport in the Philippine Archipelago, is symbolic of the missionary nature of the Church. The people in the boat, each of a different colour, symbolise the principles which have animated the faith of the Filipino people; green for hope, which blooms in adversity, blue, the colour of faith which we cling to, and red, the colour of charity, which urges us on. The aqua blue colour of the boat is reminiscent of the Christian pilgrimage to Heaven.

From where did this strong faith come? The Pilgrim Symbol, which before the Congress visited each diocese and major religious centre in the Philippines, provided an answer:

> The Local Committee has chosen as symbol of the 51st IEC a replica of the shrine that houses the Cross of

Magellan, located in the centre of Cebu. It is chosen for the following reasons:

1. The Cross of Magellan is the symbol of the beginning of the Christianisation of the Philippines. It was planted as a commemorative marker of the arrival of Magellan together with the first missionaries and the initial baptisms in the island of Cebu.

2. The Cross is the symbol of the hope that we have in Jesus Christ.

3. The Cross is the symbol of the faith that we embrace. This same faith allows us to receive Jesus in the Holy Eucharist.

4. Although the Cross of Magellan may represent the imposition of the faith on the native Filipinos at the initial stage of evangelisation, the cross itself becomes the symbol of the purification of our way of evangelisation, so that it actually points to us the way to the New Evangelisation, marked by the joy of the Gospel and the witness of our lives. The replica of the Shrine of the Cross of Magellan will contain a relic of the True Cross so that when people welcome it in their communities, they will be venerating the relic.

Small wonder therefore that we pilgrims coming from Europe were blown away by the joy and enthusiasm of the Filipino people. As Tommy Burns of the Irish group said, all day and every day during our stay we experienced 'the welcome, the smiles, the regular offers of help from the people of the Philippines'. The Irish group was led by Bishop Kevin Doran of Elphin who four years previously had been Secretary General of the 50th IEC in Dublin. It was good to make new friends, especially with Frs Pat Winkle, Paul Waldron and John Mockler. Bishop Robert Byrne, auxiliary in Birmingham, led the small English contingent.

It may be as well to say a word about the Congress theme since countless times we heard the Congress prayer or sang the Congress hymn, both repeating the theme that 'Christ is our hope of glory'. The sentence is taken from St Paul's letter to the

Colossians (1:27): 'The mystery ... Christ in you, your hope of glory.' The theological and pastoral reflections prepared for the Congress explained it like this:

> Having been told that the Colossians were 'adapting' Christianity to their culture and their beliefs, Paul had to assert with firmness that Christ possesses the fulness of redemptive power (1:19). Everything in the world is made for the sake of Christ. Right from the opening chapter of this letter, Paul applies the words 'all' and 'everything' to Christ over and over again ... By the mystery of His dying and rising Christ has indeed become our hope of glory. For the Holy Spirit whom He handed over as He breathed His last on the Cross (cf Jn 19:30) brought forth 'the wondrous sacrament of the whole Church' so that just as Christ was sent by the Father, so also does He send His Church, the community of His disciples, to continue proclaiming His work of redemption.

Immediately before the opening Mass, we were presented with a colourful drama of song and dance, depicting the bringing of Christianity to Cebu by Magellan and the missionaries who accompanied him. As the Congress hymn was sung, bearers from all the countries represented arranged their flags around the altar, followed by the processional entry. The Christ the King Youth Symphony Orchestra, formed by Archbishop Palma, accompanied the singing. Pope Francis' Legate opened the Congress and quickly fastened onto the Congress theme, which he described as 'of timeless relevance ... the source and goal of mission ... Christ in you is the Hope of Glory—taken from Colossians—is a theme that echoes through your mountains, through your beautiful rivers, soothes the heart of millions of Filipinos.' The Legate, Cardinal Charles Maung Bo, Archbishop of Yangon in Myanmar (formerly Burma), graciously thanked the Filipino people for helping the infant Church of Myanmar:

> For the last five decades, the only place that welcomed our priests, religious and laity with open arms and cared for

them is you and the Church in the Philippines. Today, Myanmar Church is a confident Church, your communion was a poignant show of Eucharistic fellowship with a suffering Church. You have shared the bread of hospitality, the bread of knowledge, the bread of your love for the people who came here ...

The [Congress] theme assigns three tasks:
1. To promote awareness of the central place of the Eucharist in life and mission.
2. To help improve our understanding and celebration of Eucharistic liturgy.
3. To draw attention to the social dimension of the Eucharist.

... a short sentence changed history. They are the words: Take and eat, This is My Body! Take and drink, This is My Blood!

The Cardinal described the Eucharist as having 'two eyes', namely Presence and Mission. The same Lord who was present in the Old Testament is with us now, and present for the whole of humanity. We adore Him present in this sacrament.

In our personal moments with Him, in our solemn Benedictions and in our adoration chapels, the Presence of Christ continues to be adored. The Eucharist and adoration is the intense faith encounter with Jesus, But this encounter needs others, the community. It was Mother Teresa who contemplated this mystery of Presence. She says every Holy Communion fills us with Jesus and we must go in haste to give Him to others. Mother Mary, whose body when she conceived Jesus became the first altar of the Eucharist, rushed in haste to meet Elizabeth.

Adoring Jesus in the Eucharist is also accepting our fellow men and women as created in the image of God. In a world that kills children in the womb, in a world that spends more on arms than on food, in a world that continues to have millions of poor, the Eucharist is a major challenge to the whole of humanity. Can we feel the presence of God in our brothers and sisters? Pope John Paul talked about the culture of death. Pope Francis spoke of a culture of indifference. Eucharist, then, cries out from the womb to tomb, human dignity. The Eucharist challenges abortion, the death penalty, euthanasia, etc. Our adoration of the Eucharist affirms our inalienable faith in human dignity. Governments and others need to appreciate our faith vision. So millions of Catholics attend Mass, adore the sacrament. As we gather, not only the bread on the altar becomes the Body of Christ. Each one of us is joined with our brothers and sisters as one body: 'We, though many, are one body' (1 Co 10:17). This great awareness brings us to the first great task: Eucharist and Mission.

Cardinal Bo explained how Eucharistic celebration leads on to Eucharistic commitment:

> Adoration alone may make us good devotees. But being a devotee in one of the easiest things. It is good. Christ is calling us to be disciples, to carry His Cross; the Mass of the devotee ends in an hour. But the Mass of the disciple is unending. The Eucharist of the devotee is confined to the clean, decorated altars of the church. The Eucharist of the disciple continues with the streets as altar.
>
> Christ died in the street, was dragged on the streets, proclaimed His good news on the streets, and affirmed human dignity in the streets. His altar was the world, He broke the bread of healing, He broke the bread of feeding, He broke the bread of reconciling, He broke the bread of Good News. His disciples carried on the task. The very act of Eucharistic assembly was revolutionary in the Acts of the Apostles. The first disciples were martyred for the act of coming together and the breaking of Bread. Pope John Paul said, 'There is one other point which I would like to emphasise, since it significantly affects the authenticity of our communal sharing in the Eucharist. It is the impulse which the Eucharist gives to the community for a practical commitment to building a more just and fraternal society'

(*Mane Nobiscum Domine* 28). And Pope Benedict in *Sacramentum Caritatis* (84) says, 'The love that we celebrate in the Sacrament is not something we can keep to ourselves. By its very nature it demands to be shared with all. What the world needs is God's love; it needs to encounter Christ and to believe in Him. The Eucharist is thus the source and summit not only of the Church's life, but also of her mission: "an authentically Eucharistic Church is a missionary Church".'

The Second Vatican Council, said the Cardinal, defined the Church's mission as three-fold: in Word, Worship and Witness. Word was knowing the Word of God and proclaiming the Good News that is the Gospel. Worship involved the community, 'affirming the oneness of the Christian community in the image of the Triune God'. Witness came through the Church's social mission and concern for the weak and vulnerable. The media then seized on the Cardinal's plea for a 'Third World War':

> Yes, we break bread in an unjust world. UNICEF says that every day 29,000 children die of starvation and malnutrition. That is 900,000 every month and 10,000,000 a year. A silent genocide, the biggest terrorism in the world; what is a greater moral sin than seeing a child dying of starvation today? The Eucharist and the poor are inseparable ... The Eucharist calls us to justice. No other religion elevates justice to this level. No other religion elevates the poor to this level, as Mary narrates after the Word was made flesh in her: 'the mighty will be brought down and the lowly will be raised up'.

> This calls for our commitment to a world of justice. Eucharist calls for a third world war, a third world war against poverty. A third world war against the cruelty of dogs fed with sumptuous organic food while poor children scramble for crumbs from the table, a third world war against a world that produces more weapons whilst more than half a billion do not get enough food every day. As long as this happens, the Eucharist will remain a revolutionary flag hoisted every day on millions of altars, crying

for justice like the prophets of old: 'The real fasting is loosing the chains of injustice, removing the yoke of oppression, sharing food with the hungry, sheltering the homeless' (cf Is 58:6–14).

The Cardinal then called on the Philippines, 'the biggest Catholic country in Asia', to declare a war against poverty and enforced migration. He called too on all who attended the Congress.

> Another world is possible. An economic system that does not treat human beings as commodities is possible, another world where the world is our common home is possible. Until that happens, the Eucharist will continue to be challenged. Our mission remains incomplete.

Cardinal Bo, coming as he did from a country which had suffered conflict and war for the past sixty years, ended his opening homily with a heartfelt plea for reconciliation and unity. The Eucharist demanded reconciliation. 'Peace is the Bread that the Catholic community waits to share with all communities.' The Cardinal's text was all of a piece with the mandate given to him by Pope Francis, who addressed the Pontifical Committee for International Eucharistic Congresses in September 2014, looking to the Cebu Congress, and said:

> The encounter with Jesus in the Eucharist will be the font of hope for the world if, transformed by the power of the Holy Spirit into the image of the One we encounter, we accept the mission to transform the world by giving the fulness of life which we ourselves have received and experienced, bringing hope, forgiveness, healing and love to those in need, especially the poor, the dispossessed and oppressed, sharing with them their life and aspirations and walking with them in the search for an authentic human life in Jesus Christ.

The Cebu Congress, like the earlier Asian one in Seoul in 1989, emphasised the importance of dialogue between the Christian community and people of other world faiths. The need for this was underlined by Archbishop Piero Marini, President of the Pontifical Committee, at a press conference in October 2015:

> The evangelical announcement and faith in the Lord Jesus professed by the Christian community are important and necessary for Asia but must be presented in accordance with the methods of dialogue, methods that have distinguished the activity of the particular Churches of the continent in the last thirty years. It is precisely this programme of dialogue with cultures, religious traditions and the multitudes of the poor that forms, in an entirely natural and evident way, the fabric of pastoral reflections contained in the basic text. The text explains that the Eucharist is the source and culmination of the mission of the Church and identifies the added value offered by the Eucharistic celebration for a mission that is committed to leavening through the enzymes of dialogue, reconciliation, peace and future, of which Asia is in great need.

These earlier interventions by Pope Francis and Archbishop Marini, about concern for the poor and about dialogue, guided so many of the presentations made at the Cebu Congress.

A fireworks display rounded off the opening ceremonies, lighting up Cebu's night sky for a full twenty minutes with cascades of brilliance. Children gazed upwards, entranced. Meanwhile, still hoping that the Holy Father would come, people chanted 'Pope Francis, we love you'. People around the world were able to share the sights as this was the first time that such a Congress had a global satellite broadcast.

Monday: hope, persecution, St Paul

On the second day of the Congress, Fr Timothy Radcliffe OP gave a well-received talk on 'The Christian Virtue of Hope'. He spoke of his visit to Iraq where he had met Christian communities who humanly speaking could see no future but who retained their hope in God. 'If you want to learn about hope, go to the hardest places.' He had learnt from the Filipinos who continued to hope despite their country being known as 'the disaster capital of the world'. He suggested four ways in which people caught in the affliction of terrible suffering could hold on to God. The first way is to stay put. 'Abide in me, and I in you' (Jn 15:4). A person refuses to despair when choosing to stay put when life at home, in the workplace, in the community or within the Congregation is terrible. In the same way, the beleaguered people of Iraq demonstrated hope by simply staying in their own country, without any prejudice to those who had decided to flee. The second way is by prayer. In the Eucharist, we gather, we pray, we sing. Fr Radcliffe recalled how in war-torn Rwanda in 1993 he had led the Christian communities in celebrating the Eucharist. He said that when Jesus celebrated the first Eucharist, it was the worst time of His life because His disciples either betrayed or denied Him and ran away. As a people of hope, we were not to be afraid of crises. The third way is simply to do the good things the Lord wants us to do today. The fourth way is to study and teach people, especially the young. Education and formation provided a positive way forward for young people. Fr Radcliffe pointed out how the children and those caring for them become clear signs of hope in our common desire for a better life today and a secure future for all.

Hope featured strongly at the Cebu Congress. The day before the Congress itself opened, I joined a 'Table of Hope' in the IEC Pavilion. Five hundred 'street children' from very poor families, some mentally or physically handicapped, shared our lunch. This was part of a long term project of catechesis and basic education for street children, geared to helping them move into mainstream education. They would be among the five thousand children making their first Holy Communion near the end of the Congress.

The distribution of food during the Congress was superbly well-organised. Fifteen thousand lunches for delegates were ready each day, with a choice of different meats, fish or vegetarian. Yet with so many delegates waiting to be fed, we never had to queue for longer than half a minute. Six thousand volunteers, many of them students, offered their services in the different Congress departments and saw to our needs with incredible efficiency.

The IEC Pavilion in Cebu was a remarkable building. Built especially for the Congress and at no cost to the Church, its main hall seated 15,000 delegates. It came as a result of an agreement between Church leaders and the Duros Development Corporation, a private company which agreed to finance the project and construct the Pavilion on the grounds of the archdiocesan seminaries, on the understanding that after the Eucharistic Congress the land would be leased so that the company might recover its investment. The Pavilion served the Congress very well, housing also a large chapel with Exposition of the Blessed Sacrament, numerous spacious rooms and an underground car park.

Monday morning's talks were shared between Archbishop Miguel Vidarte, Archbishop of Trujillo in Peru, and Cardinal Joseph Zen, retired Bishop of Hong Kong. Archbishop Vidarte gave a pastoral reflection on living a life like St Paul who strove to spread the Gospel in the face of many struggles and sufferings, and he concluded: 'We must accept sufferings for the strength of the Church, for its firmness and its growth. Trials are necessary so that human beings may understand and believe in the Gospel.'

84 year-old Cardinal Zen in an extremely moving address asked the world not to forget leading Catholics, including clergy and young members of the Legion of Mary who have suffered—and in some cases still suffer—for their faith at the hands of the communist regime in China. The Cardinal, who was born in Shanghai, urged delegates to condemn the Chinese persecution as much as they condemned Christian persecution in the Middle East. 'We should pray for the Christians of the Middle East and Africa. But don't forget the Christians in China. They are still in deep water and burning fire, a terrible reality.' The Cardinal gave as examples Bishop Cosma Shi Enxiang who had been imprisoned over sixty years by the communists and who reportedly died in 2015 at the age of 94, and Bishop Thaddeus Ma Daquin who was appointed by the communist authorities as Bishop of Shanghai,

but who was then put in prison when he renounced the Catholic Patriotic Association and declared his loyalty to Rome. 'We became a silent Church but we have not been silenced.'

Monday was the feast of the Conversion of St Paul and that afternoon Archbishop Piero Marini, President of the Pontifical Committee of International Eucharistic Congresses, celebrated Mass and preached about the Apostle:

> The life of St Paul has something to say to all of us for we, too, are called to constant conversion to the love of Jesus Christ ... Paul spent years deepening his faith by studying the Scriptures and became a tireless missionary throughout the Mediterranean ... As a free prisoner of the love of Christ, St Paul wanted to be closely conformed to His law ... With the apostle Paul may we too be able to say: the life I will live is not my own; Christ is living in me. It is a life of faith in the Son of God, Who loved me and gave Himself for me.

Featuring strongly in the Cebu Congress was service to people whose hearing is impaired. Terry O'Meara, based in the USA and Director of the International Catholic Foundation of the Service of Deaf Persons, saw this service as empowering deaf people to be missionaries in their turn. 'It's the most beautiful part of being here with the deaf community, to allow deaf people who wish to be part of this Congress to be not only participants but agents of catechesis.' The ICF is a communion of people from various countries united by the Holy Spirit out of the conviction that hearing-impaired individuals are called to the fulness of life in the Church.

Getting around Cebu was no problem, despite the lack of any bus service. One hundred and fifteen large buses had been imported for the use of delegates to the Congress. These were colour-coded to show their routes and would pick up and set down as required. The normal public transport in Cebu and throughout the Philippines is by jeepney, cheap and popular. Jeepneys were originally made from US military jeeps left over from World War II. Roofs were added for shade and protection and they were often gaudily decorated on the exterior. They are ubiquitous in Cebu and generally crowded, but they are fun to ride in. Their days however are probably numbered as anti-pollution legislation bites.

Tuesday: Eucharist, faith, poverty

Tuesday dawned, and one of the most awaited speakers took the rostrum: Bishop Robert Barron, auxiliary bishop of Los Angeles. He immediately went on the offensive. The Eucharist is the only answer to a secular, relativist culture. 'What is sad today is that so many in the Catholic Church have become blasé about the Eucharist. In my country, seventy per cent of Catholics stay away from the Eucharist.' But nothing is more important than the Eucharist. The Eucharist, in the much-quoted phrase of the Second Vatican Council, is 'the source and the summit of Christian life'. The Fathers of the Council wanted to 'revive the Eucharist, to draw people to It more and more'. If they had been told that in 2016 70%, more in Western Europe, would stay away from the Eucharist on a regular basis, they would have felt their work had been a failure.

Bishop Barron quoted the words of a Christina Aguilera song: 'I am beautiful in every single way, and words can't bring me down.' He continued: 'We'll never get a salvation religion off the ground if we believe that. So many voices in the culture insist upon it. "Don't put me down. Don't tell me I'm wrong. I've got the infinite right to define my own life, to define who I am." That is repugnant to salvation religion. It's repugnant to a Eucharistic faith.'

The Bishop called the Eucharist the 'Bread of Life which keeps us spiritually alive. We should all stretch out our hands as if we were starving for the Bread of Life.' He reminded us of the three aspects of the Eucharist: meal, sacrifice and presence. Of these, too often the sacrificial nature of the Eucharist is ignored. 'The logic of sacrifice is pretty straightforward. We take some aspect of creation and we return it to God ... If we are off-kilter, which we are, if we are worshipping in the wrong way, we need to be brought back and that process is painful. We need to go through into a painful realignment.'

Bishop Barron paid tribute to the influence of Filipino Catholics who were helping to keep the faith alive in 'the post-Christian West'. In his diocese of Los Angeles, the Filipino community was crucial to keeping the Church going. 'So to come here and be with you is a great thrill for me. In God's strange providence, He will take a particular Church, a particular people, and use them as a means to invigorate and evangelise the rest of the Catholic world. I do believe, in God's beguiling providence, that you are playing that role now.'

Bishop Barron was followed by Mrs Marianne Servaas. She was born and brought up in Belgium, in an evangelical family strongly opposed to Catholicism. After marrying an Englishman she came with her husband to the Philippines and for seven years they worked as evangelical missionaries. It was here however that

> our lives were profoundly changed in such a way that it prepared, even cleared, our hearts to begin to see the beauty of the Eucharist and Eucharistic living ... I discovered a greater depth and was unable to resist the appeal and call that was present within it because it was related to the desire to love Christ to the full. One image that came to me soon after I became a Catholic was that I grew up in an aquarium. Then I swam in the lake of a broader form of Christian tradition. Now I am in the ocean. All the water is of God, but give me the ocean. Here there is depth, diversity and unity.

That afternoon, two priests shared their insights with us about the Eucharist. First, Cardinal Orlando Quevedo, Archbishop of Cotabato in Mindonao, well-known as an advocate for social justice. His message to Catholics attending the Congress was 'practise what you preach' and 'love the poor'.

> Our faith is focused on externals and rituals, processions and private devotions. Deep down, they manifest the Filipino's authentic awareness of God's presence in everything

that is blessed or holy. But the question remains: what does
the Holy Eucharist really mean? How should we participate?
What does it tell us about how we should live?

He reminded us that the Eucharist is 'communion, the deepest
kind of union. It means a sharing in His mission—a mission to
the poor, the oppressed and marginalised—to all who are needy
and in need of love and service.' If on Sundays 'we seem to be a
nation of saints', social ills remain. 'There is massive poverty,
homelessness, street children, human trafficking, the drug problem, and other forms of criminality. And media reports speak of
horrendous corruption from top to bottom.'

Fr Luciano Ariel Felloni is an Argentine priest, working in the
Philippines for twenty-one years. He began diffidently: 'I don't
have a doctorate in anything. I don't teach anything. I'm a
professor of nothing.' It soon became obvious however that he
was well educated in the university of life. He praised the poor
and their hunger for the Eucharist, saying that often those who
have little in life are the ones more excited to receive Christ. 'I
learned that the poor feel a very special connection with Jesus in
the Eucharist. They really love and treasure Jesus so much. Jesus
is alive in the peripheries where no one wants to go.'

Fr Felloni lives in a slum on top of a huge open dump outside
Manila. He admitted that he used to look down on what he
described as 'superficial sacramentalism' in many Filipinos. 'In
twenty-one years the poor have taught me to eat my words. I
realise this is what Pope Francis calls spirituality of the people.'
Not only do the poor have devotions; they have a deep spirituality.
'They want the Lord to be there for them, in their happy moments
and not-so-happy moments. They want the Lord all the time and
everywhere, and that hunger for the Eucharist is one of the biggest
lessons I have learned from people ... Many times, the poor, not
us priests, are the ones who make the presence of the Church felt
in those places.'

Speaking of poverty, Cebu was certainly a city of contrasts. In
the same street, fine, newly-built houses and blocks would rub

shoulders with slum dwellings. We gathered that most people lived from week to week, surviving on the minimum wage. One quarter are considered as very poor and dependent on a social welfare system that does not always reach those in greatest need. In connection with the Congress, many new initiatives began through parish or other Church organisations. They included twenty-three new programmes of outreach to poor and orphaned children.

Wednesday: nourishment, caring

Wednesday, the fourth day of the Congress, brought an amazing testimony from the Ponce family. Before that, Archbishop Thomas Menamparampil of Jowai in India was the main celebrant at Mass. His homily may be summed up in this way:

> The Eucharist is Christ's greatest gift to the Church. It is His self-gift to His disciples. It is a call to oneness in the fellowship of the Triune God. It brings into existence a 'communion of believers'. This communion, however, does not stop around the Eucharistic Table or within the confines of the physical church. United with Christ, believers are exhorted not only to go out and make Him known to the world but to spring into action, to seek out the suffering and the poor ...

> The 'Go' at the end of the Eucharist is not mere ceremonial dismissal, it is a mission-laden mandate. It echoes the parting message of Jesus: 'Go, then, to all peoples everywhere and make them My disciples ... and teach them' (Mt 28:19–20), after which He adds an assurance, 'I will be with you'. Though the mandate is clear enough, this reassurance of our Divine Saviour alone can give us the courage to go beyond ourselves and reach out to the ends of the earth. For the way is long and the compulsions of the journey demanding. In an age when believers think that fidelity to the Gospel itself is strenuous enough, it calls for extraordinary courage and profound faith to take upon oneself the task of bearing Christ's Message of Hope to others ... There are more Christians under stress today

than in any other period of history. We need resolute
convictions to remain faithful in this era of persecution on
the one hand, and secularisation on the other.

There are times when a person in the service of the Gospel
feels broken and exhausted in the face of growing indifference, opposition, or outright rejection. He/she would like
to give up. 'Take away my life', he would like to say with
Elijah. Then suddenly, he hears an angel's reassuring voice:
'Arise and eat' (1 K 19:4–7). Eucharist is nourishment.
Indeed, 'God strengthens those who are weak and tired'
(Is 40:29). Pope Benedict XVI says: 'We cannot approach
the Eucharist without being drawn into the Mission'
(*Sacramentum Caritatis* 84). Jesus' example of self-giving
conceals irresistible motivating power within, so that
everyone who derives strength from Him feels drawn to
do the same (1 Jn 3:16). Faith is not an idle intellectual
conviction; it is a driving force towards self-giving, even
to the point of self-forgetfulness.

The testimony of Paul Ponce and his family gave ample proof of
that 'driving force'. I sat with them during the Statio Orbis and
saw at close range their joyful faith. Paul's testimony could have
been called 'How to juggle through life'. With his incredible
juggling act as a background, he took us through the story of his
life. He had tried to find fulfilment and happiness in fame, money,
travel, women. All of these aims he met. But he still wasn't happy.
It was only when he was confirmed, at the age of twenty-one, that
he found God, and with Him the happiness and peace he desired.
Sometime later he met Lia, his wife. They have been blessed with
three children. At the end of Paul's testimony, the whole family
was there, showing their juggling skills. With the youngest, not
everything was perfect, but 'it is in the imperfection that we
succeed. No-one is perfect. Only God is perfect.'

In the afternoon Archbishop Antonio Ledesma stood in for
Cardinal Peter Turkson and delivered the Cardinal's talk, high-
lighting the Eucharistic dimensions not just of Pope Francis'

encyclical *Laudato Si* but of Catholic Social Teachings in general—on caring for each other and for creation.

Caring for each other, either as individuals or as communities, featured in Bishop Kevin Doran's homily that evening in the Redemptorist church of Mother of Perpetual Help, and here I depend on Tommy Burns' transcript. Bishop Doran spoke about the parable of the sower:

> The good sower has spread the seed everywhere; he has prepared the ground; he has played his part; his hope is not that of wishful thinking but that of reasonable hope. However, there is also a certain amount of uncertainty about the crop with regard to the weather conditions, things which are completely outside of the farmer's control yet all conducive of a good harvest ... The seed is like the Word of God, hope-filled; God in His generosity spreads it everywhere. But there is always uncertainty about the harvest, because we lack commitment, are pre-occupied or perhaps have become lacklustre in our mission ...

> Ireland was once known as the land of saints and scholars, producing many of each. Thousands of these went abroad as missionaries to far flung lands, some of whom came to this very parish and for this we give thanks. Nourishing the soil for the reception of God's Word is essential ... But how can this be achieved?

> We must first of all prepare our own hearts by making a home there for the Word of God. St Jerome taught that we should think of the Gospel as the Body of Christ. Just as we would not allow a crumb of the Eucharist to fall to the ground, so too we must be attentive to God's Word so that nothing He says to us is ever lost. This is especially so when we gather in the communion of the Church, as when we gather in communion the power of God's Word is most effective. But we cannot just stop with ourselves; we are expected to help prepare the soil of other people, beginning with our own children and grandchildren. If you do not do it, who will? I believe the mistake we have made in

Ireland is to leave it to others. Even the best of people are
no substitute for what parents can do so effectively in this
regard. So too in our parish communities, the work place,
our whole society; God will certainly give growth, but it is
our job to prepare the soil and to sow the seed.

Bishop Doran reminded us that Pope Francis encourages us all to
be 'missionary disciples'. Whatever harvest we reap has been won
by Jesus, but not without sacrifice. We too will have to die to self
if we are to bear fruit. Then 'each of us, whether as individuals or
communities, can be carriers of that hope for each other, and so
proclaim with confidence "Christ in us, our Hope of Glory".'

One of the features of these Congresses is that they bring
Catholics from all parts of the globe together with the local faithful.
Fourteen parish churches in Cebu acted as hosts for the different
language groups. The Redemptorist parish, founded in 1929 by an
Irish priest, Fr William Byrne, was chosen for the English-speaking
group. Many Irish Redemptorists have ministered here. Bishop
Doran of Elphin was the main celebrant at Mass, concelebrated by
Bishop Robert Byrne from England, six other bishops and a large
number of priests. Two of the Irish pilgrims addressed the over-
flowing congregation at the end of Mass: John Howard spoke on
the Apostolate of Eucharistic Adoration and Catriona Heffernan
on the Pure in Heart organisation.

We were invited after Mass to a community meal, accompanied by music, song and dance, and including a musical drama
presented by the young people of the parish on the life of St
Alphonsus Liguori. We saw how seriously the Church in the
parishes is engaged in ministry to young people. Surely there must
be some connection between the active engagement of young
people in the life of the Church and the large numbers presenting
themselves as candidates for priesthood and religious life?
Enough here to provoke an examination of conscience about our
own on-going ministry involving young people!

Before we left, we were reminded of the precarious state of so
many of the poor. The parish priest asked us to pray for a number of

his parishioners who were threatened by eviction at the hands of property speculators. Developers were trying to claim the ramshackle properties the poor were living in, with a view to their demolition and the building of more expensive properties on their sites.

Thursday: cultures, migrants, youth

The fifth day featured a challenging catechesis by Cardinal Luis Antonio Tagle on 'The Eucharist and the Dialogue with Cultures'. He was tackling a section in the Basic Text for the Cebu Congress dealing with inculturation and mission as 'a theological and pastoral imperative'. What is needed is a dialogue between 'the Gospel and the Christian Faith on the one hand and the culture of the Asian people on the other, the desired result of which is faith that is inculturated and culture that is evangelised.' He saw the Eucharist as meaning 'much for most Asians, because it expresses many of the cultural values that they treasure very dearly'. Culture he defined as 'the whole complex of forms of feeling, acting and thinking shared by a society, which allows the members of the group to survive, provides them with a sense of identity and belonging, and gives meaning to their lives'.

He then suggested that we might understand the idea of 'culture' more easily by asking ourselves a few questions: How we use space in our gatherings? ('If your parish has a big space for parking but no room for pastoral formation, what does that say about the culture of your parish?') How we use language? Who are our heroes? What is our attitude to knowledge and truth? To food? To time? To money?

The Cardinal then spoke of the need for 'cultural intelligence'. Such intelligence helps dialogue, because it helps us to be aware of our own culture and how it affects us; it helps us to study and try to know from within the cultures of other people; and it explores ways for our cultures to interact and learn from each other. The Church, he asserted, 'needs cultural intelligence'. Why?

> For Mission. For the Church to exist as an effective witness
> to the Gospel before today's culture necessitates dialogue
> and cultural intelligence ... If the Gospel is to be a leaven of
> transformation, we need to know the Gospel. But we also
> need to meet people in their cultures. We need cultural
> intelligence for the sake of the Gospel and of humanity.

Cardinal Tagle asked how other cultures, outside of the Christian
culture, understood the Congress theme of 'Christ in You, Our
Hope of Glory'. For us, we are affirming the presence of Jesus,
especially in the Eucharist.

> But how do you talk about presence, real presence, in a
> world shaped by virtual reality? ... A community is being
> generated by cyber technology. Is that real? Is that virtual?
> Yet the same digital world or culture has formed many
> young people to put prominence on image ... That's one
> culture we have to contend with, the culture of the virtual,
> digital world. When you talk to young people about real
> presence, what enters into their mind? Adoration? The
> monstrance? The consecration? Or a Facebook page? ... I
> have learned from experts in the digital culture that the
> term 'real' for them means authenticity, integrity, credibil-
> ity. When we dialogue with the culture of the virtual, they
> will look for the authentic and credible presence of Jesus
> in the minister. In our words, in our Christian community,
> we assert the real presence of Jesus for those in a digital
> virtual culture. That means I will look for a credible,
> authentic manifestation of Jesus.

The Cardinal considered two other forms of culture: that of
'alienating individualism' and 'the throw-away culture'.

> One of the great gifts of our time is the value placed on the
> individual human person. The appreciation of the person
> is good and necessary for society ... Individualisation
> prevents human beings from being reduced to mere spare
> parts of a big social machinery. Unfortunately, this healthy
> process of individualistion has been pushed to an extreme
> called 'individualism', where the individual and the com-

munity become enemies ... This culture protects individual rights but does not sufficiently stress duties to other persons and to society.

Societies also can be individualistic: stigmatising persons, discriminating against them, blaming the ills of society on strangers and relegating the unwanted to ghettos. Whereas the Eucharist offers an experience of another culture, that of 'convocation', being called together. Jesus 'hosted and participated in meals by calling together the most unimaginable combination of people to a community, to become His family, His Body'. The Cardinal pleaded:

> Let us begin the dialogue with the culture of alienating individualism in our homes. Restore the family meals! The basic unit of the meal is the common table. Nowadays, the basic unit of the meal is my plate! If I have my plate with food on it, I can go anywhere and eat by myself. But that is not a meal; that is just eating! Individualistic persons know how to eat, but they don't know how to participate in a meal.

We might add that the subtle distinction between individuals and individualism by which we identify our dignity as distinct persons finds our fulfilment only in a caring community, for example in marriage, in L'Arche, in monastic communities and so on, and is a direct reflection in humankind of the Holy Trinity. There we find three distinct Persons who nevertheless are so perfectly in community with one another that we profess faith in one God and not three.

The Eucharist, with its culture of gift and sharing, was also opposed to the 'throw-away culture', which considered things and even people as disposable when they were of no further use or perceived to be a burden.

> The accumulation, the consumption of goods even when they are not needed, becomes a badge of dignity. Competitiveness, inequality and affliction emanate from this culture. Buying for the sake of having leads to throwing away, and

we throw away the goods that the poor should benefit from and that they could not afford to buy ... If we are simple, if we live by restraint, we could go against the throw-away culture ... Let us behold Jesus in the Eucharist. Let us allow Him to form in us a community of neighbours, brothers and sisters. No more barriers, only bridges! Let us allow Him to open our eyes to see in creation, in persons, in the poor, the discarded, the true gifts of God. No-one thrown away, only gifts to be treasured. This culture of communion and gifts shared will make a Eucharistic community, a real, credible presence of Christ in the cultures of the world, and provide the world a reason to hope.

Immediately after Cardinal Tagle came Mr Kei-ichi Sugawara, a member of the minority Catholic community of Japan. His town had been devastated by the tsunami which followed a huge earthquake in Japan in 2011. We saw a video showing how the seaport town was washed away in just six minutes. Before the disaster there had been little communication between the local Catholic community and the large Filipino migrant population. Mr Sugawara explained how, following the tsunami, the Japanese Catholics were spurred on by their Eucharistic faith to reach out to the migrants. His parish is now more vibrant and more inclusive, with Filipinos serving on the parish council. 'The disaster brought down not only physical walls but also walls of indifference and prejudice.'

That same day was designated as 'Youth Day'. Bishop Robert Barron gave a catechesis entitled 'Christ in the Youth, Our Hope of Glory' in which he urged his hearers to become saints. 'The most important thing and extraordinary expectation of the Church is that everybody in this room becomes a saint.' He suggested three pathways to becoming a saint: 'To find one's centre; to know that we are all sinners; and to realise that one's life is not about oneself.'

There is one centre around which everything else revolves. If Christ is not the centre of one's life, that makes us unhappy, divided, split and at war with ourselves ... To all of us sinners, everyone of us is an addict, but Jesus wants to set us free; free for joy, for fulness of life ... [Real joy lies in] giving some of yourself away for your being to grow ... Everybody in this room has a restless heart. We're searching for happiness, and we try to find it in wealth, pleasure, power, honour. It has never worked. It cannot work. We are wired for God ... What is most important? That is what you worship. Once you find that, you know how your life is structured. If you worship anything other than God, your life will become scattered ... You want to be happy? Take a good, long, prayerful look at Jesus and you'll see weirdly a formula for joy. It's a picture of freedom; Jesus on the cross is free ... God has a dream for you. When you find it, go for it, and you will find your way to happiness. We're not meant just to live our little life. There's a power already at work in you that can do infinitely more than you can ask or imagine. That power is the Holy Spirit.

Only a limited number of people, about 15,000, could be seated in the Congress Pavilion. The Congress organisers therefore arranged seven public events in which the general public could join. And join in they did, in huge numbers. One of these events was the visit to the Seven Churches on Thursday evening. Many thousands took part, carrying lighted candles or holy pictures, singing hymns and saying the rosary as they walked. We visitors were able to join them and were uplifted by seeing at first hand the fervour and joy of the locals.

Friday: street children, sacredness of food, popular piety

Friday 29 January continued the path of dialogue. At Mass, Cardinal John Onaiyekan, Archbishop of Abuja in Nigeria, spoke of dialogue with the poor and suffering. He asked: 'Can we celebrate the Eucharist together in the International Eucharistic Congress with all pomp and pageantry and (then) allow everybody to crawl back into our respective oases of poverty and misery, or affluence and indifference?' Jesus had multiplied five loaves and two fish to feed five thousand people with plenty left over. He had nudged his disciples into action. Action is needed now.

> Do something! Do not say the problem is too much, you cannot feed everybody or that what we have would not make any difference. Jesus does not want to hear that. And God is challenging us: 'Do the little you can with the right spirit and God will do the rest.' The miracle of the loaves can be repeated over and over again in our world of today if there are generous hearts among the disciples of Jesus ready to share what they have with those in greater need.

Maria Georgia (Maggie) Cogtas then gave one of the most memorable talks of the whole week. Formerly a street child and garbage scavenger, she is now a pastoral outreach worker to such children in Cebu. She and her twin brother were the youngest of seven neglected children, abandoned by their father, with an absent working mother who eventually also left them. She had scavenged for scrap from the age of eight. Her childhood broken, she soon learned to suppress her emotions.

> But there is no pain or struggle greater than God's love. I found healing; I can attest to that. For all that is broken can be repaired and with God's help can still be restored. Good people reached out to me while I was on the streets and I was given a school scholarship.

Twenty-three groups now reached out to the street children in a programme including games, meals, singing, dancing, clothing and hygiene. Catechesis and prayer helped the children to realise they are all children of God. Five hundred of them (whom we had met the day before the Congress opened) had been prepared to make their first Holy Communion at this Congress.

> They are gradually growing in dignity and now remember
> their birthdays as we have a gift for them. They now realise
> they are their brother's keeper and look out for each other.
> They tell us when one is sick, hurt or beaten. They now
> come on time to our Saturday sessions when we also teach
> them to manage their garbage. Gaining in self-respect, they
> would now be ashamed if they came unkempt or dirty.
> They no longer need to avert their eyes.

Her dream, said Maggie Cogtas, was that these children might
become public servants, such as police officers or teachers,
engineers who could build homes for the poor, or priests who
could evangelise. She said she wished their parents could find
steady work so the children would not have to go to school on
empty stomachs, without school supplies, an umbrella or shoes
for the rainy season. She called on the Church to help.

> What can we do so that they may not lose hope in God, if
> at times nobody can support them? There are a lot of street
> children that live outside our parishes. Can we not turn
> our parishes into child-friendly parishes with walk-in
> facilities, where they could take a bath, eat and study? Our
> churches are the closest place where they could see God.
> But they can also be the closest place where our children
> can see their dreams.

Cardinal Oswald Gracias of Mumbai followed with an important
paper on 'The Eucharist in the Church's Dialogue with Religions',
read for him by Archbishop Dominic Jala of Shillong. Dialogue
was repeatedly mentioned throughout the Cebu Congress. Here,
Cardinal Gracias fastened on two areas which facilitated dialogue:
food, and popular piety. Belief in the Eucharist as spiritual
nourishment could resonate with many other people. Hinduism,
Islam, Sikhism and other faiths all recognise a sacred value in
food. Through the death and resurrection of Jesus, the Eucharist
fosters reconciliation with people of every religion and culture.

> And as a community of believing persons, we reject every
> form of selfishness, sectarianism, casteism and individual-

ism and build bridges of communion with every person, association, community and nation. Our Asian reality is marked with cultural, religious, linguistic and ethnic pluralism. Hence our Eucharistic theology should help us respect these diverse groups and live with them in harmony and peace. It should also urge us to build bonds of solidarity with others.

The Eucharist invites to a fuller communion with God and with one another. The Cardinal quoted from Pope St John Paul in *Mane Nobiscum Domine* (27):

> The Eucharist is not merely an expression of communion in the Church's life; it is also a project of solidarity for all of humanity. In the celebration of the Eucharist the Church constantly renews her awareness of being a 'sign and instrument' not only of intimate union with God but also of the unity of the whole human race. ... Just as Jesus gave His Body and shed His Blood for us, we are invited to break ourselves for others and live for others. Nourished by the Body and Blood of Christ, we must grow in awareness of the dignity and value of every person.

The Cardinal also addressed the issue of social justice and the Eucharist.

Popular piety could also promote friendship and dialogue with people of other religions. 'Asia is the continent where the spiritual is held in high esteem and where the religious sense is deep and innate: the preservation of this precious heritage must be the common task of all'. Public devotions and processions had great value as enculturating local religious practice.

Friday ended on a very high note. Archbishop Diarmuid Martin of Dublin celebrated the late afternoon open-air Mass before an immense crowd in front of the Cebu Capitol Building which was followed by a procession of the Blessed Sacrament. In his homily, the Archbishop reminded us that 'There is no Church without the Eucharist. The Eucharist builds the Church.' He urged Catholics to model their lives as a celebration of the mystery of the life and love of Jesus Christ. 'We are called to understand, love and assimilate the very love of Jesus ... Our lives too must be offered in sacrifice.' He spoke of two bishops he had known, both of whom had spent time in concentration camps in Dachau or in Vietnam. Both experienced a deep sense of loss at being deprived of the Eucharist and, when they eventually managed to make simple arrangements for the celebration of the Eucharist, they also found that the Church became present in a new way in the camp. The Archbishop's message was clear: the Eucharist makes the Church.

The procession brought back memories of Guadalajara. The specially designed monstrance was carried on a pedestal in an open-top truck decked with flowers. The impressive river of faithful accompanying the Blessed Sacrament reached as far as the eye could see and took three hours to pass through the city's streets which were flanked on both sides by throngs of young people. The route was decorated throughout and benefited from a most effective sound system along the whole length. The police estimate of the crowd was a million and a half. Benediction was given in the Plaza Independencia, beside the beach where the Gospel reached the Philippines for the first time, nearly five hundred years ago.

Saturday: first Communions

Saturday 30 January featured a catechesis by Cardinal Timothy Dolan of New York on 'The Eucharist and Mary'. He spoke of the Eucharist as sacrifice, meal and presence, themes delivered by other speakers, but this time emphasising Mary's unique contribution. To quote some of his sentences: 'The Mass is our family meal, especially on Sundays. The mother of our family, Mary, is always at the table with Jesus, with us ... You want to be closer to Jesus? Then be close to Mary, because she is right there next to Him.' Mary, said the Cardinal, gave birth to the Son of God in Bethlehem, which means 'House of Bread'. She placed Him in a manger, which means a 'feed box', because 'Jesus was intended as bread for the world in the Eucharist'.

Mass that afternoon was offered in the Cebu City Sports Centre, with retired Cardinal Ricardo Vidal as main celebrant. Five thousand children made their first Holy Communion at this Mass. At the only previous IEC held in the Philippines, in Manila in 1937, Ricardo Vidal as a little boy had made his first Holy Communion. Here he was, seventy-nine years later and now looking very frail, presiding at another such Eucharist.

> I know very well the feeling of these children here because I was once in their place. I was one of those children who received First Communion during Children's Day at Luneta. I was amazed at the beauty of the priest and the many people. I was even more amazed at the papal legate looking like a king with his long red robe. But above all as a young boy I felt very big ... My dear children, strive to live as true children of God. Faith in God brings out the best in us and faith in others brings out the best in them. So have faith in the Real Presence of the Lord in the Eucharist. Believe that the Real Presence is in our midst. Realise the presence of Jesus in others. Believe. Have faith.

One hundred bishops helped to give Communion to the children, including the five hundred street children we had met the day before the Congress opened. All were beautifully but simply dressed in white. One little girl, Maryst Norña Donque of Cebu South, asked how she felt, said 'I'm happy and glad' because she was about to have what St Thérèse of Lisieux called the first 'kiss of love' with the Lord.

Does that seem too sentimental in this twenty-first century? That would be a pity, for many reasons. St Thérèse herself cultivated a personal relationship with the child Jesus, no doubt helped by her older sister Pauline who had written to her: 'I still think that for little girls, very good, very sweet . . . the Holy Child in the crib reserves all kinds of divine caresses.' She used the image of childhood or littleness in communicating her own spiritual journey. St Bernard of Clairvaux also used the theme of the Child Jesus in his sermons and composed this lovely Christmas prayer:

> Let Your goodness Lord appear to us that we, made in your image, conform ourselves to it. In our own strength we cannot imitate Your majesty, power, and wonder, nor is it fitting for us to try. But Your mercy reaches from the heavens through the clouds to the earth below. You have come to us as a small child, but you have brought us the greatest of all gifts, the gift of eternal love. Caress us with Your tiny hands, embrace us with Your tiny arms and pierce our hearts with Your soft, sweet cries.

Christ in fact is present in the Eucharist in all the mysteries of His human life, not only in His Holy Childhood but in all His human forms. The Benedictine Abbot Bl Columba Marmion in *Christ in His Mysteries* has shown how the Eucharist includes the whole life of Christ:

> Since it is the Body and Blood of Christ that we receive, the Eucharist presupposes the Incarnation and the mysteries which are founded upon or flow from it. Christ is upon the altar with the divine life which never ceases, with His mortal life of which the historical form has doubtless ceased, but of which the substance and merits remain, with His glorious life which shall have no end. All this, as you know, is really contained in the Sacred Host and given in Communion to our souls. In communicating Himself to us, Christ Jesus gives Himself in the substantial totality of His works and mysteries, as in the oneness of His Person … The Eucharist is like the synthesis of the marvels of the love of the Incarnate Word towards us.

That little first communicant, Maryst, can perhaps teach even us adults.

The celebrations continued in the Sports Centre with an amazing show of the Sinulog, a ritual prayer-dance honouring Señor Santo Niño, the Child Jesus. The Portuguese explorer

Ferdinand Magellan gave a small statue of the Child Jesus to the local Queen in Cebu in April 1521. It is now venerated at the Basilica of the Santo Niño in downtown Cebu City and is a most important symbol of the faith of the Filipino people, with replicas kept and honoured in their homes.

The Statio Orbis

After such a Congress week many people were sad when the final day dawned. The weather had been very wet for the first two days of the Congress and had threatened to turn the venue for the Statio Orbis into a quagmire. Thankfully, the rain cleared and a hot sun shone. The Statio was held at the San Pedro Calungsod Templete in Cebu City's South Road Properties, fronting an open area of twenty-six hectares capable of holding up to one million people. The site was approached from the north by a two kilometre-long viaduct crossing the sea and from the south from Cebu's main thoroughfare. The crowds converged, and by four o'clock the sun-drenched venue was filled to capacity.

Cardinal Charles Bo, Papal Legate, had clearly been deeply moved by all he had witnessed during the Congress week. In his homily he praised the Filipino people:

> What great hosts you are! What a great experience! For the last seven days you made us all proud to be Catholics. You broke the bread of hospitality, warmth and your smile. You are apostles of smiling! How can we forget your meticulous organisation? How can we forget the warmth, the smile, the dance, the piety and the fellowship of all of you? What a deep experience of table fellowship! For seven days we were on Mount Tabor.
>
> Seven intense days are coming to an end, my dear friends from all over the world. We have explored the Eucharist in all dimensions with the theme—Christ in Us, our Hope of Glory; Eucharist, the source and the goal of Mission. More than seventy countries have savoured the spiritual food that nourished us through our sharing, our adoration, our

beautiful liturgy, our enriching fellowship, our wonderful lectures, our grand Eucharistic procession. A global table was laid and we broke the Word and the Bread. It was almost an eschatological moment of universal brotherhood.

The Cardinal insisted that as the disciples had to come down from Mount Tabor, so we all had to return to our daily life. What will this Eucharistic Congress have achieved? He answered his own question by saying 'Renewed apostolic and missionary zeal'. Contact with the Filipino Church had re-energised our Christian hope. 'This nation holds great promises to the Catholic world.' Cardinal Bo urged his Philippine hearers 'to proclaim the Christian hope to every soul ... Your time of destiny has arrived ... Go to countries that have more pets than children!' He then spoke to the families and the youth, 'bringing in mercy and love as the core values of the Eucharist'.

> Not only in the Philippines but all over the world, the family needs to be protected and promoted and nurtured. The death of the family is the death of humanity. Pope Francis has been concerned these last three years with three major dangers to the world: environmental injustice; economic injustice; and the greatest danger to humanity today, the destruction of the family ... More than any nuclear bomb, more than any terrorism, a mortal danger awaits humanity because some countries have chosen a path of destroying families through laws ... This Congress needs to end with the strong resolve to strengthen Catholic families, to uphold the priesthood of the laity. Catholic families—Christ in you—you are the hope of glory. The future of the Church depends on the Catholic family. As Pope St John Paul II said, 'the future of humanity passes by way of the family'.

Noting that 52% of the people in the Philippines were under the age of 25, the Cardinal said 'What a blessing! This is the future of the Church. What a young nation! ... The Youth are not only the hope of the future; they are the present precious treasures.'

Urging other Churches not to neglect young people, he told the Philippine people that they had 'two great graces. Your family integrity is strong ... [and] the number of your young people ... The future does not belong to countries that have oil or weapons. The future belongs to nations with young people.'

The Cardinal drew warm applause from the Filipinos when he said he found it hard to leave them.

> As we go, part of us refuses to come with us. Our hearts wish to stay with you. You have loved us so intensely and the thought of going shakes us. You have made us proud to be Catholics and you made us realise the intense fellowship that comes through Eucharist ... Rejoice today! ... Hope in your hearts, hope in your families, let hope flow like a radiant river in your mountains, let hope spread like a morning sun on your people.

At the end of the Statio Orbis, Pope Francis gave a video message to those present. He called the Congress theme, 'Christ in you, our hope of glory',

> a very timely reminder for all the faithful. It reminds us that the risen Jesus is always alive and present in His Church, above all in the Eucharist, the sacrament of His Body and Blood. Christ's presence among us is not only a consolation, but also a promise and a summons. It is a promise that everlasting joy and peace will one day be ours in the fullness of His Kingdom. But it is also a summons to go forth, as missionaries, to bring the message of the Father's tenderness, forgiveness and mercy to every man, woman and child.

> How much our world needs this message! When we think of the conflicts, the injustices and the urgent humanitarian crises which mark our time, we realize how important it is for every Christian to be a true missionary disciple, bringing the good news of Christ's redemptive love to a world in such need of reconciliation, justice and peace.

Pope Francis asked us to reflect on two gestures of Jesus at the Last Supper: table fellowship and the washing of feet. Both were connected with the missionary dimension of the Eucharist.

> We know how important it was for Jesus to share meals with His disciples, but also, and especially, with sinners and the outcast. Sitting at table, Jesus was able to listen to others, to hear their stories, to appreciate their hopes and aspirations, and to speak to them of the Father's love. At each Eucharist, the table of the Lord's Supper, we should be inspired to follow His example, by reaching out to others, in a spirit of respect and openness, in order to share with them the gift we ourselves have received.

> In Asia, where the Church is committed to respectful dialogue with the followers of other religions, this prophetic witness most often takes place, as we know, through the dialogue of life. Through the testimony of lives transformed by God's love, we best proclaim the Kingdom's promise of reconciliation, justice and unity for the human family. Our example can open hearts to the grace of the Holy Spirit, who leads them to Christ the Saviour.

> The other image which the Lord offers us at the Last Supper is the washing of feet. On the eve of His passion, Jesus washed the feet of His disciples as a sign of humble service, of the unconditional love with which He gave His life on the Cross for the salvation of the world. The Eucharist is a school of humble service. It teaches us readiness to be there for others. This too is at the heart of missionary discipleship.

Pope Francis had visited the Philippines twelve months previously in the wake of Typhoon Yolanda which had brought immense devastation but also 'an immense outpouring of solidarity, generosity and goodness ... The Eucharist speaks to us of that power which flows from the Cross and constantly brings new life. It changes hearts. It enables us to be caring, to protect the poor and the vulnerable, and to be sensitive to the cry of our brothers and sisters in need. It teaches us to act with integrity and to reject the injustice and corruption which poison the roots of society.'

Before ending his message Pope Francis announced that the next International Eucharistic Congress will take place in 2020 in Budapest, Hungary.

Because of the frequent and severe natural disasters they suffer, the Philippines have been described as 'the disaster capital of the world'. Nevertheless, after each setback the Filipino people have shown their resilience and their faith. Symbolic of this was the altar table built for the Cebu Congress. It was made of wood from the boats and houses destroyed in northern Cebu two years previously in the fierce winds and waves of Typhoon Yolanda.

Clayton Tugonon, a furniture maker of Mandaue City, designed the altar table. It stood on five legs, symbolising the five wounds of Jesus. The front three legs displayed images of a chalice, with grapes for wine and wheat for bread. Simeon Dumdum Jr, a former Regional Trial Court Judge in Cebu City and a renowned poet, described the devastation wrought by the typhoon in a poem entitled 'The Wood of Sacrifice'. The storm had taken homes and lives away, the wreckage had been stored, and then a stranger came

> And asked for wood, the bits
> Of boats, the pieces of the
> The posts and walls, and even
> The tree where someone died,
> And then put them together,
> Chiselled them, sawed and hammered,
> And when the man had finished
> The people saw an altar.
> The lives of those who died
> The folk could not retrieve,
> But through the odds and ends
> Of what remained of them
> Was formed a table for
> What they had sacrificed.
> They knew that if there was

A dying on the altar
There was also a rising.

What better epitaph could there be for such a challenging and enriching Congress?

Returning to England via Hong Kong was unquestionably like coming down from Mount Tabor. Hong Kong is one of the world's leading financial, banking and trading centres. Someone described it as a 'colourful, chaotic, fantastic place to live and visit'. A few days at the Bishop Lei International House on Robinson Road, however, maintained continuity with the Cebu Congress. The House is next to the Catholic cathedral in Hong Kong and has a connection with that diocese.

References

1) Pontifical Commission for International Eucharistic Congresses, *Christ in You, Our Hope of Glory and The Eucharist: Source and Goal of the Church's Mission*. Basic Text, Theological and Pastoral Reflections in preparation for the 51st International Eucharistic Congress, Cebu, Philippines 24–31 January 2016.

2) Allen, J. F., Personal notes and diaries and Congress releases.

3) Boccardi, V. S.S.S., Plenary Assembly in preparation for the 51st IEC Cebu, *International Eucharistic Congresses: Between history and the modern times* (2015).

4) Congress publications:
   - Program Guide
   - Living with Christ: The Word of God, Daily Prayer & the Bread of Life
   - Visita Iglesia Prayers
   - Daily Bulletins

5) Bersales, J. E. R. (Ed), *Days of Hope and Glory*, The 51st International Eucharistic Congress Commemorative Book (Cebu 2016).

6) Burns, T., *The 51st International Eucharistic Congress: A Personal Pilgrimage* (Privately printed, Ireland 2016).

7) Pangan, J. K., Pontifical Commission for International Eucharistic Congresses, Cebu: la culla del cristianesimo filippino.

8) Rosica, T., http:// www.saltandlighttv.org

9) http://iec2016.ph

10) http://www.vatican.va/roman_curia/pont_committees/eucharist-congr/archive/index_en.htm

11) CBCP Monitor Special Congress issues (Manila 2016).

EPILOGUE

SOMEONE ASKED 'WHAT has attending the last twelve International Eucharistic Congresses meant to you?' A challenging question but a fair one. Taking part in these events for nearly half a century, one has heard many things said about the Eucharist in so many ways, times and places. All have shown that the mystery of the Eucharist is a wellspring of freshness, newness, that constantly rejuvenates, inspires, provokes awe. It never ceases to energise, re-invigorating our lives, inviting us into the brightness of a never-ending Easter.

To attend has been an enriching humanising experience. Seeing so many parts of our beautiful world lifts the heart; meeting with people of different cultures stretches the mind.

It has been a luminous academic experience. Listening and talking to some of the leading scholars of the day deepens one's grasp of the intellectual content of faith.

It has been a heightened spiritual experience. The Congresses have shown how the Eucharist is indeed the 'source and summit' of Christian life.

It has been a valuable pastoral experience, observing how the faith is lived and put into action.

It has been a truly Catholic experience, sharing communion with a plurality of peoples.

It has been a profoundly unifying experience, brought to pass at the Statio Orbis and by the presence of the Pope or his Legate.

It has been an experience which makes sense of the life of a priest, drawing out the timeless significance of words that changed the world: 'This is My Body, given for you. This is My Blood, poured out for you. Do this in memory of Me.'

See you at Budapest 2020, God willing.

INDEX

The Blessed Trinity, Jesus Christ and the Blessed Virgin Mary are mentioned throughout the book. They are not included in this index.

Abitene, Martyrs of 258, 267
Adalbert, St 194
Adam 158
Adamakis, Metropolitan
    Emmanuel 307
Adenauer, Konrad 19
Agagianian, Cardinal Gregory
    26–27
Aglipay, Gregorio 17
Agrippa, King 197
Aguilera, Christina 348
Albert the Great, St 295
Alla, Fr Henrique 15
Allende, General Ignacio 232
Allin, Bishop John 61
Aloysius, Mother 98
Alphonsus Liguori, St 354
Amos 164
Andrew, Bishop Agnellus 27
Aniagwu, Fr John 91
Anthony of Padua, St 315–316
Arinze, Cardinal Francis 104,
    181, 241–242, 292
Aristotle 209
Arnold, Bishop John 308
Arrupe, Fr Pedro 54
Asquith, Herbert Henry 7
Augustine, St 13, 44, 158, 208,
    295
Ayella, Anne Healy 54

Badano, Chiara 'Luce' 309
Balthasar, Hans Urs von 152
Barankitse, Marguerite 291
Barbarin, Cardinal Philippe
    273–277
Barron, Bishop Robert 348–349,
    358
Barry, Commodore John 60
Basil, Fr 3
Baum, Cardinal William W 61
Bea, Cardinal Augustin 20, 25
Bede, St 151
Benedict XV, Pope 10, 16
Benedict XVI, Pope 24, 152,
    176, 265, 269, 292–297, 303,
    306, 309–311, 314, 317, 323,
    331–335, 342, 352
Bergoglio, Cardinal Jorge see
    Francis, Pope
Bergoglio, Mario Jose and
    Regina Maria 15
Berlie, Archbishop Emilio 239
Bernadette, St 83
Bernard of Clairvaux, St 365
Bernardin, Cardinal Joseph 65,
    108–110
Bignardi, Paola 220–221
Blaiha family 194
Bo, Cardinal Charles Maung
    339–343, 366–368
Boccafola, Ken 69

Bock, Lawrence 69
Bonaparte, Joseph 232
Bonaparte, Napoleon 174, 232
Bonsevicius, Bishop Vincent 204
Bonzano, Cardinal Giovanni 12
Bossuet, Bishop 31
Bourassa, Henri 8–9
Bourne, Archbishop Francis 6–8
Brady, Cardinal Sean 320–321
Brain, Bishop Terence 301
Brown, Archbishop Charles 314
Burke, Bishop Geoffrey 292
Burns, Tommy 338, 353
Buttet, Fr Nicolas 278
Byrne, Bishop Robert 338, 354
Byrne, Celine 331
Byrne, Fr William 354

Caesar 197
Cahill, Edie, Bill and Mary 68–69
Cahill, Mary Ann 68
Cain, Fr Joseph 116
Calles, Plutarco 247
Camara, Archbishop Dom
    Helder 22, 54, 57, 91, 126, 128
Candreva, Tom 69
Carney, Fr Joseph 98
Carrera, Cardinal Norbert 222
Carroll, Bishop John 67
Carroll, Fr Joseph 123
Carroll, Mrs Noreen 316
Cassidy, Cardinal Edward 186,
    188
Cerretti, Cardinal Bonaventura
    13
Cervera, Fr Jesus Castellano 173
Charles IV, King 232
Charles, Prince 73

Chavez, Cesar 54
Christophe, Paul 9
Churchill, Winston 171–172
Cody, Cardinal John 46
Cogtas, Maria Georgia (Maggie)
    360–361
Collins, Bishop Barry 205–206
Columbus, Christopher 145
Conlon, Fr Anthony 171
Conrad, Joseph 38
Conway, Cardinal William 64
Cooke, Cardinal Terence 54, 57
Cordeiro, Cardinal Joseph 100–
    102
Cortés, Hernán 231
Cotton, Fr Jonathan 73
Couve de Murville, Archbishop
    216
Cull, Fr Kevin 206, 264
Cunningham, Fr Paul 99
Cusick, Fr John 315
Cyprian, St 13
Cyril of Alexandria, St 208, 295
Cyril of Jerusalem, St 6

Dale, Fr John 104
Daly, Bishop Edward 64
Dante Alighieri 151
Daquin, Bishop Thaddeus Ma
    346
Darwin, Charles 1
David, King 150
Davies, Bishop Colin 99
Davies, Bishop Mark 308–309
Davin, Sean and Margaret 301
Day, Dorothy 54, 62
de Bolonia, Miguel 240
de Champlain, Samuel 265

De Gaspari, Alcide 19
de la Vergne, Cardinal Francois-Marie-Benjamin Richard 2
de Lamennais, Ven Jean-Marie 1
de Laval, Bl Bishop François 264, 267
de Reeper, Fr Joannes 103
de Segovia, Antonio 240
de Segur, Mgr Louis Gaston Adrien 2
De Smedt, Bishop Emile 39
de Veuster, St Damien 142
Diana, Princess 98
Dolan, Cardinal Timothy 363–364
Dolfini, Giuseppe and Silvia 222
Donque, Maryst Norña 364–365
Doran, Bishop Kevin 303, 317, 338, 353–354
Dougherty, Cardinal Dennis Joseph 16–17
Downes, Tom 69
Dubois, Bishop John 62
Dumdum, Simeon Jr 370
Durand, Fr 5
Dziwisz, Cardinal Stanislaw 278

Eastwood, Fr Michael 171
Elijah 352
Elizabeth I, Queen 246
Elizabeth II, Queen 53
Elizabeth, St 63, 184–185, 328, 340
Enxiang, Bishop Cosma Shi 346
Eric 270–271
Eric, Fr 69
Erlebacher, Walter 56

Etchegaray, Cardinal Roger 71, 126–127
Eymard, St Peter Julian 1

Felloni, Fr Luciano Ariel 350
Fernandez, Alejo 145
Ferrari, Cardinal 7
Fischer, Prof Balthazar 77, 79, 86, 91
Flores, José 291
Ford, Gerald R 66
Francis of Assisi, St 126, 278
Francis, Pope 15, 142, 222, 278–281, 339–341, 343–344, 350, 352–354, 367–370
Frost, Mgr Prof Francis 91

Gabriel, Archangel 328
Gachambi, Sister Theresa 110–111
Gagnon, Cardinal Edouard 166, 183
Gallaraga, Fr John 146
Gantin, Cardinal Bernardin 71–72, 75–76, 80, 94, 107
Garrigou-Lagrange, Pere Reginald 20
Gaudoin-Parker, Fr Michael 121
Genevieve, Sr 318
George, Cardinal Francis 206–209, 255–256
Gibbons, Cardinal 7
Gilroy, Cardinal 40
Glemp, Cardinal Jozef 180
Glendon, Mary Ann 222
Goldie, Rosemary 132
Gorbachev, Mikhail 59
Goulet, Mgr Emilius 206

Grace, Princess 54, 57
Gracias, Cardinal Oswald 361–362
Gracias, Cardinal Valerian 28, 132
Greene, Graham 246
Griffin, Anne 303
Griffin, Fr Kevin 264, 298
Grocholewski, Archbishop Zenon 182
Guevara, Che 29
Guinness, Alec 38
Gulbinowicz, Cardinal Henryk 173, 180

Haigh, Fr Martin 73
Hakim, Patriarch Maximos V 45
Hamao, Cardinal Stephen Fumio 253
Han, Thomas 253
Hanlon, Bishop Henry 97–98, 116–117
Harmel, Leon 3
Harty, Bishop Michael 99
Hassig, Ross 231
Hawkins, Jack 38
Hawthorne, Mary 65
Hayes, Cardinal Patrick Joseph 12
Heakin, Fr Dermot 116
Heffernan, Catriona 354
Heylen, Bishop 9
Hickey, Archbishop Barry James 86–87, 236–237, 309
Hidalgo y Costilla, Don Miguel 232
Hitler, Adolf 18
Holden, William 38

Holland, Bishop Thomas 24, 27–28, 32, 37–38, 41–42, 53, 57, 65–68, 72, 85–86, 97–99, 112, 145–146, 166–168
Hong Yong-ho, Bishop Francis 142
Horgan, Denis, Darlene and Marie 298
Howard, John 354
Huculak, Archbishop Lawrence 281
Hyun Sok Mun, Charles, St 120

Ingham, Alice 98
Iñiguez, Cardinal Juan Sandoval 240
Isaiah 160–161, 165
Iscariot, Judas 285
Isidore, St 151–152

Jackson, Archbishop Michael 308
Jaeger, Archbishop Lorenz 25
Jala, Archbishop Dominic 361
Jaluag, Jayson 337
James, St 165
Jerome, St 353
Joan, Sr 98
Joanna, Sr 98
John Paul II, Pope St 54, 58–59, 64, 71–75, 81–84, 88, 90, 92, 97, 100–101, 105, 107, 112–117, 121, 124, 131–142, 146, 152, 156, 165–170, 172–176, 184, 186–194, 198–200, 210, 212, 215–216, 222–226, 231, 234, 237, 239, 248, 251, 259–

261, 264, 278–281, 298, 306, 310, 341, 362, 367
John the Baptist, St 185
John the Evangelist, St 325–326
John XXIII, Pope St 22–25, 160
John, St 175, 191, 207–208, 257
Jones, Rev Dr Percy 44
Joseph, son of the patriarch Jacob 134
Joseph, St 328
Joyce, James 301
Juan Carlos, King 73, 167, 169
Juan Diego, St 230–231
Jungmann, Fr Josef 23–24, 30, 43, 77

Kang, Bishop Peter 123
Keep, Fr Graham 221, 298
Kelly, Archbishop Patrick 99, 323
Kelly, Bob, Bernadette and Benjamin 65
Kennedy, John F 126
Kenyatta, Jomo 98
Kim, Cardinal Stephen 122–123, 126–127, 142
King, Martin Luther 57, 68
King, Triona 335
Kleiter, Fr Ralph 229
Knox, Cardinal James 39, 45, 51, 54–55, 66–67, 74, 88
Koch, Cardinal Kurt 307
Krol, Cardinal John 54, 61, 65

Lagrange, Fr Marie-Joseph 4
Lamont, Bishop Donal 99
Lane, Fr Dermot 88–90
Langenieux, Cardinal 4
Lauri, Cardinal Lorenzo 14, 301

LaVerdiere, Fr Eugene 91
Lavigerie, Cardinal Charles 13
Law, Cardinal Bernard 181–182, 184, 238
Lawless, Fr Anthony 46
Lazarus of Bethany 327
Lecour, Prof Guzman Carriquiury 151–152
Ledesma, Archbishop Antonio 352
LeGatt, Bishop Albert 229
Lehmann, Bishop Karl 181
Leiza, Sr Juana Elizondo 164
Lelievre, Fr 288
Leo the Great, Pope St 306
Leo XIII, Pope 2, 4, 16, 278
Leonard, Fr Tony 171
Lercaro, Cardinal Giacomo 33
Lievens, Fr Constant 288
Lima, Dr Alceu Amoroso 21
Logue, Cardinal 7
Lombardi, Fr Riccardo 20
Löser, Br Alois 308
Louis XVI, King 267
Lubac, Henri de 153
Luke, St 224
Lustiger, Cardinal Jean Marie 211–214
Lydia 37

Mabry, Donald 246
Macharski, Cardinal Franciszek 84, 181
Magellan, Ferdinand 338–339, 366
Maguire, Fr 46
Maida, Cardinal Adam Joseph 181

Majella, Archbishop Agnelo
Geraldo 202
Maradiaga, Cardinal Rodriguez
315
Marini, Archbishop Piero 344,
347
Marmion, Abbot Bl Columba 365
Marshall, Alan 45
Marshall, Robert 61
Martha of Bethany, St 268, 326
Martin, Archbishop Diarmuid
301–303, 308, 362–363
Martin, Cardinal Marcelo
Gonzalez 167
Martin, Pauline 365
Martini, Cardinal Carlo 104–107,
154–157
Marty, Cardinal François 91–93
Mary of Bethany 326
Mary of Magdala, St 274, 326
Masella, Cardinal Benedetto
Aloisi 22
Mathieu, Cardinal 7
Matulionis, Bishop Theophile
204
Mbinda, Fr Mutiso 111
McCloskey, Matt III 65
McCormack, Count John 14, 64,
301, 331
McCusker, Fr John 176
McDonald, Fr Brendan 98
McDonnell, Sr Conchita 316
McGarry, Fr Cecil 116
McGough, Bishop David 308
McNamara, Fr Edward 79
McSweeney, Fr Anthony 158, 162
Meisner, Cardinal Joachim 147–
150, 174–180, 254

Melchizedek 215
Menamparampil, Archbishop
Thomas 351
Mercier, Cardinal 7
Mickiewicz, Adam 173
Miller, Archbishop Michael 315
Mindszenty, Cardinal 21
Mockler, Fr John 338
Modrego Casaus, Archbishop
Gregorio 20
Monaghan, John 330–331
Montcalm, General 292
Montezuma II 231
Morelos, Archbishop Carmelo
235–236, 238
Moses 197, 224, 305, 311
Muheria, Bishop Anthony 103
Mulheran, Fr Thomas 98
Mundelein, Cardinal George 11
Munoz Vega, Cardinal 73

Napoleon Bonaparte 174, 232
Neumann, St John 61–62
Neves, Cardinal Lucas 183
Newman, Cardinal John Henry,
Bl 130, 308
Nguyen Thi Thu Hong, Eliza-
beth 287
Niedringhaus, Paul 65
Noman, Hasan ibn 13
Nzeki, Bishop Raphael 107

O'Brien, Bishop James 98
O'Connell, Daniel 317
O'Connor, Canon Kevin 229,
233, 264, 298, 301
O'Connor, Fr Richard 116
Ó Fiaich, Cardinal Tomás 99

O'Hara, Archbishop Gerald Patrick 24, 65–66
O'Meara, Terry 347
Onaiyekan, Cardinal John 359–360
Otunga, Cardinal Maurice 103–104, 107, 116
Ouellet, Cardinal Marc 206, 255, 263, 272, 292, 297, 304–307, 314, 331–332
Ozanam, Bl Frederick 1

Pacelli, Cardinal Eugenio see Pius XII, Pope Ven
Pak, Fr Thomas 120
Palma, Archbishop 339
Parkinson, Fr Francis 146
Parsch, Dr Pius 20
Patrick, St 13, 332
Paul VI, Pope Bl 26–33, 39–44, 51, 55, 62, 67, 72, 104, 146, 164, 189, 202
Paul, St 37, 47, 74, 137, 153, 159, 182, 193, 197–199, 211, 245, 253, 266, 268, 272, 283, 295, 309–310, 317–318, 326, 338, 344–347
Penn, William 59
Perugini, Mother Antonella 221
Peter, St 185, 204, 215, 218, 235, 268, 326
Philip, Prince 53
Philip, St 326
Picher, Abbé Jean 229
Pignatelli di Belmonte, Cardinal 9
Pilate, Pontius 285
Pius X, Pope St 5–6, 8–10, 85, 238

Pius XI, Pope 5, 10–18, 247
Pius XII, Pope Ven 5, 14, 18, 20–22, 44, 65–66, 103
Pole, Cardinal 7
Ponce, Paul and Lia 351–352
Potter, Mary, Ven 135
Poupard, Cardinal Paul 146–147
Pro, Bl Miguel 247

Quevedo, Cardinal Orlando 349

Radcliffe, Fr Timothy 344–345
Rahner, Karl 176
Ratzinger, Cardinal Joseph see Benedict XVI, Pope
Re, Cardinal Giovanni Battista 256–257
Reinys, Bishop Metchislovas 204
Renan, Ernest 1
Riber, Don Lorenzo 20
Rice, Fr Francis 171
Richard of St Victor 151
Rivera, Cardinal José Garibi 262
Rizzo, Frank L 54
Robinson, Fr Jonathan 262
Rodríguez, Cardinal Nicolás de Jesus López 150
Roosevelt, Franklin D 171
Rosica, Fr Thomas 265, 297, 319
Ross, Betsy 60
Rossi, Cardinal Agnelo 110
Rugambwa, Cardinal Laurean 108
Ruini, Cardinal Camillo 174, 184, 199–200, 206
Ryu, Catherine 253

Sancha y Hervas, Cardinal 7
Sanon, Mgr Anselme 93
Santamaria, Mr Bob 48–50
Sarah, Cardinal Robert 324–325
Sarpong, Bishop Peter 200
Schlembach, Bishop Anton 128–
    129
Schonborn, Cardinal Christoph
    216–220
Schuman, Robert 19–20
Servaas, Mrs Marianne 349
Shallow, Jim and Victoria 65
Sharrocks, Fr Peter 104
Sheen, Archbishop Fulton 54–55
Shehan, Cardinal Lawrence
    Joseph 41, 45, 51
Simeon 328
Simonis, Cardinal Adrianus 131
Sin, Cardinal Jaime 110, 158–160
Slipyj, Cardinal Josyf 45
Smith, Mgr Paul 146
Sodano, Cardinal Angelo 180
Sofia, Queen 73, 167, 169
Some, Bishop Jean Baptiste
    Kpiele 235
Spencer, Lady Diana 73
Stalin, Josef 171
Stanelyte, Sr Edwige 204
Stein, Edith (Teresa Benedicta of
    the Cross, St) 296
Stephen, Mother 104
Stephen, St 326
Stephen, St, King of Hungary 18
Stephenson, George 2
Stepinac, Cardinal 21
Strauss, David 1
Sudi 103–104
Sugawara, Mr Kei-ichi 358

Swiatek, Cardinal Kazimierz 183

Tagle, Cardinal Luis Antonio
    282–287, 325–330, 355–358
Talamayan, Archbishop Dios-
    dado 202–203
Tamisier, Emelie 1–2, 75
Tamkevicius, Archbishop
    Sigitas 203
Tedeschini, Cardinal Federico
    20
Teresa Benedicta of the Cross,
    St see Stein
Teresa of Calcutta, Mother St
    48, 53–54, 62–64, 97, 108–
    109, 130, 164, 179, 289, 340
Testa, Cardinal Gustavo 24
Theisen, Prof Sylvester 47–48
Thérèse of Lisieux, St 242, 364–
    365
Thiandoum, Cardinal Hya-
    cinthe 93
Thomas Aquinas, St 175, 209–
    210, 225, 242, 295
Thomas, St 274
Tibhirine, Cistercian monks of
    277
Tomko, Cardinal Jozef 210–211,
    233, 258, 264–267, 292–293,
    297
Toomey, Mgr Kevin 39
Toppo, Cardinal Telesphore
    Placidus 288–291
Torres, Fr Camilo 29
Truman, Harry 171
Tugonon, Clayton 370
Tumi, Cardinal Christian 291

Turkson, Cardinal Peter 242–
245, 318–319, 352
Twal, Archbishop Fouad 321–
323

Ustrzycki, Bishop Matthew 221

Vallejo, Cardinal Carlos 237, 254
Van Thuan, Cardinal Francis
Xavier Nguyen 214–215, 287
Vanier, Jean 209, 270–272
Vannutelli, Cardinal Vincenzo
7–9
Vianney, St John 1, 177
Vidal, Cardinal Ricardo 248–251,
364
Vidarte, Archbishop Miguel 346
Vincent de Paul, St 165
Vingt-Trois, Cardinal Andre 312
Vischer, the Reverend Dr Lukas
47
Vlk, Cardinal Miloslav 183
Vrau, Philibert 2

Wako, Archbishop Gabriel
Zubeir 107
Waldron, Fr Paul 38
Walesa, Lech 180
Walmsley, Bishop Charles 67
Walsh, Mgr Brian 39–40, 221,
298, 335
Wendel, Cardinal Joseph 24
Westendorf, Omer 56
Willebrands, Cardinal Johannes
47, 61, 131
Winkle, Fr Pat 338
Winstone, Fr Harold 45

Wojtyla, Cardinal Karol see
John Paul II, Pope St
Wolfe, General 292
Wright, Cardinal John 46, 50, 60
Wuerl, Archbishop Donald 60,
267
Wyszynski, Cardinal Stefan 21,
180

Yeom Soo-jung, Cardinal
Andrew 142
Yeom, Seok-tae Peter and Kim
Maria 142

Zacchaeus 327
Zdebskis, Fr Joseph 204
Zen Ze-Kiun, Cardinal Joseph
291, 346
Zumarraga, Bishop 230–231

Lightning Source UK Ltd.
Milton Keynes UK
UKHW01f1319120718
325611UK00002B/6/P